GIRL GENIUS ®

AGATHA HETERODYNE
& THE
HEIRS OF THE STORM

A Gaslamp Fantasy
with
ADVENTURE, ROMANCE & MAD SCIENCE

Story by Kaja & Phil...
Pencils by Phil Fog...
Colors by Cheyenne W...

AIRSHIP
ENTERTAINMENT

OTHER BOOKS FROM AIRSHIP ENTERTAINMENT AND STUDIO FOGLIO

Girl Genius® Graphic Novels

Girl Genius Volume One:
Agatha Heterodyne and the Beetleburg Clank

Girl Genius Volume Two:
Agatha Heterodyne and the Airship City

Girl Genius Volume Three:
Agatha Heterodyne and the Monster Engine

Girl Genius Volume Four:
Agatha Heterodyne and the Circus of Dreams

Girl Genius Volume Five:
Agatha Heterodyne and the Clockwork Princess

Girl Genius Volume Six:
Agatha Heterodyne and the Golden Trilobite

Girl Genius Volume Seven:
Agatha Heterodyne and the Voice of the Castle

Girl Genius Volume Eight:
Agatha Heterodyne and the Chapel of Bones

Girl Genius Volume Nine:
Agatha Heterodyne and the Heirs of the Storm

Other Graphic Novels

What's New with Phil & Dixie Collection

Robert Asprin's MythAdventures®

Buck Godot, zap gun for hire:
• *Three Short Stories*
• *PSmIth*
• *The Gallimaufry*

Girl Genius® is published by:
Airship Entertainment™: a happy part of Studio Foglio, LLC
2400 NW 80th St #129 Seattle WA 98117-4449, USA

Please visit our Web sites at www.airshipbooks.com and www.girlgenius.net

Story by Phil & Kaja Foglio. Pencils by Phil Foglio. Main story colors by Cheyenne Wright. Selected spot illustrations colored by Kaja Foglio and/or Cheyenne Wright. Logos, Lettering, Artist Bullying & Book Design by Kaja. Fonts mostly by Comicraft– www.comicbookfonts.com.

This material originally appeared January-November 2009 at www.girlgenius.net.

Published simultaneously in Hardcover (ISBN 978-1-890856-51-9) and Softcover (ISBN 978-1-890856-52-6) editions.

First Printing: May 2010   PRINTED IN THE USA

This book is dedicated to John & Carol, who knew perfectly well what we were up to, and still failed to "forget" the jelly; and to Nora, who at that point, simply didn't care.

KAJA FOGLIO

Professoressa Foglio is the daughter of The Grumbly Witch of Băneasa Forest, who lived in self-imposed exile after a curse involving giant snails backfired–causing her great embarrassment within the witching world. Kaja's early life was spent exploring the forests, caves and occasional ruined laboratories of her mother's domain while learning the witch business. This knowledge served her well when she made the transition to academia, as any number of troublesome department heads found themselves stricken with warts, goiters, lycanthropy, or in the case of a legendary argument about the placement of a water cooler, transformed into amphibians. It is, however, embarrassing; as she has trouble fitting all this into her scientific world view. Luckily, at a young age, she discovered good Sherry.

PHIL FOGLIO

Professor Foglio is the son of Cleonicus Foglio, a man who made a fine living selling large, dangerous-looking machinery to various laboratories, each unit supplied with a guarantee that it would never actually *function*. After the inevitable, comedic-in-retrospect accident, Cleonicus found himself in Mechanicsburg, where he fell in love with Dorothea Vodenicharova: the daughter of a prosperous macaroni farmer. Cleonicus was initially rejected by her father for being "too euphoric." Things looked bleak, until Farmer Vodenicharova's farm, along with the farms of most of his neighbors, was overrun by giant snails. Famine loomed until Cleonicus created an advertising campaign extolling said snails as a delicacy. Thus, the town's most profitable export–the Mechanicsburg Giant Snail–was born. Today, giant snails grace tables throughout the known world. Amazingly, they taste *nothing* like chicken.

CHEYENNE WRIGHT

As a young lad, Professor Wright sent away for a wonderful and mysterious kit. Soon, he was raising giant snails in his bathtub. He became intrigued by the vibrant shell colors of the different varieties, and as a result of meticulously planned breeding programs, created several popular new varieties, including The Cerulean Giant, The Orange Snap-Shell, The Variegated Spine-Tail, the Phosphorescent Devil, and the Great White Inedible. His full scholarship to Prague's Institute of Coloring Heresies was paid by The Mechanicsburg Giant Snail Collective on the condition that he permanently dismantle his breeding programs. This was acceptable, as he had recently discovered girls and started dating. He does however, still keep his bathtub full of snails. Beautiful, beautiful, non-judgmental snails.

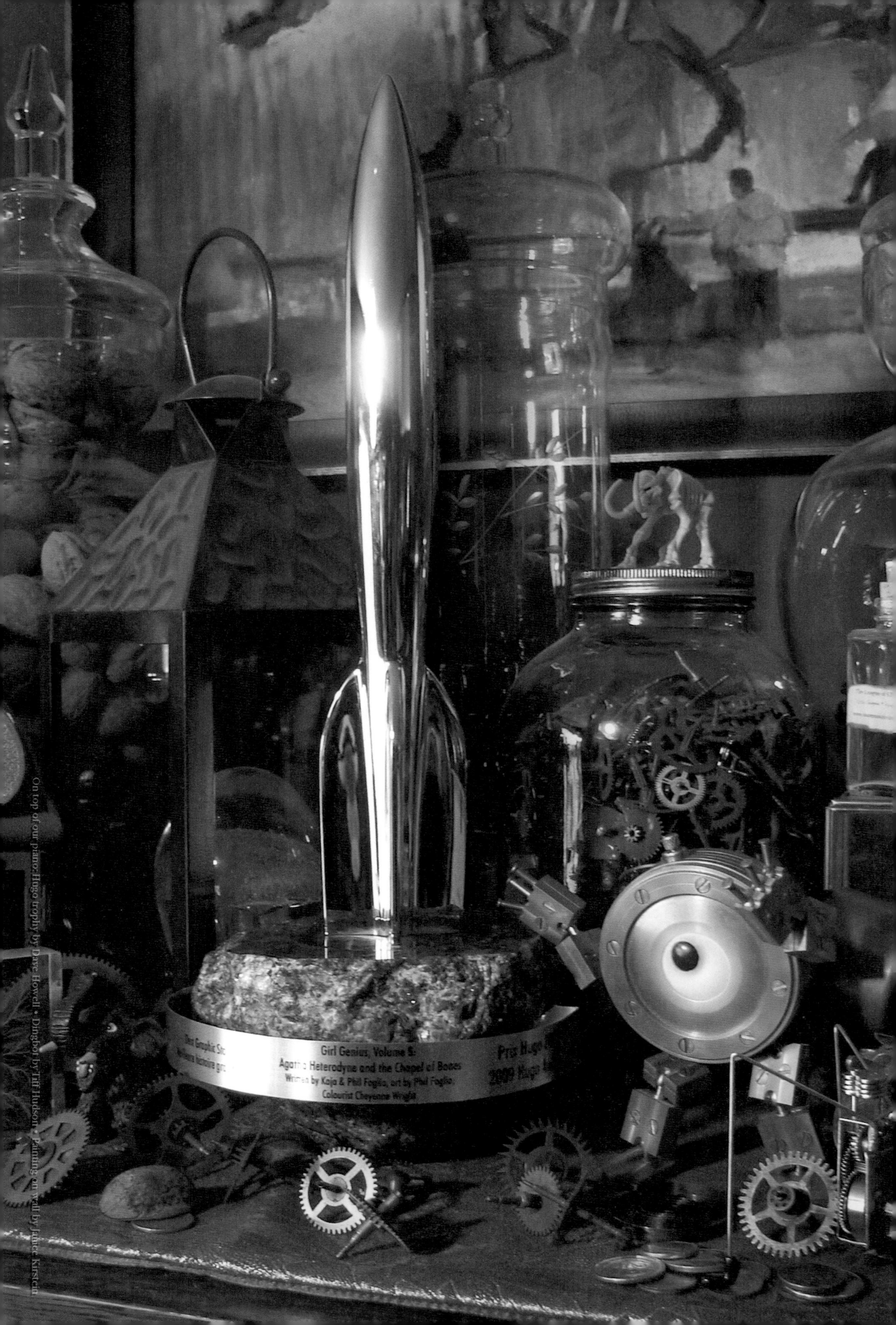
Girl Genius, Volume 8:
Agatha Heterodyne and the Chapel of Bones
Written by Kaja & Phil Foglio, art by Phil Foglio,
Colourist Cheyenne Wright

On top of our piano: Hugo trophy by Dave Howell • Dingbot by Tiff Hudson • Painting on wall by Janet Kirstein

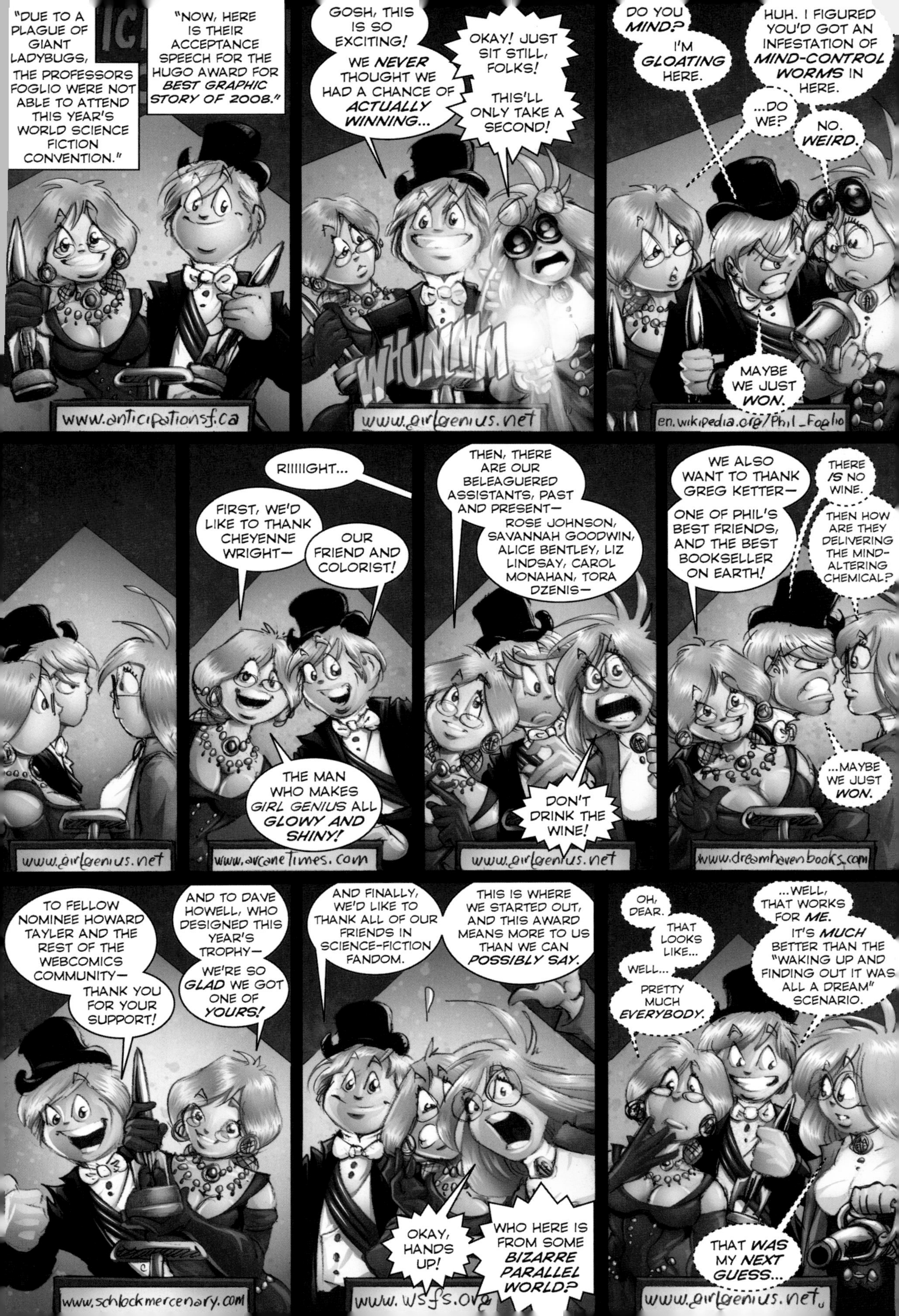
"DUE TO A PLAGUE OF GIANT LADYBUGS, THE PROFESSORS FOGLIO WERE NOT ABLE TO ATTEND THIS YEAR'S WORLD SCIENCE FICTION CONVENTION."
"NOW, HERE IS THEIR ACCEPTANCE SPEECH FOR THE HUGO AWARD FOR BEST GRAPHIC STORY OF 2008."
www.anticipationsf.ca
GOSH, THIS IS SO EXCITING!
WE NEVER THOUGHT WE HAD A CHANCE OF ACTUALLY WINNING...
OKAY! JUST SIT STILL, FOLKS!
THIS'LL ONLY TAKE A SECOND!
WHUMMM
www.girlgenius.net
DO YOU MIND? I'M GLOATING HERE.
HUH. I FIGURED YOU'D GOT AN INFESTATION OF MIND-CONTROL WORMS IN HERE.
...DO WE?
NO. WEIRD.
MAYBE WE JUST WON.
en.wikipedia.org/Phil_Foglio
www.girlgenius.net
RIIIIIGHT...
FIRST, WE'D LIKE TO THANK CHEYENNE WRIGHT—
OUR FRIEND AND COLORIST!
THE MAN WHO MAKES GIRL GENIUS ALL GLOWY AND SHINY!
www.arcanetimes.com
THEN, THERE ARE OUR BELEAGUERED ASSISTANTS, PAST AND PRESENT— ROSE JOHNSON, SAVANNAH GOODWIN, ALICE BENTLEY, LIZ LINDSAY, CAROL MONAHAN, TORA DZENIS—
DON'T DRINK THE WINE!
www.girlgenius.net
WE ALSO WANT TO THANK GREG KETTER—
ONE OF PHIL'S BEST FRIENDS, AND THE BEST BOOKSELLER ON EARTH!
THERE IS NO WINE.
THEN HOW ARE THEY DELIVERING THE MIND-ALTERING CHEMICAL?
...MAYBE WE JUST WON.
www.dreamhavenbooks.com
TO FELLOW NOMINEE HOWARD TAYLER AND THE REST OF THE WEBCOMICS COMMUNITY—
THANK YOU FOR YOUR SUPPORT!
AND TO DAVE HOWELL, WHO DESIGNED THIS YEAR'S TROPHY—
WE'RE SO GLAD WE GOT ONE OF YOURS!
www.schlockmercenary.com
AND FINALLY, WE'D LIKE TO THANK ALL OF OUR FRIENDS IN SCIENCE-FICTION FANDOM.
THIS IS WHERE WE STARTED OUT, AND THIS AWARD MEANS MORE TO US THAN WE CAN POSSIBLY SAY.
OKAY, HANDS UP!
WHO HERE IS FROM SOME BIZARRE PARALLEL WORLD?
www.wsfs.org
OH, DEAR.
THAT LOOKS LIKE...
WELL...
PRETTY MUCH EVERYBODY.
...WELL, THAT WORKS FOR ME.
IT'S MUCH BETTER THAN THE "WAKING UP AND FINDING OUT IT WAS ALL A DREAM" SCENARIO.
THAT WAS MY NEXT GUESS...
www.girlgenius.net

· THE STORY SO FAR ·

Agatha Clay was an unlucky student at Transylvania Polygnostic University, until an accident revealed her hidden "spark:" a capacity for mad science beyond the reach of all but the most gifted. This alone would have been enough to bring her to the attention of Baron Wulfenbach, the powerful Spark who held the fractious ruling houses of Europa under his thumb, but Agatha was *also* the last of the famous Heterodyne family–beloved folk heroes who disappeared many years ago. This troubled the Baron. The return of a Heterodyne would have a destabilizing effect upon the peace he had spent the last two decades building. The Baron was also displeased because his only son, Gilgamesh, had fallen in love with Agatha. While uniting the houses of Wulfenbach and Heterodyne would have solved many political problems, The Baron had excellent reasons to believe that Agatha was actually a malevolent entity known as "The Other," who almost destroyed Europa twenty years before.

Now, after many adventures, Agatha has made her way across Europa to Mechanicsburg, the ancestral home of the Heterodyne family–and she's not the only one. The Baron is also in the town, but as a patient in Mechanicsburg's famous hospital. Attempts have already been made to conquer the town, most notably an invasion of war clanks which was single-handedly stopped by Gilgamesh Wulfenbach. Another faction has just flown in a charismatic girl claiming to be Agatha. This imposter has already entered Castle Heterodyne, with Agatha close behind.

The Castle itself is a self-aware mechanical fortress which was badly damaged in the war with the "Other." Ongoing repairs are made by the Baron's worst convicts. Agatha has disguised herself as one of these, hoping to repair the castle and activate the town's defenses. Unfortunately, the false Heterodyne has set a pack of cutthroats after her. After being chased deep into a dangerously unmapped part of the castle, Agatha has managed to make the Castle accept her as the true Heterodyne. Still, the Castle can't control all of the autonomous security systems and booby traps that fill its halls. To complicate things further, Agatha's friends are starting to come into the Castle after her, hoping to lend her their help. But how much help will they be, when they're in so much danger themselves?

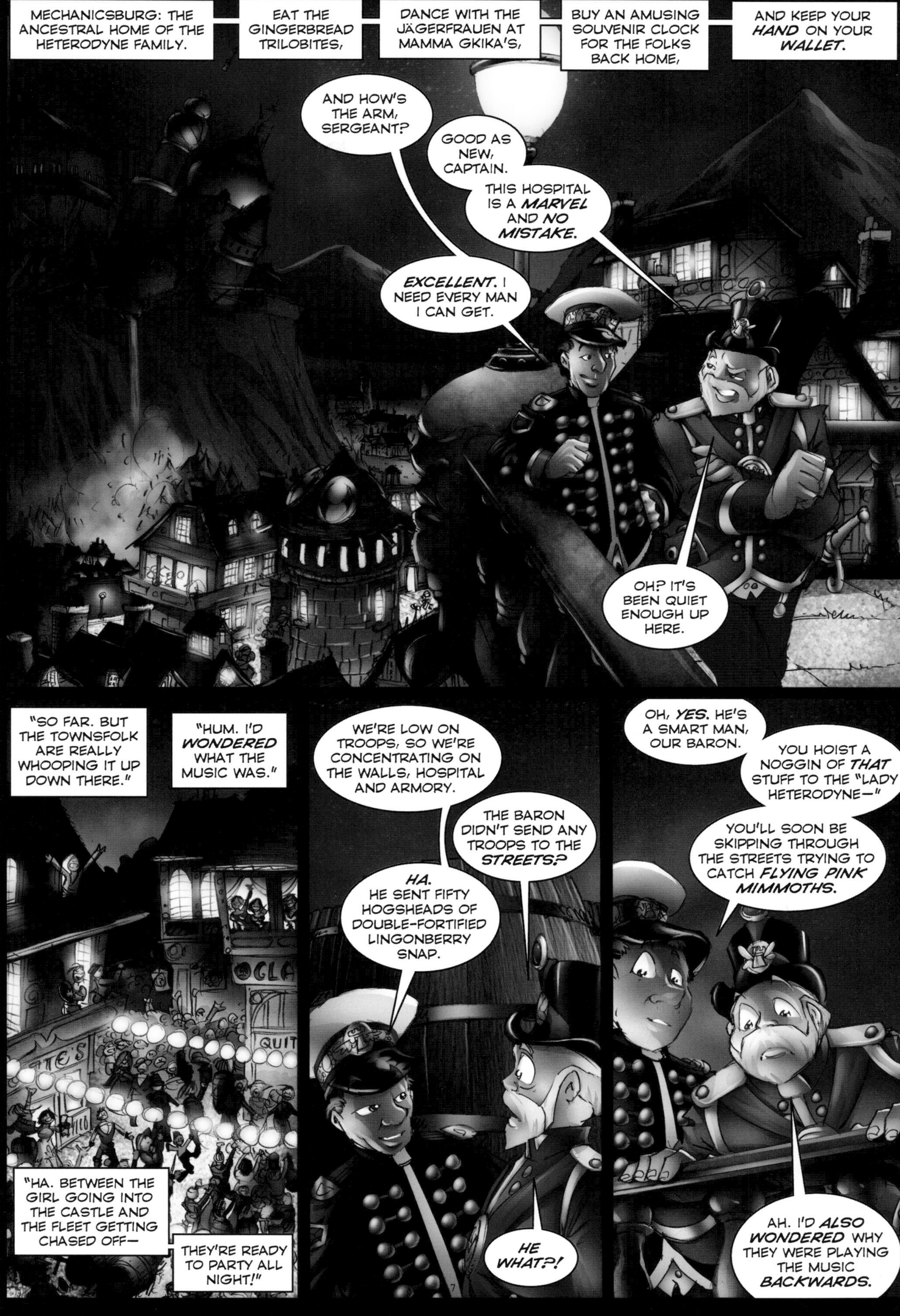
MECHANICSBURG: THE ANCESTRAL HOME OF THE HETERODYNE FAMILY.
EAT THE GINGERBREAD TRILOBITES,
DANCE WITH THE JÄGERFRAUEN AT MAMMA GKIKA'S,
BUY AN AMUSING SOUVENIR CLOCK FOR THE FOLKS BACK HOME,
AND KEEP YOUR *HAND* ON YOUR *WALLET*.
AND HOW'S THE ARM, SERGEANT?
GOOD AS NEW, CAPTAIN.
THIS HOSPITAL IS A *MARVEL* AND *NO MISTAKE*.
EXCELLENT. I NEED EVERY MAN I CAN GET.
OH? IT'S BEEN QUIET ENOUGH UP HERE.
"SO FAR. BUT THE TOWNSFOLK ARE REALLY WHOOPING IT UP DOWN THERE."
"HUM. I'D *WONDERED* WHAT THE MUSIC WAS."
"HA. BETWEEN THE GIRL GOING INTO THE CASTLE AND THE FLEET GETTING CHASED OFF—
THEY'RE READY TO PARTY ALL NIGHT!"
WE'RE LOW ON TROOPS, SO WE'RE CONCENTRATING ON THE WALLS, HOSPITAL AND ARMORY.
THE BARON DIDN'T SEND ANY TROOPS TO THE *STREETS?*
HA. HE SENT FIFTY HOGSHEADS OF DOUBLE-FORTIFIED LINGONBERRY SNAP.
HE WHAT?!
OH, *YES.* HE'S A SMART MAN, OUR BARON.
YOU HOIST A NOGGIN OF *THAT* STUFF TO THE "LADY HETERODYNE—"
YOU'LL SOON BE SKIPPING THROUGH THE STREETS TRYING TO CATCH *FLYING PINK MIMMOTHS*.
AH. I'D *ALSO WONDERED* WHY THEY WERE PLAYING THE MUSIC *BACKWARDS*.

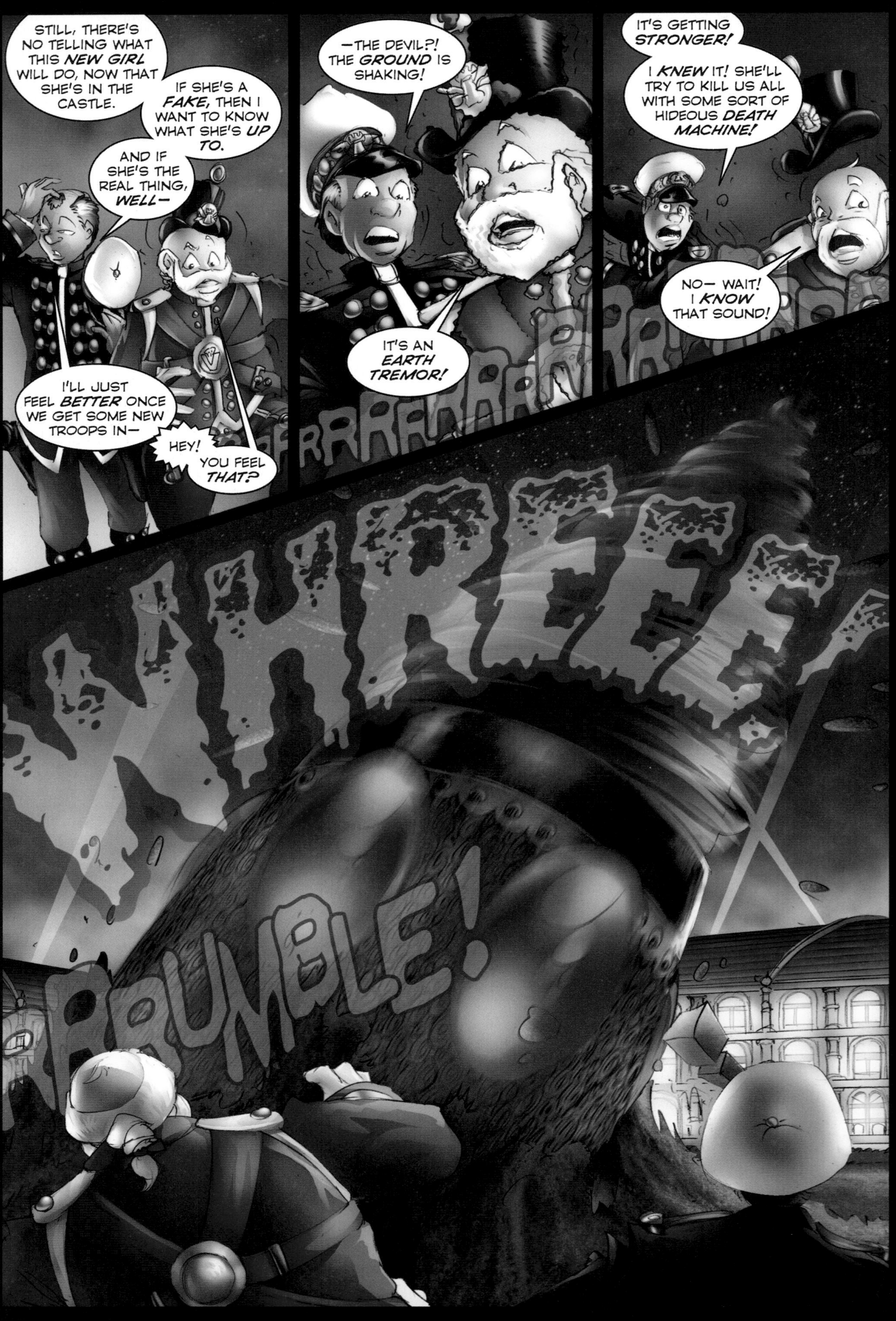
STILL, THERE'S NO TELLING WHAT THIS NEW GIRL WILL DO, NOW THAT SHE'S IN THE CASTLE.
IF SHE'S A FAKE, THEN I WANT TO KNOW WHAT SHE'S UP TO.
AND IF SHE'S THE REAL THING, WELL—
I'LL JUST FEEL BETTER ONCE WE GET SOME NEW TROOPS IN—
HEY!
YOU FEEL THAT?
—THE DEVIL?! THE GROUND IS SHAKING!
IT'S AN EARTH TREMOR!
IT'S GETTING STRONGER!
I KNEW IT! SHE'LL TRY TO KILL US ALL WITH SOME SORT OF HIDEOUS DEATH MACHINE!
NO— WAIT! I KNOW THAT SOUND!
RRUMBLE!

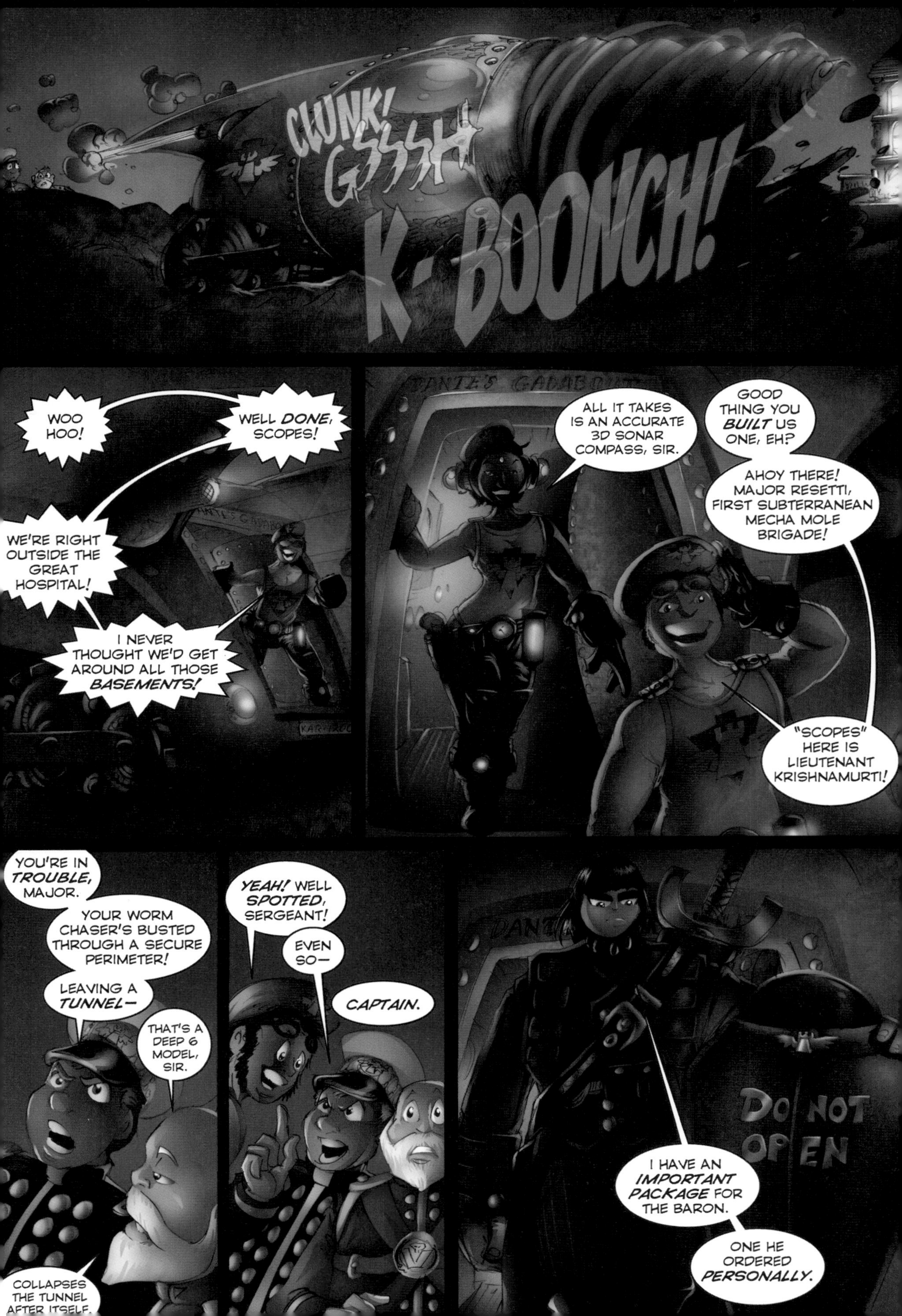
CLUNK!
GSSSH
K-BOONCH!
WOO HOO!
WELL DONE, SCOPES!
WE'RE RIGHT OUTSIDE THE GREAT HOSPITAL!
I NEVER THOUGHT WE'D GET AROUND ALL THOSE BASEMENTS!
ALL IT TAKES IS AN ACCURATE 3D SONAR COMPASS, SIR.
GOOD THING YOU BUILT US ONE, EH?
AHOY THERE! MAJOR RESETTI, FIRST SUBTERRANEAN MECHA MOLE BRIGADE!
"SCOPES" HERE IS LIEUTENANT KRISHNAMURTI!
YOU'RE IN TROUBLE, MAJOR.
YOUR WORM CHASER'S BUSTED THROUGH A SECURE PERIMETER!
LEAVING A TUNNEL—
THAT'S A DEEP 6 MODEL, SIR.
COLLAPSES THE TUNNEL AFTER ITSELF.
YEAH! WELL SPOTTED, SERGEANT!
EVEN SO—
CAPTAIN.
I HAVE AN IMPORTANT PACKAGE FOR THE BARON.
ONE HE ORDERED PERSONALLY.
DO NOT OPEN

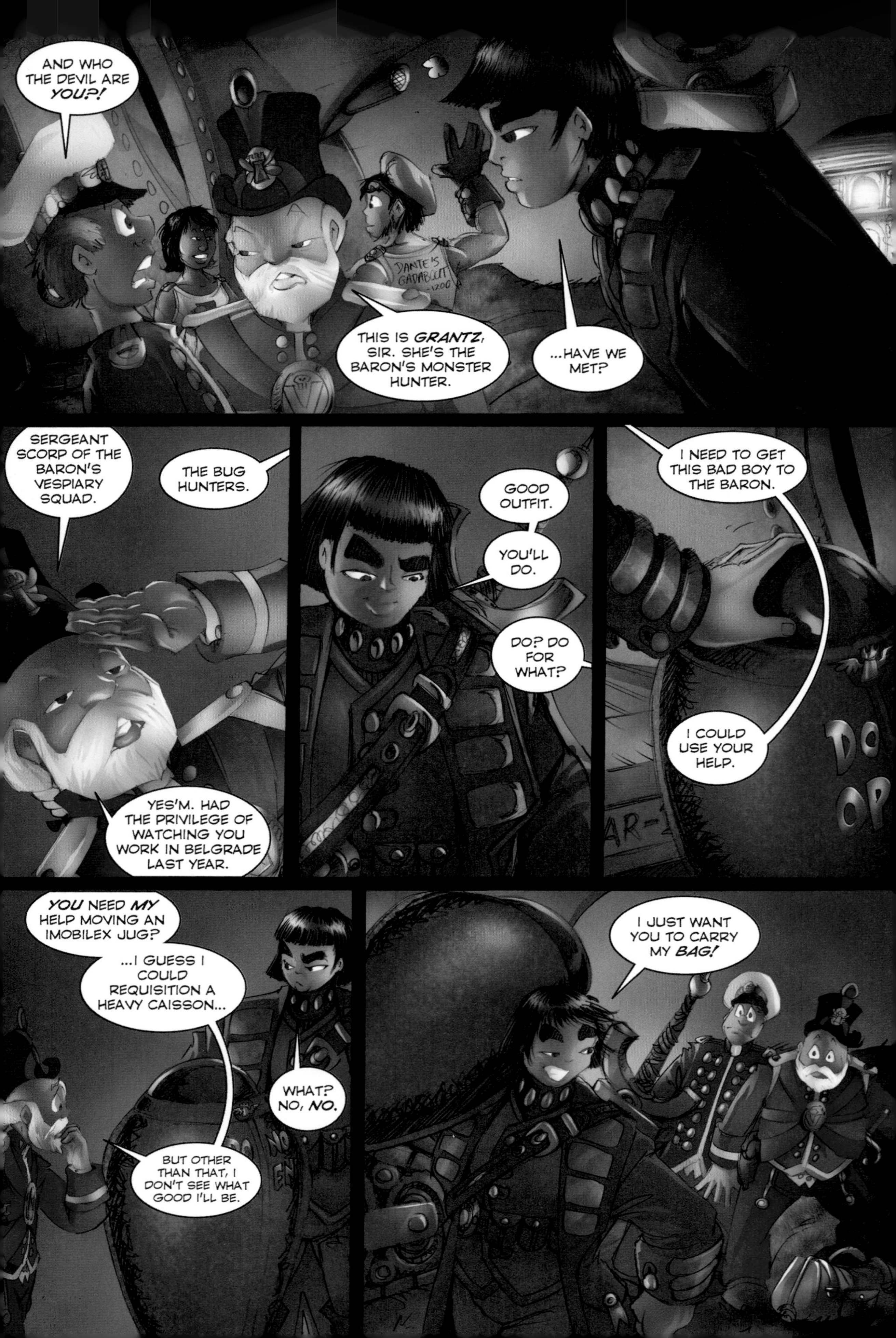
AND WHO THE DEVIL ARE *YOU?!*
DANTE'S GADABOUT
THIS IS ***GRANTZ***, SIR. SHE'S THE BARON'S MONSTER HUNTER.
...HAVE WE MET?
SERGEANT SCORP OF THE BARON'S VESPIARY SQUAD.
THE BUG HUNTERS.
YES'M. HAD THE PRIVILEGE OF WATCHING YOU WORK IN BELGRADE LAST YEAR.
GOOD OUTFIT.
YOU'LL DO.
DO? DO FOR WHAT?
I NEED TO GET THIS BAD BOY TO THE BARON.
I COULD USE YOUR HELP.
YOU NEED ***MY*** HELP MOVING AN IMOBILEX JUG?
...I GUESS I COULD REQUISITION A HEAVY CAISSON...
WHAT? NO, ***NO.***
BUT OTHER THAN THAT, I DON'T SEE WHAT GOOD I'LL BE.
I JUST WANT YOU TO CARRY MY ***BAG!***

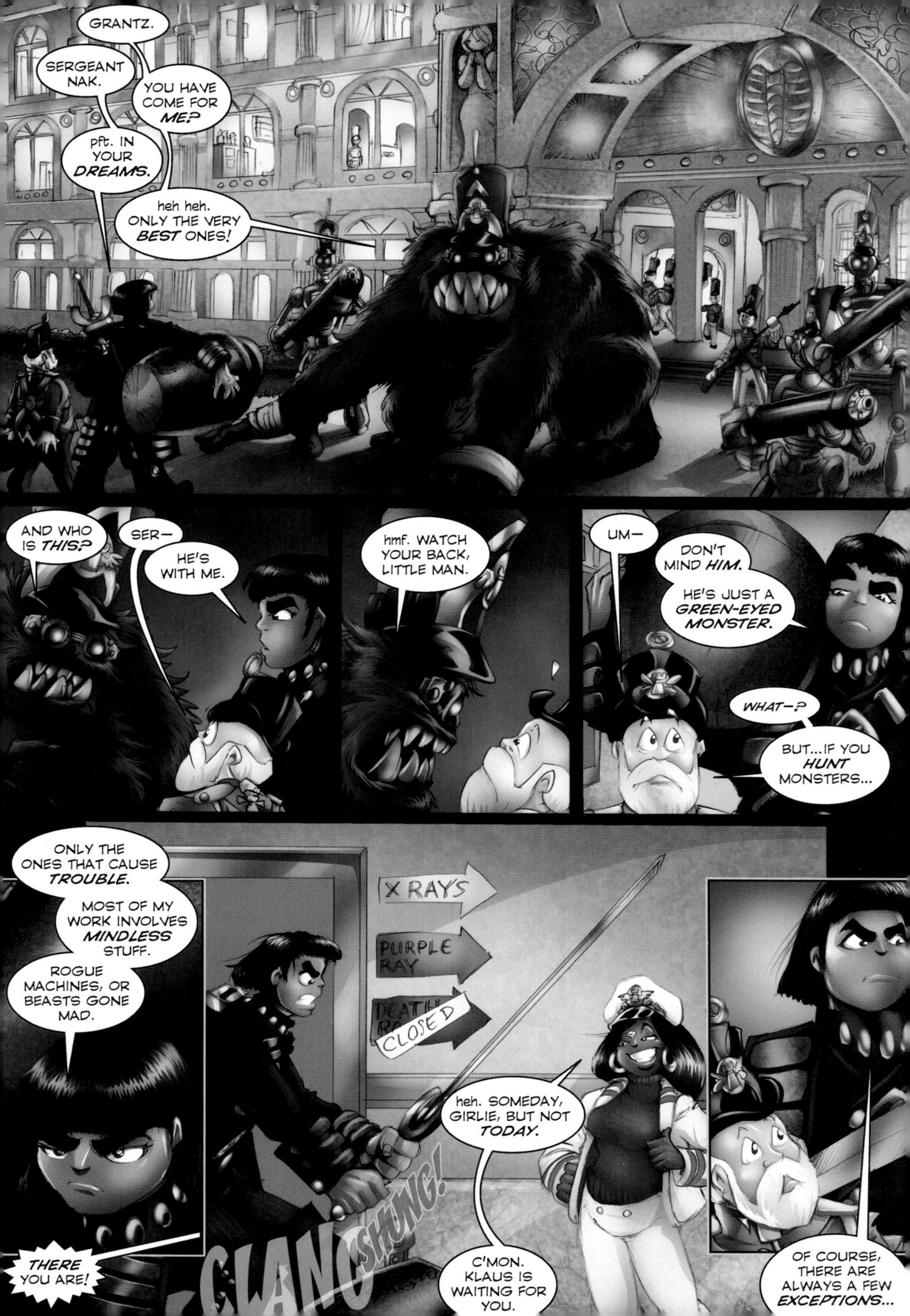
GRANTZ.
SERGEANT NAK.
YOU HAVE COME FOR ME?
pft. IN YOUR DREAMS.
heh heh. ONLY THE VERY BEST ONES!
AND WHO IS THIS?
SER—
HE'S WITH ME.
hmf. WATCH YOUR BACK, LITTLE MAN.
UM—
DON'T MIND HIM.
HE'S JUST A GREEN-EYED MONSTER.
WHAT—?
BUT...IF YOU HUNT MONSTERS...
ONLY THE ONES THAT CAUSE TROUBLE.
MOST OF MY WORK INVOLVES MINDLESS STUFF.
ROGUE MACHINES, OR BEASTS GONE MAD.
X RAYS
PURPLE RAY
CLOSED
THERE YOU ARE!
CLANG
SHUNG!
heh. SOMEDAY, GIRLIE, BUT NOT TODAY.
C'MON. KLAUS IS WAITING FOR YOU.
OF COURSE, THERE ARE ALWAYS A FEW EXCEPTIONS...

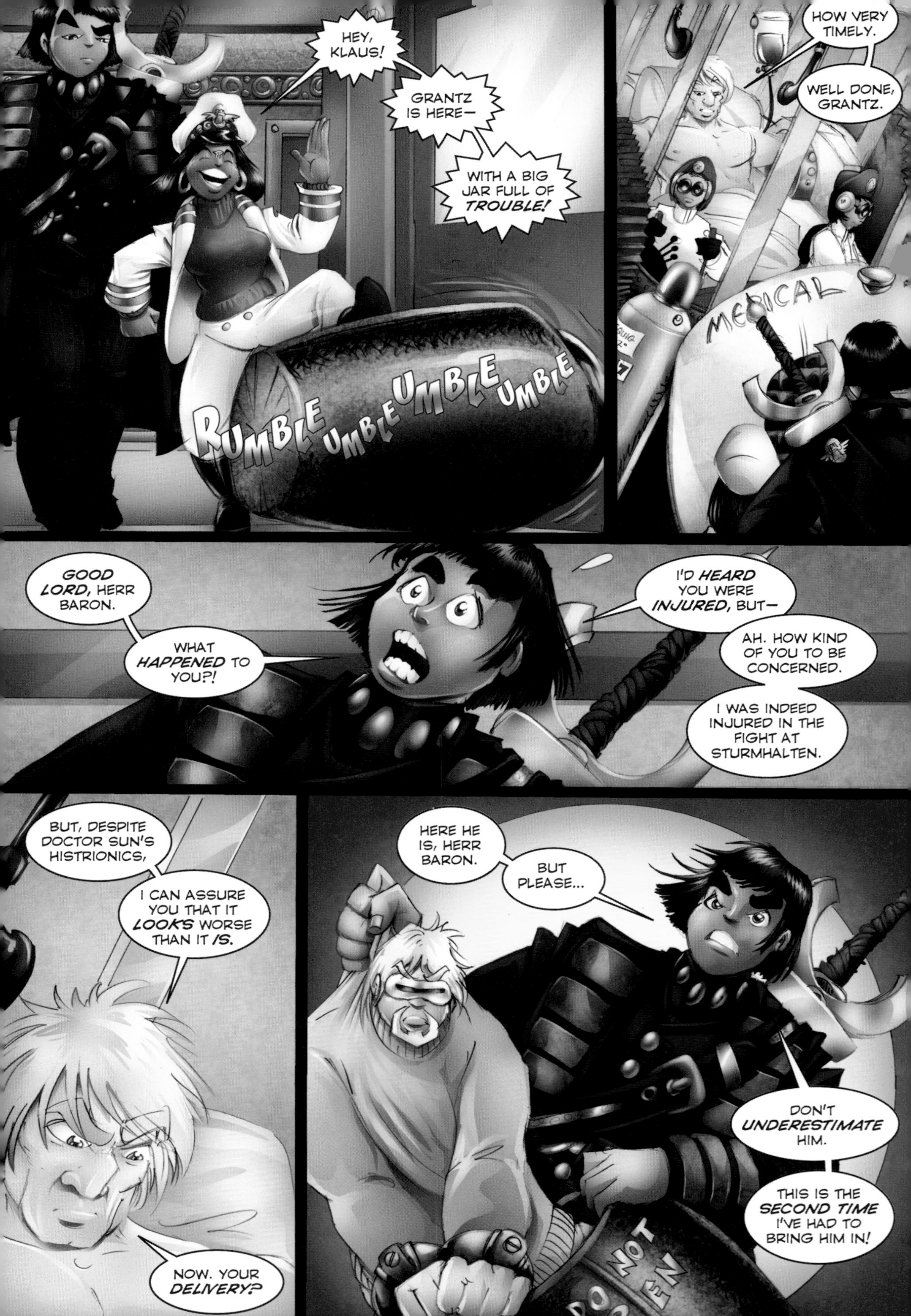
HEY, KLAUS!
GRANTZ IS HERE—
WITH A BIG JAR FULL OF TROUBLE!
RUMBLE UMBLE UMBLE UMBLE
HOW VERY TIMELY.
WELL DONE, GRANTZ.
MEDICAL
GOOD LORD, HERR BARON.
WHAT HAPPENED TO YOU?!
I'D HEARD YOU WERE INJURED, BUT—
AH. HOW KIND OF YOU TO BE CONCERNED.
I WAS INDEED INJURED IN THE FIGHT AT STURMHALTEN.
BUT, DESPITE DOCTOR SUN'S HISTRIONICS,
I CAN ASSURE YOU THAT IT LOOKS WORSE THAN IT IS.
NOW. YOUR DELIVERY?
HERE HE IS, HERR BARON.
BUT PLEASE...
DON'T UNDERESTIMATE HIM.
THIS IS THE SECOND TIME I'VE HAD TO BRING HIM IN!

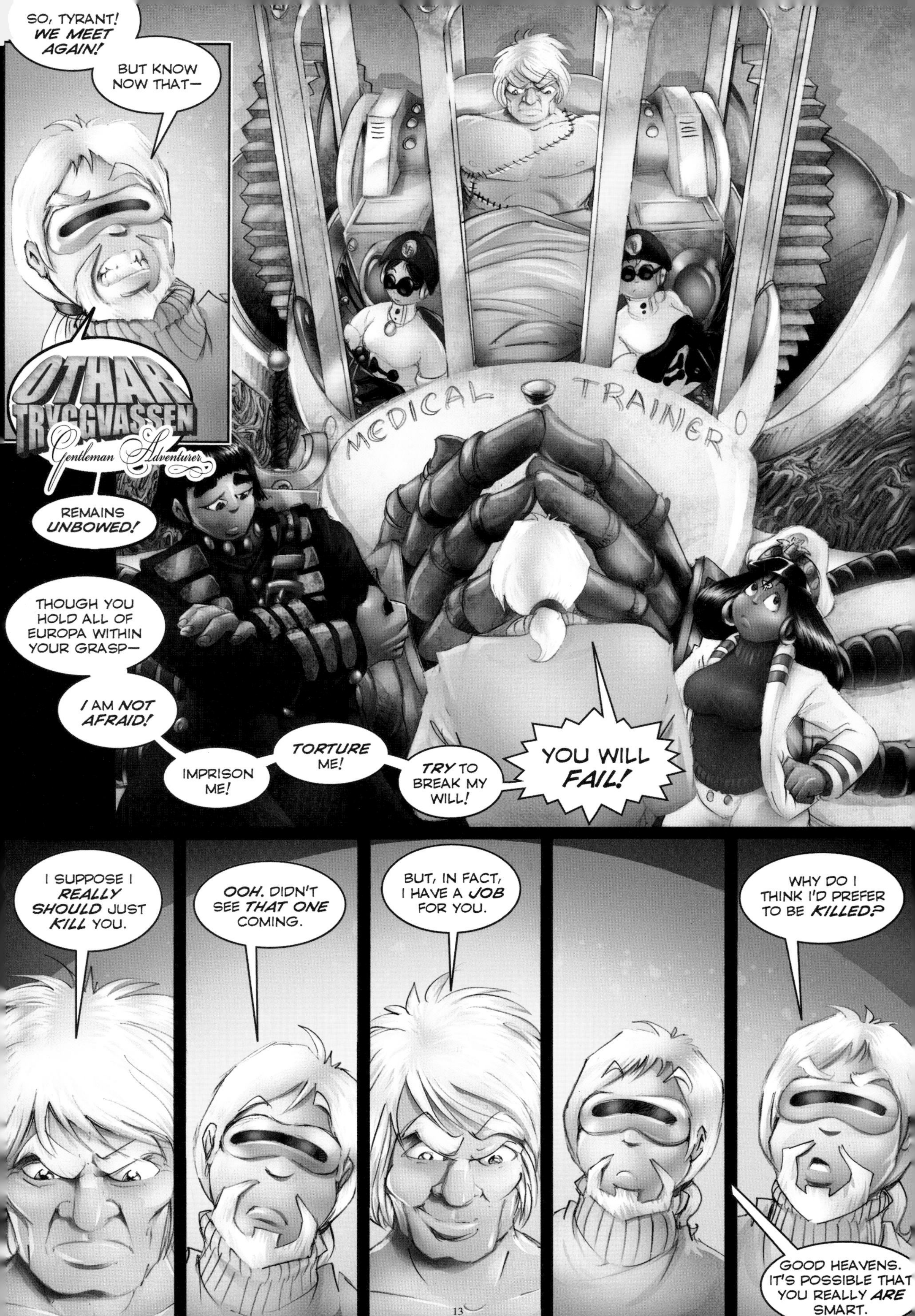
SO, TYRANT! WE MEET AGAIN!
BUT KNOW NOW THAT—
OTHAR TRYGGVASSEN Gentleman Adventurer
REMAINS UNBOWED!
MEDICAL TRAINER
THOUGH YOU HOLD ALL OF EUROPA WITHIN YOUR GRASP—
I AM NOT AFRAID!
IMPRISON ME!
TORTURE ME!
TRY TO BREAK MY WILL!
YOU WILL FAIL!
I SUPPOSE I REALLY SHOULD JUST KILL YOU.
OOH. DIDN'T SEE THAT ONE COMING.
BUT, IN FACT, I HAVE A JOB FOR YOU.
WHY DO I THINK I'D PREFER TO BE KILLED?
GOOD HEAVENS. IT'S POSSIBLE THAT YOU REALLY ARE SMART.

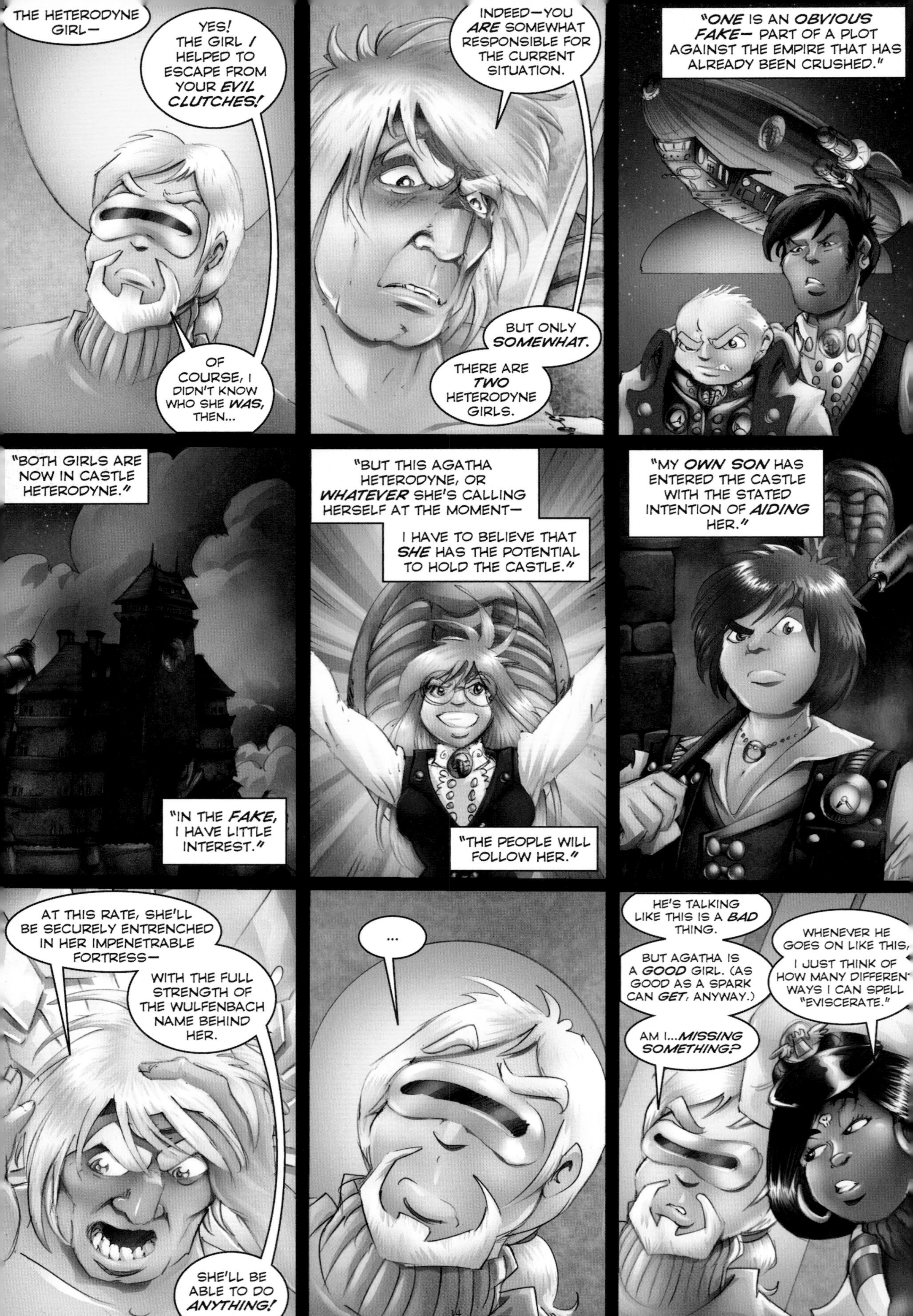
THE HETERODYNE GIRL—
YES! THE GIRL *I* HELPED TO ESCAPE FROM YOUR *EVIL CLUTCHES!*
OF COURSE, I DIDN'T KNOW WHO SHE *WAS*, THEN...
INDEED—YOU *ARE* SOMEWHAT RESPONSIBLE FOR THE CURRENT SITUATION.
BUT ONLY *SOMEWHAT*.
THERE ARE *TWO* HETERODYNE GIRLS.
"*ONE* IS AN *OBVIOUS FAKE*— PART OF A PLOT AGAINST THE EMPIRE THAT HAS ALREADY BEEN CRUSHED."
"BOTH GIRLS ARE NOW IN CASTLE HETERODYNE."
"IN THE *FAKE*, I HAVE LITTLE INTEREST."
"BUT THIS AGATHA HETERODYNE, OR *WHATEVER* SHE'S CALLING HERSELF AT THE MOMENT—
I HAVE TO BELIEVE THAT *SHE* HAS THE POTENTIAL TO HOLD THE CASTLE."
"THE PEOPLE WILL FOLLOW HER."
"MY *OWN SON* HAS ENTERED THE CASTLE WITH THE STATED INTENTION OF *AIDING* HER."
AT THIS RATE, SHE'LL BE SECURELY ENTRENCHED IN HER IMPENETRABLE FORTRESS—
WITH THE FULL STRENGTH OF THE WULFENBACH NAME BEHIND HER.
SHE'LL BE ABLE TO DO *ANYTHING!*
...
HE'S TALKING LIKE THIS IS A *BAD* THING.
BUT AGATHA IS A *GOOD* GIRL. (AS GOOD AS A SPARK CAN *GET*, ANYWAY.)
AM I...*MISSING SOMETHING?*
WHENEVER HE GOES ON LIKE THIS,
I JUST THINK OF HOW MANY DIFFEREN WAYS I CAN SPELL "EVISCERATE."

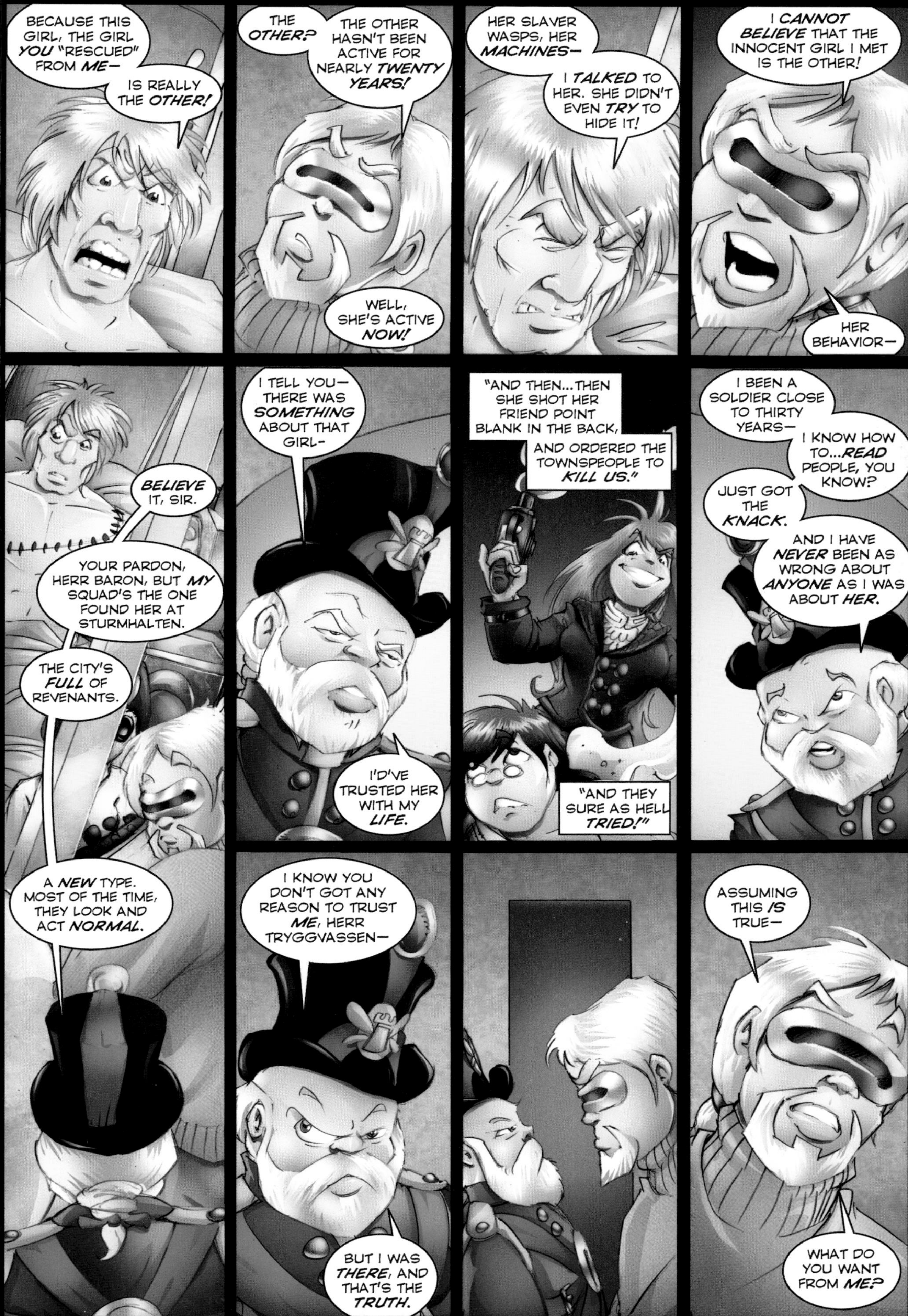
BECAUSE THIS GIRL, THE GIRL YOU "RESCUED" FROM ME—
IS REALLY THE OTHER!
THE OTHER?
THE OTHER HASN'T BEEN ACTIVE FOR NEARLY TWENTY YEARS!
WELL, SHE'S ACTIVE NOW!
HER SLAVER WASPS, HER MACHINES—
I TALKED TO HER. SHE DIDN'T EVEN TRY TO HIDE IT!
I CANNOT BELIEVE THAT THE INNOCENT GIRL I MET IS THE OTHER!
HER BEHAVIOR—
BELIEVE IT, SIR.
YOUR PARDON, HERR BARON, BUT MY SQUAD'S THE ONE FOUND HER AT STURMHALTEN.
THE CITY'S FULL OF REVENANTS.
I TELL YOU—THERE WAS SOMETHING ABOUT THAT GIRL-
I'D'VE TRUSTED HER WITH MY LIFE.
"AND THEN...THEN SHE SHOT HER FRIEND POINT BLANK IN THE BACK,
AND ORDERED THE TOWNSPEOPLE TO KILL US."
"AND THEY SURE AS HELL TRIED!"
I BEEN A SOLDIER CLOSE TO THIRTY YEARS—
I KNOW HOW TO...READ PEOPLE, YOU KNOW?
JUST GOT THE KNACK.
AND I HAVE NEVER BEEN AS WRONG ABOUT ANYONE AS I WAS ABOUT HER.
A NEW TYPE. MOST OF THE TIME, THEY LOOK AND ACT NORMAL.
I KNOW YOU DON'T GOT ANY REASON TO TRUST ME, HERR TRYGGVASSEN—
BUT I WAS THERE, AND THAT'S THE TRUTH.
ASSUMING THIS IS TRUE—
WHAT DO YOU WANT FROM ME?

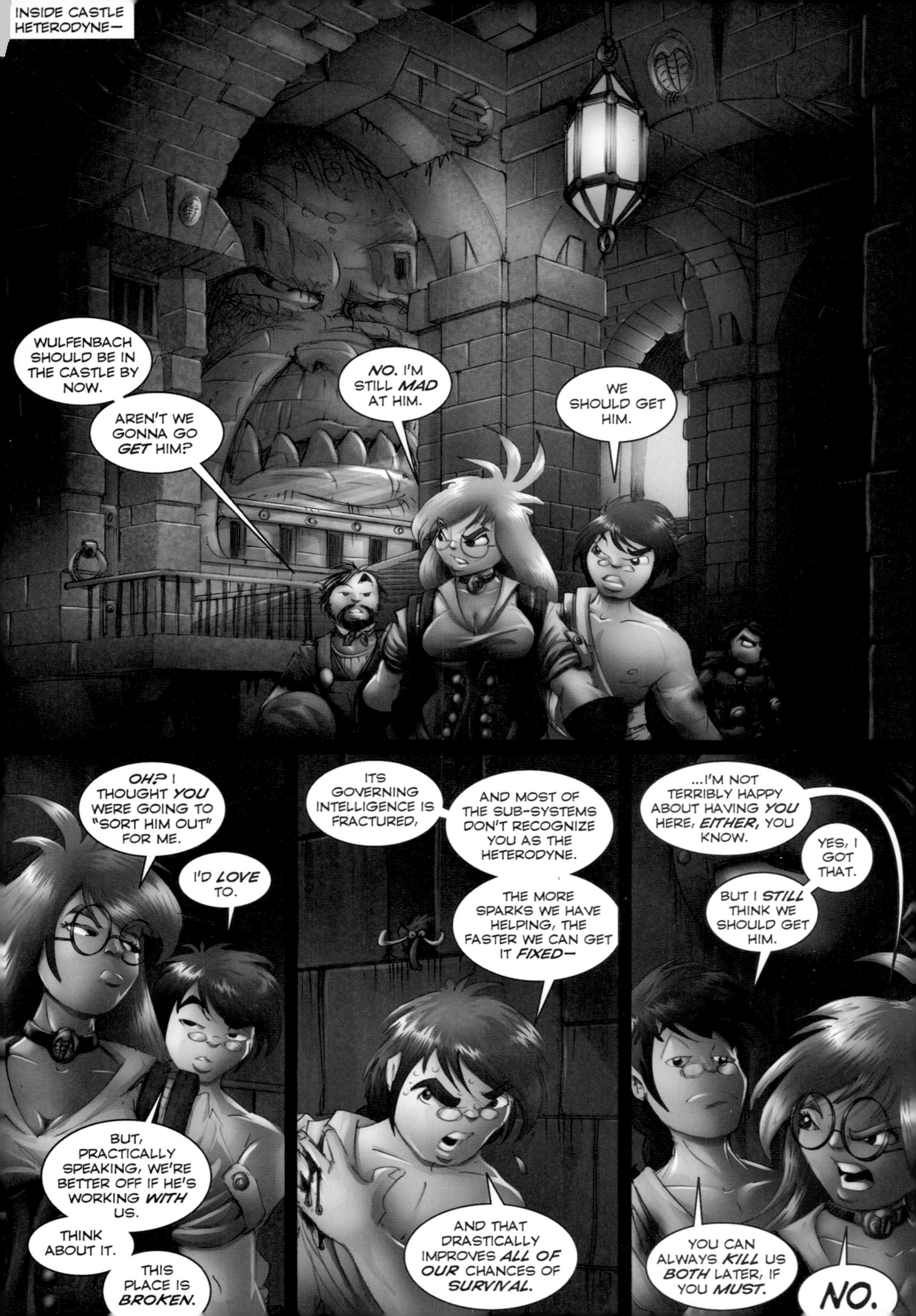
INSIDE CASTLE HETERODYNE—
WULFENBACH SHOULD BE IN THE CASTLE BY NOW.
AREN'T WE GONNA GO GET HIM?
NO. I'M STILL MAD AT HIM.
WE SHOULD GET HIM.
OH? I THOUGHT YOU WERE GOING TO "SORT HIM OUT" FOR ME.
I'D LOVE TO.
BUT, PRACTICALLY SPEAKING, WE'RE BETTER OFF IF HE'S WORKING WITH US.
THINK ABOUT IT.
THIS PLACE IS BROKEN.
ITS GOVERNING INTELLIGENCE IS FRACTURED,
AND MOST OF THE SUB-SYSTEMS DON'T RECOGNIZE YOU AS THE HETERODYNE.
THE MORE SPARKS WE HAVE HELPING, THE FASTER WE CAN GET IT FIXED—
AND THAT DRASTICALLY IMPROVES ALL OF OUR CHANCES OF SURVIVAL.
...I'M NOT TERRIBLY HAPPY ABOUT HAVING YOU HERE, EITHER, YOU KNOW.
YES, I GOT THAT.
BUT I STILL THINK WE SHOULD GET HIM.
YOU CAN ALWAYS KILL US BOTH LATER, IF YOU MUST.
NO.

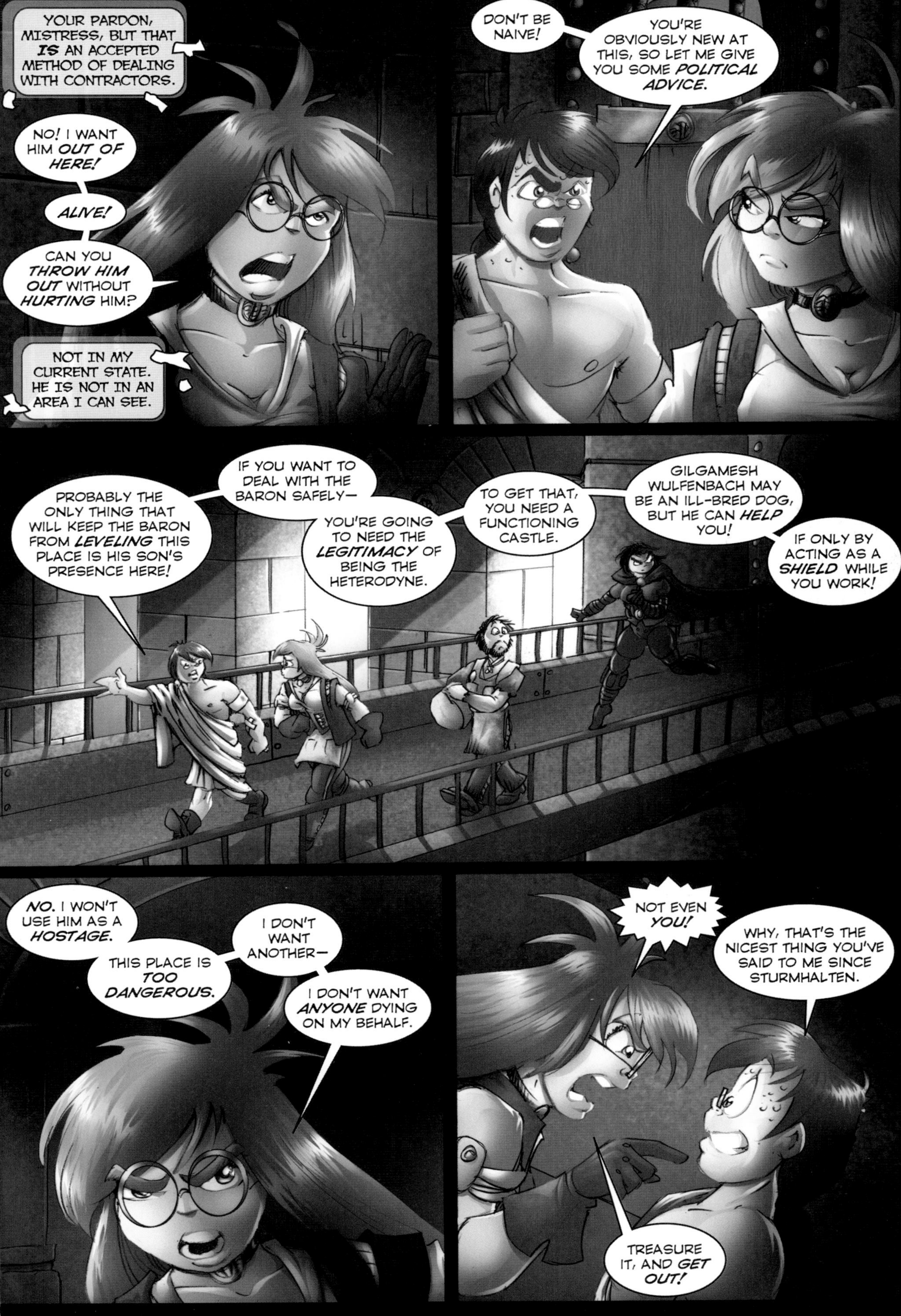
YOUR PARDON, MISTRESS, BUT THAT *IS* AN ACCEPTED METHOD OF DEALING WITH CONTRACTORS.
NO! I WANT HIM *OUT OF HERE!*
ALIVE!
CAN YOU *THROW HIM OUT* WITHOUT *HURTING* HIM?
NOT IN MY CURRENT STATE. HE IS NOT IN AN AREA I CAN SEE.
DON'T BE NAIVE!
YOU'RE OBVIOUSLY NEW AT THIS, SO LET ME GIVE YOU SOME *POLITICAL ADVICE*.
PROBABLY THE ONLY THING THAT WILL KEEP THE BARON FROM *LEVELING* THIS PLACE IS HIS SON'S PRESENCE HERE!
IF YOU WANT TO DEAL WITH THE BARON SAFELY—
YOU'RE GOING TO NEED THE *LEGITIMACY* OF BEING THE HETERODYNE.
TO GET THAT, YOU NEED A FUNCTIONING CASTLE.
GILGAMESH WULFENBACH MAY BE AN ILL-BRED DOG, BUT HE CAN *HELP* YOU!
IF ONLY BY ACTING AS A *SHIELD* WHILE YOU WORK!
NO. I WON'T USE HIM AS A *HOSTAGE*.
THIS PLACE IS *TOO DANGEROUS*.
I DON'T WANT ANOTHER—
I DON'T WANT *ANYONE* DYING ON MY BEHALF.
NOT EVEN *YOU!*
WHY, THAT'S THE NICEST THING YOU'VE SAID TO ME SINCE STURMHALTEN.
TREASURE IT, AND *GET OUT!*

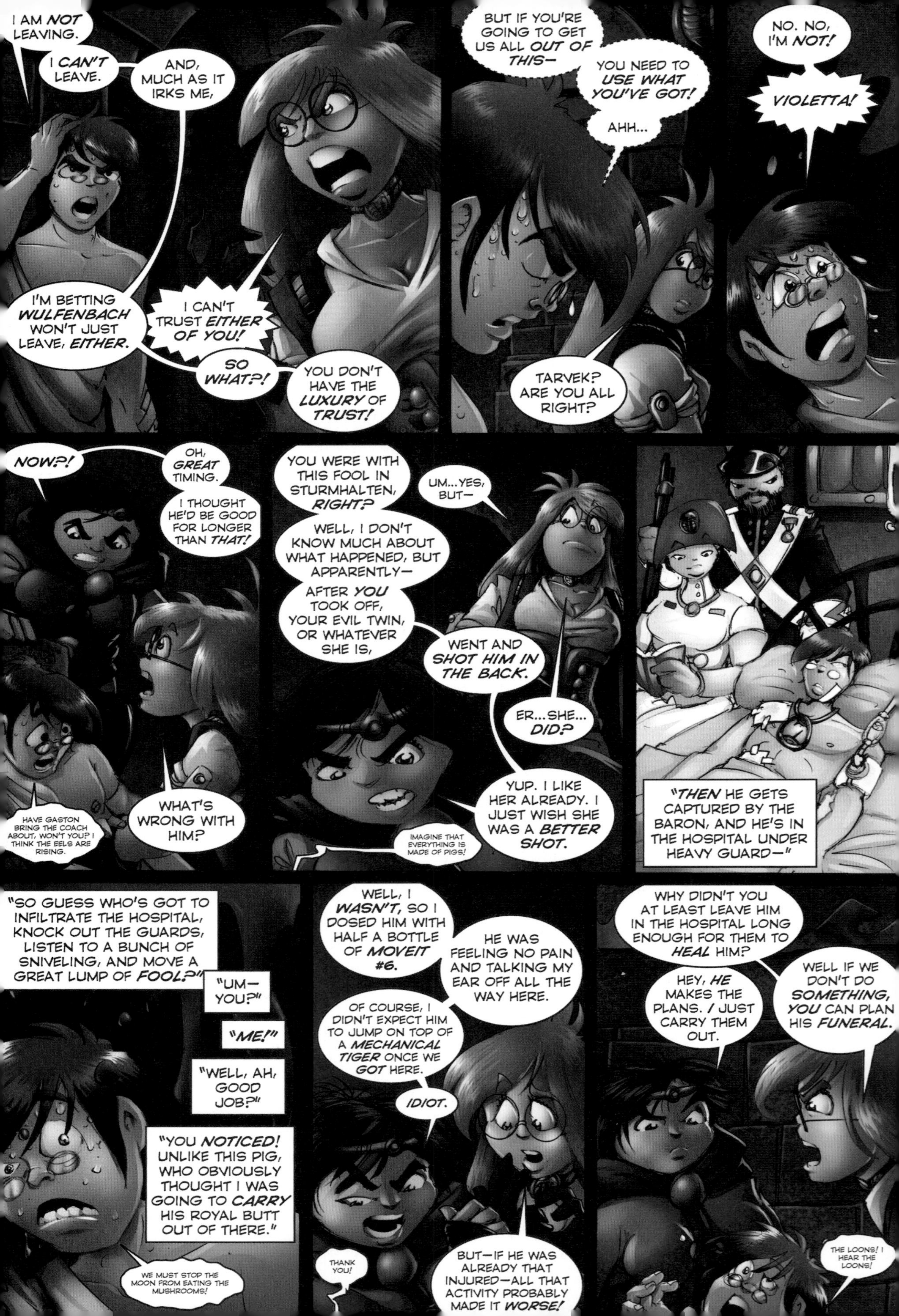

I AM NOT LEAVING.
I CAN'T LEAVE.
AND, MUCH AS IT IRKS ME,
I'M BETTING WULFENBACH WON'T JUST LEAVE, EITHER.
I CAN'T TRUST EITHER OF YOU!
SO WHAT?!
YOU DON'T HAVE THE LUXURY OF TRUST!
BUT IF YOU'RE GOING TO GET US ALL OUT OF THIS—
YOU NEED TO USE WHAT YOU'VE GOT!
AHH...
TARVEK? ARE YOU ALL RIGHT?
NO. NO, I'M NOT!
VIOLETTA!
NOW?!
OH, GREAT TIMING.
I THOUGHT HE'D BE GOOD FOR LONGER THAN THAT!
HAVE GASTON BRING THE COACH ABOUT, WON'T YOU? I THINK THE EELS ARE RISING.
WHAT'S WRONG WITH HIM?
YOU WERE WITH THIS FOOL IN STURMHALTEN, RIGHT?
UM...YES, BUT—
WELL, I DON'T KNOW MUCH ABOUT WHAT HAPPENED, BUT APPARENTLY—
AFTER YOU TOOK OFF, YOUR EVIL TWIN, OR WHATEVER SHE IS,
WENT AND SHOT HIM IN THE BACK.
ER...SHE... DID?
YUP. I LIKE HER ALREADY. I JUST WISH SHE WAS A BETTER SHOT.
IMAGINE THAT EVERYTHING IS MADE OF PIGS!
"THEN HE GETS CAPTURED BY THE BARON, AND HE'S IN THE HOSPITAL UNDER HEAVY GUARD—"
"SO GUESS WHO'S GOT TO INFILTRATE THE HOSPITAL, KNOCK OUT THE GUARDS, LISTEN TO A BUNCH OF SNIVELING, AND MOVE A GREAT LUMP OF FOOL?"
"UM— YOU?"
"ME!"
"WELL, AH, GOOD JOB?"
"YOU NOTICED! UNLIKE THIS PIG, WHO OBVIOUSLY THOUGHT I WAS GOING TO CARRY HIS ROYAL BUTT OUT OF THERE."
WE MUST STOP THE MOON FROM EATING THE MUSHROOMS!
WELL, I WASN'T, SO I DOSED HIM WITH HALF A BOTTLE OF MOVEIT #6.
HE WAS FEELING NO PAIN AND TALKING MY EAR OFF ALL THE WAY HERE.
OF COURSE, I DIDN'T EXPECT HIM TO JUMP ON TOP OF A MECHANICAL TIGER ONCE WE GOT HERE.
IDIOT.
THANK YOU!
BUT—IF HE WAS ALREADY THAT INJURED—ALL THAT ACTIVITY PROBABLY MADE IT WORSE!
WHY DIDN'T YOU AT LEAST LEAVE HIM IN THE HOSPITAL LONG ENOUGH FOR THEM TO HEAL HIM?
HEY, HE MAKES THE PLANS. I JUST CARRY THEM OUT.
WELL IF WE DON'T DO SOMETHING, YOU CAN PLAN HIS FUNERAL.
THE LOONS! I HEAR THE LOONS!

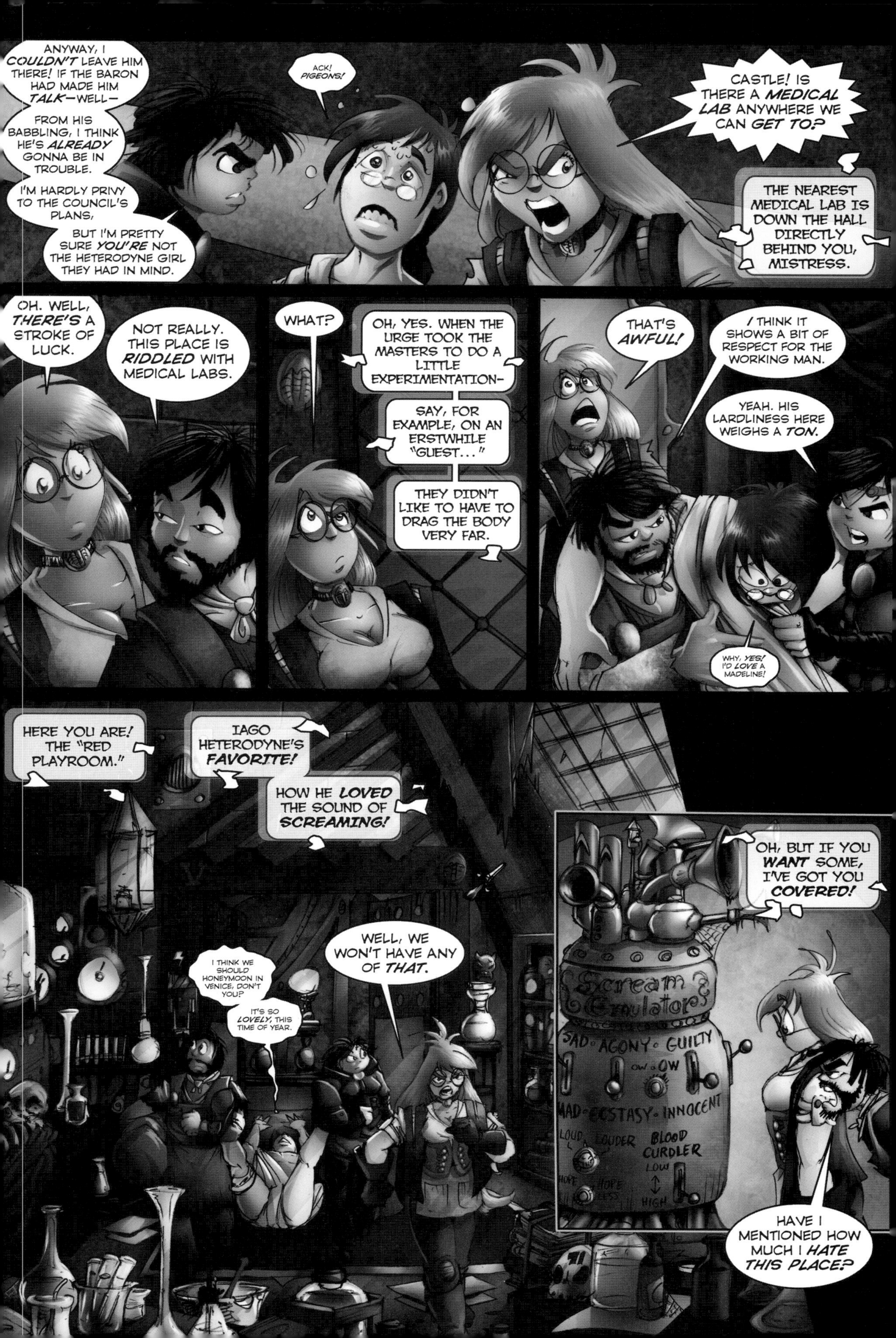
ANYWAY, I COULDN'T LEAVE HIM THERE! IF THE BARON HAD MADE HIM TALK—WELL—
FROM HIS BABBLING, I THINK HE'S ALREADY GONNA BE IN TROUBLE.
ACK! PIGEONS!
I'M HARDLY PRIVY TO THE COUNCIL'S PLANS,
BUT I'M PRETTY SURE YOU'RE NOT THE HETERODYNE GIRL THEY HAD IN MIND.
CASTLE! IS THERE A MEDICAL LAB ANYWHERE WE CAN GET TO?
THE NEAREST MEDICAL LAB IS DOWN THE HALL DIRECTLY BEHIND YOU, MISTRESS.
OH. WELL, THERE'S A STROKE OF LUCK.
NOT REALLY. THIS PLACE IS RIDDLED WITH MEDICAL LABS.
WHAT?
OH, YES. WHEN THE URGE TOOK THE MASTERS TO DO A LITTLE EXPERIMENTATION-
SAY, FOR EXAMPLE, ON AN ERSTWHILE "GUEST..."
THEY DIDN'T LIKE TO HAVE TO DRAG THE BODY VERY FAR.
THAT'S AWFUL!
I THINK IT SHOWS A BIT OF RESPECT FOR THE WORKING MAN.
YEAH. HIS LARDLINESS HERE WEIGHS A TON.
WHY, YES! I'D LOVE A MADELINE!
HERE YOU ARE! THE "RED PLAYROOM."
IAGO HETERODYNE'S FAVORITE!
HOW HE LOVED THE SOUND OF SCREAMING!
I THINK WE SHOULD HONEYMOON IN VENICE, DON'T YOU?
IT'S SO LOVELY, THIS TIME OF YEAR.
WELL, WE WON'T HAVE ANY OF THAT.
OH, BUT IF YOU WANT SOME, I'VE GOT YOU COVERED!
Scream Emulator
SAD
AGONY
GUILTY
OW OW
MAD
ECSTASY
INNOCENT
LOUD
LOUDER
BLOOD CURDLER
LOW
HIGH
HOPE
HOPELESS
HAVE I MENTIONED HOW MUCH I HATE THIS PLACE?

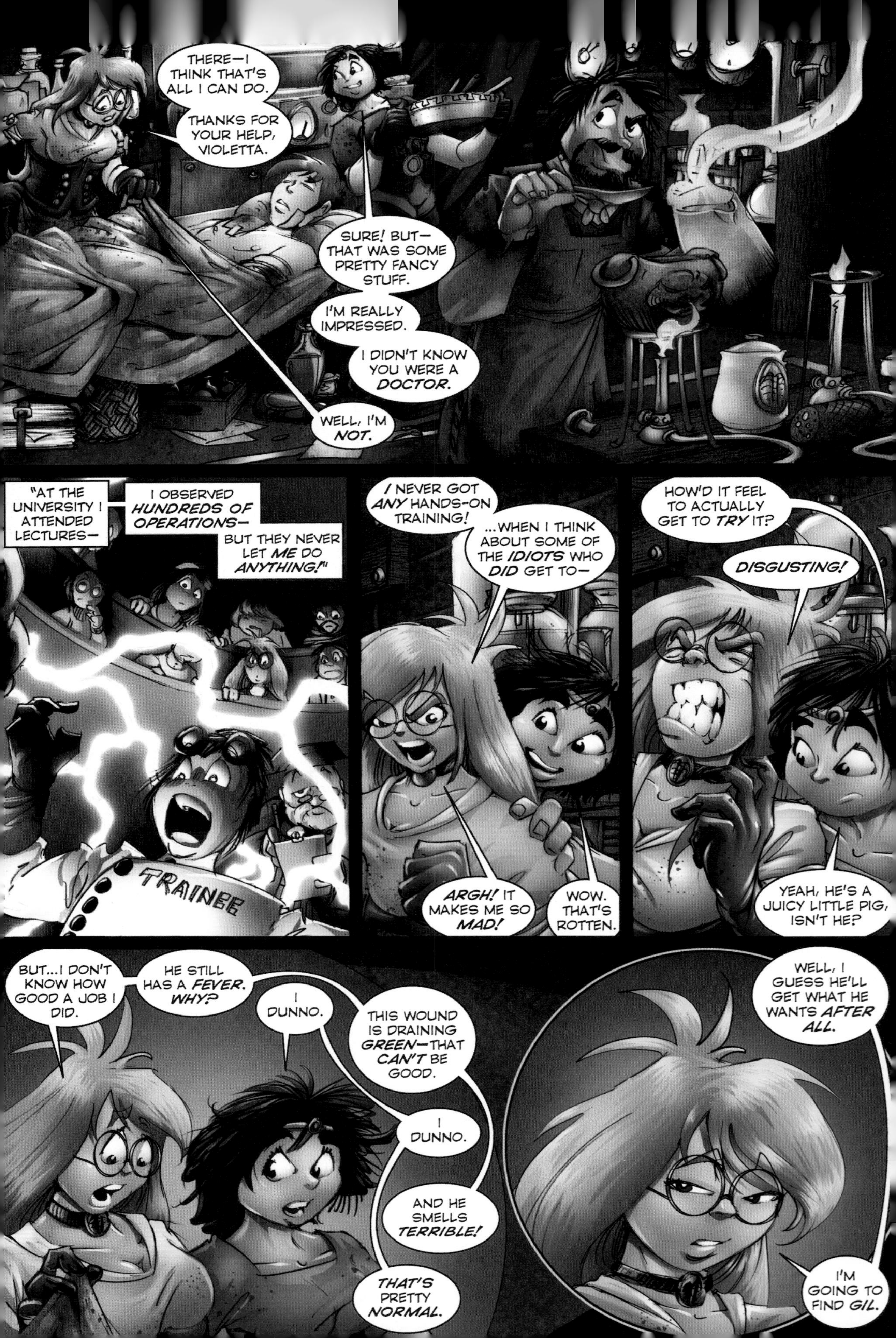
THERE—I THINK THAT'S ALL I CAN DO.
THANKS FOR YOUR HELP, VIOLETTA.
SURE! BUT—THAT WAS SOME PRETTY FANCY STUFF.
I'M REALLY IMPRESSED.
I DIDN'T KNOW YOU WERE A *DOCTOR*.
WELL, I'M *NOT*.
"AT THE UNIVERSITY I ATTENDED LECTURES—
I OBSERVED *HUNDREDS OF OPERATIONS*—
BUT THEY NEVER LET *ME* DO *ANYTHING!*"
TRAINEE
I NEVER GOT *ANY* HANDS-ON TRAINING!
...WHEN I THINK ABOUT SOME OF THE *IDIOTS* WHO *DID* GET TO—
ARGH! IT MAKES ME SO *MAD!*
WOW. THAT'S ROTTEN.
HOW'D IT FEEL TO ACTUALLY GET TO *TRY* IT?
DISGUSTING!
YEAH, HE'S A JUICY LITTLE PIG, ISN'T HE?
BUT...I DON'T KNOW HOW GOOD A JOB I DID.
HE STILL HAS A *FEVER*. *WHY?*
I DUNNO.
THIS WOUND IS DRAINING *GREEN*—THAT *CAN'T* BE GOOD.
I DUNNO.
AND HE SMELLS *TERRIBLE!*
THAT'S PRETTY *NORMAL*.
WELL, I GUESS HE'LL GET WHAT HE WANTS *AFTER ALL*.
I'M GOING TO FIND *GIL*.

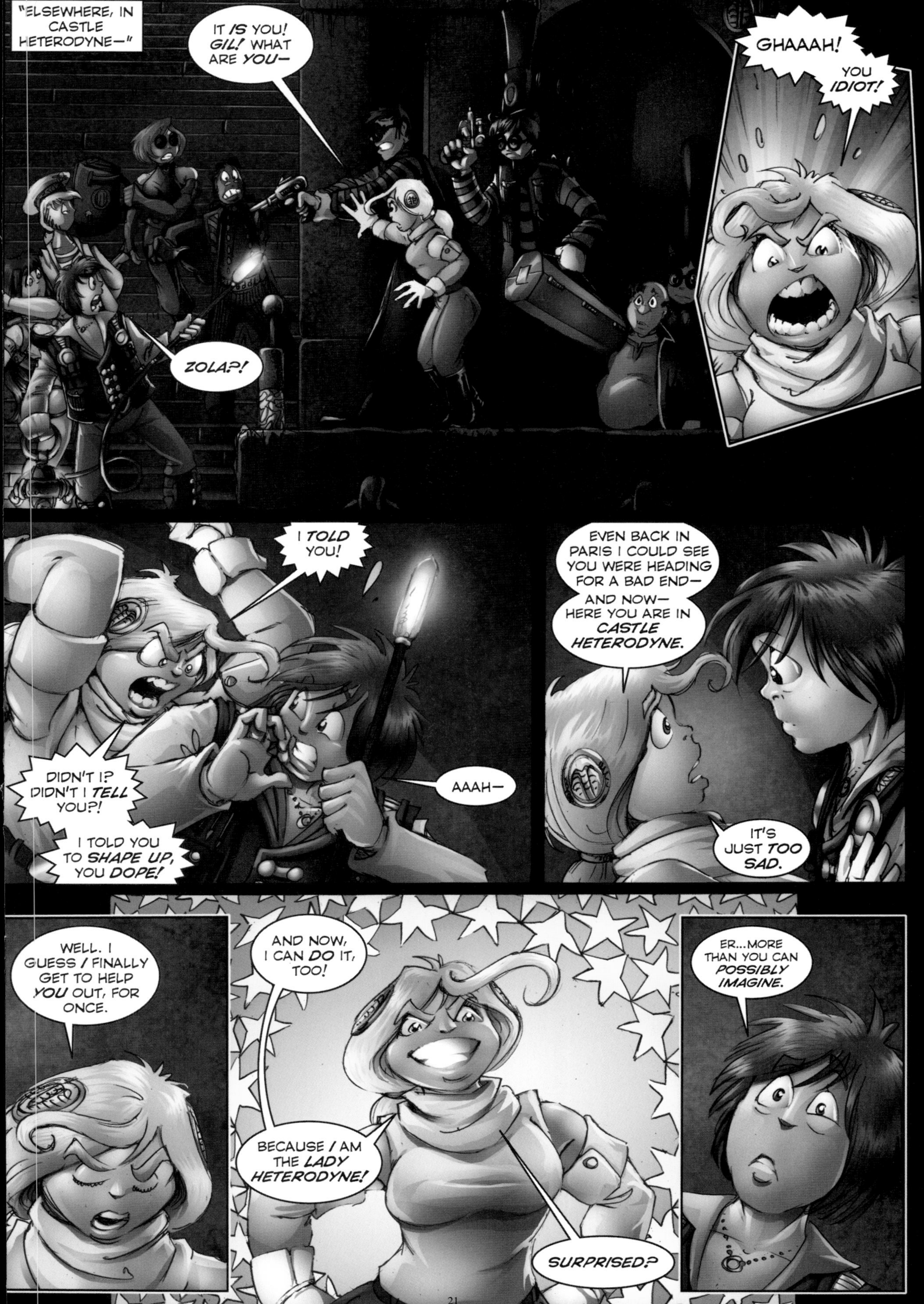
"ELSEWHERE, IN CASTLE HETERODYNE—"
IT IS YOU! GIL! WHAT ARE YOU—
ZOLA?!
GHAAAH!
YOU IDIOT!
I TOLD YOU!
DIDN'T I? DIDN'T I TELL YOU?!
I TOLD YOU TO SHAPE UP, YOU DOPE!
AAAH—
EVEN BACK IN PARIS I COULD SEE YOU WERE HEADING FOR A BAD END—
AND NOW— HERE YOU ARE IN CASTLE HETERODYNE.
IT'S JUST TOO SAD.
WELL. I GUESS I FINALLY GET TO HELP YOU OUT, FOR ONCE.
AND NOW, I CAN DO IT, TOO!
BECAUSE I AM THE LADY HETERODYNE!
SURPRISED?
ER...MORE THAN YOU CAN POSSIBLY IMAGINE.

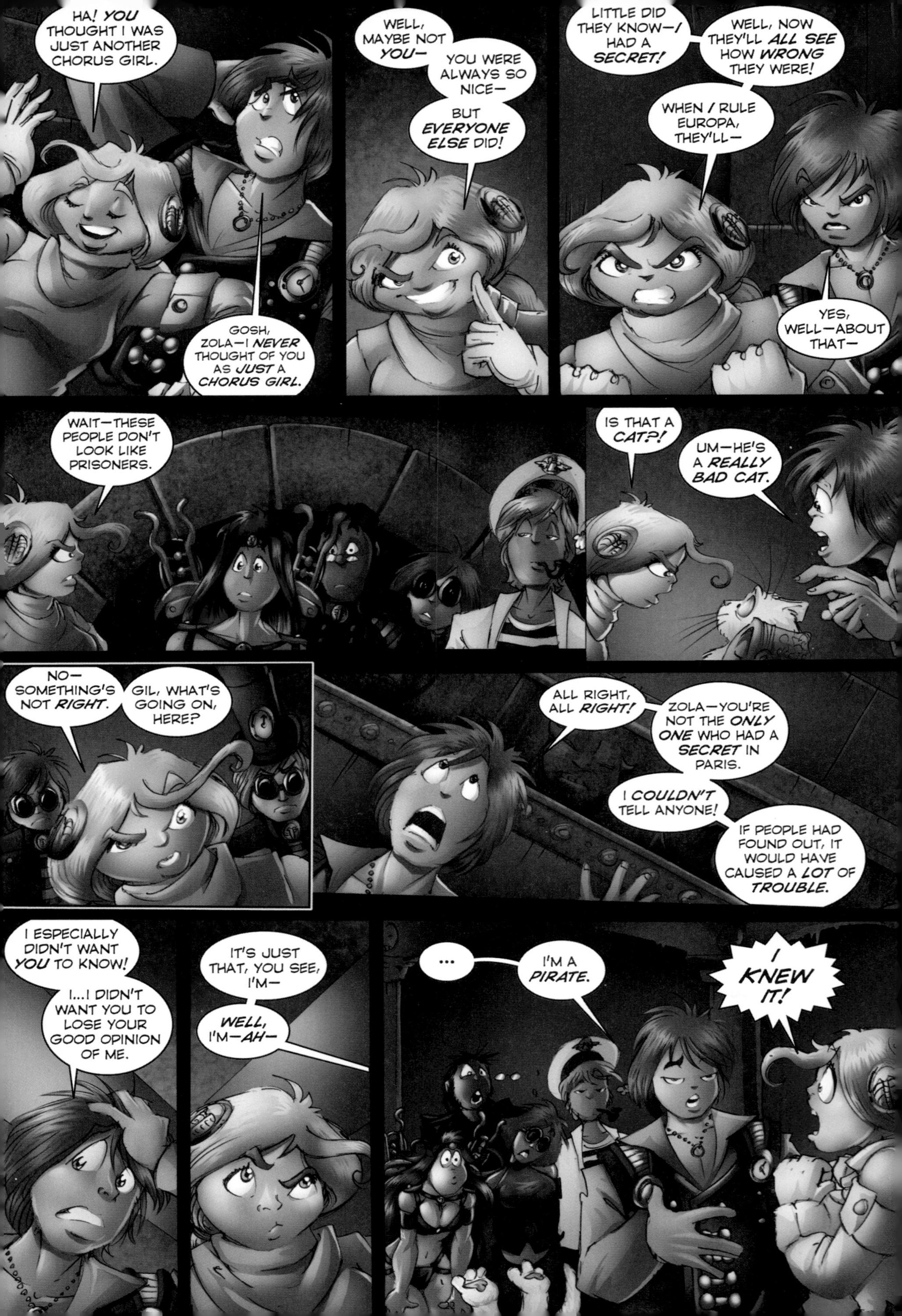
HA! YOU THOUGHT I WAS JUST ANOTHER CHORUS GIRL.
GOSH, ZOLA—I NEVER THOUGHT OF YOU AS JUST A CHORUS GIRL.
WELL, MAYBE NOT YOU—
YOU WERE ALWAYS SO NICE—
BUT EVERYONE ELSE DID!
LITTLE DID THEY KNOW—I HAD A SECRET!
WELL, NOW THEY'LL ALL SEE HOW WRONG THEY WERE!
WHEN I RULE EUROPA, THEY'LL—
YES, WELL—ABOUT THAT—
WAIT—THESE PEOPLE DON'T LOOK LIKE PRISONERS.
IS THAT A CAT?!
UM—HE'S A REALLY BAD CAT.
NO—SOMETHING'S NOT RIGHT.
GIL, WHAT'S GOING ON, HERE?
ALL RIGHT, ALL RIGHT!
ZOLA—YOU'RE NOT THE ONLY ONE WHO HAD A SECRET IN PARIS.
I COULDN'T TELL ANYONE!
IF PEOPLE HAD FOUND OUT, IT WOULD HAVE CAUSED A LOT OF TROUBLE.
I ESPECIALLY DIDN'T WANT YOU TO KNOW!
I...I DIDN'T WANT YOU TO LOSE YOUR GOOD OPINION OF ME.
IT'S JUST THAT, YOU SEE, I'M—
WELL, I'M—AH—
...
I'M A PIRATE.
I KNEW IT!

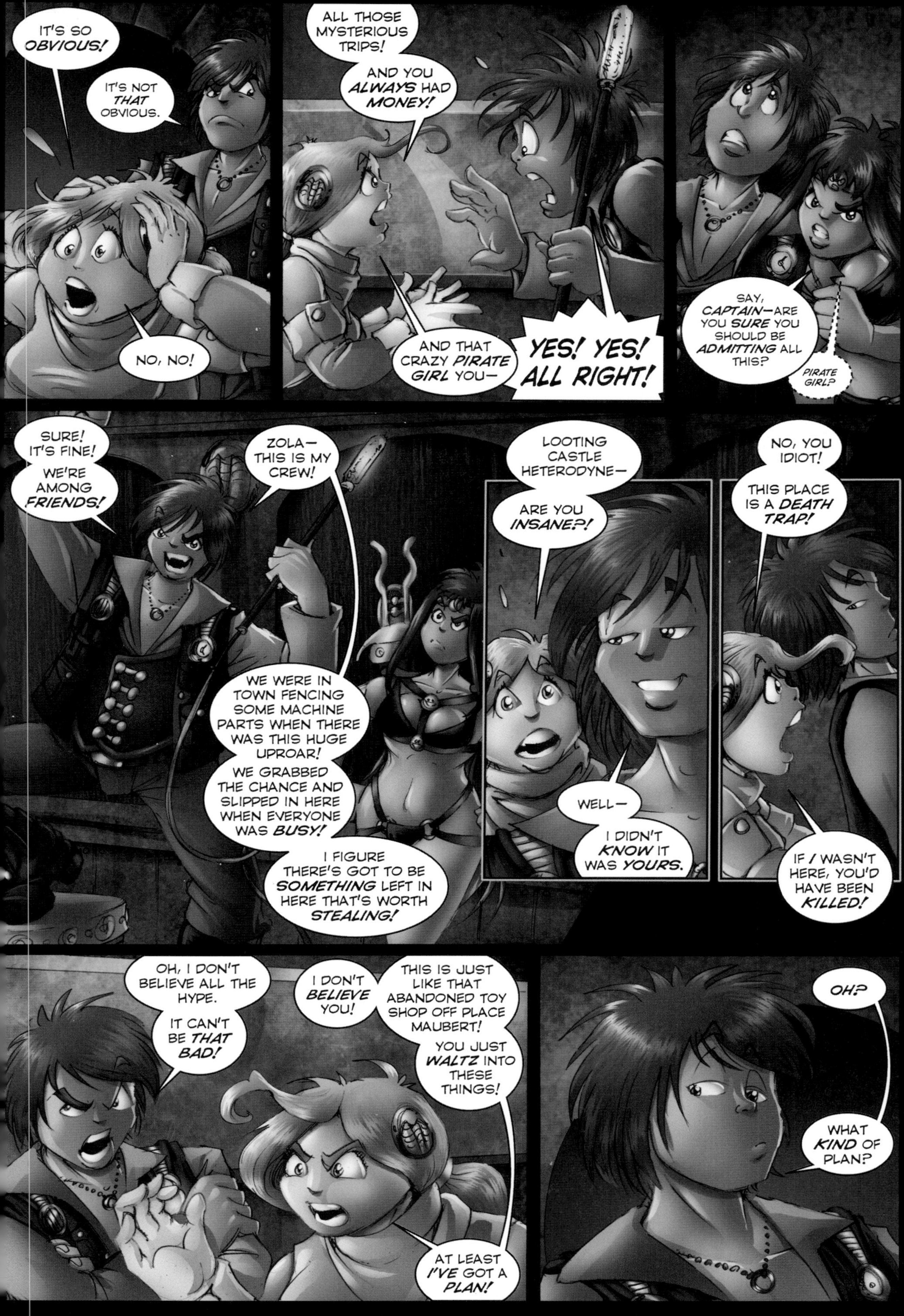

IT'S SO OBVIOUS!
IT'S NOT THAT OBVIOUS.
NO, NO!
ALL THOSE MYSTERIOUS TRIPS!
AND YOU ALWAYS HAD MONEY!
AND THAT CRAZY PIRATE GIRL YOU—
YES! YES! ALL RIGHT!
SAY, CAPTAIN—ARE YOU SURE YOU SHOULD BE ADMITTING ALL THIS?
PIRATE GIRL?
SURE! IT'S FINE!
WE'RE AMONG FRIENDS!
ZOLA—THIS IS MY CREW!
WE WERE IN TOWN FENCING SOME MACHINE PARTS WHEN THERE WAS THIS HUGE UPROAR!
WE GRABBED THE CHANCE AND SLIPPED IN HERE WHEN EVERYONE WAS BUSY!
I FIGURE THERE'S GOT TO BE SOMETHING LEFT IN HERE THAT'S WORTH STEALING!
LOOTING CASTLE HETERODYNE—
ARE YOU INSANE?!
WELL—
I DIDN'T KNOW IT WAS YOURS.
NO, YOU IDIOT!
THIS PLACE IS A DEATH TRAP!
IF I WASN'T HERE, YOU'D HAVE BEEN KILLED!
OH, I DON'T BELIEVE ALL THE HYPE.
IT CAN'T BE THAT BAD!
I DON'T BELIEVE YOU!
THIS IS JUST LIKE THAT ABANDONED TOY SHOP OFF PLACE MAUBERT!
YOU JUST WALTZ INTO THESE THINGS!
AT LEAST I'VE GOT A PLAN!
OH?
WHAT KIND OF PLAN?

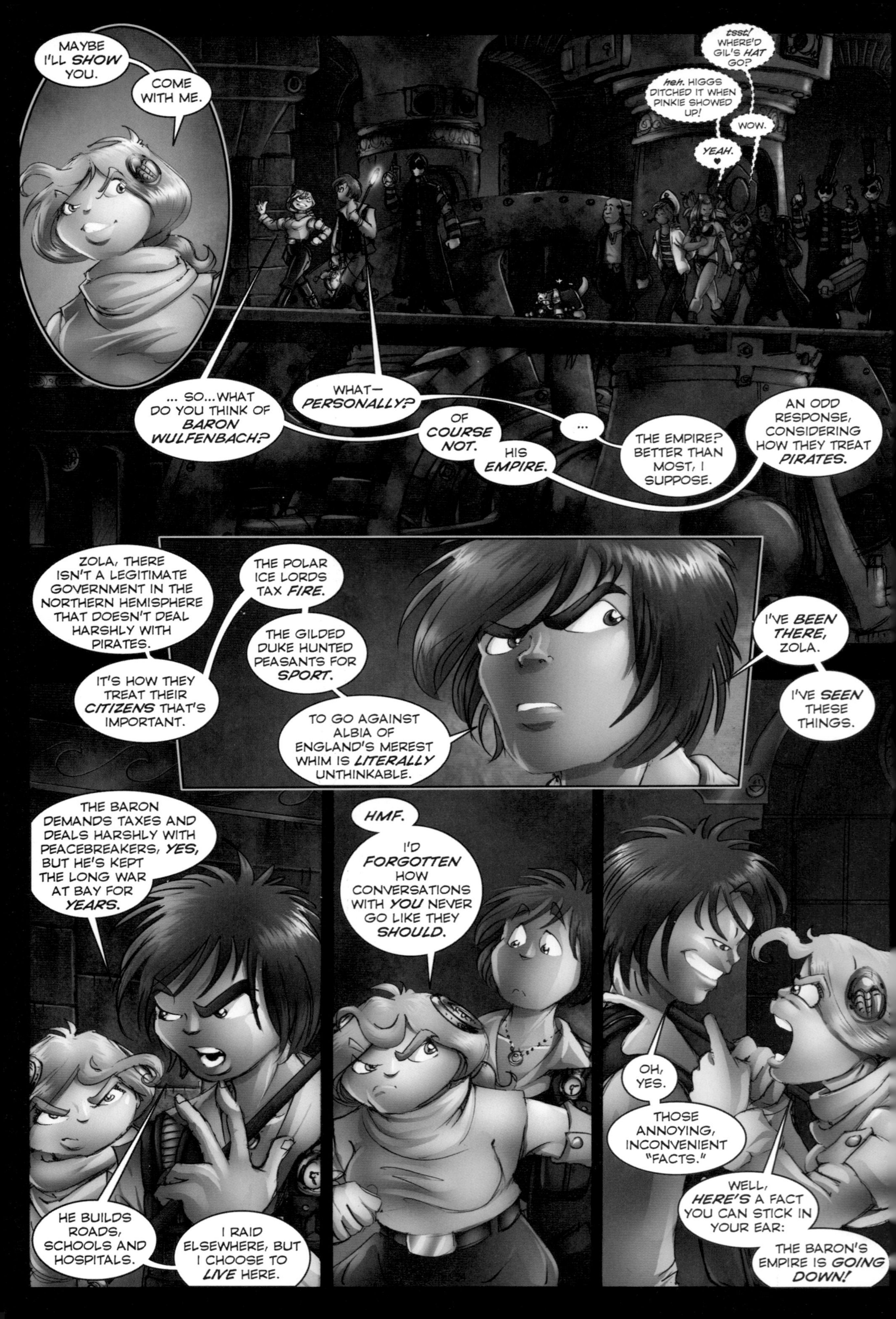
MAYBE I'LL *SHOW* YOU.
COME WITH ME.
tsst! WHERE'D GIL'S *HAT* GO?
heh. HIGGS DITCHED IT WHEN PINKIE SHOWED UP!
WOW.
YEAH. ♥
... SO...WHAT DO YOU THINK OF *BARON WULFENBACH?*
WHAT— *PERSONALLY?*
OF *COURSE NOT.*
HIS *EMPIRE.*
...
THE EMPIRE? BETTER THAN MOST, I SUPPOSE.
AN ODD RESPONSE, CONSIDERING HOW THEY TREAT *PIRATES.*
ZOLA, THERE ISN'T A LEGITIMATE GOVERNMENT IN THE NORTHERN HEMISPHERE THAT DOESN'T DEAL HARSHLY WITH PIRATES.
IT'S HOW THEY TREAT THEIR *CITIZENS* THAT'S IMPORTANT.
THE POLAR ICE LORDS TAX *FIRE.*
THE GILDED DUKE HUNTED PEASANTS FOR *SPORT.*
TO GO AGAINST ALBIA OF ENGLAND'S MEREST WHIM IS *LITERALLY* UNTHINKABLE.
I'VE *BEEN THERE,* ZOLA.
I'VE *SEEN* THESE THINGS.
THE BARON DEMANDS TAXES AND DEALS HARSHLY WITH PEACEBREAKERS, *YES,* BUT HE'S KEPT THE LONG WAR AT BAY FOR *YEARS.*
HE BUILDS ROADS, SCHOOLS AND HOSPITALS.
I RAID ELSEWHERE, BUT I CHOOSE TO *LIVE* HERE.
HMF.
I'D *FORGOTTEN* HOW CONVERSATIONS WITH *YOU* NEVER GO LIKE THEY *SHOULD.*
OH, YES.
THOSE ANNOYING, INCONVENIENT "FACTS."
WELL, *HERE'S* A FACT YOU CAN STICK IN YOUR EAR:
THE BARON'S EMPIRE IS *GOING DOWN!*

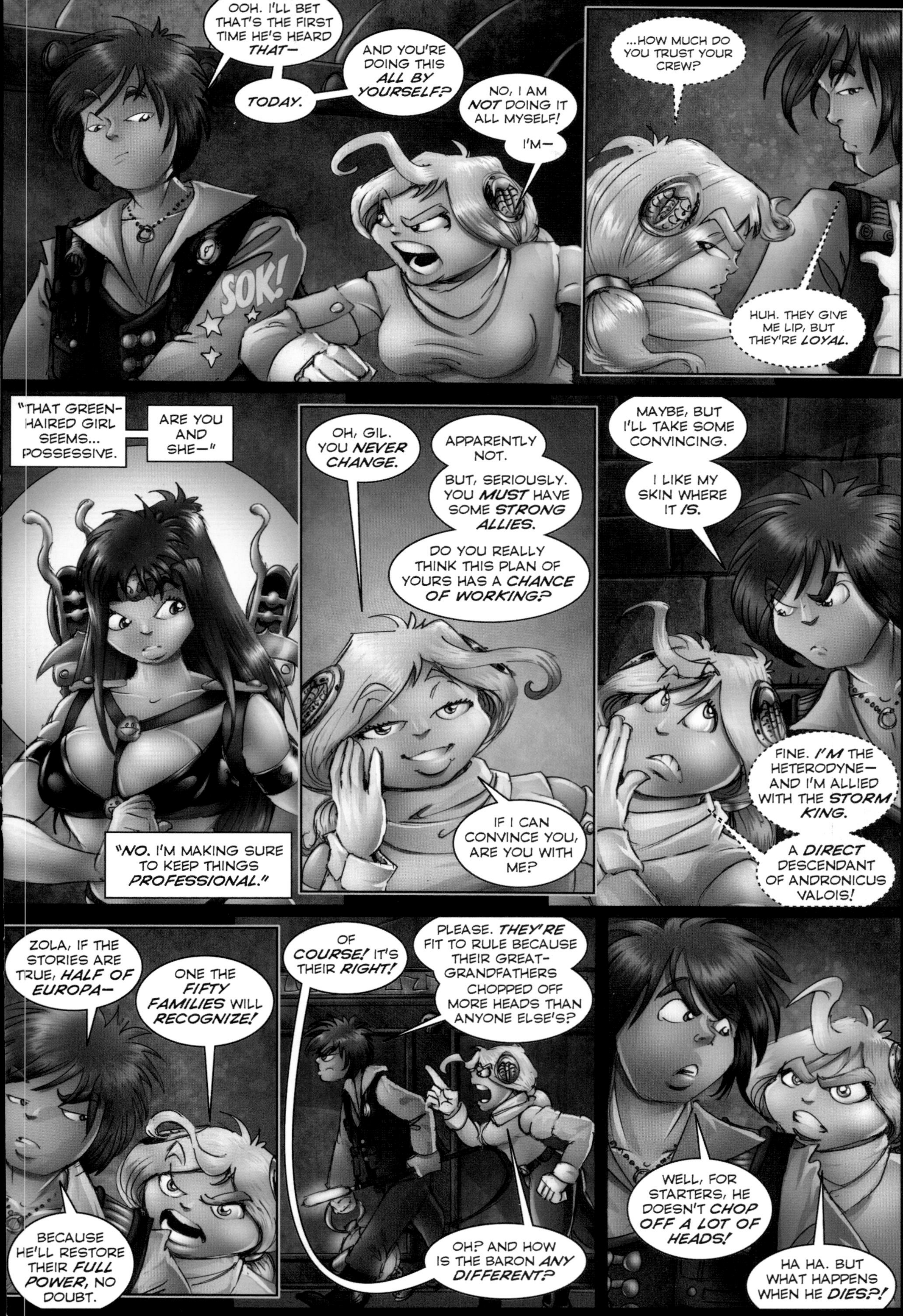
OOH. I'LL BET THAT'S THE FIRST TIME HE'S HEARD THAT—
TODAY.
AND YOU'RE DOING THIS ALL BY YOURSELF?
NO, I AM NOT DOING IT ALL MYSELF!
I'M—
SOK!
...HOW MUCH DO YOU TRUST YOUR CREW?
HUH. THEY GIVE ME LIP, BUT THEY'RE LOYAL.
"THAT GREEN-HAIRED GIRL SEEMS... POSSESSIVE.
ARE YOU AND SHE—"
"NO. I'M MAKING SURE TO KEEP THINGS PROFESSIONAL."
OH, GIL. YOU NEVER CHANGE.
APPARENTLY NOT.
BUT, SERIOUSLY. YOU MUST HAVE SOME STRONG ALLIES.
DO YOU REALLY THINK THIS PLAN OF YOURS HAS A CHANCE OF WORKING?
IF I CAN CONVINCE YOU, ARE YOU WITH ME?
MAYBE, BUT I'LL TAKE SOME CONVINCING.
I LIKE MY SKIN WHERE IT IS.
FINE. I'M THE HETERODYNE— AND I'M ALLIED WITH THE STORM KING.
A DIRECT DESCENDANT OF ANDRONICUS VALOIS!
ZOLA, IF THE STORIES ARE TRUE, HALF OF EUROPA—
ONE THE FIFTY FAMILIES WILL RECOGNIZE!
BECAUSE HE'LL RESTORE THEIR FULL POWER, NO DOUBT.
OF COURSE! IT'S THEIR RIGHT!
PLEASE. THEY'RE FIT TO RULE BECAUSE THEIR GREAT-GRANDFATHERS CHOPPED OFF MORE HEADS THAN ANYONE ELSE'S?
OH? AND HOW IS THE BARON ANY DIFFERENT?
WELL, FOR STARTERS, HE DOESN'T CHOP OFF A LOT OF HEADS!
HA HA. BUT WHAT HAPPENS WHEN HE DIES?!

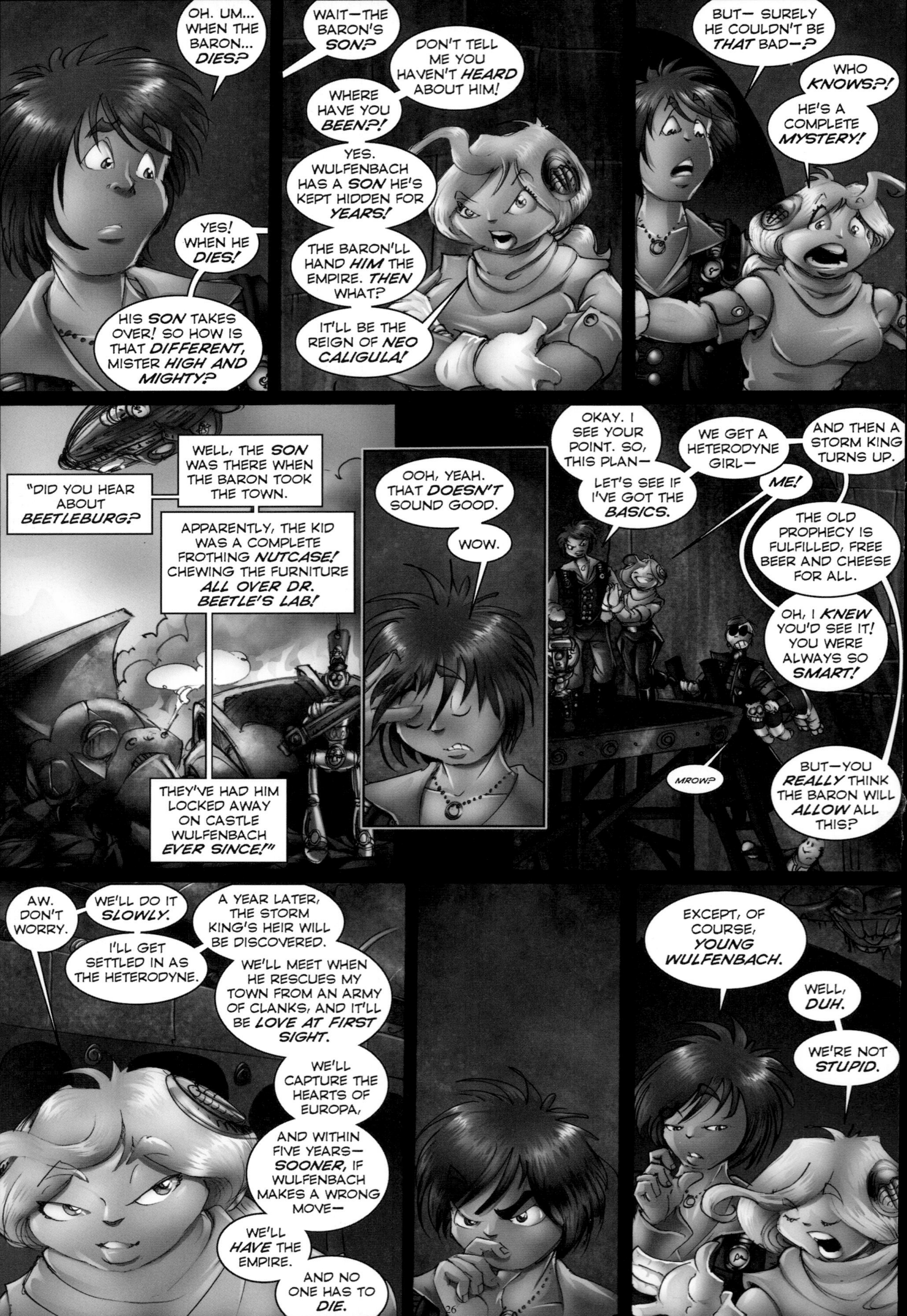
OH. UM... WHEN THE BARON... DIES?
YES! WHEN HE DIES!
HIS SON TAKES OVER! SO HOW IS THAT DIFFERENT, MISTER HIGH AND MIGHTY?
WAIT—THE BARON'S SON?
DON'T TELL ME YOU HAVEN'T HEARD ABOUT HIM!
WHERE HAVE YOU BEEN?!
YES. WULFENBACH HAS A SON HE'S KEPT HIDDEN FOR YEARS!
THE BARON'LL HAND HIM THE EMPIRE. THEN WHAT?
IT'LL BE THE REIGN OF NEO CALIGULA!
BUT— SURELY HE COULDN'T BE THAT BAD—?
WHO KNOWS?!
HE'S A COMPLETE MYSTERY!
"DID YOU HEAR ABOUT BEETLEBURG?
WELL, THE SON WAS THERE WHEN THE BARON TOOK THE TOWN.
APPARENTLY, THE KID WAS A COMPLETE FROTHING NUTCASE! CHEWING THE FURNITURE ALL OVER DR. BEETLE'S LAB!
THEY'VE HAD HIM LOCKED AWAY ON CASTLE WULFENBACH EVER SINCE!"
OOH, YEAH. THAT DOESN'T SOUND GOOD.
WOW.
OKAY. I SEE YOUR POINT. SO, THIS PLAN—
LET'S SEE IF I'VE GOT THE BASICS.
WE GET A HETERODYNE GIRL—
ME!
AND THEN A STORM KING TURNS UP.
THE OLD PROPHECY IS FULFILLED, FREE BEER AND CHEESE FOR ALL.
OH, I KNEW YOU'D SEE IT! YOU WERE ALWAYS SO SMART!
MROW?
BUT—YOU REALLY THINK THE BARON WILL ALLOW ALL THIS?
AW. DON'T WORRY.
WE'LL DO IT SLOWLY.
I'LL GET SETTLED IN AS THE HETERODYNE.
A YEAR LATER, THE STORM KING'S HEIR WILL BE DISCOVERED.
WE'LL MEET WHEN HE RESCUES MY TOWN FROM AN ARMY OF CLANKS, AND IT'LL BE LOVE AT FIRST SIGHT.
WE'LL CAPTURE THE HEARTS OF EUROPA,
AND WITHIN FIVE YEARS— SOONER, IF WULFENBACH MAKES A WRONG MOVE—
WE'LL HAVE THE EMPIRE.
AND NO ONE HAS TO DIE.
EXCEPT, OF COURSE, YOUNG WULFENBACH.
WELL, DUH.
WE'RE NOT STUPID.

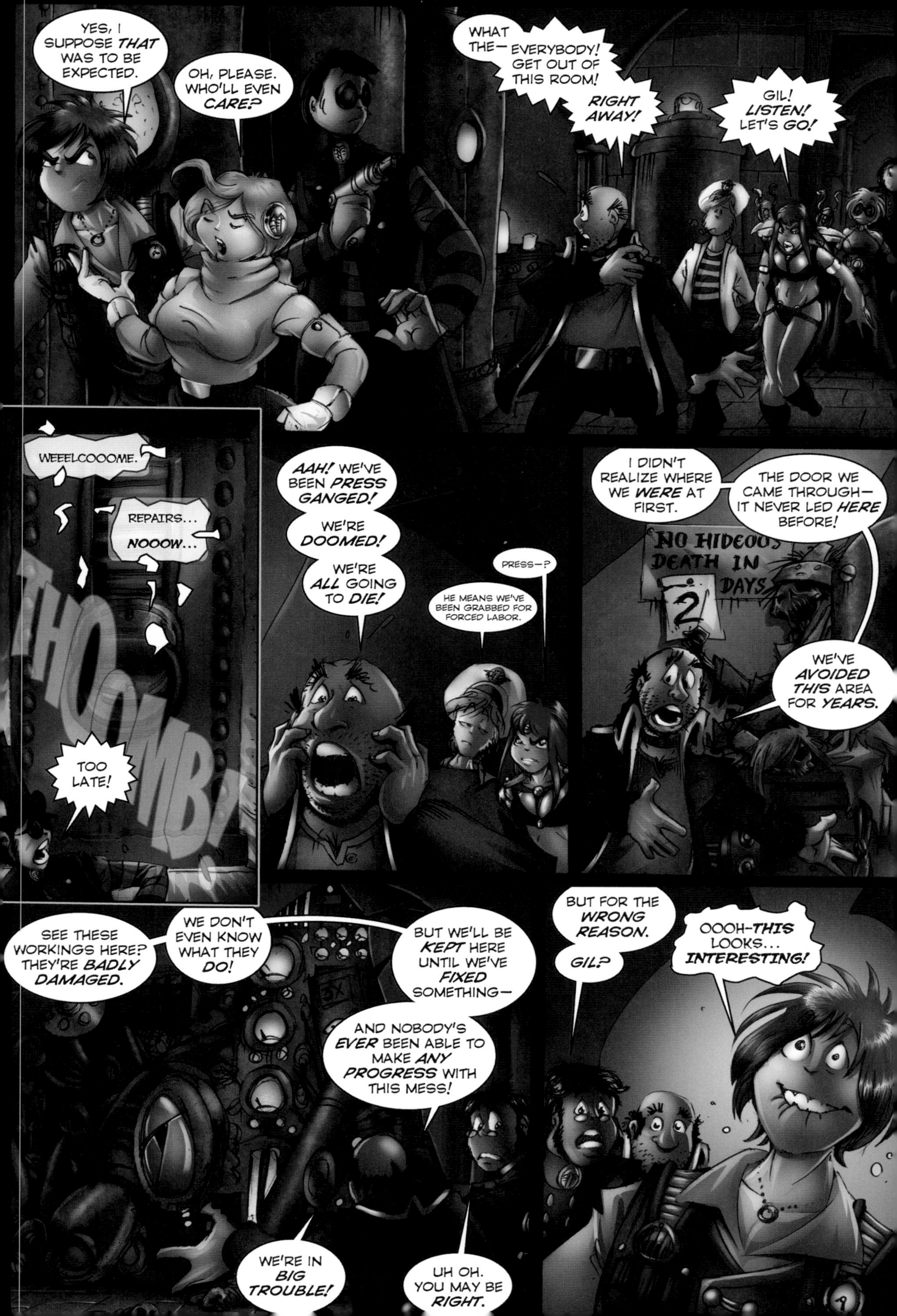
YES, I SUPPOSE THAT WAS TO BE EXPECTED.
OH, PLEASE. WHO'LL EVEN CARE?
WHAT THE—
EVERYBODY! GET OUT OF THIS ROOM!
RIGHT AWAY!
GIL! LISTEN! LET'S GO!
WEEELCOOOME.
REPAIRS... NOOOW...
THOOOMB!
TOO LATE!
AAH! WE'VE BEEN PRESS GANGED!
WE'RE DOOMED!
WE'RE ALL GOING TO DIE!
PRESS—?
HE MEANS WE'VE BEEN GRABBED FOR FORCED LABOR.
I DIDN'T REALIZE WHERE WE WERE AT FIRST.
THE DOOR WE CAME THROUGH— IT NEVER LED HERE BEFORE!
NO HIDEOUS DEATH IN 2 DAYS
WE'VE AVOIDED THIS AREA FOR YEARS.
SEE THESE WORKINGS HERE? THEY'RE BADLY DAMAGED.
WE DON'T EVEN KNOW WHAT THEY DO!
BUT WE'LL BE KEPT HERE UNTIL WE'VE FIXED SOMETHING—
AND NOBODY'S EVER BEEN ABLE TO MAKE ANY PROGRESS WITH THIS MESS!
WE'RE IN BIG TROUBLE!
UH OH. YOU MAY BE RIGHT.
BUT FOR THE WRONG REASON.
GIL?
OOOH-THIS LOOKS... INTERESTING!

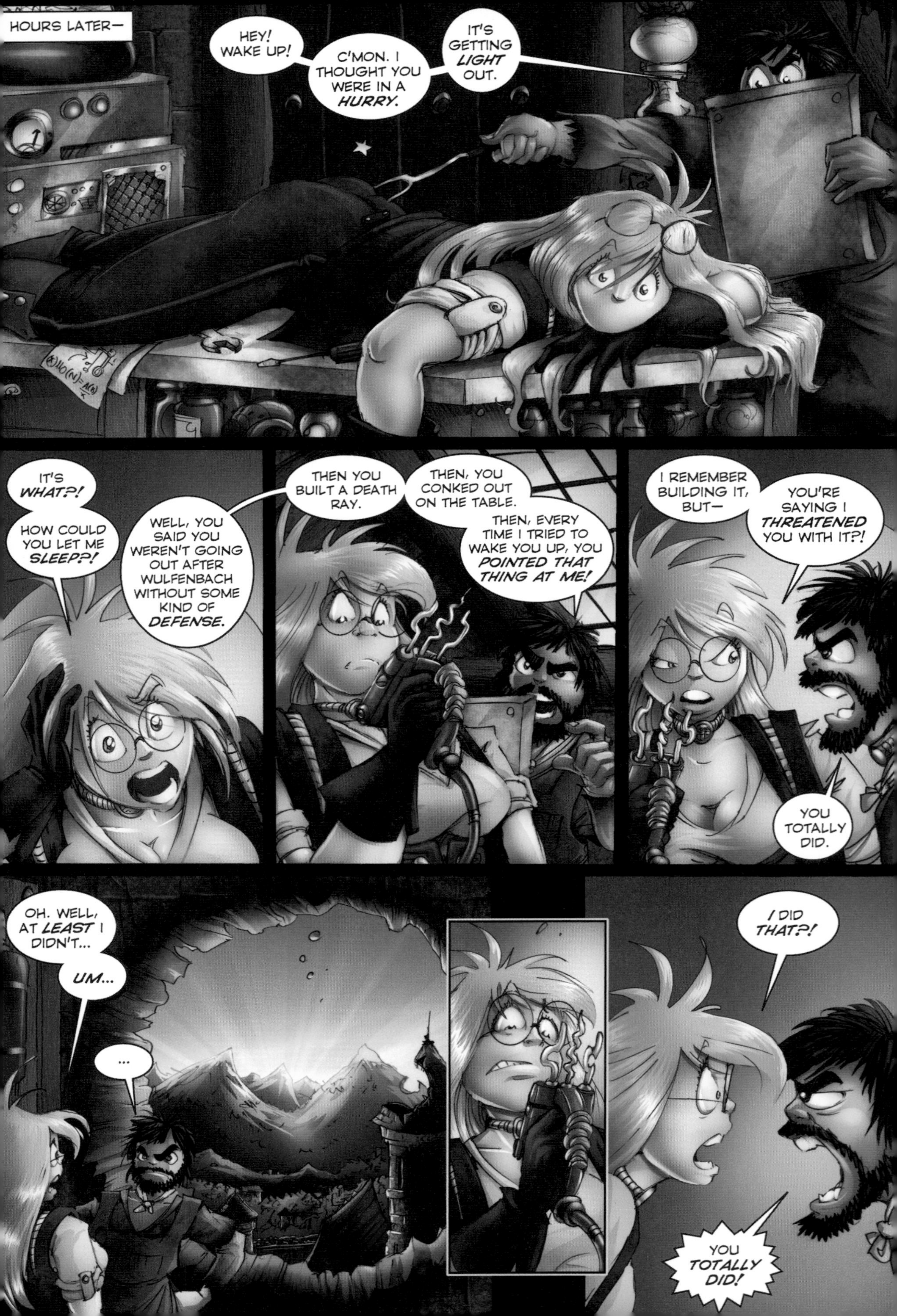
HOURS LATER—
HEY! WAKE UP!
C'MON. I THOUGHT YOU WERE IN A HURRY.
IT'S GETTING LIGHT OUT.
IT'S WHAT?!
HOW COULD YOU LET ME SLEEP?!
WELL, YOU SAID YOU WEREN'T GOING OUT AFTER WULFENBACH WITHOUT SOME KIND OF DEFENSE.
THEN YOU BUILT A DEATH RAY.
THEN, YOU CONKED OUT ON THE TABLE.
THEN, EVERY TIME I TRIED TO WAKE YOU UP, YOU POINTED THAT THING AT ME!
I REMEMBER BUILDING IT, BUT—
YOU'RE SAYING I THREATENED YOU WITH IT?!
YOU TOTALLY DID.
OH. WELL, AT LEAST I DIDN'T...
UM...
...
I DID THAT?!
YOU TOTALLY DID!

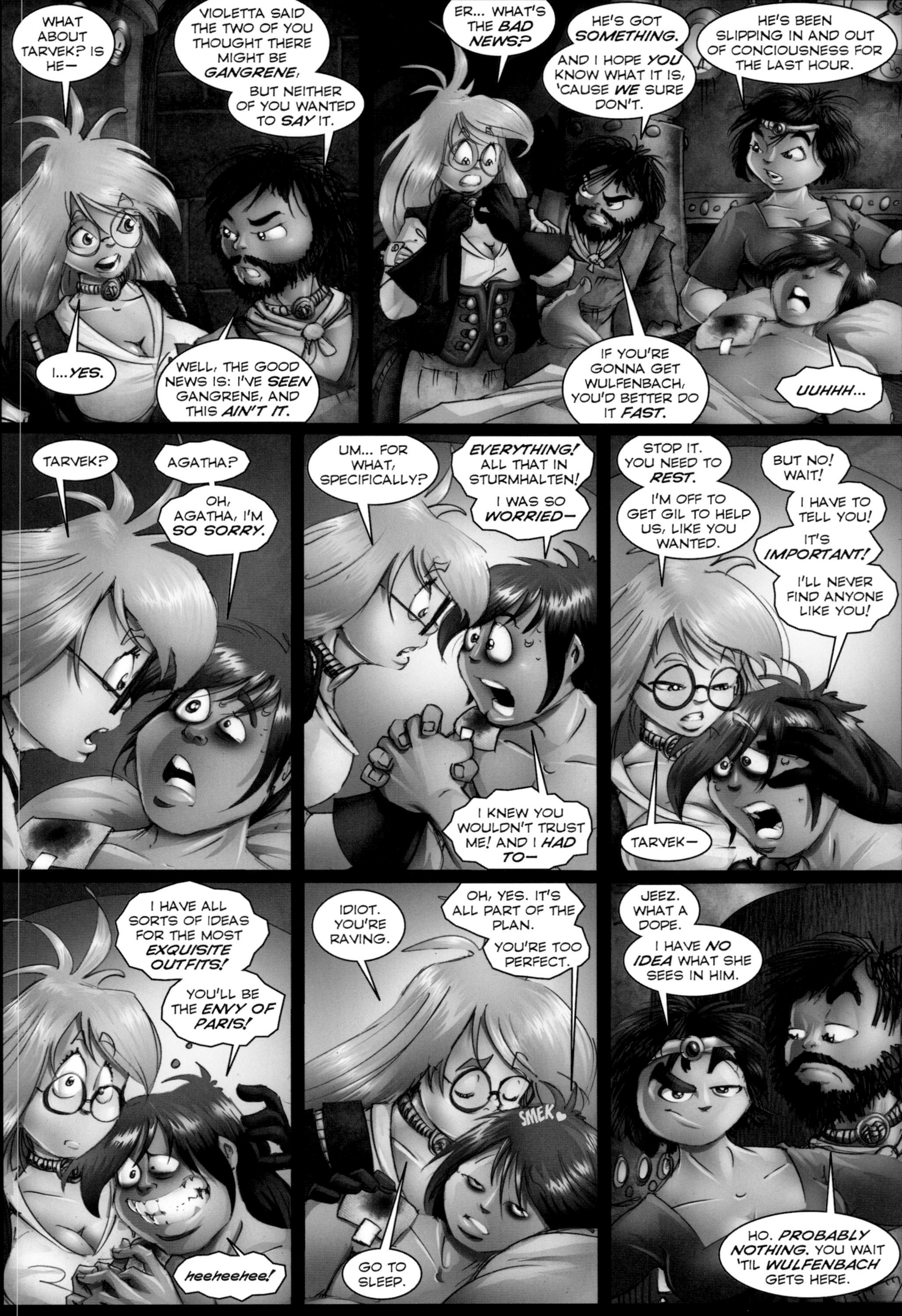

WHAT ABOUT TARVEK? IS HE—
VIOLETTA SAID THE TWO OF YOU THOUGHT THERE MIGHT BE GANGRENE,
BUT NEITHER OF YOU WANTED TO SAY IT.
I...YES.
WELL, THE GOOD NEWS IS: I'VE SEEN GANGRENE, AND THIS AIN'T IT.
ER... WHAT'S THE BAD NEWS?
HE'S GOT SOMETHING.
AND I HOPE YOU KNOW WHAT IT IS, 'CAUSE WE SURE DON'T.
HE'S BEEN SLIPPING IN AND OUT OF CONCIOUSNESS FOR THE LAST HOUR.
IF YOU'RE GONNA GET WULFENBACH, YOU'D BETTER DO IT FAST.
UUHHH...
TARVEK?
AGATHA?
OH, AGATHA, I'M SO SORRY.
UM... FOR WHAT, SPECIFICALLY?
EVERYTHING! ALL THAT IN STURMHALTEN!
I WAS SO WORRIED—
I KNEW YOU WOULDN'T TRUST ME! AND I HAD TO—
STOP IT. YOU NEED TO REST.
I'M OFF TO GET GIL TO HELP US, LIKE YOU WANTED.
BUT NO! WAIT!
I HAVE TO TELL YOU!
IT'S IMPORTANT!
I'LL NEVER FIND ANYONE LIKE YOU!
TARVEK—
I HAVE ALL SORTS OF IDEAS FOR THE MOST EXQUISITE OUTFITS!
YOU'LL BE THE ENVY OF PARIS!
heeheehee!
IDIOT. YOU'RE RAVING.
OH, YES. IT'S ALL PART OF THE PLAN.
YOU'RE TOO PERFECT.
SMEK
GO TO SLEEP.
JEEZ. WHAT A DOPE.
I HAVE NO IDEA WHAT SHE SEES IN HIM.
HO. PROBABLY NOTHING. YOU WAIT 'TIL WULFENBACH GETS HERE.

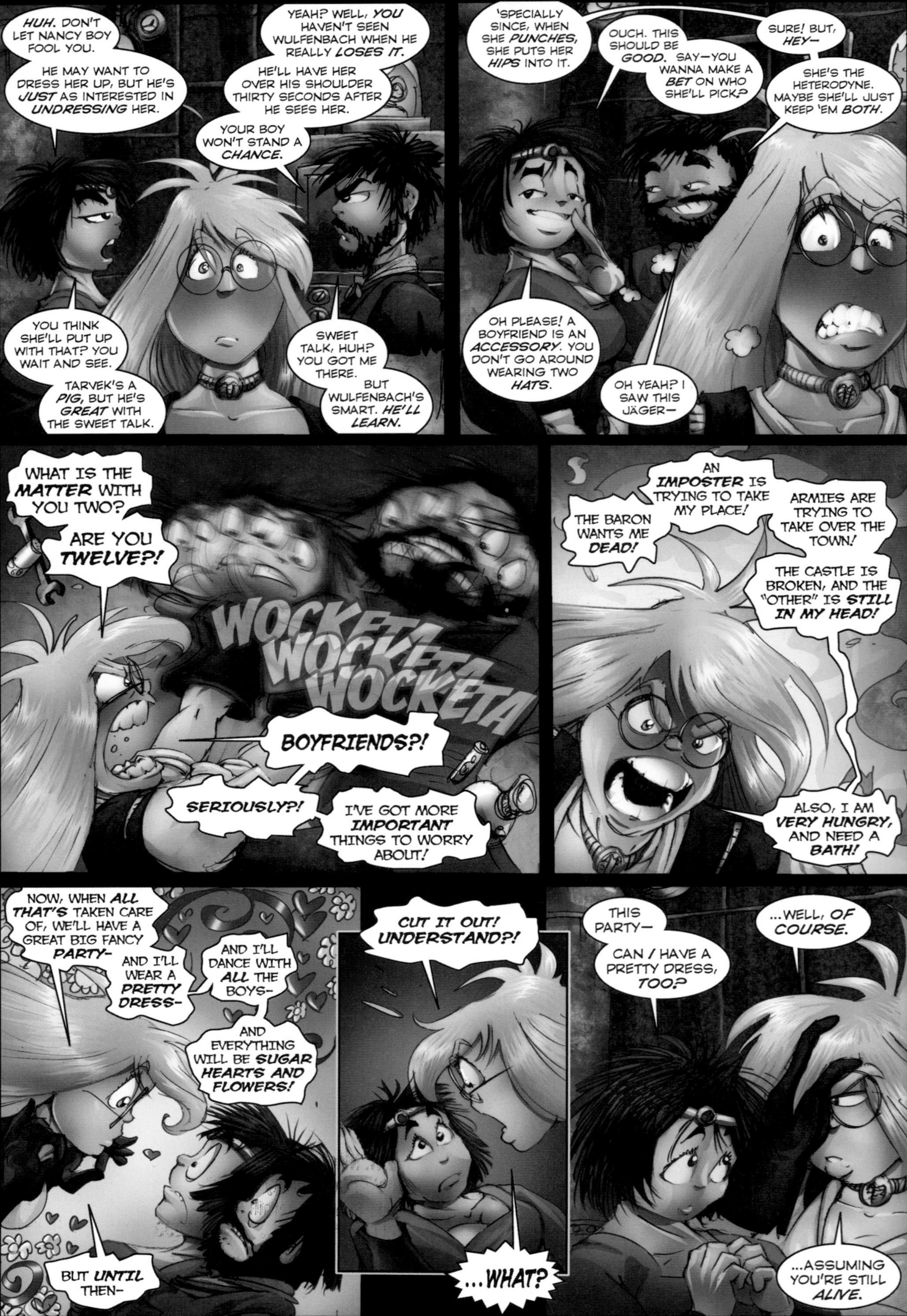
HUH. DON'T LET NANCY BOY FOOL YOU.
HE MAY WANT TO DRESS HER UP, BUT HE'S JUST AS INTERESTED IN UNDRESSING HER.
YEAH? WELL, YOU HAVEN'T SEEN WULFENBACH WHEN HE REALLY LOSES IT.
HE'LL HAVE HER OVER HIS SHOULDER THIRTY SECONDS AFTER HE SEES HER.
YOUR BOY WON'T STAND A CHANCE.
YOU THINK SHE'LL PUT UP WITH THAT? YOU WAIT AND SEE.
TARVEK'S A PIG, BUT HE'S GREAT WITH THE SWEET TALK.
SWEET TALK, HUH? YOU GOT ME THERE.
BUT WULFENBACH'S SMART. HE'LL LEARN.
'SPECIALLY SINCE, WHEN SHE PUNCHES, SHE PUTS HER HIPS INTO IT.
OUCH. THIS SHOULD BE GOOD. SAY—YOU WANNA MAKE A BET ON WHO SHE'LL PICK?
SURE! BUT, HEY—
SHE'S THE HETERODYNE. MAYBE SHE'LL JUST KEEP 'EM BOTH.
OH PLEASE! A BOYFRIEND IS AN ACCESSORY. YOU DON'T GO AROUND WEARING TWO HATS.
OH YEAH? I SAW THIS JÄGER—
WHAT IS THE MATTER WITH YOU TWO?
ARE YOU TWELVE?!
WOCKETA WOCKETA WOCKETA
BOYFRIENDS?!
SERIOUSLY?!
I'VE GOT MORE IMPORTANT THINGS TO WORRY ABOUT!
THE BARON WANTS ME DEAD!
AN IMPOSTER IS TRYING TO TAKE MY PLACE!
ARMIES ARE TRYING TO TAKE OVER THE TOWN!
THE CASTLE IS BROKEN, AND THE "OTHER" IS STILL IN MY HEAD!
ALSO, I AM VERY HUNGRY, AND NEED A BATH!
NOW, WHEN ALL THAT'S TAKEN CARE OF, WE'LL HAVE A GREAT BIG FANCY PARTY-
AND I'LL WEAR A PRETTY DRESS-
AND I'LL DANCE WITH ALL THE BOYS-
AND EVERYTHING WILL BE SUGAR HEARTS AND FLOWERS!
BUT UNTIL THEN-
CUT IT OUT! UNDERSTAND?!
...WHAT?
THIS PARTY—
CAN I HAVE A PRETTY DRESS, TOO?
...WELL, OF COURSE.
...ASSUMING YOU'RE STILL ALIVE.

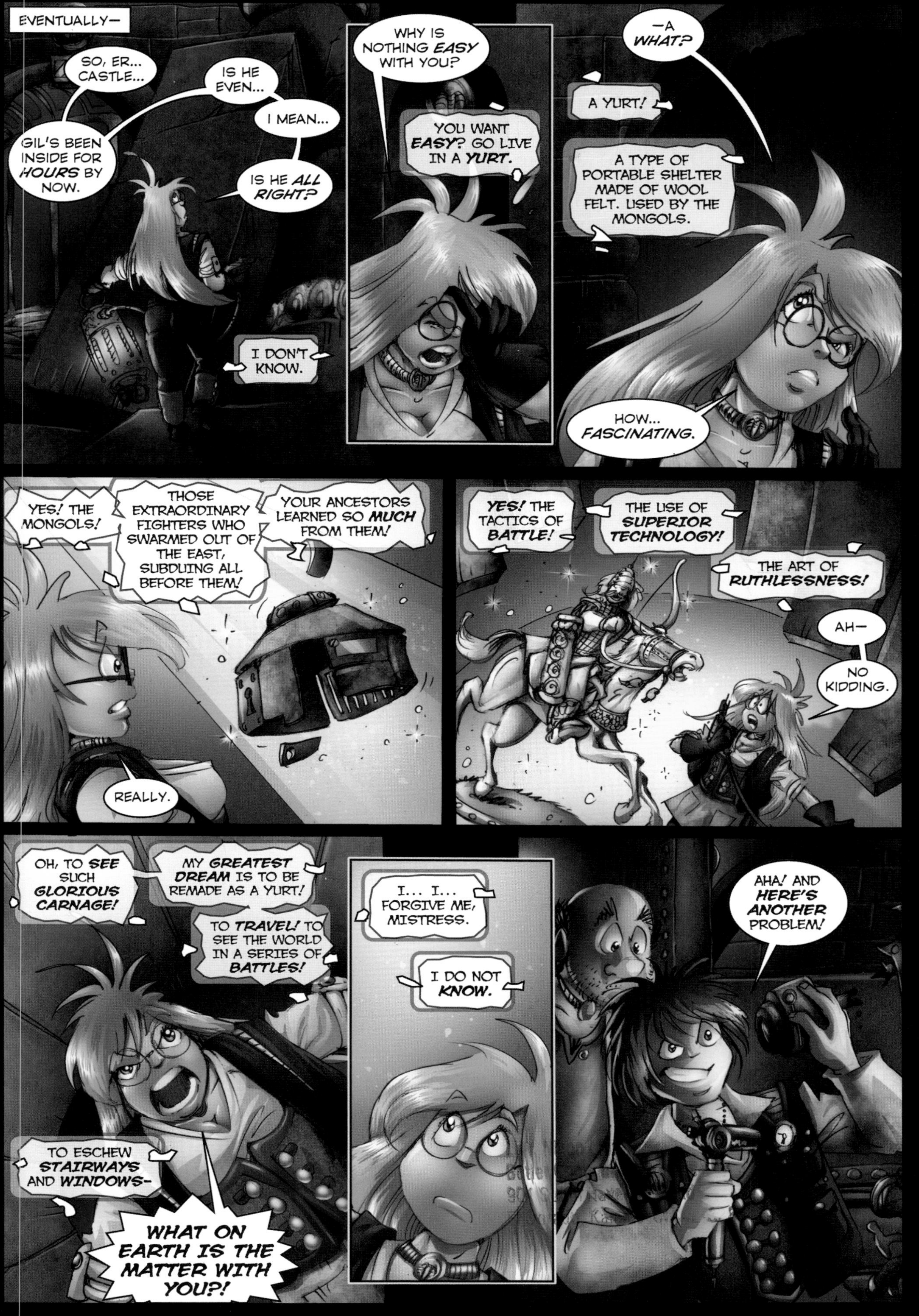
EVENTUALLY—
SO, ER... CASTLE...
GIL'S BEEN INSIDE FOR HOURS BY NOW.
IS HE EVEN...
I MEAN...
IS HE ALL RIGHT?
I DON'T KNOW.
WHY IS NOTHING EASY WITH YOU?
YOU WANT EASY? GO LIVE IN A YURT.
—A WHAT?
A YURT!
A TYPE OF PORTABLE SHELTER MADE OF WOOL FELT. USED BY THE MONGOLS.
HOW... FASCINATING.
YES! THE MONGOLS!
THOSE EXTRAORDINARY FIGHTERS WHO SWARMED OUT OF THE EAST, SUBDUING ALL BEFORE THEM!
YOUR ANCESTORS LEARNED SO MUCH FROM THEM!
REALLY.
YES! THE TACTICS OF BATTLE!
THE USE OF SUPERIOR TECHNOLOGY!
THE ART OF RUTHLESSNESS!
AH—
NO KIDDING.
OH, TO SEE SUCH GLORIOUS CARNAGE!
MY GREATEST DREAM IS TO BE REMADE AS A YURT!
TO TRAVEL! TO SEE THE WORLD IN A SERIES OF BATTLES!
TO ESCHEW STAIRWAYS AND WINDOWS-
WHAT ON EARTH IS THE MATTER WITH YOU?!
I... I... FORGIVE ME, MISTRESS.
I DO NOT KNOW.
AHA! AND HERE'S ANOTHER PROBLEM!

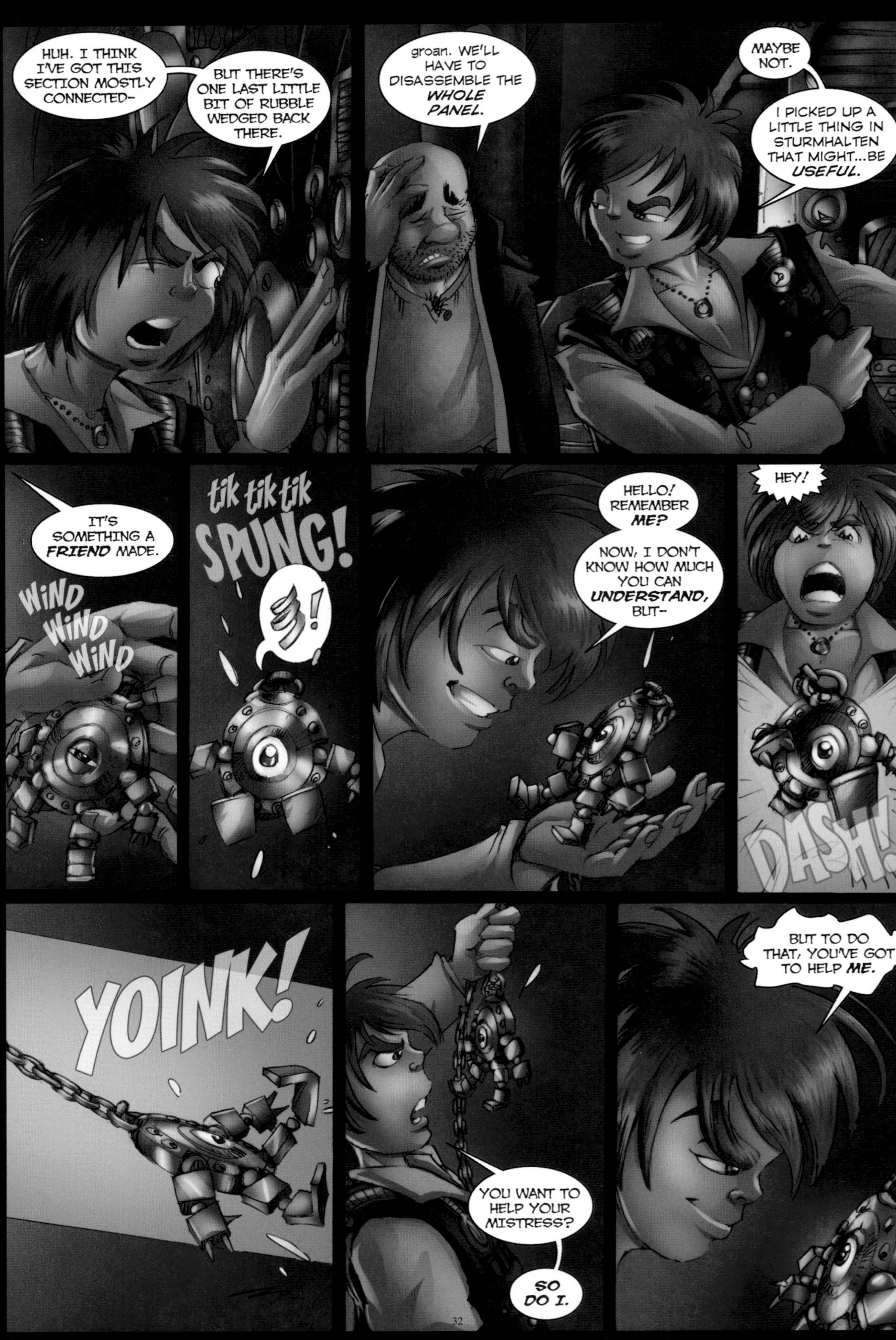

HUH. I THINK I'VE GOT THIS SECTION MOSTLY CONNECTED-
BUT THERE'S ONE LAST LITTLE BIT OF RUBBLE WEDGED BACK THERE.
groan. WE'LL HAVE TO DISASSEMBLE THE *WHOLE PANEL*.
MAYBE NOT.
I PICKED UP A LITTLE THING IN STURMHALTEN THAT MIGHT...BE *USEFUL*.
IT'S SOMETHING A *FRIEND* MADE.
WIND WIND WIND
tik tik tik
SPUNG!
!
HELLO! REMEMBER *ME?*
NOW, I DON'T KNOW HOW MUCH YOU CAN *UNDERSTAND*, BUT-
HEY!
DASH!
YOINK!
YOU WANT TO HELP YOUR MISTRESS?
SO DO I.
BUT TO DO THAT, YOU'VE GOT TO HELP *ME.*

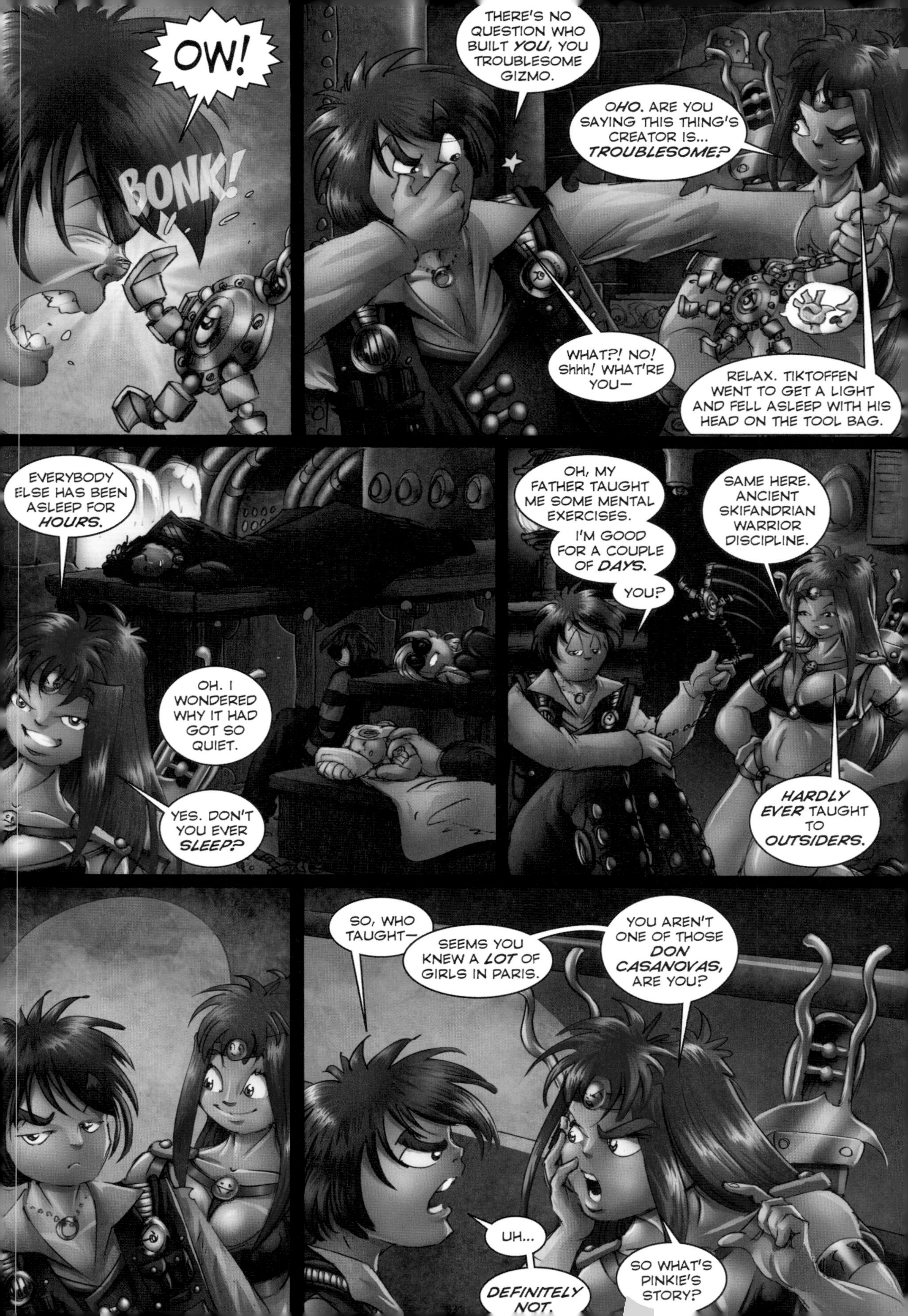
OW!
BONK!
THERE'S NO QUESTION WHO BUILT *YOU*, YOU TROUBLESOME GIZMO.
OHO. ARE YOU SAYING THIS THING'S CREATOR IS... *TROUBLESOME?*
WHAT?! NO! Shhh! WHAT'RE YOU—
RELAX. TIKTOFFEN WENT TO GET A LIGHT AND FELL ASLEEP WITH HIS HEAD ON THE TOOL BAG.
EVERYBODY ELSE HAS BEEN ASLEEP FOR *HOURS.*
OH. I WONDERED WHY IT HAD GOT SO QUIET.
YES. DON'T YOU EVER *SLEEP?*
OH, MY FATHER TAUGHT ME SOME MENTAL EXERCISES.
I'M GOOD FOR A COUPLE OF *DAYS.*
YOU?
SAME HERE. ANCIENT SKIFANDRIAN WARRIOR DISCIPLINE.
HARDLY EVER TAUGHT TO *OUTSIDERS.*
SO, WHO TAUGHT—
SEEMS YOU KNEW A *LOT* OF GIRLS IN PARIS.
YOU AREN'T ONE OF THOSE *DON CASANOVAS,* ARE YOU?
UH...
DEFINITELY NOT.
SO WHAT'S PINKIE'S STORY?

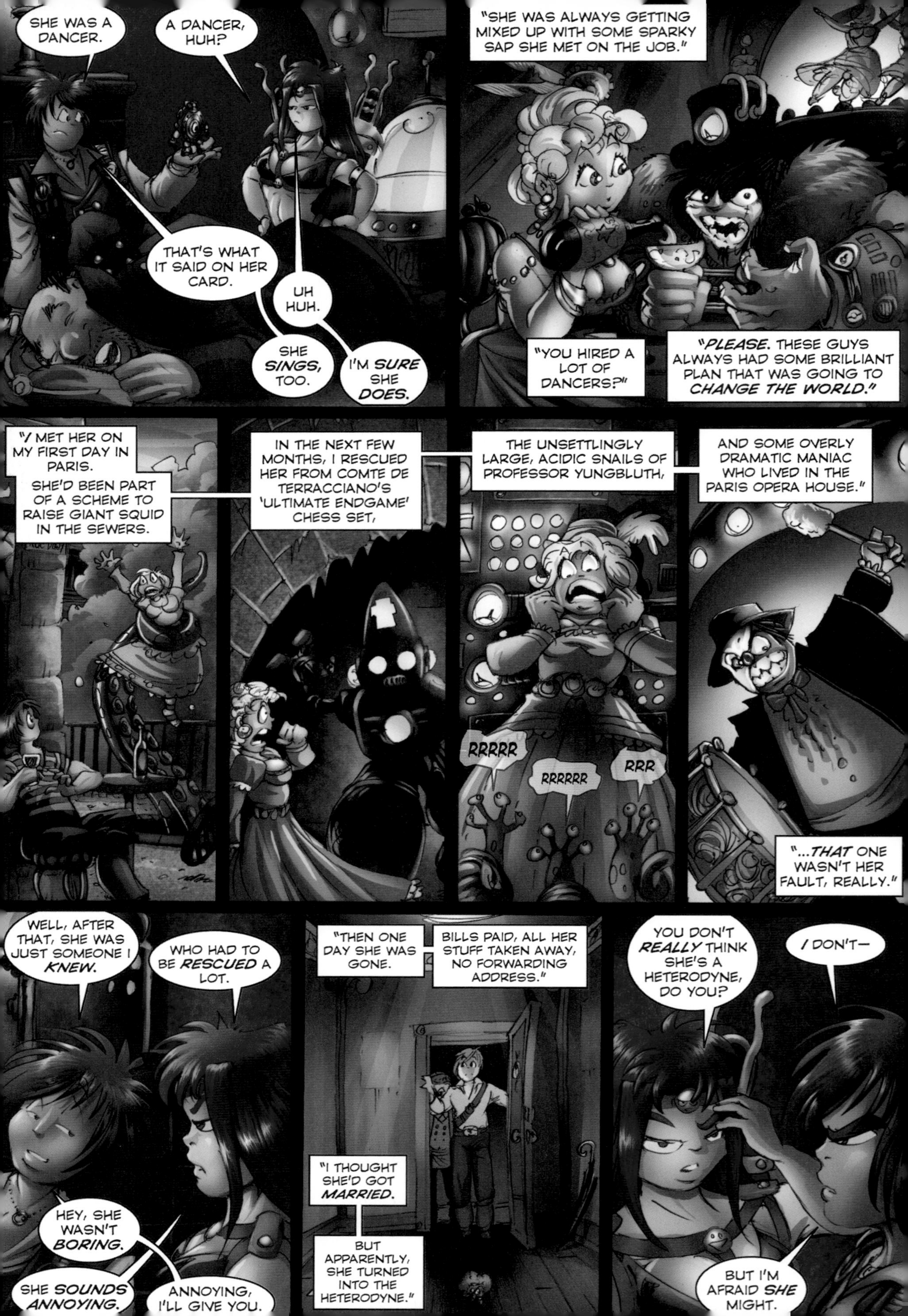

SHE WAS A DANCER.
A DANCER, HUH?
THAT'S WHAT IT SAID ON HER CARD.
UH HUH.
SHE *SINGS,* TOO.
I'M *SURE* SHE *DOES.*
"SHE WAS ALWAYS GETTING MIXED UP WITH SOME SPARKY SAP SHE MET ON THE JOB."
"YOU HIRED A LOT OF DANCERS?"
"*PLEASE.* THESE GUYS ALWAYS HAD SOME BRILLIANT PLAN THAT WAS GOING TO *CHANGE THE WORLD.*"
"*I* MET HER ON MY FIRST DAY IN PARIS.
SHE'D BEEN PART OF A SCHEME TO RAISE GIANT SQUID IN THE SEWERS.
IN THE NEXT FEW MONTHS, I RESCUED HER FROM COMTE DE TERRACCIANO'S 'ULTIMATE ENDGAME' CHESS SET,
THE UNSETTLINGLY LARGE, ACIDIC SNAILS OF PROFESSOR YUNGBLUTH,
AND SOME OVERLY DRAMATIC MANIAC WHO LIVED IN THE PARIS OPERA HOUSE."
RRRRR
RRRRRR
RRR
"...*THAT* ONE WASN'T HER FAULT, REALLY."
WELL, AFTER THAT, SHE WAS JUST SOMEONE I *KNEW.*
WHO HAD TO BE *RESCUED* A LOT.
HEY, SHE WASN'T *BORING.*
SHE *SOUNDS ANNOYING.*
ANNOYING, I'LL GIVE YOU.
"THEN ONE DAY SHE WAS GONE.
BILLS PAID, ALL HER STUFF TAKEN AWAY, NO FORWARDING ADDRESS."
"I THOUGHT SHE'D GOT *MARRIED.*
BUT APPARENTLY, SHE TURNED INTO THE HETERODYNE."
YOU DON'T *REALLY* THINK SHE'S A HETERODYNE, DO YOU?
I DON'T—
BUT I'M AFRAID *SHE* MIGHT.

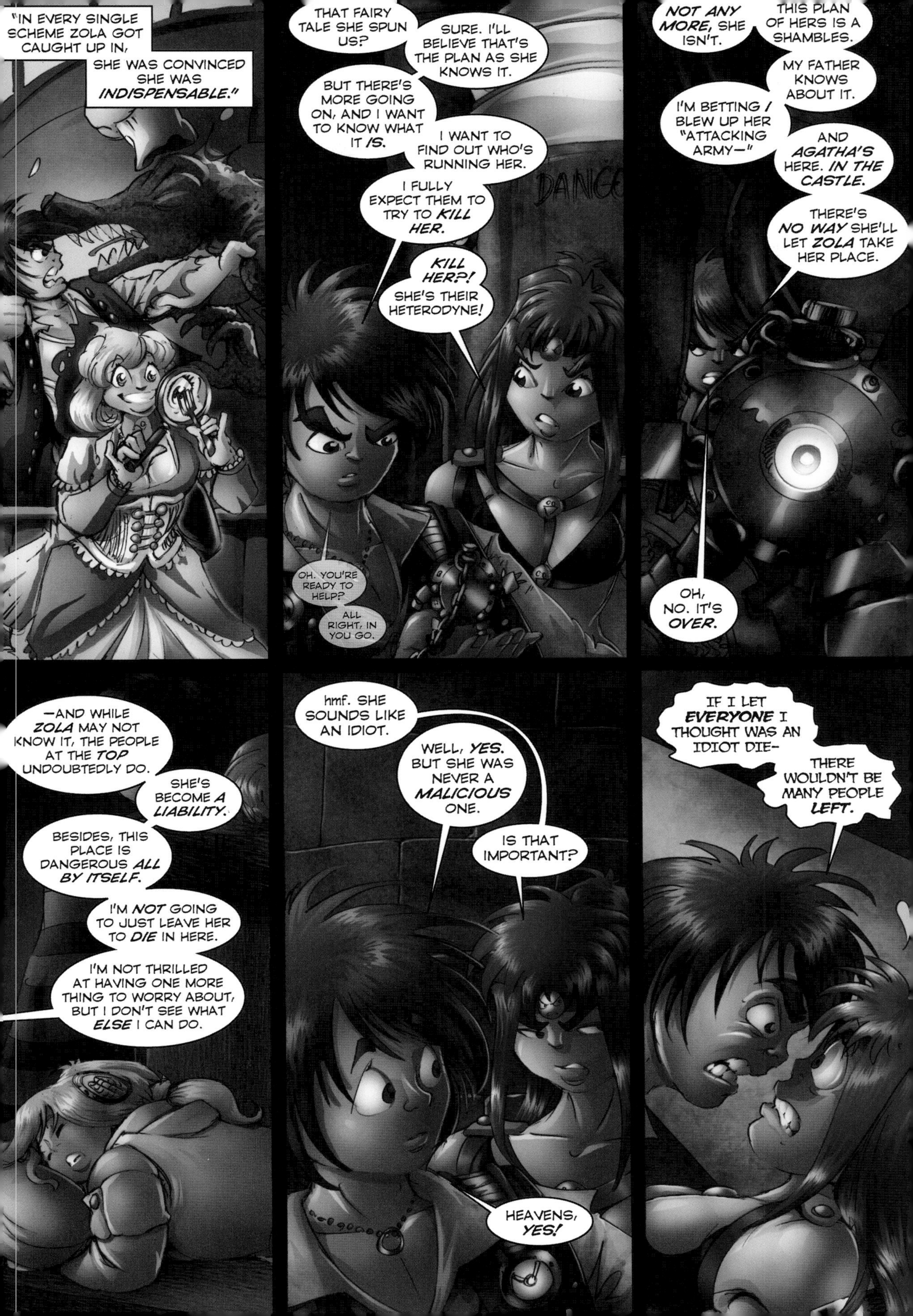
"IN EVERY SINGLE SCHEME ZOLA GOT CAUGHT UP IN,
SHE WAS CONVINCED SHE WAS INDISPENSABLE."
THAT FAIRY TALE SHE SPUN US?
SURE. I'LL BELIEVE THAT'S THE PLAN AS SHE KNOWS IT.
BUT THERE'S MORE GOING ON, AND I WANT TO KNOW WHAT IT IS.
I WANT TO FIND OUT WHO'S RUNNING HER.
I FULLY EXPECT THEM TO TRY TO KILL HER.
KILL HER?! SHE'S THEIR HETERODYNE!
OH. YOU'RE READY TO HELP?
ALL RIGHT, IN YOU GO.
NOT ANY MORE, SHE ISN'T.
THIS PLAN OF HERS IS A SHAMBLES.
MY FATHER KNOWS ABOUT IT.
I'M BETTING I BLEW UP HER "ATTACKING ARMY—"
AND AGATHA'S HERE. IN THE CASTLE.
THERE'S NO WAY SHE'LL LET ZOLA TAKE HER PLACE.
OH, NO. IT'S OVER.
—AND WHILE ZOLA MAY NOT KNOW IT, THE PEOPLE AT THE TOP UNDOUBTEDLY DO.
SHE'S BECOME A LIABILITY.
BESIDES, THIS PLACE IS DANGEROUS ALL BY ITSELF.
I'M NOT GOING TO JUST LEAVE HER TO DIE IN HERE.
I'M NOT THRILLED AT HAVING ONE MORE THING TO WORRY ABOUT, BUT I DON'T SEE WHAT ELSE I CAN DO.
hmf. SHE SOUNDS LIKE AN IDIOT.
WELL, YES. BUT SHE WAS NEVER A MALICIOUS ONE.
IS THAT IMPORTANT?
HEAVENS, YES!
IF I LET EVERYONE I THOUGHT WAS AN IDIOT DIE-
THERE WOULDN'T BE MANY PEOPLE LEFT.

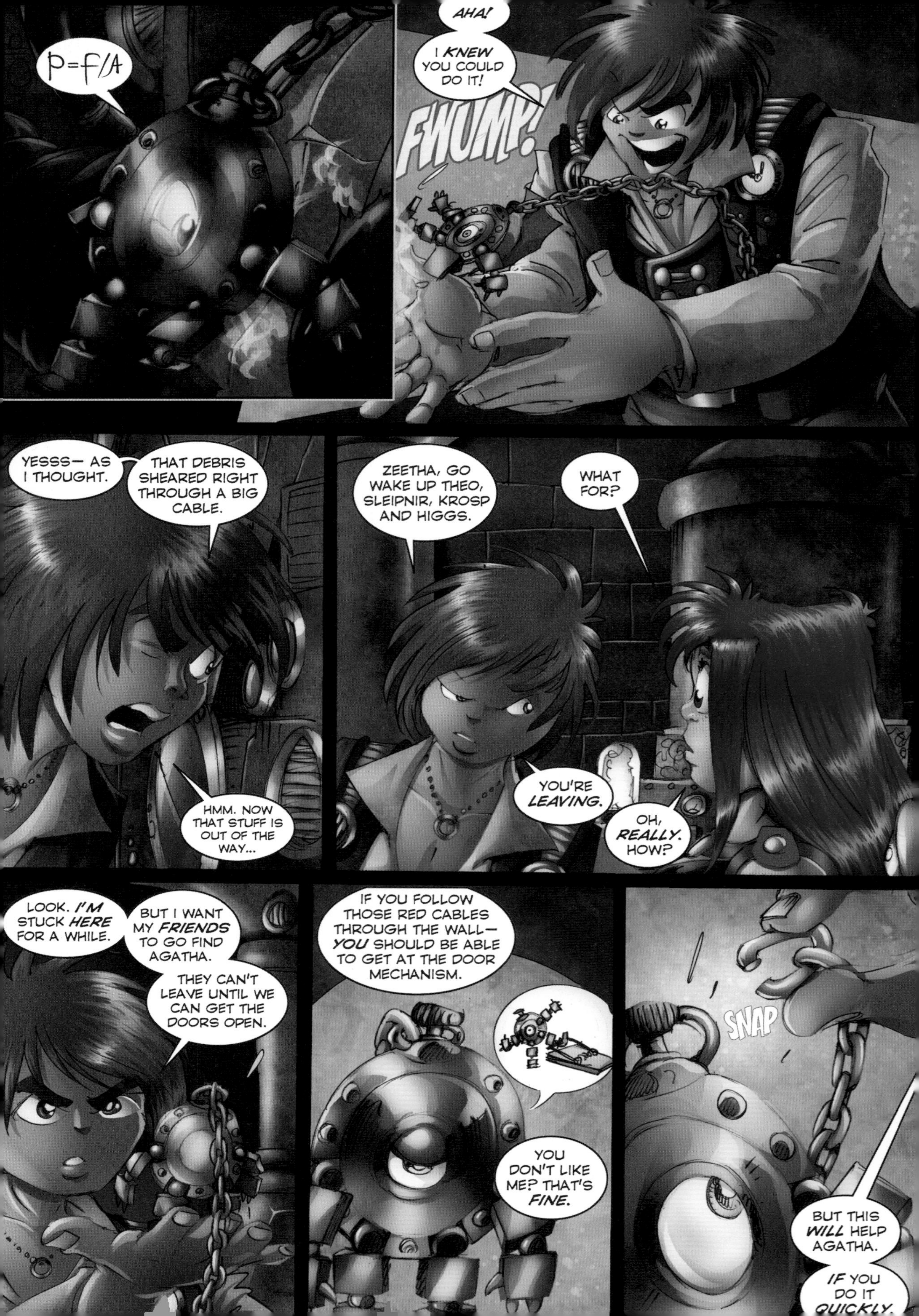

P=F/A
AHA!
I KNEW YOU COULD DO IT!
FWUMP!
YESSS— AS I THOUGHT.
THAT DEBRIS SHEARED RIGHT THROUGH A BIG CABLE.
HMM. NOW THAT STUFF IS OUT OF THE WAY...
ZEETHA, GO WAKE UP THEO, SLEIPNIR, KROSP AND HIGGS.
WHAT FOR?
YOU'RE LEAVING.
OH, REALLY. HOW?
LOOK. I'M STUCK HERE FOR A WHILE.
BUT I WANT MY FRIENDS TO GO FIND AGATHA.
THEY CAN'T LEAVE UNTIL WE CAN GET THE DOORS OPEN.
IF YOU FOLLOW THOSE RED CABLES THROUGH THE WALL— YOU SHOULD BE ABLE TO GET AT THE DOOR MECHANISM.
YOU DON'T LIKE ME? THAT'S FINE.
SNAP
BUT THIS WILL HELP AGATHA.
IF YOU DO IT QUICKLY.

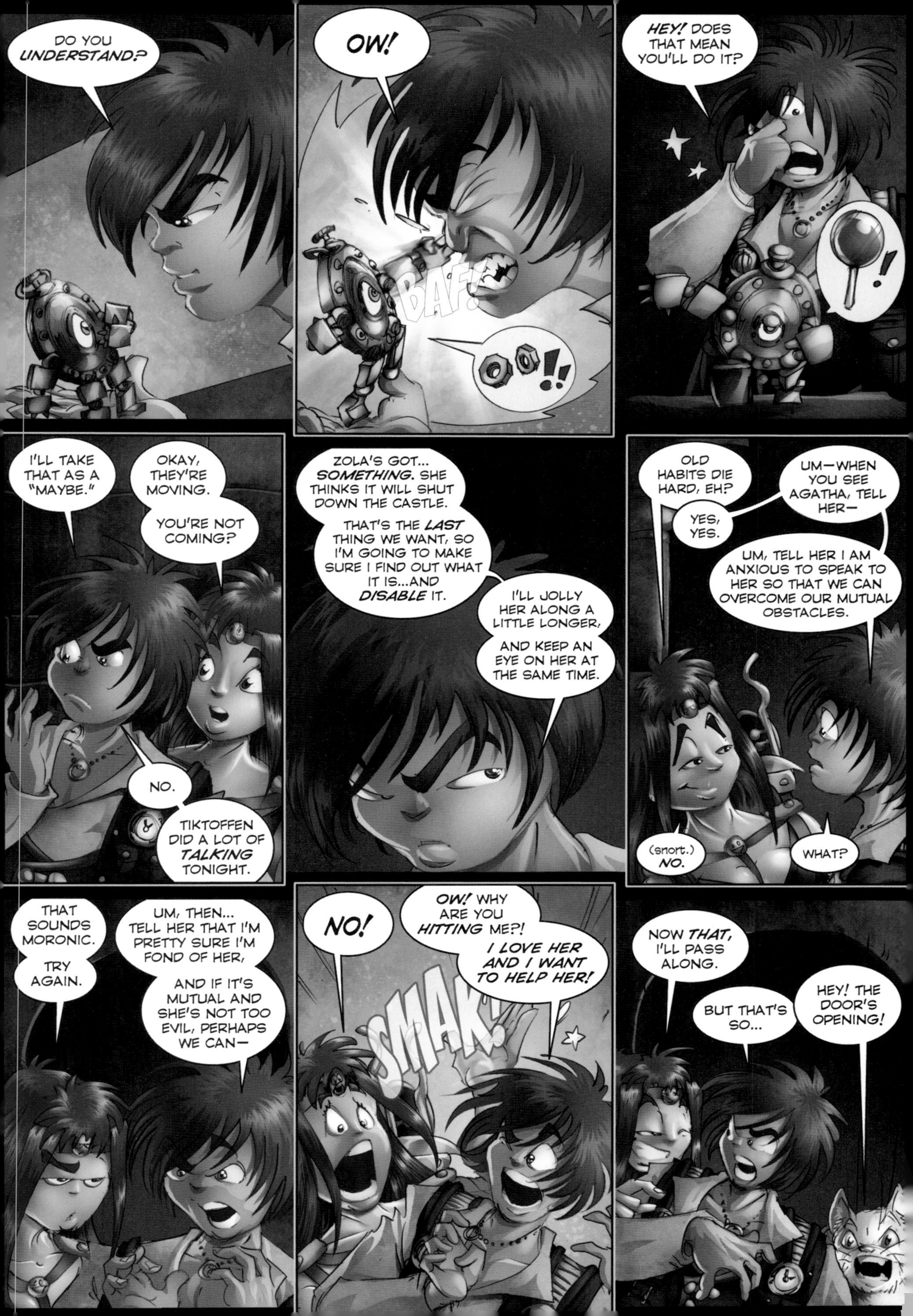
DO YOU UNDERSTAND?
OW!
BAF!
!!
HEY! DOES THAT MEAN YOU'LL DO IT?
!
I'LL TAKE THAT AS A "MAYBE."
OKAY, THEY'RE MOVING.
YOU'RE NOT COMING?
NO.
TIKTOFFEN DID A LOT OF TALKING TONIGHT.
ZOLA'S GOT... SOMETHING. SHE THINKS IT WILL SHUT DOWN THE CASTLE.
THAT'S THE LAST THING WE WANT, SO I'M GOING TO MAKE SURE I FIND OUT WHAT IT IS...AND DISABLE IT.
I'LL JOLLY HER ALONG A LITTLE LONGER,
AND KEEP AN EYE ON HER AT THE SAME TIME.
OLD HABITS DIE HARD, EH?
YES, YES.
UM—WHEN YOU SEE AGATHA, TELL HER—
UM, TELL HER I AM ANXIOUS TO SPEAK TO HER SO THAT WE CAN OVERCOME OUR MUTUAL OBSTACLES.
(snort.) NO.
WHAT?
THAT SOUNDS MORONIC.
TRY AGAIN.
UM, THEN... TELL HER THAT I'M PRETTY SURE I'M FOND OF HER,
AND IF IT'S MUTUAL AND SHE'S NOT TOO EVIL, PERHAPS WE CAN—
NO!
SMAK!
OW! WHY ARE YOU HITTING ME?!
I LOVE HER AND I WANT TO HELP HER!
NOW THAT, I'LL PASS ALONG.
BUT THAT'S SO...
HEY! THE DOOR'S OPENING!

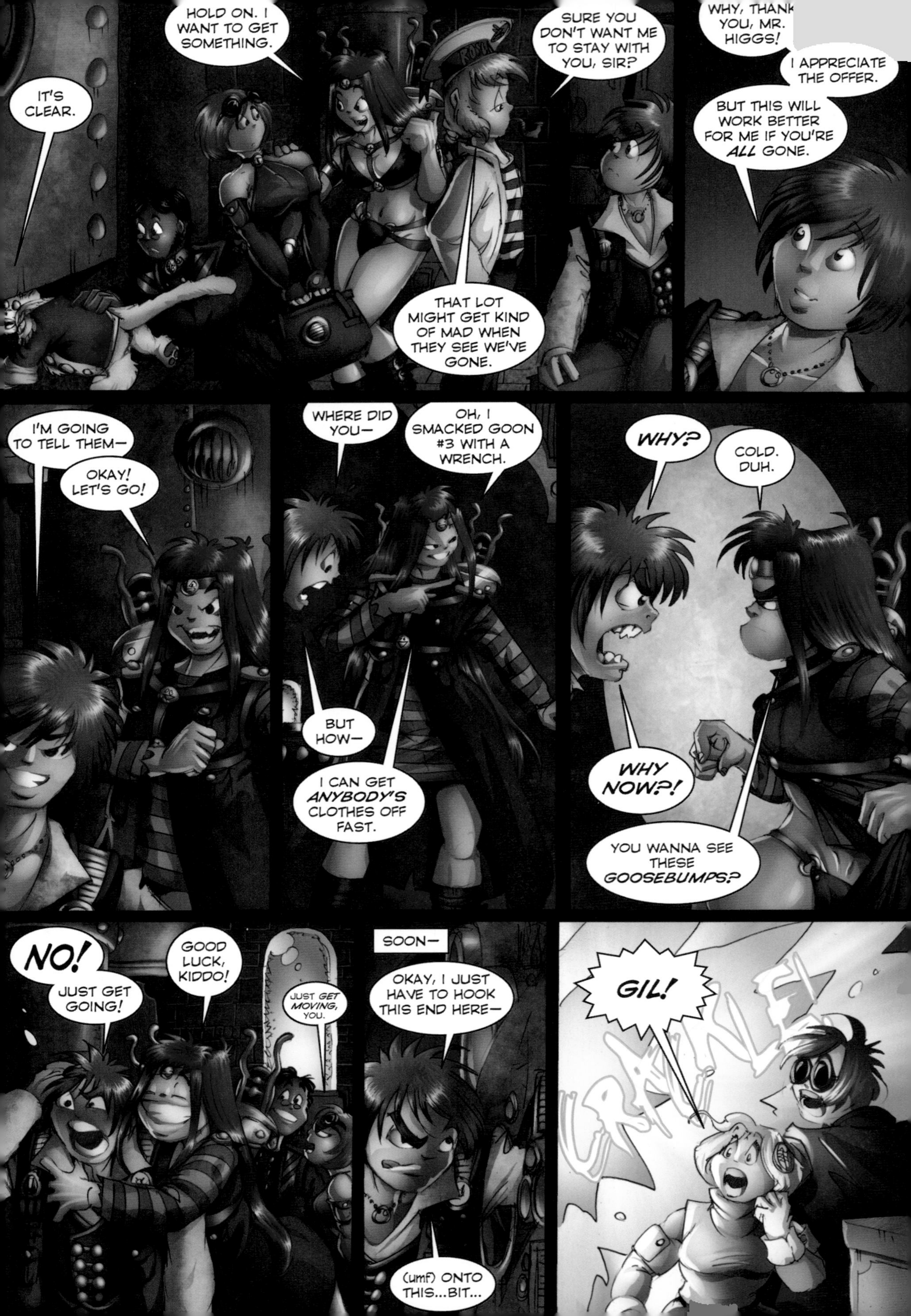

IT'S CLEAR.
HOLD ON. I WANT TO GET SOMETHING.
SURE YOU DON'T WANT ME TO STAY WITH YOU, SIR?
THAT LOT MIGHT GET KIND OF MAD WHEN THEY SEE WE'VE GONE.
WHY, THANK YOU, MR. HIGGS!
I APPRECIATE THE OFFER.
BUT THIS WILL WORK BETTER FOR ME IF YOU'RE *ALL* GONE.
I'M GOING TO TELL THEM—
OKAY! LET'S GO!
WHERE DID YOU—
OH, I SMACKED GOON #3 WITH A WRENCH.
BUT HOW—
I CAN GET *ANYBODY'S* CLOTHES OFF FAST.
WHY?
COLD. DUH.
WHY NOW?!
YOU WANNA SEE THESE *GOOSEBUMPS*?
NO!
JUST GET GOING!
GOOD LUCK, KIDDO!
JUST *GET MOVING*, YOU.
SOON—
OKAY, I JUST HAVE TO HOOK THIS END HERE—
(umf) ONTO THIS...BIT...
GIL!

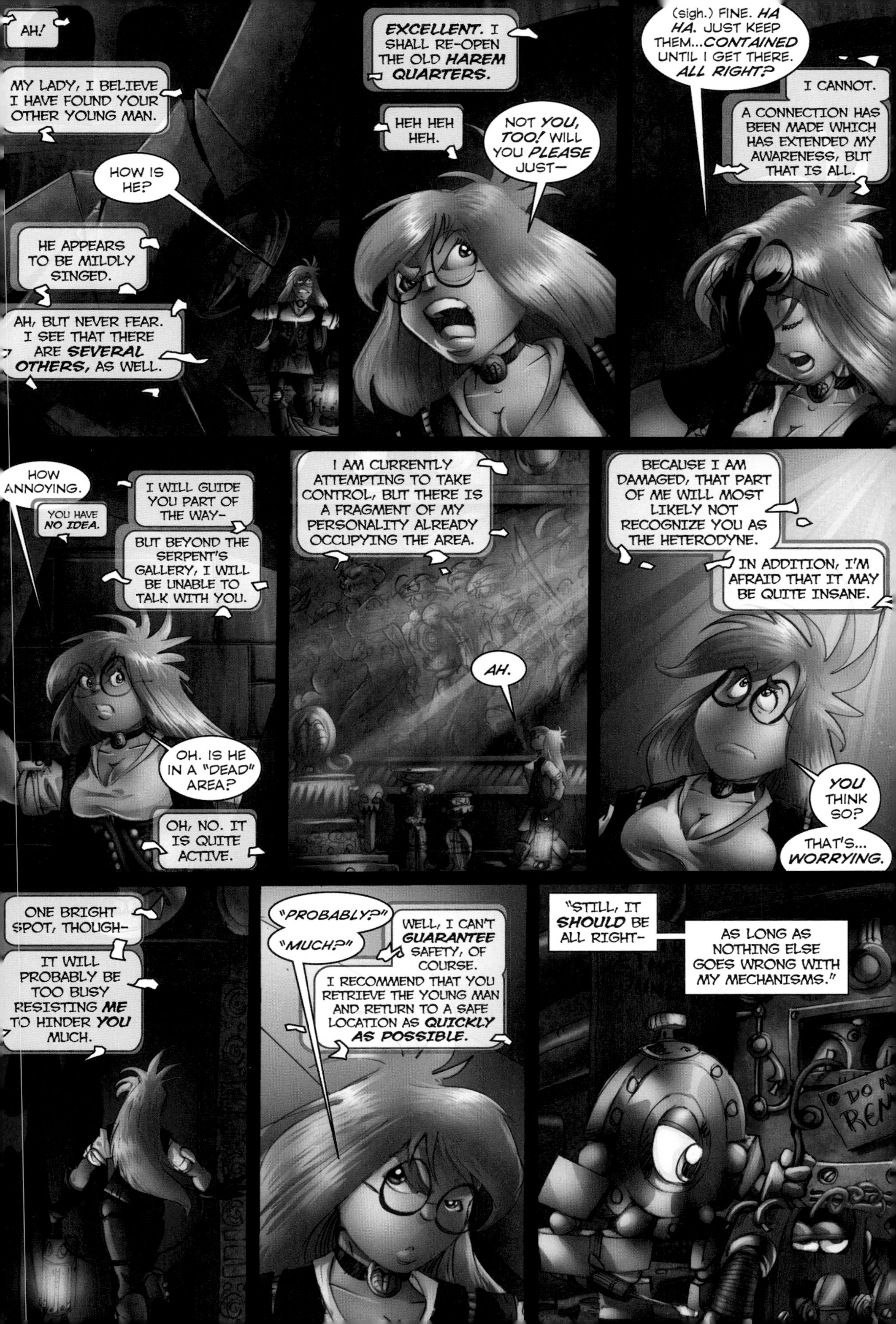

AH!
MY LADY, I BELIEVE I HAVE FOUND YOUR OTHER YOUNG MAN.
HOW IS HE?
HE APPEARS TO BE MILDLY SINGED.
AH, BUT NEVER FEAR. I SEE THAT THERE ARE SEVERAL OTHERS, AS WELL.
EXCELLENT. I SHALL RE-OPEN THE OLD HAREM QUARTERS.
HEH HEH HEH.
NOT YOU, TOO! WILL YOU PLEASE JUST—
(sigh.) FINE. HA HA. JUST KEEP THEM...CONTAINED UNTIL I GET THERE. ALL RIGHT?
I CANNOT.
A CONNECTION HAS BEEN MADE WHICH HAS EXTENDED MY AWARENESS, BUT THAT IS ALL.
HOW ANNOYING.
YOU HAVE NO IDEA.
I WILL GUIDE YOU PART OF THE WAY-
BUT BEYOND THE SERPENT'S GALLERY, I WILL BE UNABLE TO TALK WITH YOU.
OH. IS HE IN A "DEAD" AREA?
OH, NO. IT IS QUITE ACTIVE.
I AM CURRENTLY ATTEMPTING TO TAKE CONTROL, BUT THERE IS A FRAGMENT OF MY PERSONALITY ALREADY OCCUPYING THE AREA.
AH.
BECAUSE I AM DAMAGED, THAT PART OF ME WILL MOST LIKELY NOT RECOGNIZE YOU AS THE HETERODYNE.
IN ADDITION, I'M AFRAID THAT IT MAY BE QUITE INSANE.
YOU THINK SO?
THAT'S... WORRYING.
ONE BRIGHT SPOT, THOUGH-
IT WILL PROBABLY BE TOO BUSY RESISTING ME TO HINDER YOU MUCH.
"PROBABLY?"
"MUCH?"
WELL, I CAN'T GUARANTEE SAFETY, OF COURSE.
I RECOMMEND THAT YOU RETRIEVE THE YOUNG MAN AND RETURN TO A SAFE LOCATION AS QUICKLY AS POSSIBLE.
"STILL, IT SHOULD BE ALL RIGHT-
AS LONG AS NOTHING ELSE GOES WRONG WITH MY MECHANISMS."

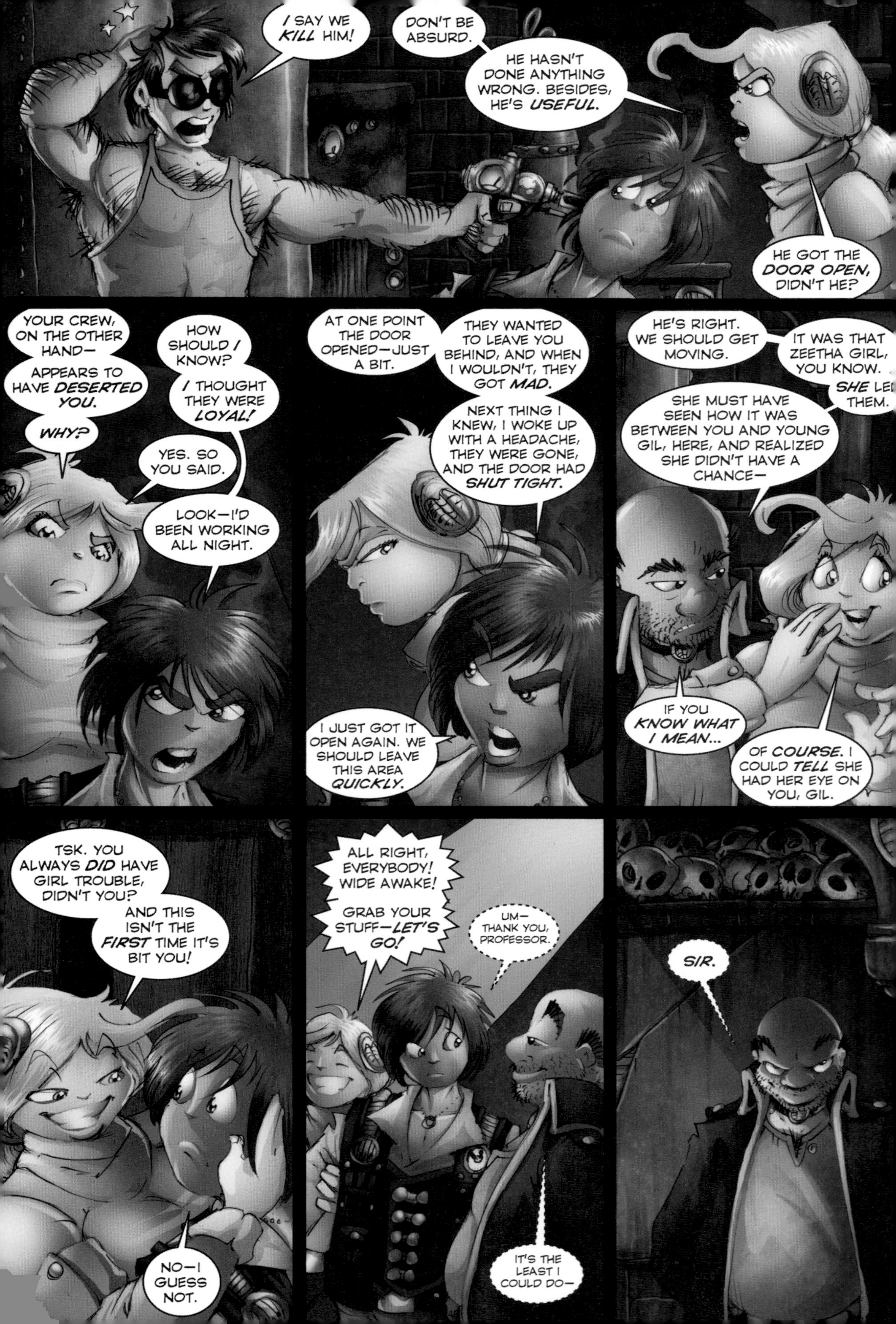

I SAY WE KILL HIM!
DON'T BE ABSURD.
HE HASN'T DONE ANYTHING WRONG. BESIDES, HE'S USEFUL.
HE GOT THE DOOR OPEN, DIDN'T HE?
YOUR CREW, ON THE OTHER HAND—
APPEARS TO HAVE DESERTED YOU.
WHY?
HOW SHOULD I KNOW?
I THOUGHT THEY WERE LOYAL!
YES. SO YOU SAID.
LOOK—I'D BEEN WORKING ALL NIGHT.
AT ONE POINT THE DOOR OPENED—JUST A BIT.
THEY WANTED TO LEAVE YOU BEHIND, AND WHEN I WOULDN'T, THEY GOT MAD.
NEXT THING I KNEW, I WOKE UP WITH A HEADACHE, THEY WERE GONE, AND THE DOOR HAD SHUT TIGHT.
I JUST GOT IT OPEN AGAIN. WE SHOULD LEAVE THIS AREA QUICKLY.
HE'S RIGHT. WE SHOULD GET MOVING.
IT WAS THAT ZEETHA GIRL, YOU KNOW.
SHE MUST HAVE SEEN HOW IT WAS BETWEEN YOU AND YOUNG GIL, HERE, AND REALIZED SHE DIDN'T HAVE A CHANCE—
IF YOU KNOW WHAT I MEAN...
OF COURSE. I COULD TELL SHE HAD HER EYE ON YOU, GIL.
TSK. YOU ALWAYS DID HAVE GIRL TROUBLE, DIDN'T YOU?
AND THIS ISN'T THE FIRST TIME IT'S BIT YOU!
NO—I GUESS NOT.
ALL RIGHT, EVERYBODY! WIDE AWAKE!
GRAB YOUR STUFF—LET'S GO!
UM—THANK YOU, PROFESSOR.
IT'S THE LEAST I COULD DO—
SIR.

Panel 1:
I KNEW YOU COULD DO IT. YOU'RE GOING TO BE HANDY TO HAVE ALONG!

HANDY, *HOW?* I STILL DON'T KNOW WHAT YOU'RE GOING TO DO!

Panel 2:
OH, *THAT.*

WHAT AM I GOING TO DO, PROFESSOR?

HM. HAVE A *PARTY,* I THINK.

HAVE A *WHAT?!*

A PARTY!

ONCE I'M SETTLED IN AS THE HETERODYNE, I SHALL HAVE A BIG, FANCY PARTY!

Panel 3:
AND I'LL WEAR A *PRETTY DRESS—*

AND I'LL DANCE WITH *ALL* THE BOYS—

BUT MOSTLY *YOU,* OF COURSE.

Panel 4:
AN ETERNITY LATER—

...AND GOLD AND PEARL BEADS ON THE LACE TRIM!

AND FOR *YOU*—

SWEET, SWEET DEATH?

NO, NO. A CLOTH OF GOLD COAT, AND—

WE'RE SAFE, MY LADY.

Panel 5:
THANK *GOODNESS.*

SAFE FROM *WHAT?*

THE *FASHION POLICE?*

THE CASTLE. WE'RE IN A DEAD ZONE NOW.

BEFORE, IT COULD HEAR EVERYTHING WE SAID.

Panel 6:
YOU MEAN—ALL OF THAT—

I *WANT* THE CASTLE TO UNDERESTIMATE ME.

SURELY *YOU* DIDN'T AS WELL?

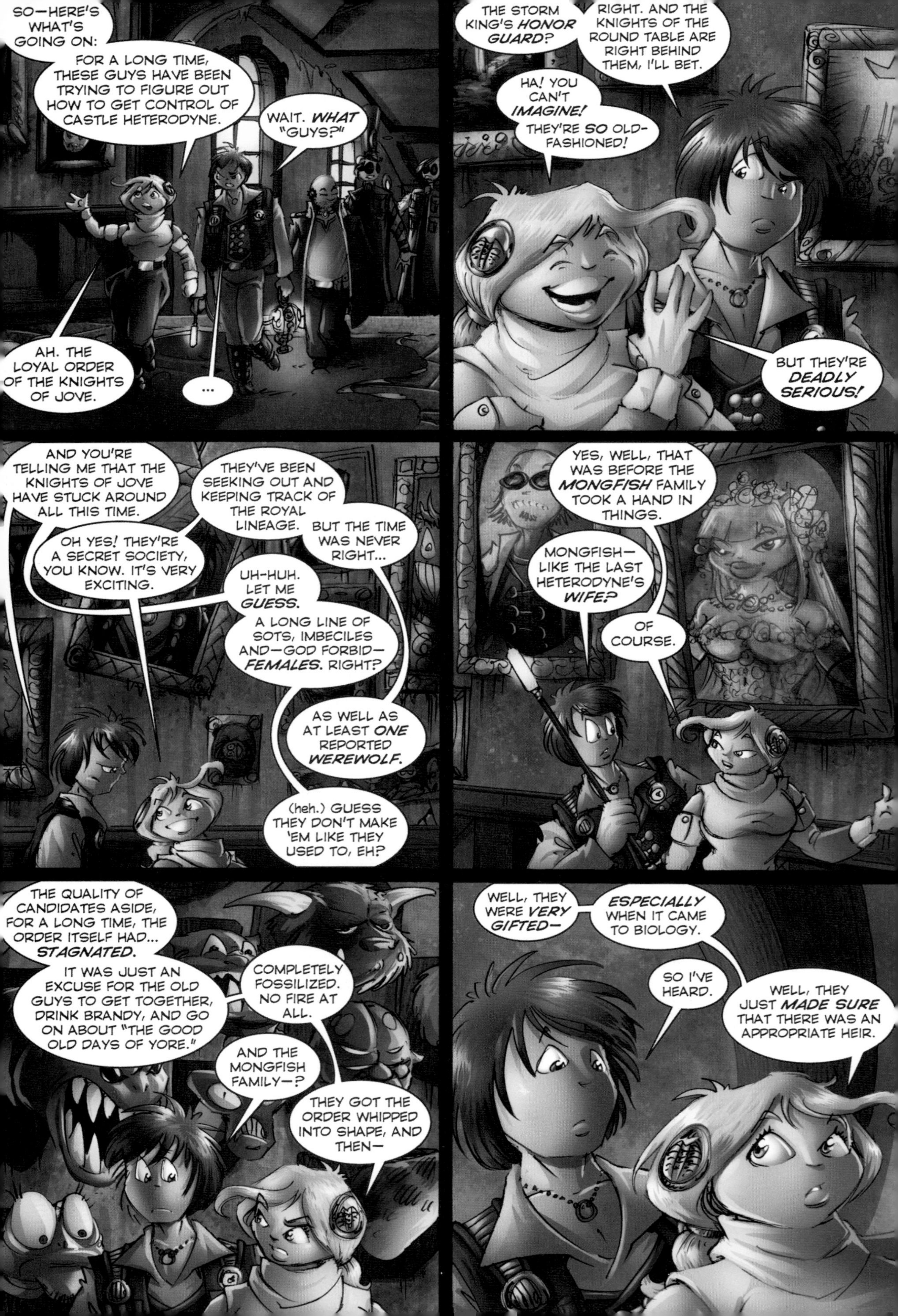
SO—HERE'S WHAT'S GOING ON:
FOR A LONG TIME, THESE GUYS HAVE BEEN TRYING TO FIGURE OUT HOW TO GET CONTROL OF CASTLE HETERODYNE.
WAIT. WHAT "GUYS?"
AH. THE LOYAL ORDER OF THE KNIGHTS OF JOVE.
...
THE STORM KING'S HONOR GUARD?
RIGHT. AND THE KNIGHTS OF THE ROUND TABLE ARE RIGHT BEHIND THEM, I'LL BET.
HA! YOU CAN'T IMAGINE!
THEY'RE SO OLD-FASHIONED!
BUT THEY'RE DEADLY SERIOUS!
AND YOU'RE TELLING ME THAT THE KNIGHTS OF JOVE HAVE STUCK AROUND ALL THIS TIME.
OH YES! THEY'RE A SECRET SOCIETY, YOU KNOW. IT'S VERY EXCITING.
THEY'VE BEEN SEEKING OUT AND KEEPING TRACK OF THE ROYAL LINEAGE.
BUT THE TIME WAS NEVER RIGHT...
UH-HUH. LET ME GUESS.
A LONG LINE OF SOTS, IMBECILES AND—GOD FORBID—FEMALES. RIGHT?
AS WELL AS AT LEAST ONE REPORTED WEREWOLF.
(heh.) GUESS THEY DON'T MAKE 'EM LIKE THEY USED TO, EH?
YES, WELL, THAT WAS BEFORE THE MONGFISH FAMILY TOOK A HAND IN THINGS.
MONGFISH—LIKE THE LAST HETERODYNE'S WIFE?
OF COURSE.
THE QUALITY OF CANDIDATES ASIDE, FOR A LONG TIME, THE ORDER ITSELF HAD... STAGNATED.
IT WAS JUST AN EXCUSE FOR THE OLD GUYS TO GET TOGETHER, DRINK BRANDY, AND GO ON ABOUT "THE GOOD OLD DAYS OF YORE."
COMPLETELY FOSSILIZED. NO FIRE AT ALL.
AND THE MONGFISH FAMILY—?
THEY GOT THE ORDER WHIPPED INTO SHAPE, AND THEN—
WELL, THEY WERE VERY GIFTED—
ESPECIALLY WHEN IT CAME TO BIOLOGY.
SO I'VE HEARD.
WELL, THEY JUST MADE SURE THAT THERE WAS AN APPROPRIATE HEIR.

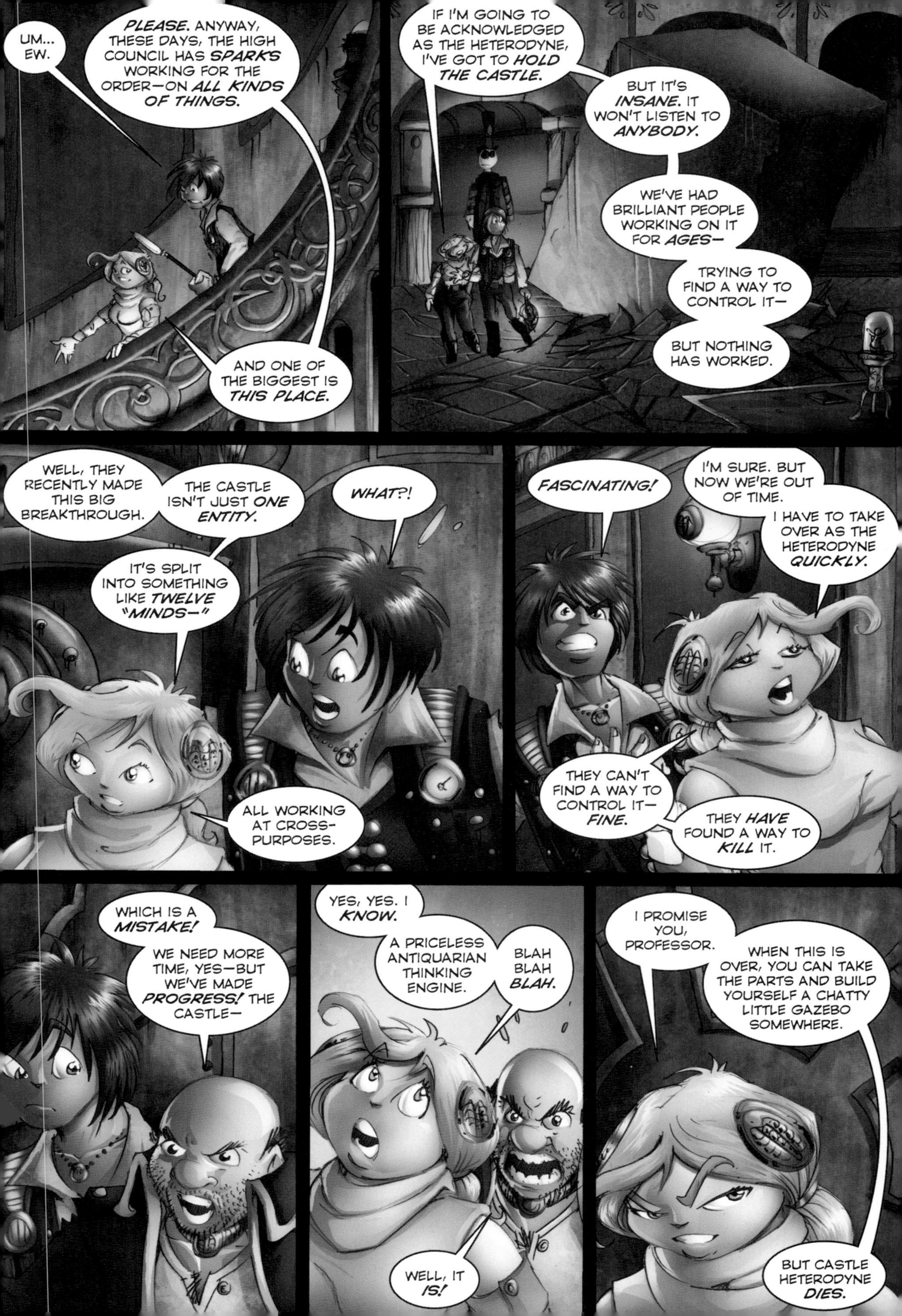
UM... EW.
PLEASE. ANYWAY, THESE DAYS, THE HIGH COUNCIL HAS *SPARKS* WORKING FOR THE ORDER—ON *ALL KINDS OF THINGS.*
AND ONE OF THE BIGGEST IS *THIS PLACE.*
IF I'M GOING TO BE ACKNOWLEDGED AS THE HETERODYNE, I'VE GOT TO *HOLD THE CASTLE.*
BUT IT'S *INSANE.* IT WON'T LISTEN TO *ANYBODY.*
WE'VE HAD BRILLIANT PEOPLE WORKING ON IT FOR *AGES*—
TRYING TO FIND A WAY TO CONTROL IT—
BUT NOTHING HAS WORKED.
WELL, THEY RECENTLY MADE THIS BIG BREAKTHROUGH.
THE CASTLE ISN'T JUST *ONE ENTITY.*
IT'S SPLIT INTO SOMETHING LIKE *TWELVE "MINDS—"*
WHAT?!
ALL WORKING AT CROSS-PURPOSES.
FASCINATING!
I'M SURE. BUT NOW WE'RE OUT OF TIME.
I HAVE TO TAKE OVER AS THE HETERODYNE *QUICKLY.*
THEY CAN'T FIND A WAY TO CONTROL IT—*FINE.*
THEY *HAVE* FOUND A WAY TO *KILL* IT.
WHICH IS A *MISTAKE!*
WE NEED MORE TIME, YES—BUT WE'VE MADE *PROGRESS!* THE CASTLE—
YES, YES. I *KNOW.*
A PRICELESS ANTIQUARIAN THINKING ENGINE.
BLAH BLAH *BLAH.*
WELL, IT *IS!*
I PROMISE YOU, PROFESSOR.
WHEN THIS IS OVER, YOU CAN TAKE THE PARTS AND BUILD YOURSELF A CHATTY LITTLE GAZEBO SOMEWHERE.
BUT CASTLE HETERODYNE *DIES.*

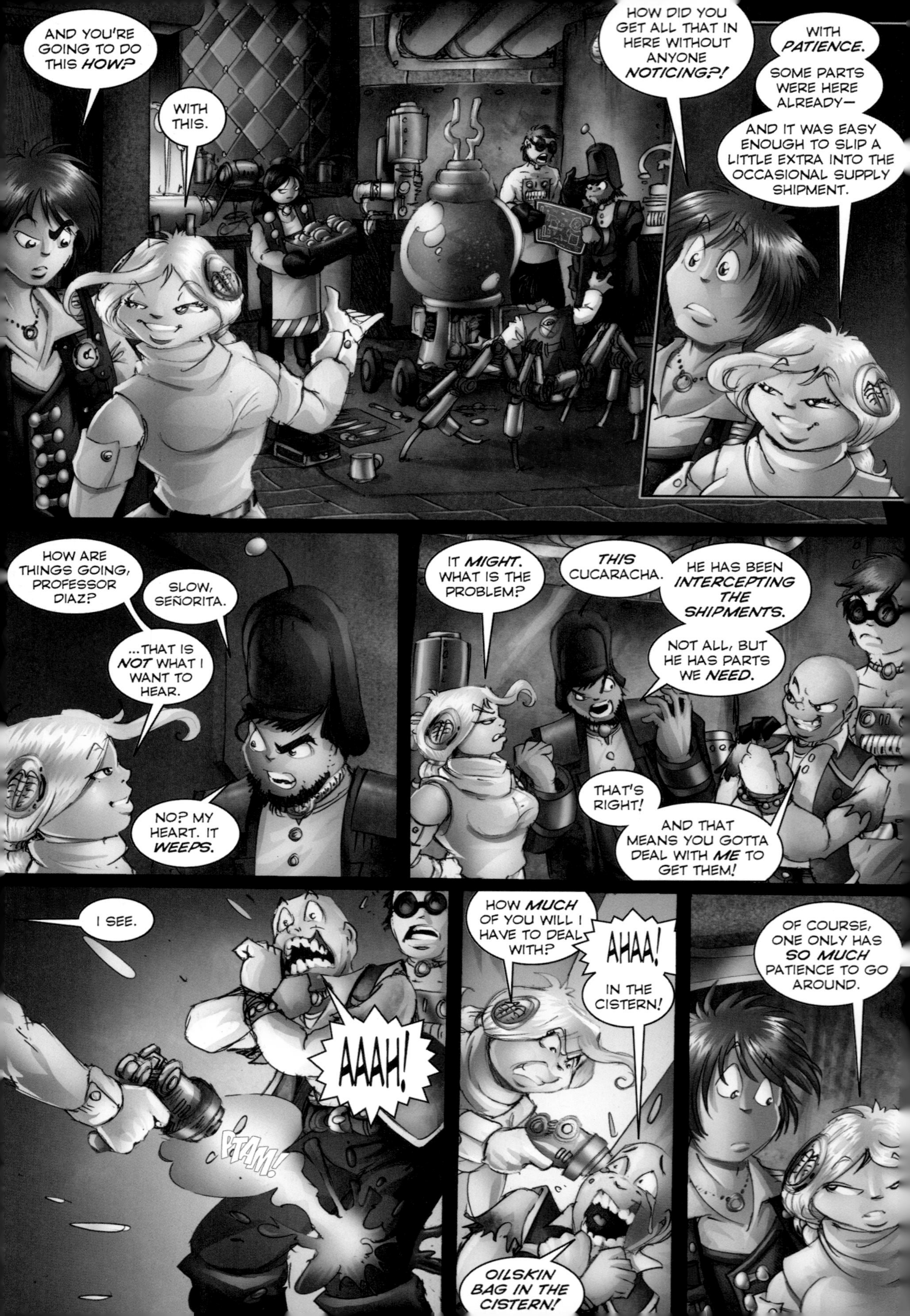
AND YOU'RE GOING TO DO THIS HOW?
WITH THIS.
HOW DID YOU GET ALL THAT IN HERE WITHOUT ANYONE NOTICING?!
WITH PATIENCE.
SOME PARTS WERE HERE ALREADY—
AND IT WAS EASY ENOUGH TO SLIP A LITTLE EXTRA INTO THE OCCASIONAL SUPPLY SHIPMENT.
HOW ARE THINGS GOING, PROFESSOR DIAZ?
SLOW, SEÑORITA.
...THAT IS NOT WHAT I WANT TO HEAR.
NO? MY HEART. IT WEEPS.
IT MIGHT. WHAT IS THE PROBLEM?
THIS CUCARACHA.
HE HAS BEEN INTERCEPTING THE SHIPMENTS.
NOT ALL, BUT HE HAS PARTS WE NEED.
THAT'S RIGHT!
AND THAT MEANS YOU GOTTA DEAL WITH ME TO GET THEM!
I SEE.
AAAH!
PTAM!
HOW MUCH OF YOU WILL I HAVE TO DEAL WITH?
AHAA!
IN THE CISTERN!
OILSKIN BAG IN THE CISTERN!
OF COURSE, ONE ONLY HAS SO MUCH PATIENCE TO GO AROUND.

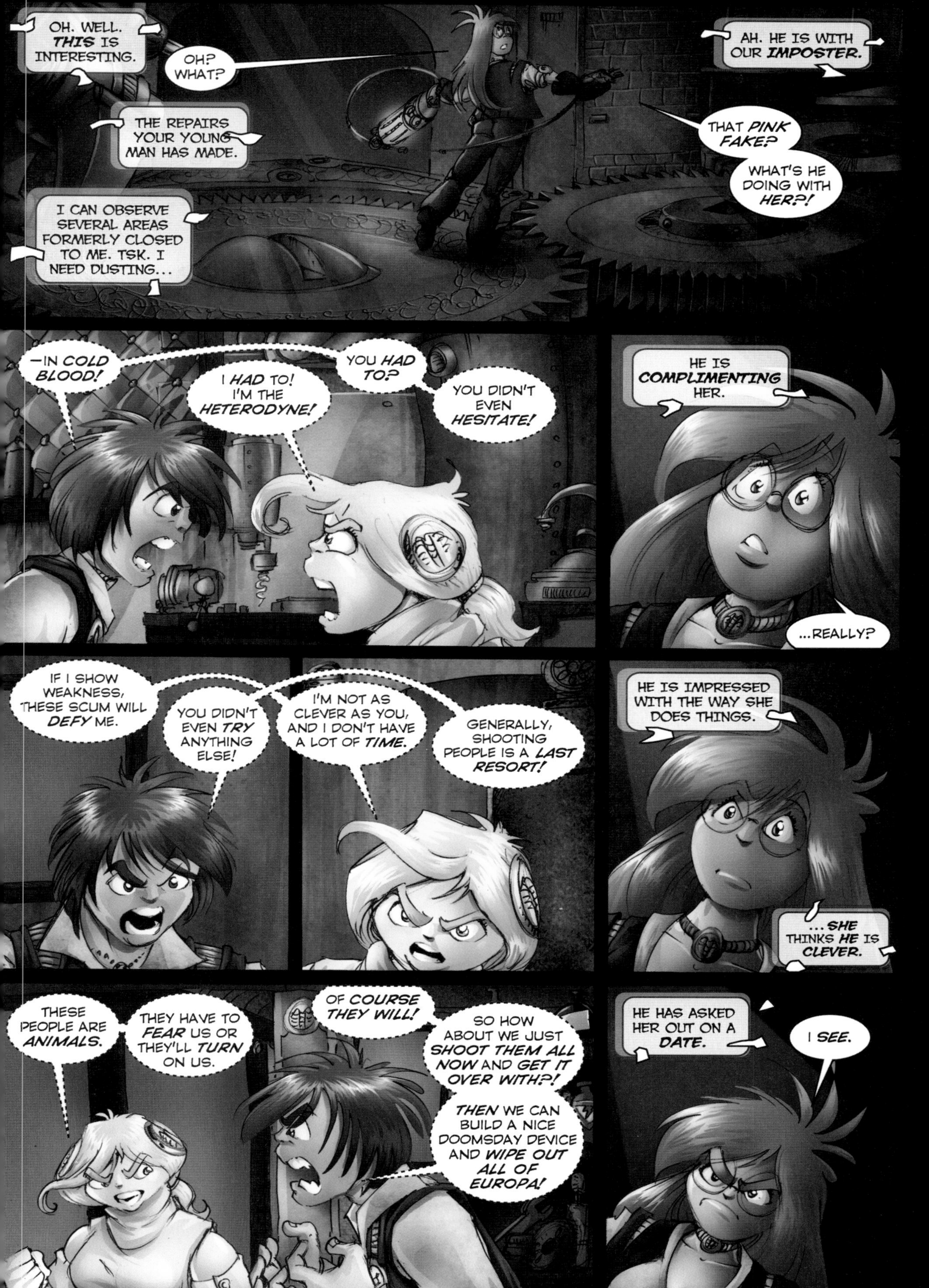

OH. WELL. *THIS* IS INTERESTING.
OH? WHAT?
THE REPAIRS YOUR YOUNG MAN HAS MADE.
I CAN OBSERVE SEVERAL AREAS FORMERLY CLOSED TO ME. TSK. I NEED DUSTING...
AH. HE IS WITH OUR *IMPOSTER.*
THAT *PINK FAKE?*
WHAT'S HE DOING WITH *HER?!*
—IN *COLD BLOOD!*
I *HAD* TO! I'M THE *HETERODYNE!*
YOU *HAD TO?*
YOU DIDN'T EVEN *HESITATE!*
HE IS *COMPLIMENTING* HER.
...REALLY?
IF I SHOW WEAKNESS, THESE SCUM WILL *DEFY* ME.
YOU DIDN'T EVEN *TRY* ANYTHING ELSE!
I'M NOT AS CLEVER AS YOU, AND I DON'T HAVE A LOT OF *TIME.*
GENERALLY, SHOOTING PEOPLE IS A *LAST RESORT!*
HE IS IMPRESSED WITH THE WAY SHE DOES THINGS.
...*SHE* THINKS *HE* IS *CLEVER.*
THESE PEOPLE ARE *ANIMALS.*
THEY HAVE TO *FEAR* US OR THEY'LL *TURN* ON US.
OF *COURSE THEY WILL!*
SO HOW ABOUT WE JUST *SHOOT THEM ALL NOW* AND *GET IT OVER WITH?!*
THEN WE CAN BUILD A NICE DOOMSDAY DEVICE AND *WIPE OUT ALL OF EUROPA!*
HE HAS ASKED HER OUT ON A *DATE.*
I *SEE.*

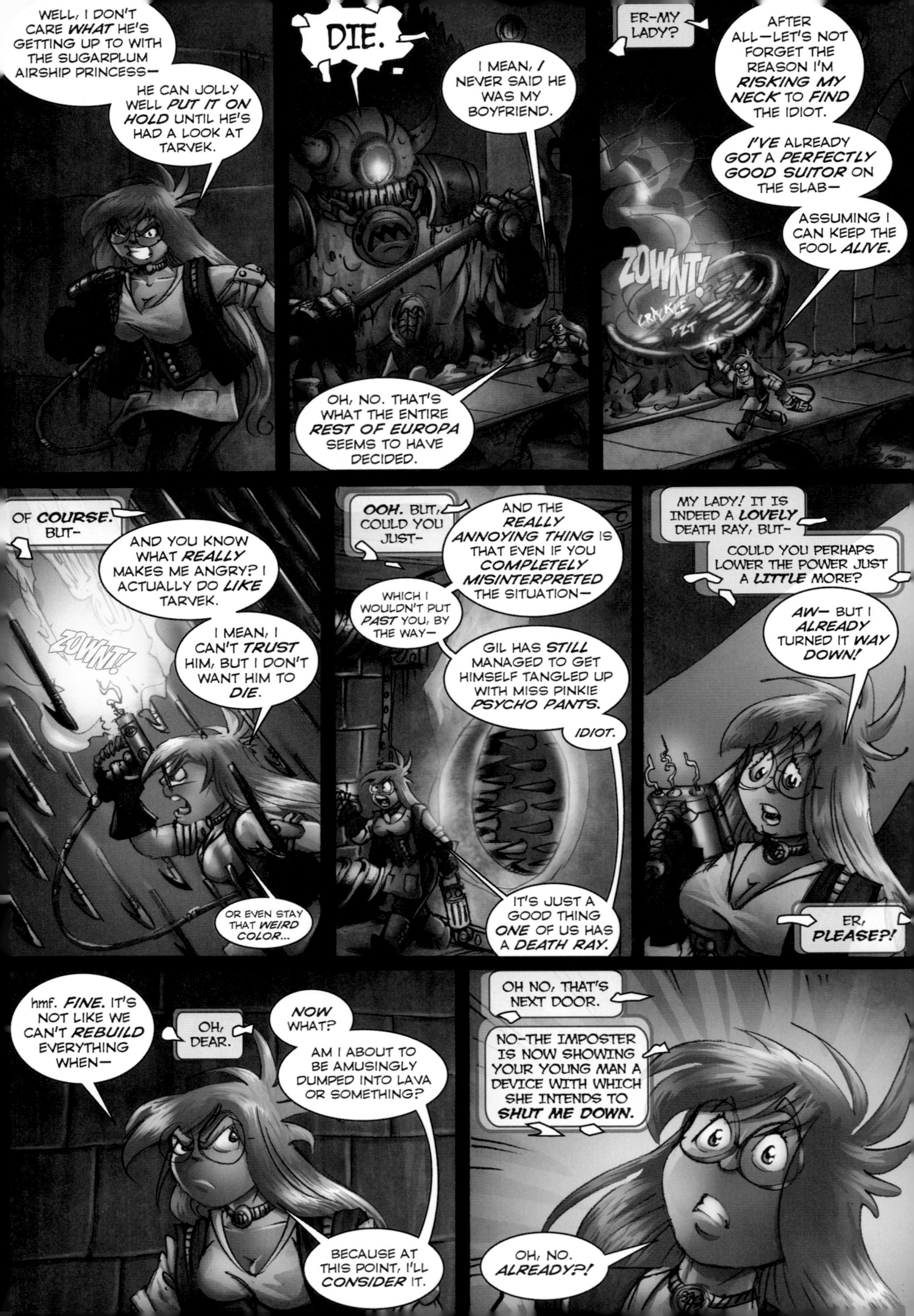

WELL, I DON'T CARE WHAT HE'S GETTING UP TO WITH THE SUGARPLUM AIRSHIP PRINCESS—
HE CAN JOLLY WELL PUT IT ON HOLD UNTIL HE'S HAD A LOOK AT TARVEK.
DIE.
I MEAN, I NEVER SAID HE WAS MY BOYFRIEND.
OH, NO. THAT'S WHAT THE ENTIRE REST OF EUROPA SEEMS TO HAVE DECIDED.
ER-MY LADY?
AFTER ALL—LET'S NOT FORGET THE REASON I'M RISKING MY NECK TO FIND THE IDIOT.
I'VE ALREADY GOT A PERFECTLY GOOD SUITOR ON THE SLAB—
ASSUMING I CAN KEEP THE FOOL ALIVE.
ZOWNT!
CRACKLE
FZT
OF COURSE. BUT-
AND YOU KNOW WHAT REALLY MAKES ME ANGRY? I ACTUALLY DO LIKE TARVEK.
ZOWNT!
I MEAN, I CAN'T TRUST HIM, BUT I DON'T WANT HIM TO DIE.
OR EVEN STAY THAT WEIRD COLOR...
OOH. BUT, COULD YOU JUST-
AND THE REALLY ANNOYING THING IS THAT EVEN IF YOU COMPLETELY MISINTERPRETED THE SITUATION—
WHICH I WOULDN'T PUT PAST YOU, BY THE WAY—
GIL HAS STILL MANAGED TO GET HIMSELF TANGLED UP WITH MISS PINKIE PSYCHO PANTS.
IDIOT.
IT'S JUST A GOOD THING ONE OF US HAS A DEATH RAY.
MY LADY! IT IS INDEED A LOVELY DEATH RAY, BUT-
COULD YOU PERHAPS LOWER THE POWER JUST A LITTLE MORE?
AW— BUT I ALREADY TURNED IT WAY DOWN!
ER, PLEASE?!
hmf. FINE. IT'S NOT LIKE WE CAN'T REBUILD EVERYTHING WHEN—
OH, DEAR.
NOW WHAT?
AM I ABOUT TO BE AMUSINGLY DUMPED INTO LAVA OR SOMETHING?
BECAUSE AT THIS POINT, I'LL CONSIDER IT.
OH NO, THAT'S NEXT DOOR.
NO-THE IMPOSTER IS NOW SHOWING YOUR YOUNG MAN A DEVICE WITH WHICH SHE INTENDS TO SHUT ME DOWN.
OH, NO. ALREADY?!

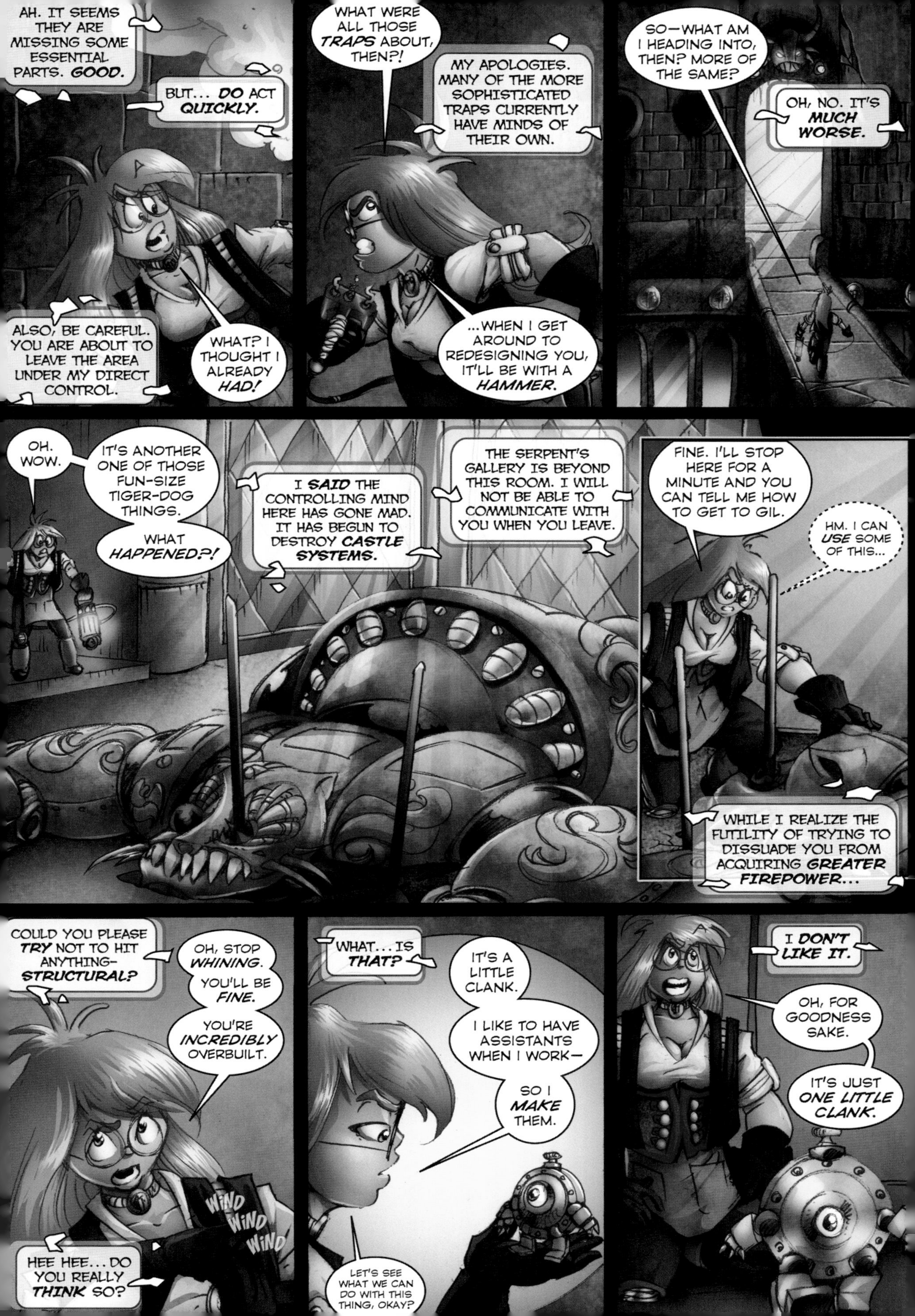

AH. IT SEEMS THEY ARE MISSING SOME ESSENTIAL PARTS. GOOD.
BUT... DO ACT QUICKLY.
ALSO, BE CAREFUL. YOU ARE ABOUT TO LEAVE THE AREA UNDER MY DIRECT CONTROL.
WHAT? I THOUGHT I ALREADY HAD!
WHAT WERE ALL THOSE TRAPS ABOUT, THEN?!
MY APOLOGIES. MANY OF THE MORE SOPHISTICATED TRAPS CURRENTLY HAVE MINDS OF THEIR OWN.
...WHEN I GET AROUND TO REDESIGNING YOU, IT'LL BE WITH A HAMMER.
SO—WHAT AM I HEADING INTO, THEN? MORE OF THE SAME?
OH, NO. IT'S MUCH WORSE.
OH. WOW.
IT'S ANOTHER ONE OF THOSE FUN-SIZE TIGER-DOG THINGS.
WHAT HAPPENED?!
I SAID THE CONTROLLING MIND HERE HAS GONE MAD. IT HAS BEGUN TO DESTROY CASTLE SYSTEMS.
THE SERPENT'S GALLERY IS BEYOND THIS ROOM. I WILL NOT BE ABLE TO COMMUNICATE WITH YOU WHEN YOU LEAVE.
FINE. I'LL STOP HERE FOR A MINUTE AND YOU CAN TELL ME HOW TO GET TO GIL.
HM. I CAN USE SOME OF THIS...
WHILE I REALIZE THE FUTILITY OF TRYING TO DISSUADE YOU FROM ACQUIRING GREATER FIREPOWER...
COULD YOU PLEASE TRY NOT TO HIT ANYTHING–STRUCTURAL?
OH, STOP WHINING. YOU'LL BE FINE.
YOU'RE INCREDIBLY OVERBUILT.
WIND WIND WIND
HEE HEE... DO YOU REALLY THINK SO?
WHAT... IS THAT?
IT'S A LITTLE CLANK.
I LIKE TO HAVE ASSISTANTS WHEN I WORK—
SO I MAKE THEM.
LET'S SEE WHAT WE CAN DO WITH THIS THING, OKAY?
I DON'T LIKE IT.
OH, FOR GOODNESS SAKE.
IT'S JUST ONE LITTLE CLANK.

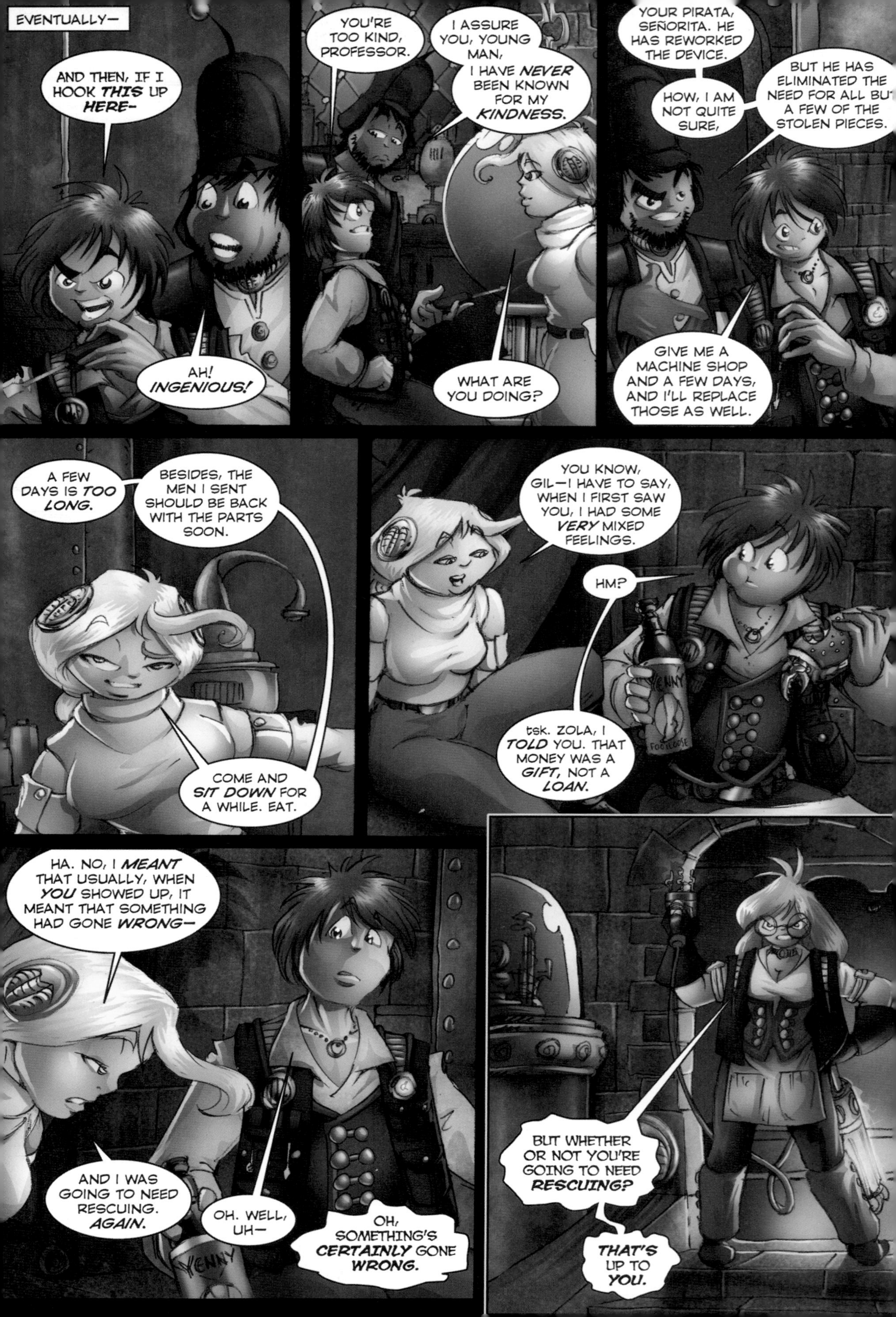
EVENTUALLY—
AND THEN, IF I HOOK THIS UP HERE-
AH! INGENIOUS!
YOU'RE TOO KIND, PROFESSOR.
I ASSURE YOU, YOUNG MAN, I HAVE NEVER BEEN KNOWN FOR MY KINDNESS.
WHAT ARE YOU DOING?
YOUR PIRATA, SEÑORITA. HE HAS REWORKED THE DEVICE.
HOW, I AM NOT QUITE SURE,
BUT HE HAS ELIMINATED THE NEED FOR ALL BUT A FEW OF THE STOLEN PIECES.
GIVE ME A MACHINE SHOP AND A FEW DAYS, AND I'LL REPLACE THOSE AS WELL.
A FEW DAYS IS TOO LONG.
BESIDES, THE MEN I SENT SHOULD BE BACK WITH THE PARTS SOON.
COME AND SIT DOWN FOR A WHILE. EAT.
YOU KNOW, GIL—I HAVE TO SAY, WHEN I FIRST SAW YOU, I HAD SOME VERY MIXED FEELINGS.
HM?
tsk. ZOLA, I TOLD YOU. THAT MONEY WAS A GIFT, NOT A LOAN.
HA. NO, I MEANT THAT USUALLY, WHEN YOU SHOWED UP, IT MEANT THAT SOMETHING HAD GONE WRONG—
AND I WAS GOING TO NEED RESCUING. AGAIN.
OH. WELL, UH—
OH, SOMETHING'S CERTAINLY GONE WRONG.
BUT WHETHER OR NOT YOU'RE GOING TO NEED RESCUING?
THAT'S UP TO YOU.

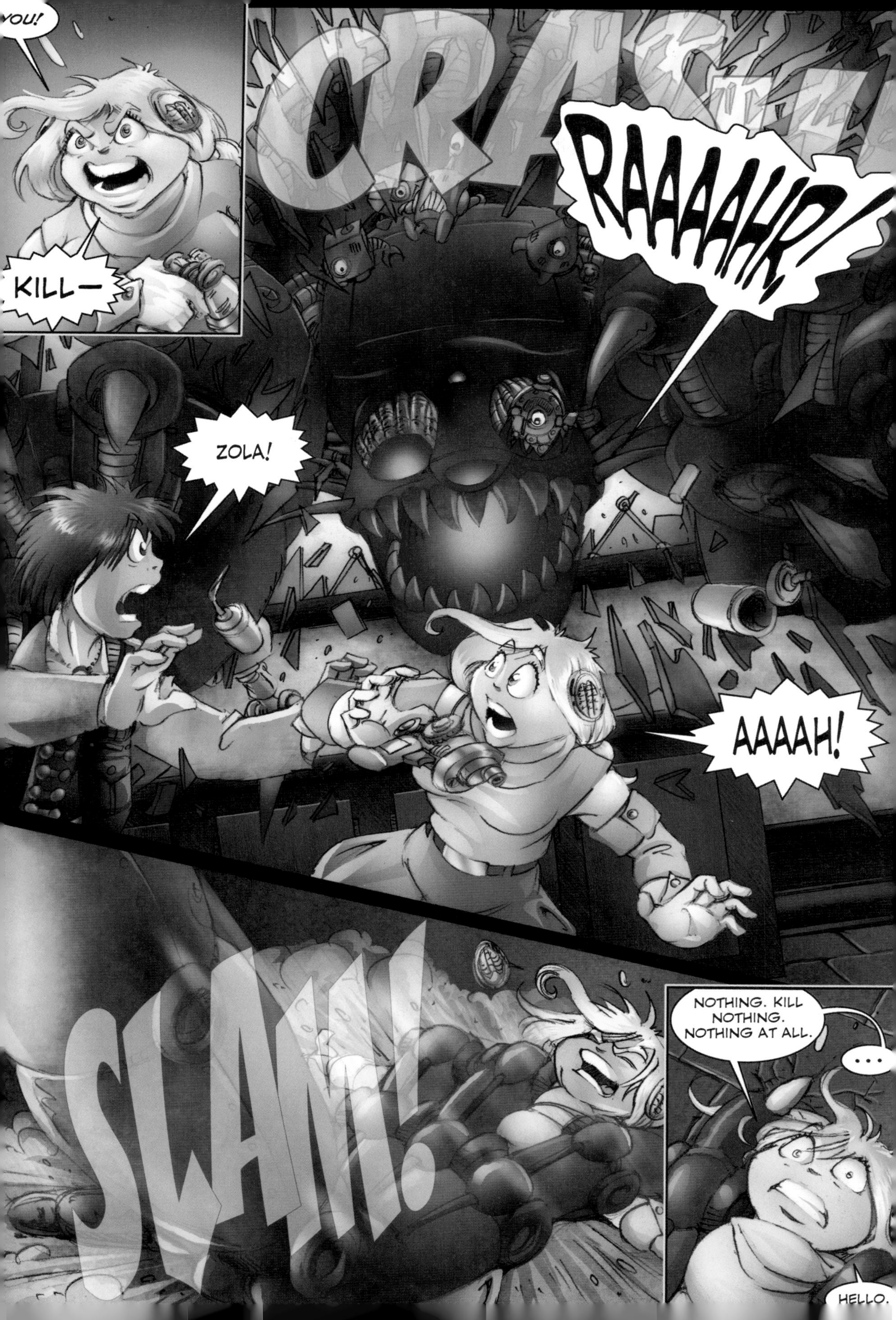
YOU!
KILL—
CRASH!
RAAAAHR!!
ZOLA!
AAAAH!
SLAM!
NOTHING. KILL NOTHING. NOTHING AT ALL.
...
HELLO.

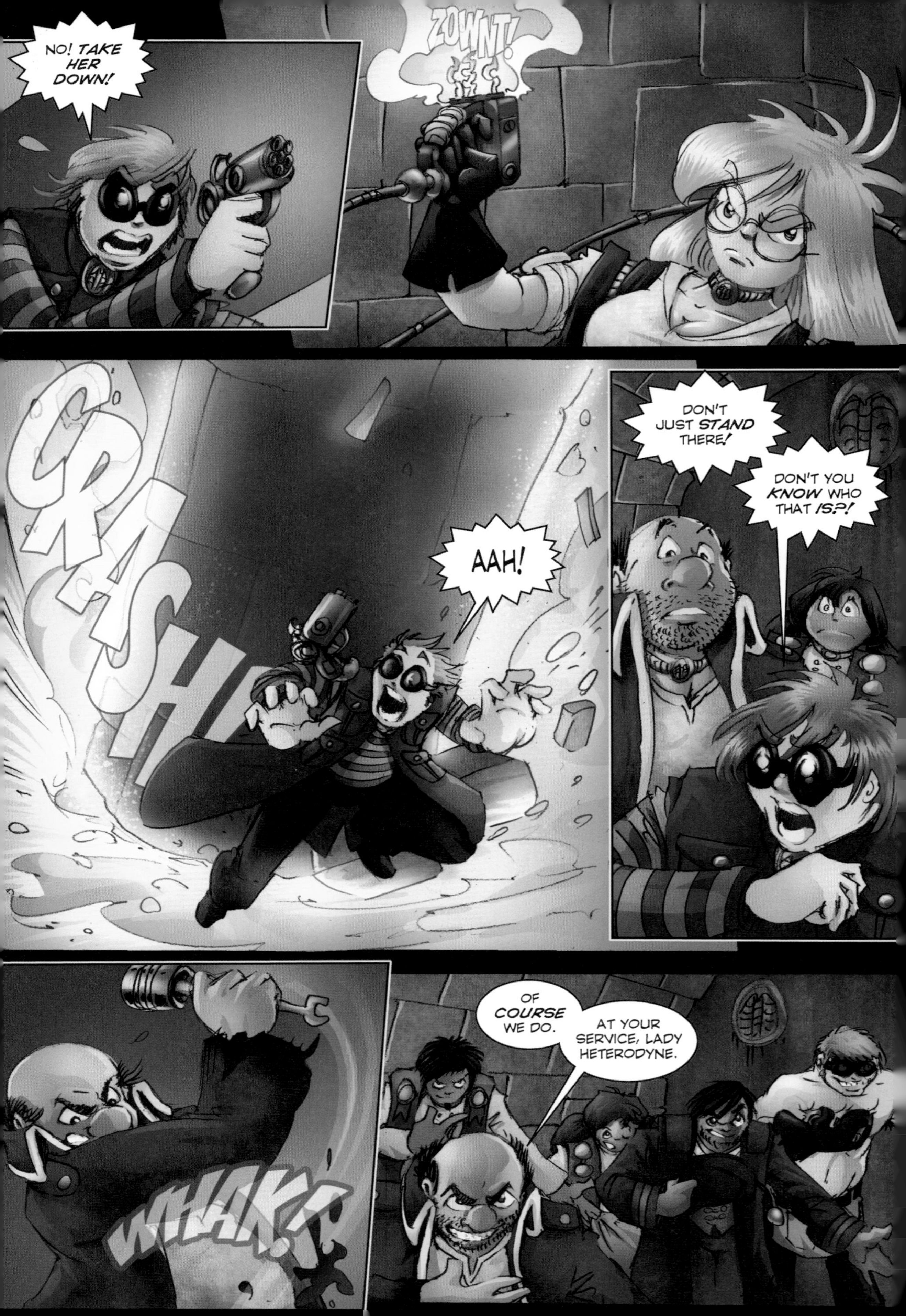

NO! TAKE HER DOWN!
ZOWNT!
CRASH
AAH!
DON'T JUST STAND THERE!
DON'T YOU KNOW WHO THAT IS?!
WHAK!
OF COURSE WE DO.
AT YOUR SERVICE, LADY HETERODYNE.

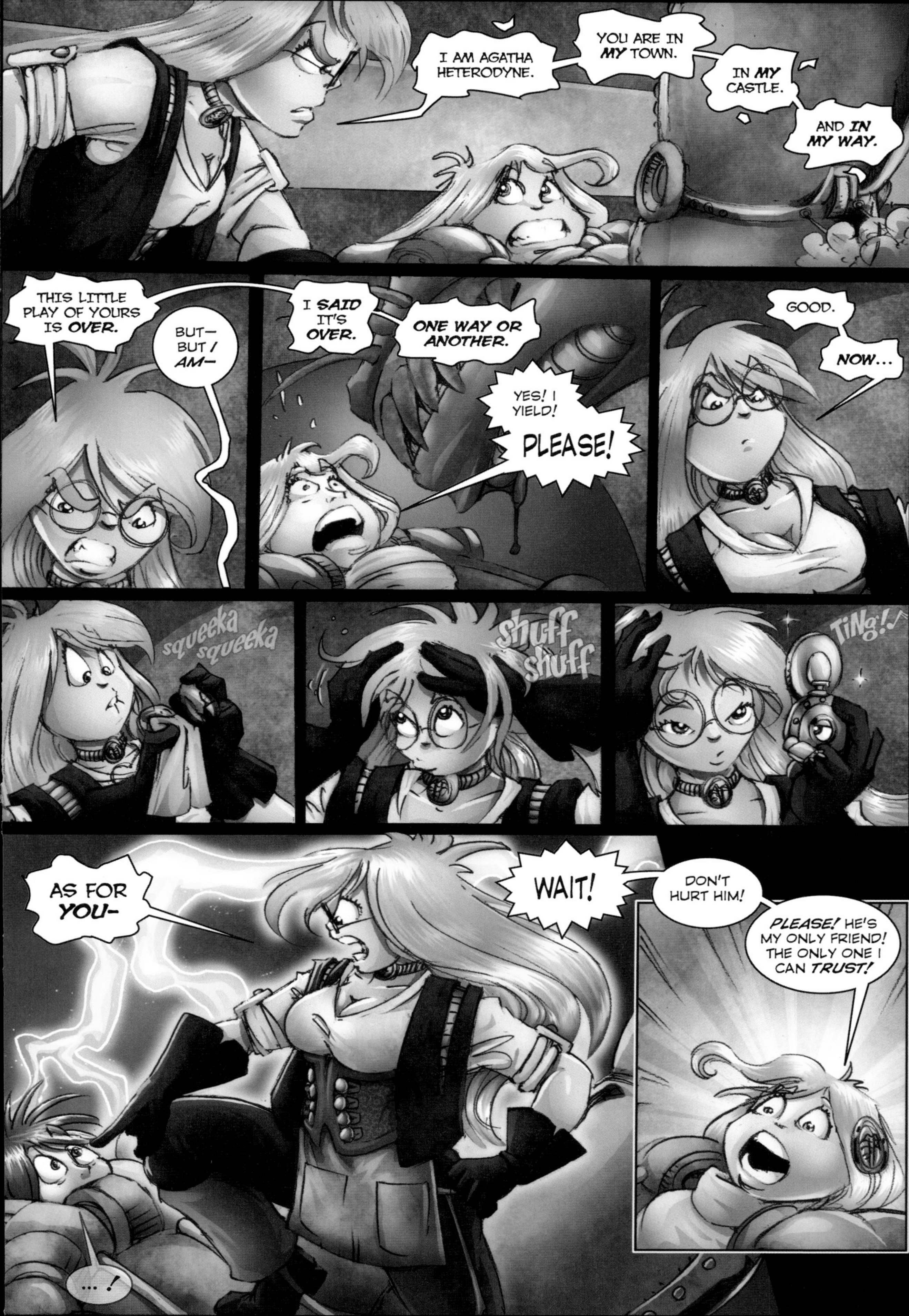
I AM AGATHA HETERODYNE.
YOU ARE IN *MY* TOWN.
IN *MY* CASTLE.
AND *IN MY WAY.*
THIS LITTLE PLAY OF YOURS IS *OVER.*
BUT— BUT *I AM—*
I *SAID* IT'S *OVER.*
ONE WAY OR ANOTHER.
YES! I YIELD!
PLEASE!
GOOD.
NOW...
squeeka squeeka
shuff shuff
TiNg!
AS FOR *YOU-*
WAIT!
DON'T HURT HIM!
PLEASE! HE'S MY ONLY FRIEND! THE ONLY ONE I CAN *TRUST!*
...!

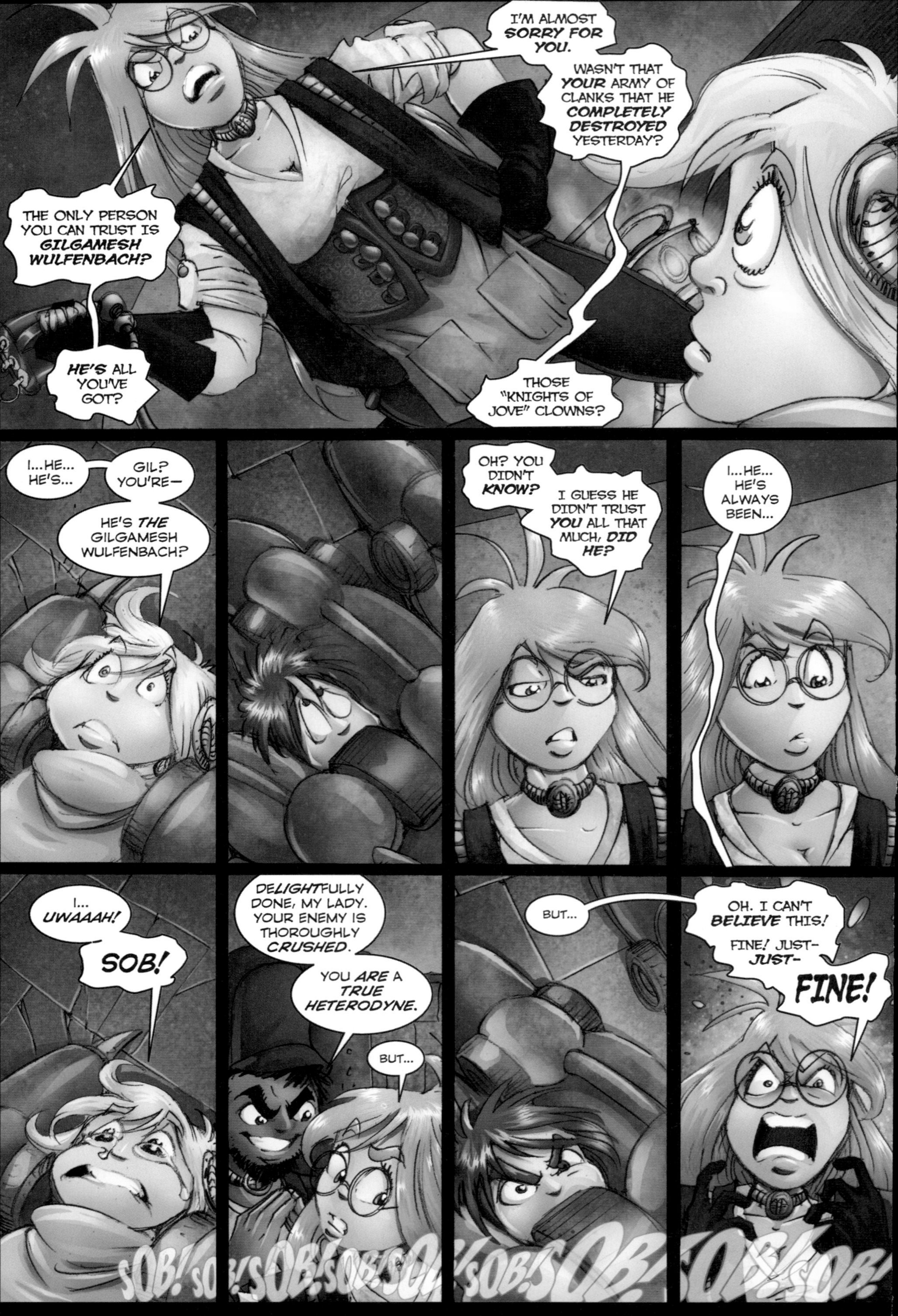
I'M ALMOST SORRY FOR YOU.
WASN'T THAT YOUR ARMY OF CLANKS THAT HE COMPLETELY DESTROYED YESTERDAY?
THE ONLY PERSON YOU CAN TRUST IS GILGAMESH WULFENBACH?
HE'S ALL YOU'VE GOT?
THOSE "KNIGHTS OF JOVE" CLOWNS?
I...HE... HE'S...
GIL? YOU'RE—
HE'S THE GILGAMESH WULFENBACH?
OH? YOU DIDN'T KNOW?
I GUESS HE DIDN'T TRUST YOU ALL THAT MUCH, DID HE?
I...HE... HE'S ALWAYS BEEN...
I... UWAAAH!
SOB!
DELIGHTFULLY DONE, MY LADY. YOUR ENEMY IS THOROUGHLY CRUSHED.
YOU ARE A TRUE HETERODYNE.
BUT...
BUT...
OH. I CAN'T BELIEVE THIS!
FINE! JUST- JUST-
FINE!
SOB! SOB! SOB! SOB! SOB! SOB! SOB! SOB! SOB!

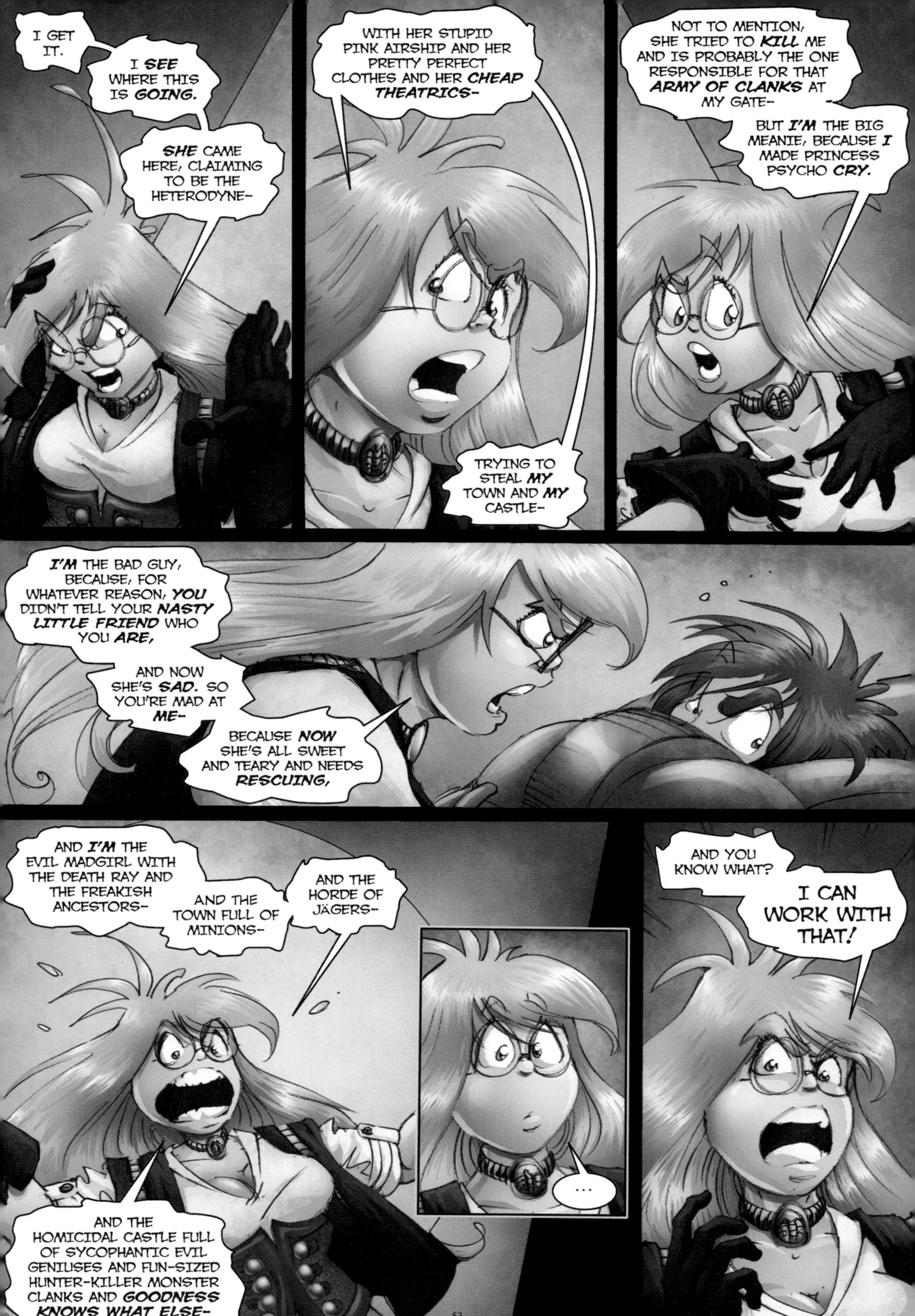

I GET IT.
I *SEE* WHERE THIS IS *GOING.*
SHE CAME HERE, CLAIMING TO BE THE HETERODYNE-
WITH HER STUPID PINK AIRSHIP AND HER PRETTY PERFECT CLOTHES AND HER *CHEAP THEATRICS-*
TRYING TO STEAL *MY* TOWN AND *MY* CASTLE-
NOT TO MENTION, SHE TRIED TO *KILL* ME AND IS PROBABLY THE ONE RESPONSIBLE FOR THAT *ARMY OF CLANKS* AT MY GATE-
BUT *I'M* THE BIG MEANIE, BECAUSE *I* MADE PRINCESS PSYCHO *CRY.*
I'M THE BAD GUY, BECAUSE, FOR WHATEVER REASON, *YOU* DIDN'T TELL YOUR *NASTY LITTLE FRIEND* WHO YOU *ARE,*
AND NOW SHE'S *SAD.* SO YOU'RE MAD AT *ME-*
BECAUSE *NOW* SHE'S ALL SWEET AND TEARY AND NEEDS *RESCUING,*
AND *I'M* THE EVIL MADGIRL WITH THE DEATH RAY AND THE FREAKISH ANCESTORS-
AND THE TOWN FULL OF MINIONS-
AND THE HORDE OF JÄGERS-
AND THE HOMICIDAL CASTLE FULL OF SYCOPHANTIC EVIL GENIUSES AND FUN-SIZED HUNTER-KILLER MONSTER CLANKS AND *GOODNESS KNOWS WHAT ELSE-*
...
AND YOU KNOW WHAT?
I CAN WORK WITH THAT!

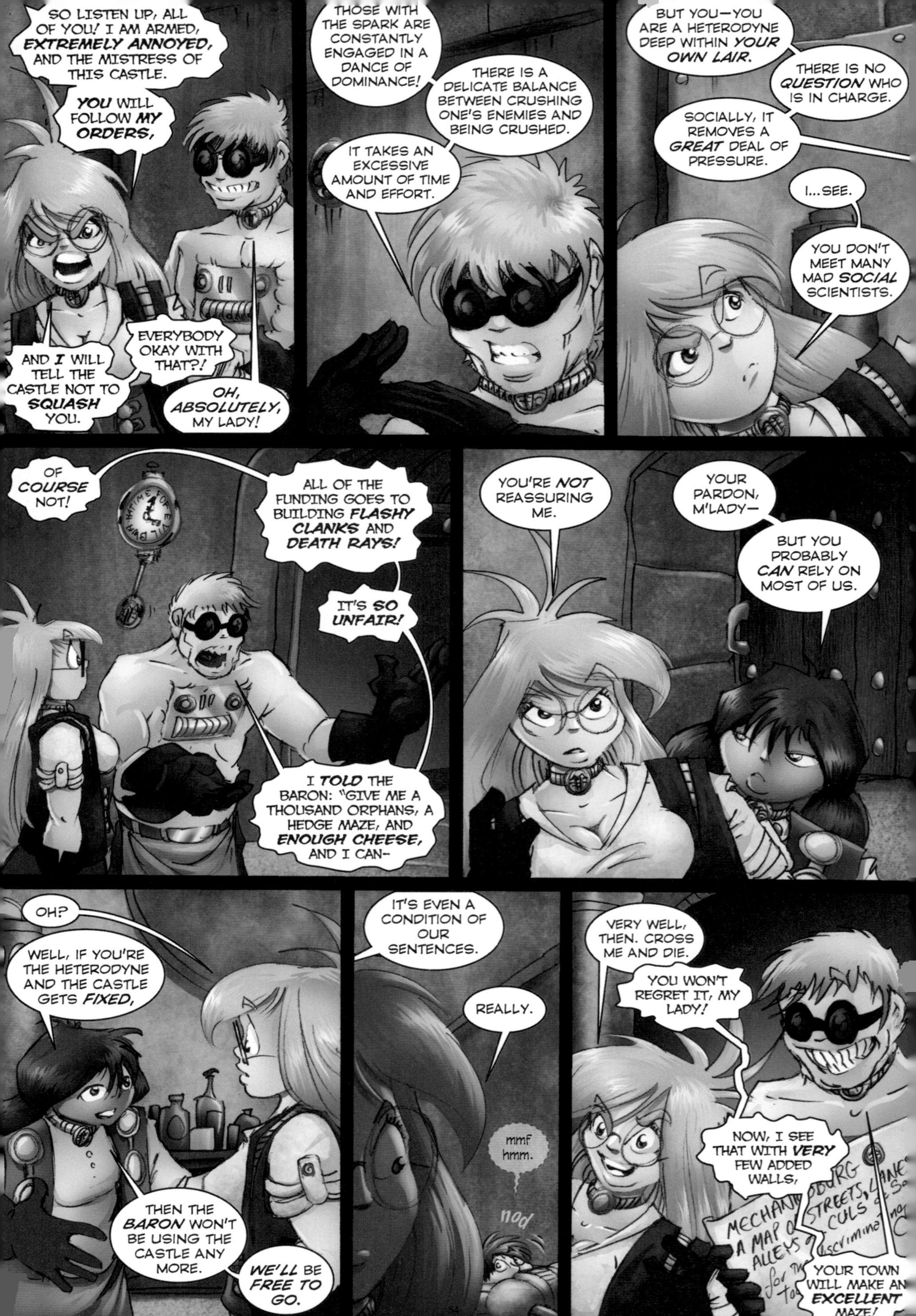
SO LISTEN UP, ALL OF YOU! I AM ARMED, **EXTREMELY ANNOYED,** AND THE MISTRESS OF THIS CASTLE.
YOU WILL FOLLOW ***MY ORDERS,***
AND ***I*** WILL TELL THE CASTLE NOT TO ***SQUASH*** YOU.
EVERYBODY OKAY WITH THAT?!
OH, ABSOLUTELY, MY LADY!
THOSE WITH THE SPARK ARE CONSTANTLY ENGAGED IN A DANCE OF DOMINANCE!
THERE IS A DELICATE BALANCE BETWEEN CRUSHING ONE'S ENEMIES AND BEING CRUSHED.
IT TAKES AN EXCESSIVE AMOUNT OF TIME AND EFFORT.
BUT YOU—YOU ARE A HETERODYNE DEEP WITHIN ***YOUR OWN LAIR.***
THERE IS NO ***QUESTION*** WHO IS IN CHARGE.
SOCIALLY, IT REMOVES A ***GREAT*** DEAL OF PRESSURE.
I...SEE.
YOU DON'T MEET MANY MAD ***SOCIAL*** SCIENTISTS.
OF ***COURSE*** NOT!
ALL OF THE FUNDING GOES TO BUILDING ***FLASHY CLANKS*** AND ***DEATH RAYS!***
IT'S ***SO UNFAIR!***
I ***TOLD*** THE BARON: "GIVE ME A THOUSAND ORPHANS, A HEDGE MAZE, AND ***ENOUGH CHEESE,*** AND I CAN-
YOU'RE ***NOT*** REASSURING ME.
YOUR PARDON, M'LADY—
BUT YOU PROBABLY ***CAN*** RELY ON MOST OF US.
OH?
WELL, IF YOU'RE THE HETERODYNE AND THE CASTLE GETS ***FIXED,***
THEN THE ***BARON*** WON'T BE USING THE CASTLE ANY MORE.
WE'LL BE ***FREE TO GO.***
IT'S EVEN A CONDITION OF OUR SENTENCES.
REALLY.
mmf hmm.
nod
VERY WELL, THEN. CROSS ME AND DIE.
YOU WON'T REGRET IT, MY LADY!
NOW, I SEE THAT WITH ***VERY*** FEW ADDED WALLS,
YOUR TOWN WILL MAKE AN ***EXCELLENT*** MAZE!

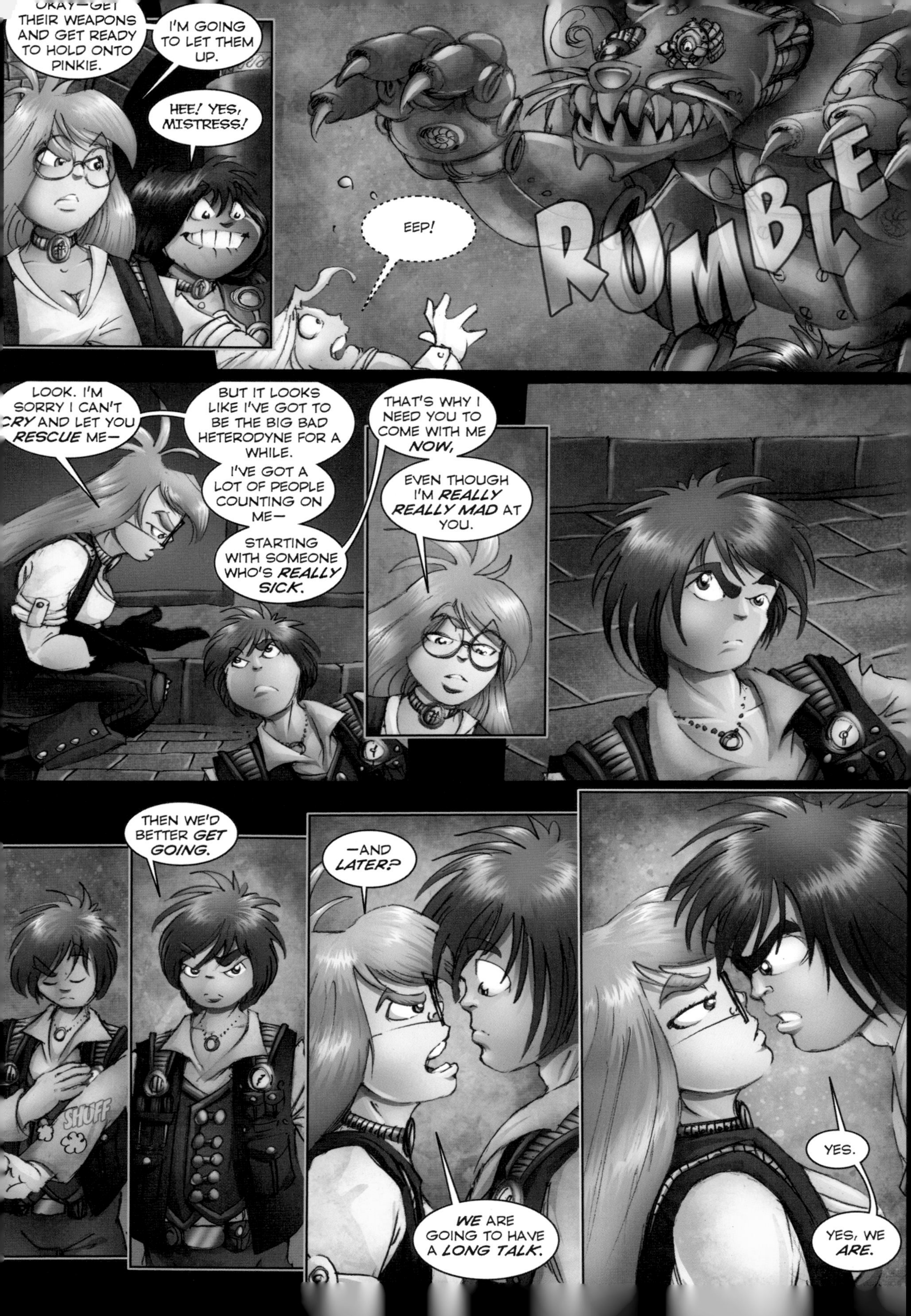

OKAY—GET THEIR WEAPONS AND GET READY TO HOLD ONTO PINKIE.
I'M GOING TO LET THEM UP.
HEE! YES, MISTRESS!
EEP!
RUMBLE
LOOK. I'M SORRY I CAN'T CRY AND LET YOU RESCUE ME—
BUT IT LOOKS LIKE I'VE GOT TO BE THE BIG BAD HETERODYNE FOR A WHILE.
I'VE GOT A LOT OF PEOPLE COUNTING ON ME—
STARTING WITH SOMEONE WHO'S REALLY SICK.
THAT'S WHY I NEED YOU TO COME WITH ME NOW,
EVEN THOUGH I'M REALLY REALLY MAD AT YOU.
SHUFF
THEN WE'D BETTER GET GOING.
—AND LATER?
WE ARE GOING TO HAVE A LONG TALK.
YES.
YES, WE ARE.

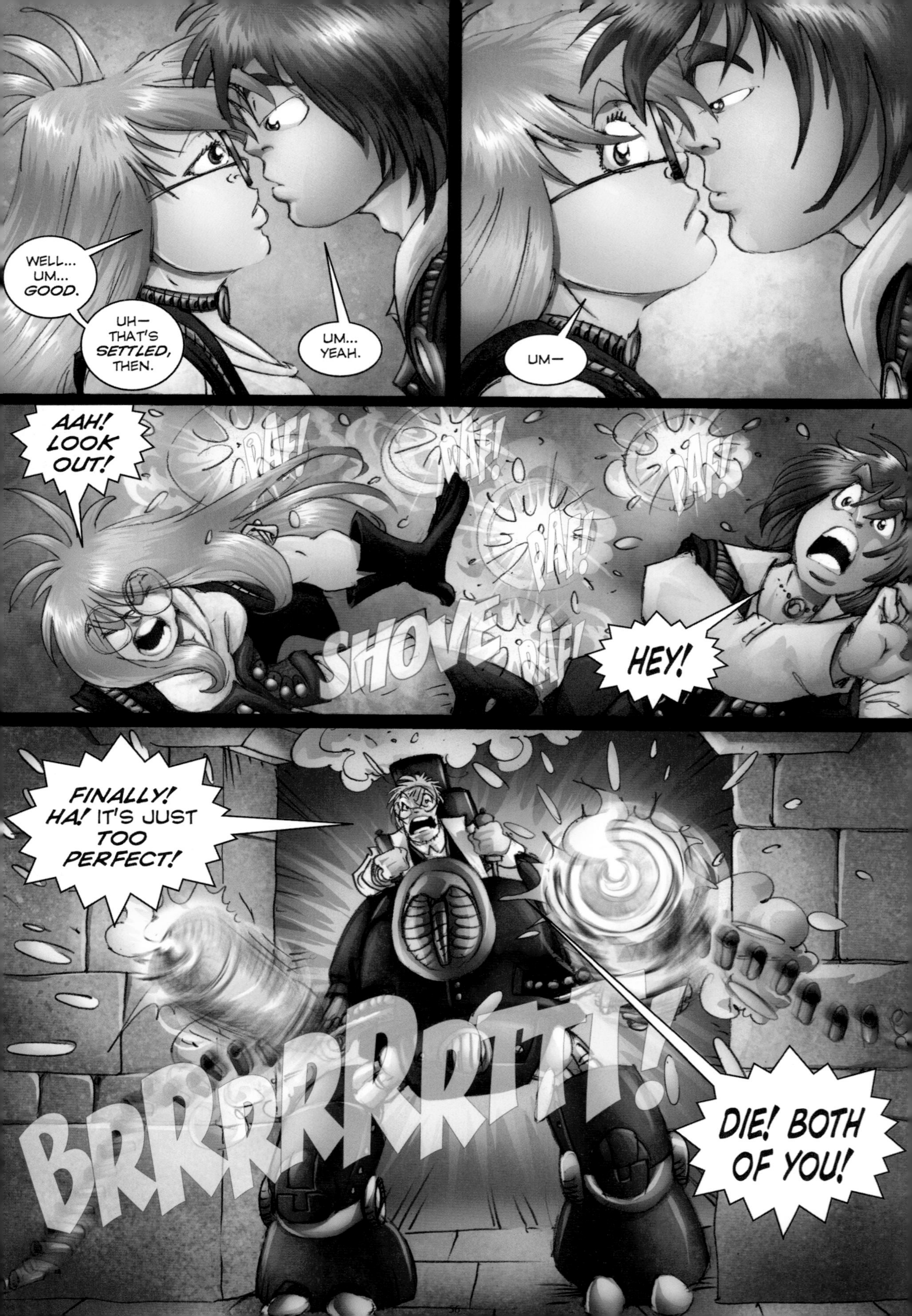

WELL... UM... GOOD.
UH— THAT'S SETTLED, THEN.
UM... YEAH.
UM—
AAH! LOOK OUT!
PAF!
PAF!
PAF!
PAF!
PAF!
SHOVE
HEY!
FINALLY! HA! IT'S JUST TOO PERFECT!
BRRRRRRTTT!
DIE! BOTH OF YOU!

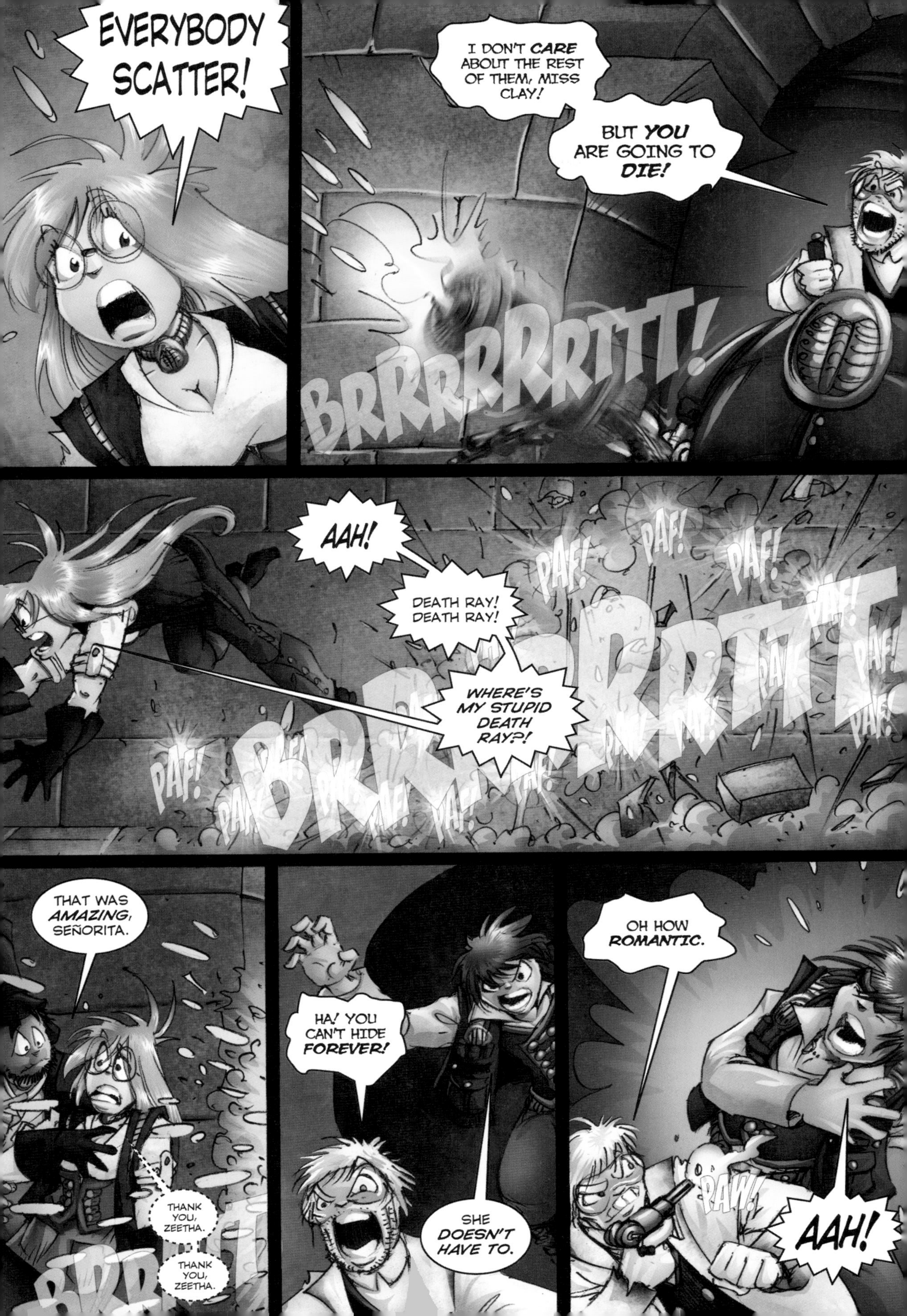
EVERYBODY SCATTER!
I DON'T CARE ABOUT THE REST OF THEM, MISS CLAY!
BUT YOU ARE GOING TO DIE!
BRRRRRRRTTT!
AAH!
DEATH RAY! DEATH RAY!
WHERE'S MY STUPID DEATH RAY?!
BRRRRRTTT!
PAF!
THAT WAS AMAZING, SEÑORITA.
THANK YOU, ZEETHA.
THANK YOU, ZEETHA.
HA! YOU CAN'T HIDE FOREVER!
SHE DOESN'T HAVE TO.
OH HOW ROMANTIC.
PAW!
AAH!

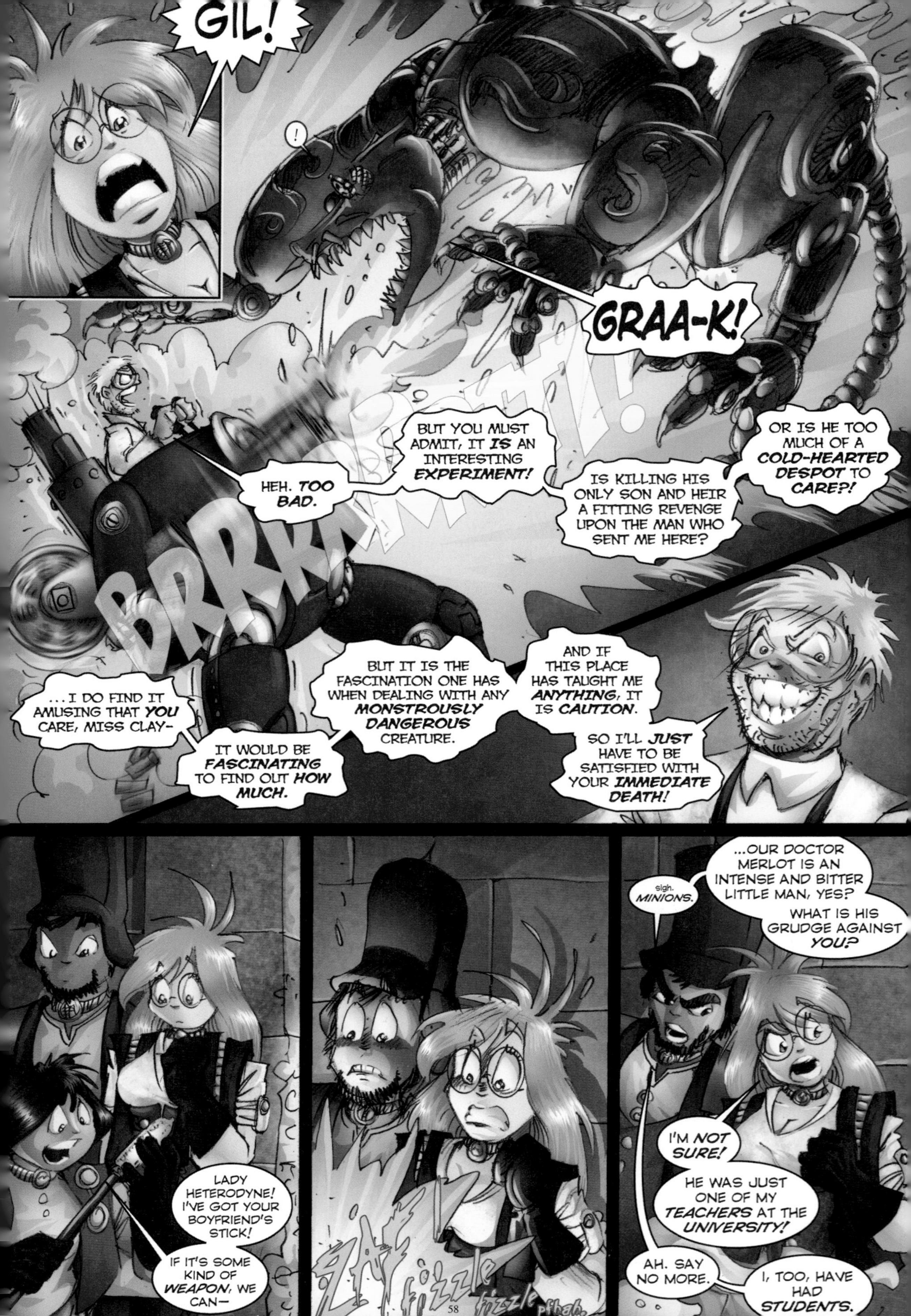
GIL!
!
GRAA-K!
BRRKA
HEH. TOO BAD.
BUT YOU MUST ADMIT, IT IS AN INTERESTING EXPERIMENT!
IS KILLING HIS ONLY SON AND HEIR A FITTING REVENGE UPON THE MAN WHO SENT ME HERE?
OR IS HE TOO MUCH OF A COLD-HEARTED DESPOT TO CARE?!
. . . I DO FIND IT AMUSING THAT YOU CARE, MISS CLAY-
IT WOULD BE FASCINATING TO FIND OUT HOW MUCH.
BUT IT IS THE FASCINATION ONE HAS WHEN DEALING WITH ANY MONSTROUSLY DANGEROUS CREATURE.
AND IF THIS PLACE HAS TAUGHT ME ANYTHING, IT IS CAUTION.
SO I'LL JUST HAVE TO BE SATISFIED WITH YOUR IMMEDIATE DEATH!
LADY HETERODYNE! I'VE GOT YOUR BOYFRIEND'S STICK!
IF IT'S SOME KIND OF WEAPON, WE CAN—
fizzle
fizzle
pfhah.
sigh. MINIONS.
...OUR DOCTOR MERLOT IS AN INTENSE AND BITTER LITTLE MAN, YES?
WHAT IS HIS GRUDGE AGAINST YOU?
I'M NOT SURE!
HE WAS JUST ONE OF MY TEACHERS AT THE UNIVERSITY!
AH. SAY NO MORE.
I, TOO, HAVE HAD STUDENTS.

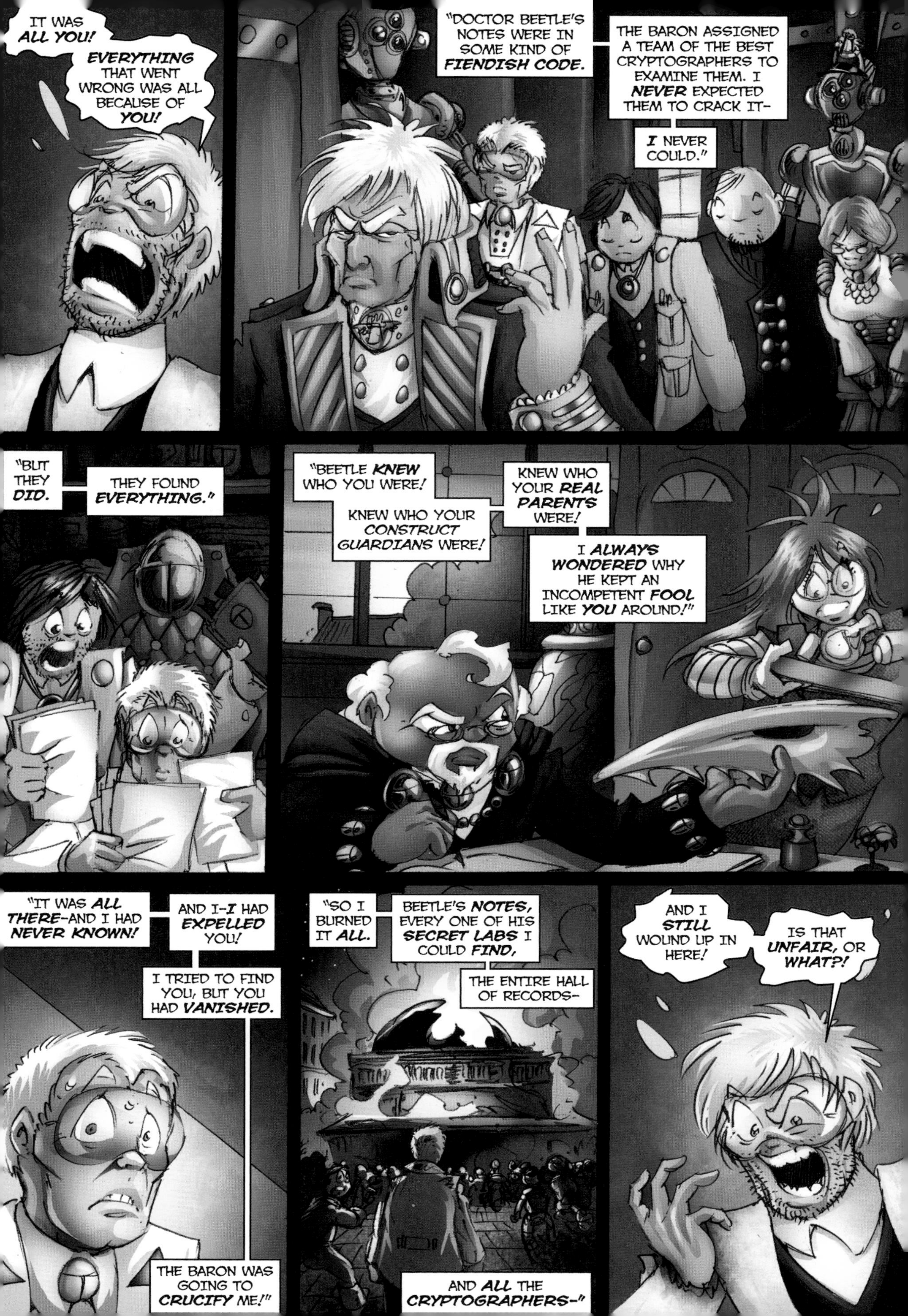
IT WAS ALL YOU!
EVERYTHING THAT WENT WRONG WAS ALL BECAUSE OF YOU!
"DOCTOR BEETLE'S NOTES WERE IN SOME KIND OF FIENDISH CODE.
THE BARON ASSIGNED A TEAM OF THE BEST CRYPTOGRAPHERS TO EXAMINE THEM. I NEVER EXPECTED THEM TO CRACK IT-
I NEVER COULD."
"BUT THEY DID.
THEY FOUND EVERYTHING."
"BEETLE KNEW WHO YOU WERE!
KNEW WHO YOUR CONSTRUCT GUARDIANS WERE!
KNEW WHO YOUR REAL PARENTS WERE!
I ALWAYS WONDERED WHY HE KEPT AN INCOMPETENT FOOL LIKE YOU AROUND!"
"IT WAS ALL THERE-AND I HAD NEVER KNOWN!
AND I-I HAD EXPELLED YOU!
I TRIED TO FIND YOU, BUT YOU HAD VANISHED.
THE BARON WAS GOING TO CRUCIFY ME!"
"SO I BURNED IT ALL.
BEETLE'S NOTES, EVERY ONE OF HIS SECRET LABS I COULD FIND,
THE ENTIRE HALL OF RECORDS-
AND ALL THE CRYPTOGRAPHERS-"
AND I STILL WOUND UP IN HERE!
IS THAT UNFAIR, OR WHAT?!

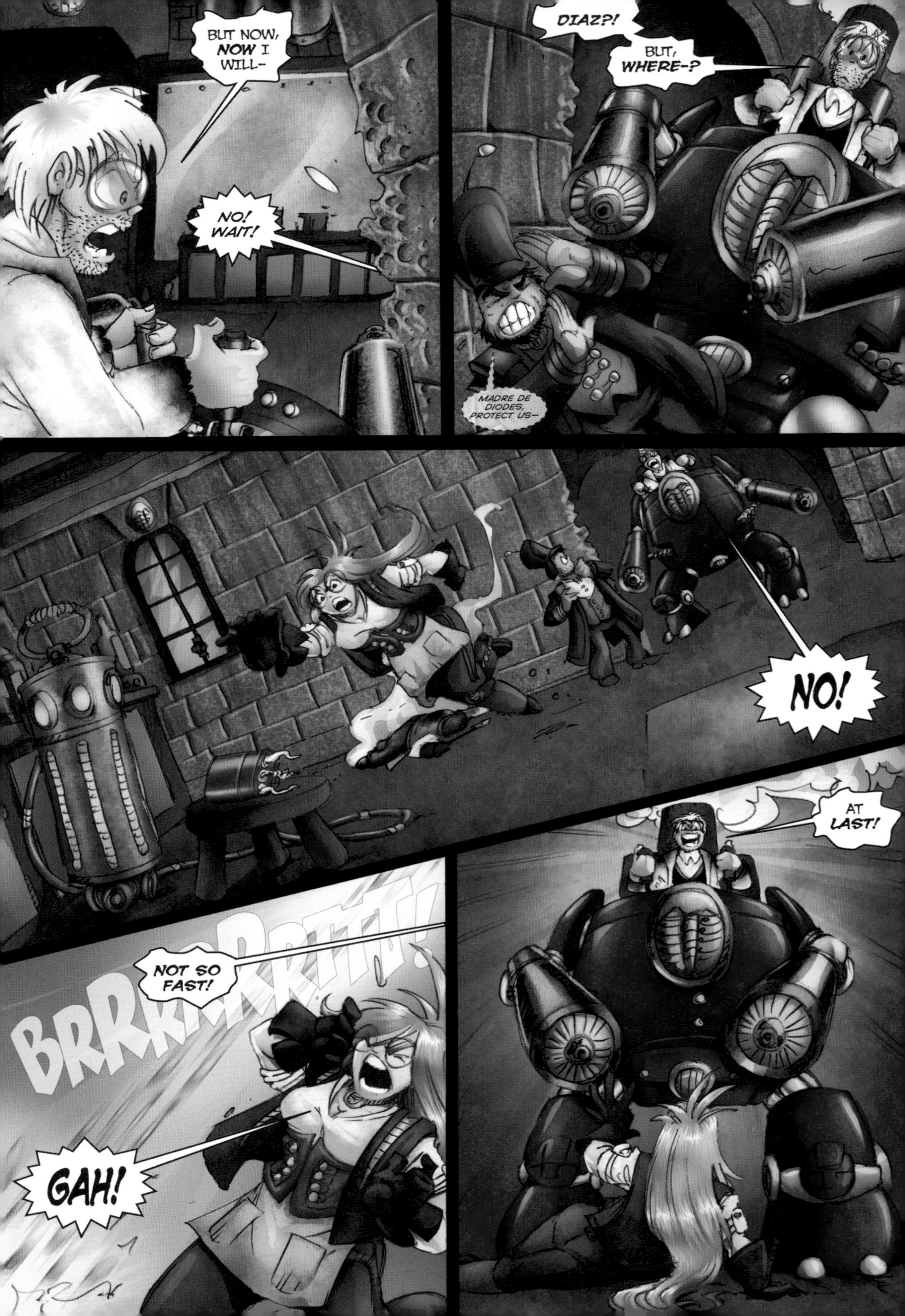

BUT NOW, NOW I WILL-
NO! WAIT!
DIAZ?!
BUT, WHERE-?
MADRE DE DIODES, PROTECT US-
NO!
AT LAST!
BRRRRRRRTTTT!
NOT SO FAST!
GAH!

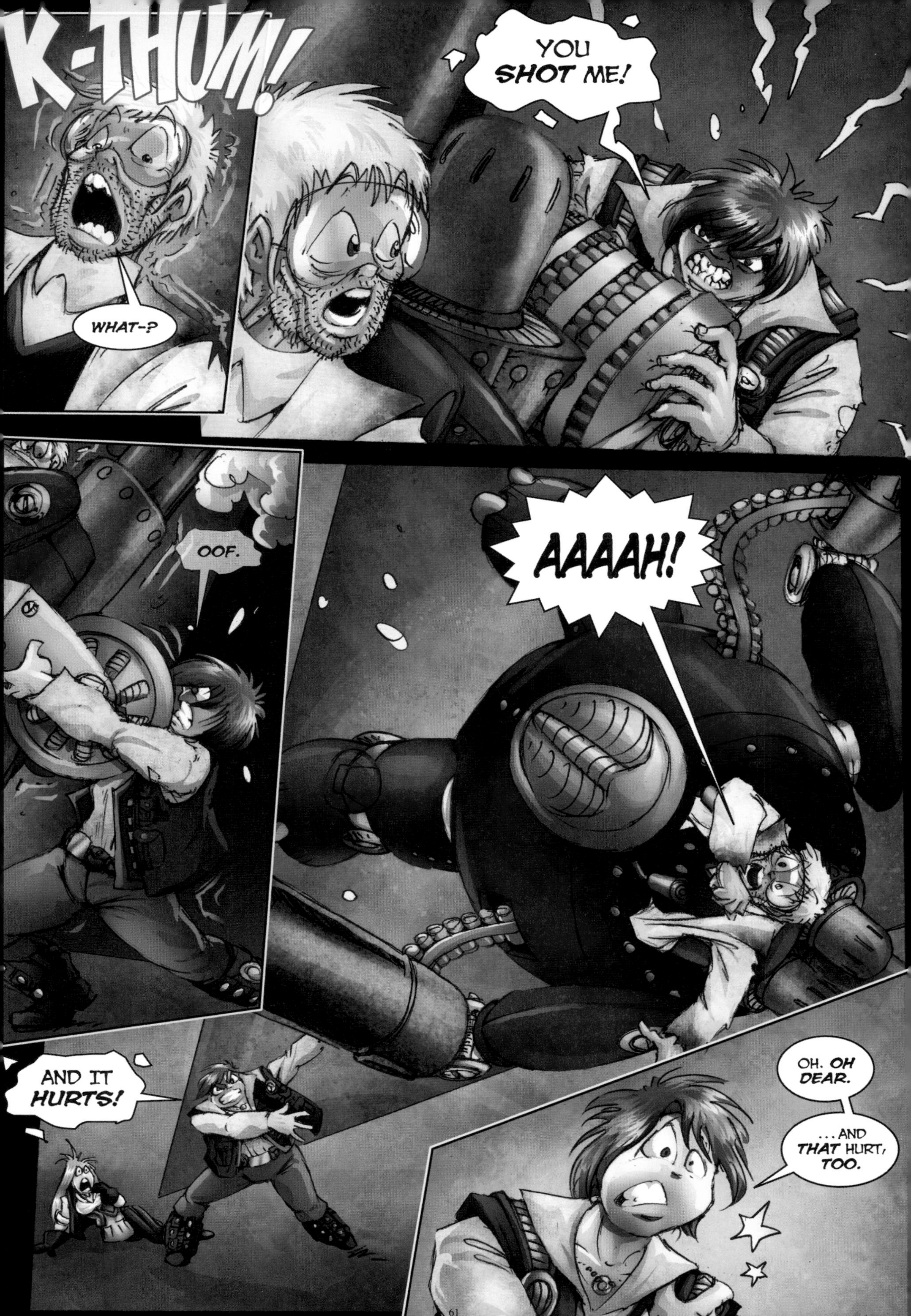
K-THUM!
WHAT-?
YOU SHOT ME!
OOF.
AAAAH!
AND IT HURTS!
OH. OH DEAR.
...AND THAT HURT, TOO.

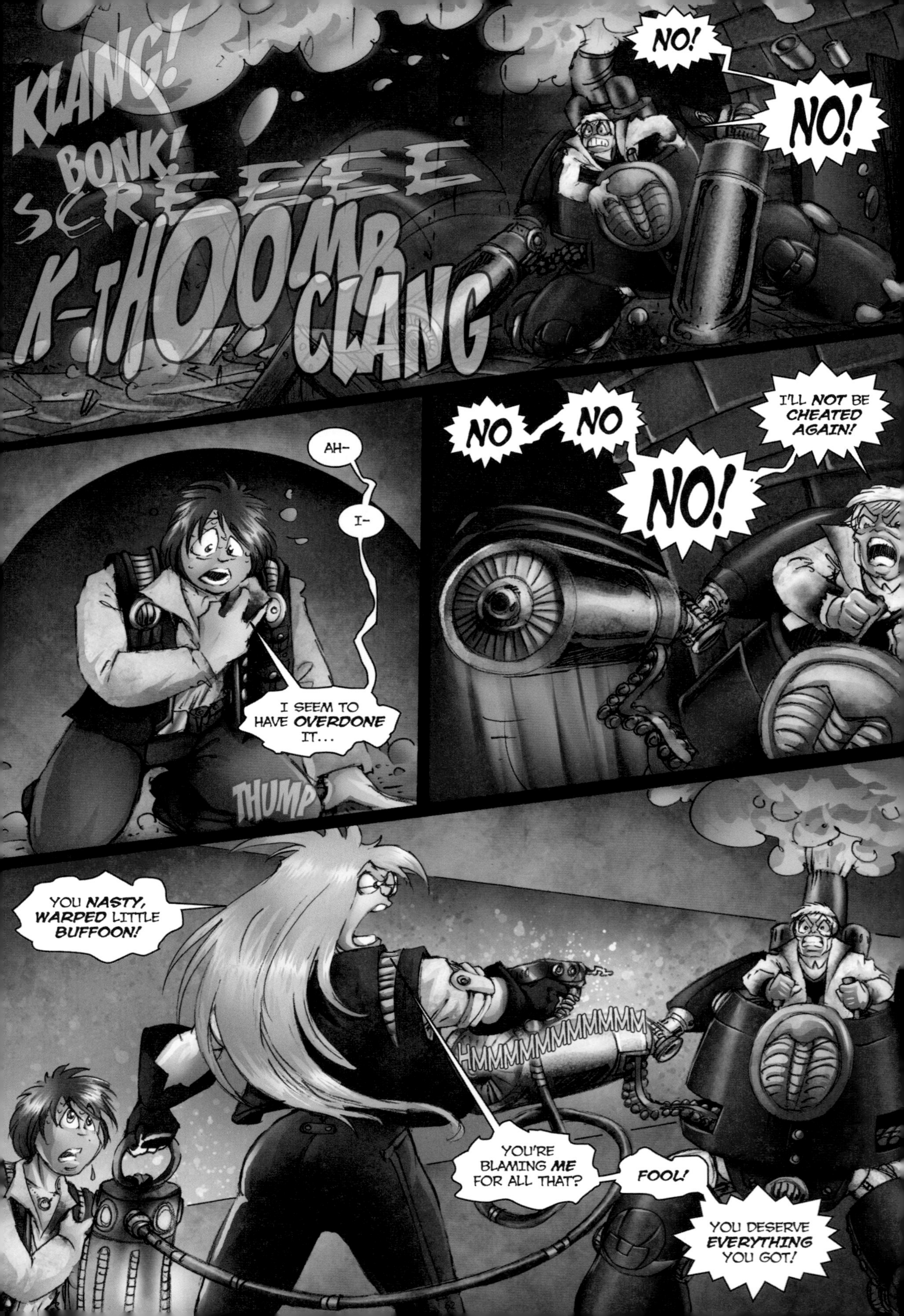
KLANG!
BONK!
SCREEEEE
K-THOOMB
CLANG
NO!
NO!
AH-
I-
I SEEM TO HAVE OVERDONE IT...
THUMP
NO
NO
NO!
I'LL NOT BE CHEATED AGAIN!
YOU NASTY, WARPED LITTLE BUFFOON!
HMMMMMMMMMMMMMM
YOU'RE BLAMING ME FOR ALL THAT?
FOOL!
YOU DESERVE EVERYTHING YOU GOT!

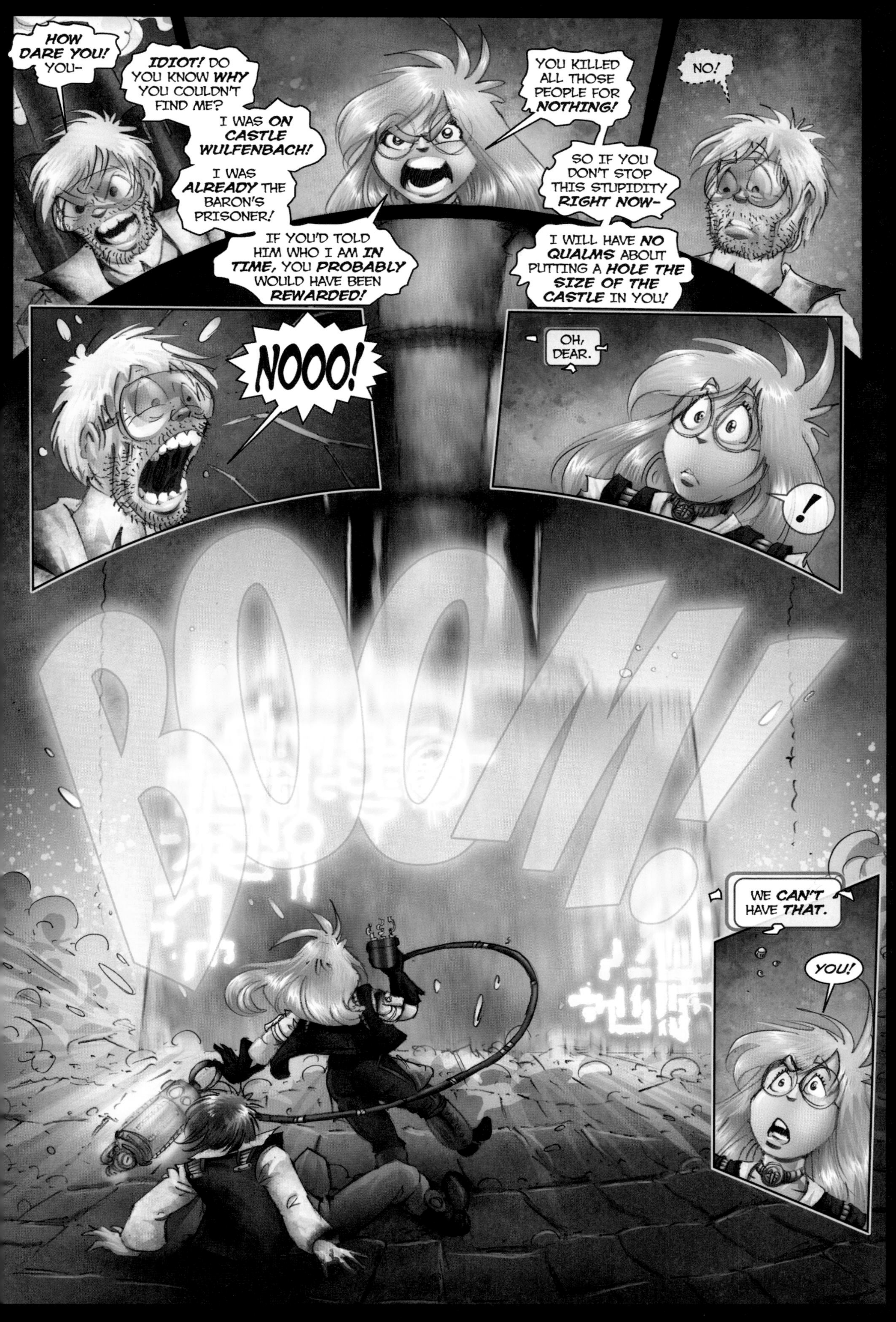
HOW DARE YOU! YOU-
IDIOT! DO YOU KNOW WHY YOU COULDN'T FIND ME?
I WAS ON CASTLE WULFENBACH!
I WAS ALREADY THE BARON'S PRISONER!
IF YOU'D TOLD HIM WHO I AM IN TIME, YOU PROBABLY WOULD HAVE BEEN REWARDED!
YOU KILLED ALL THOSE PEOPLE FOR NOTHING!
NO!
SO IF YOU DON'T STOP THIS STUPIDITY RIGHT NOW-
I WILL HAVE NO QUALMS ABOUT PUTTING A HOLE THE SIZE OF THE CASTLE IN YOU!
NOOO!
OH, DEAR.
!
BOOM!
WE CAN'T HAVE THAT.
YOU!

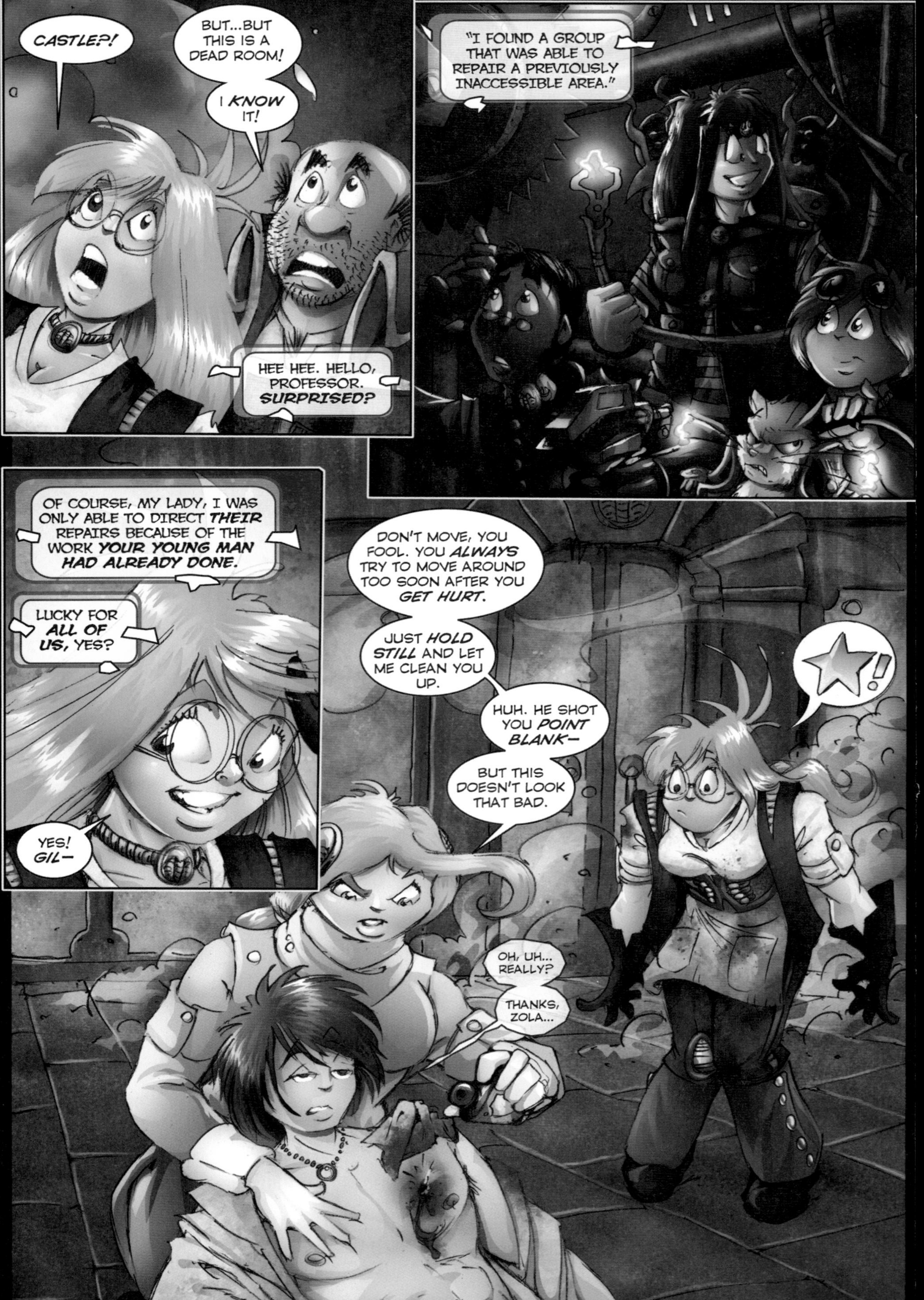

CASTLE?!
BUT...BUT THIS IS A DEAD ROOM!
I KNOW IT!
HEE HEE. HELLO, PROFESSOR. SURPRISED?
"I FOUND A GROUP THAT WAS ABLE TO REPAIR A PREVIOUSLY INACCESSIBLE AREA."
OF COURSE, MY LADY, I WAS ONLY ABLE TO DIRECT THEIR REPAIRS BECAUSE OF THE WORK YOUR YOUNG MAN HAD ALREADY DONE.
LUCKY FOR ALL OF US, YES?
YES! GIL—
DON'T MOVE, YOU FOOL. YOU ALWAYS TRY TO MOVE AROUND TOO SOON AFTER YOU GET HURT.
JUST HOLD STILL AND LET ME CLEAN YOU UP.
HUH. HE SHOT YOU POINT BLANK—
BUT THIS DOESN'T LOOK THAT BAD.
!
OH, UH... REALLY?
THANKS, ZOLA...

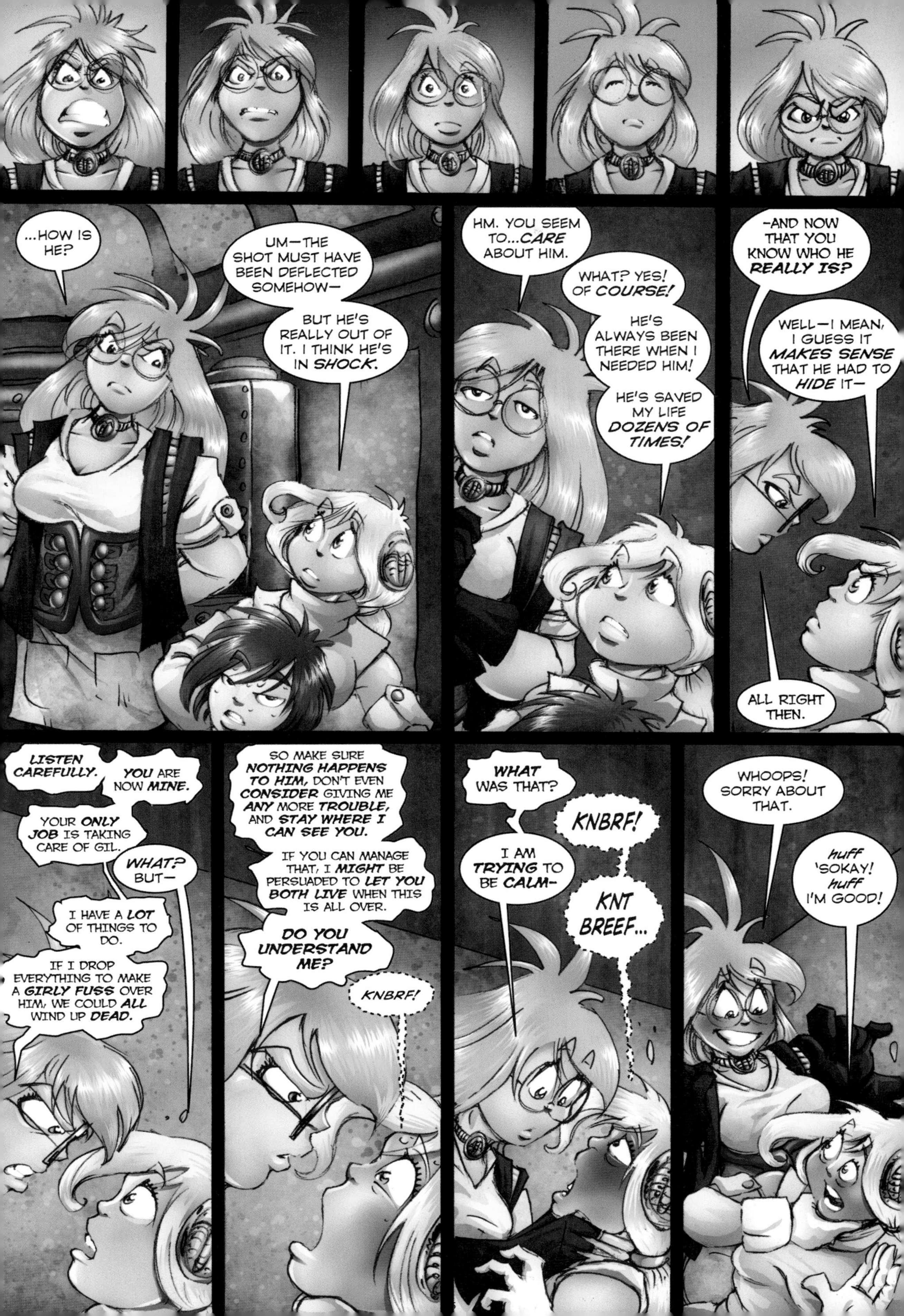

...HOW IS HE?
UM—THE SHOT MUST HAVE BEEN DEFLECTED SOMEHOW—
BUT HE'S REALLY OUT OF IT. I THINK HE'S IN SHOCK.
HM. YOU SEEM TO...CARE ABOUT HIM.
WHAT? YES! OF COURSE!
HE'S ALWAYS BEEN THERE WHEN I NEEDED HIM!
HE'S SAVED MY LIFE DOZENS OF TIMES!
-AND NOW THAT YOU KNOW WHO HE REALLY IS?
WELL—I MEAN, I GUESS IT MAKES SENSE THAT HE HAD TO HIDE IT—
ALL RIGHT THEN.
LISTEN CAREFULLY.
YOU ARE NOW MINE.
YOUR ONLY JOB IS TAKING CARE OF GIL.
WHAT? BUT—
I HAVE A LOT OF THINGS TO DO.
IF I DROP EVERYTHING TO MAKE A GIRLY FUSS OVER HIM, WE COULD ALL WIND UP DEAD.
SO MAKE SURE NOTHING HAPPENS TO HIM, DON'T EVEN CONSIDER GIVING ME ANY MORE TROUBLE, AND STAY WHERE I CAN SEE YOU.
IF YOU CAN MANAGE THAT, I MIGHT BE PERSUADED TO LET YOU BOTH LIVE WHEN THIS IS ALL OVER.
DO YOU UNDERSTAND ME?
KNBRF!
WHAT WAS THAT?
KNBRF!
I AM TRYING TO BE CALM-
KNT BREEF...
WHOOPS! SORRY ABOUT THAT.
huff 'SOKAY! huff I'M GOOD!

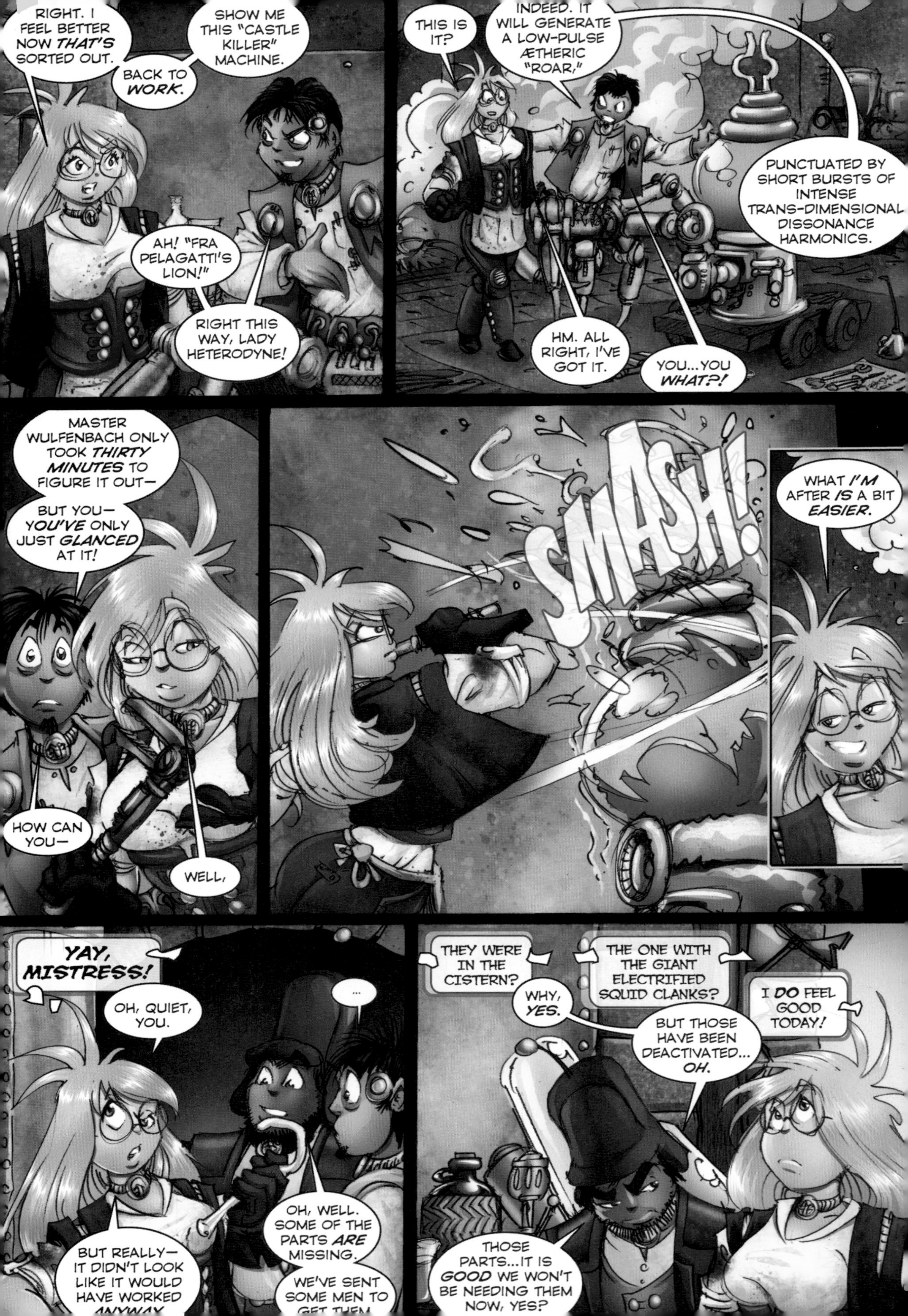

RIGHT. I FEEL BETTER NOW THAT'S SORTED OUT.
BACK TO WORK.
SHOW ME THIS "CASTLE KILLER" MACHINE.
AH! "FRA PELAGATTI'S LION!"
RIGHT THIS WAY, LADY HETERODYNE!
THIS IS IT?
INDEED. IT WILL GENERATE A LOW-PULSE ÆTHERIC "ROAR,"
PUNCTUATED BY SHORT BURSTS OF INTENSE TRANS-DIMENSIONAL DISSONANCE HARMONICS.
HM. ALL RIGHT, I'VE GOT IT.
YOU...YOU WHAT?!
MASTER WULFENBACH ONLY TOOK THIRTY MINUTES TO FIGURE IT OUT—
BUT YOU— YOU'VE ONLY JUST GLANCED AT IT!
HOW CAN YOU—
WELL,
SMASH!
WHAT I'M AFTER IS A BIT EASIER.
YAY, MISTRESS!
OH, QUIET, YOU.
...
BUT REALLY— IT DIDN'T LOOK LIKE IT WOULD HAVE WORKED ANYWAY.
OH, WELL. SOME OF THE PARTS ARE MISSING.
WE'VE SENT SOME MEN TO GET THEM.
THEY WERE IN THE CISTERN?
WHY, YES.
THE ONE WITH THE GIANT ELECTRIFIED SQUID CLANKS?
BUT THOSE HAVE BEEN DEACTIVATED... OH.
I DO FEEL GOOD TODAY!
THOSE PARTS...IT IS GOOD WE WON'T BE NEEDING THEM NOW, YES?

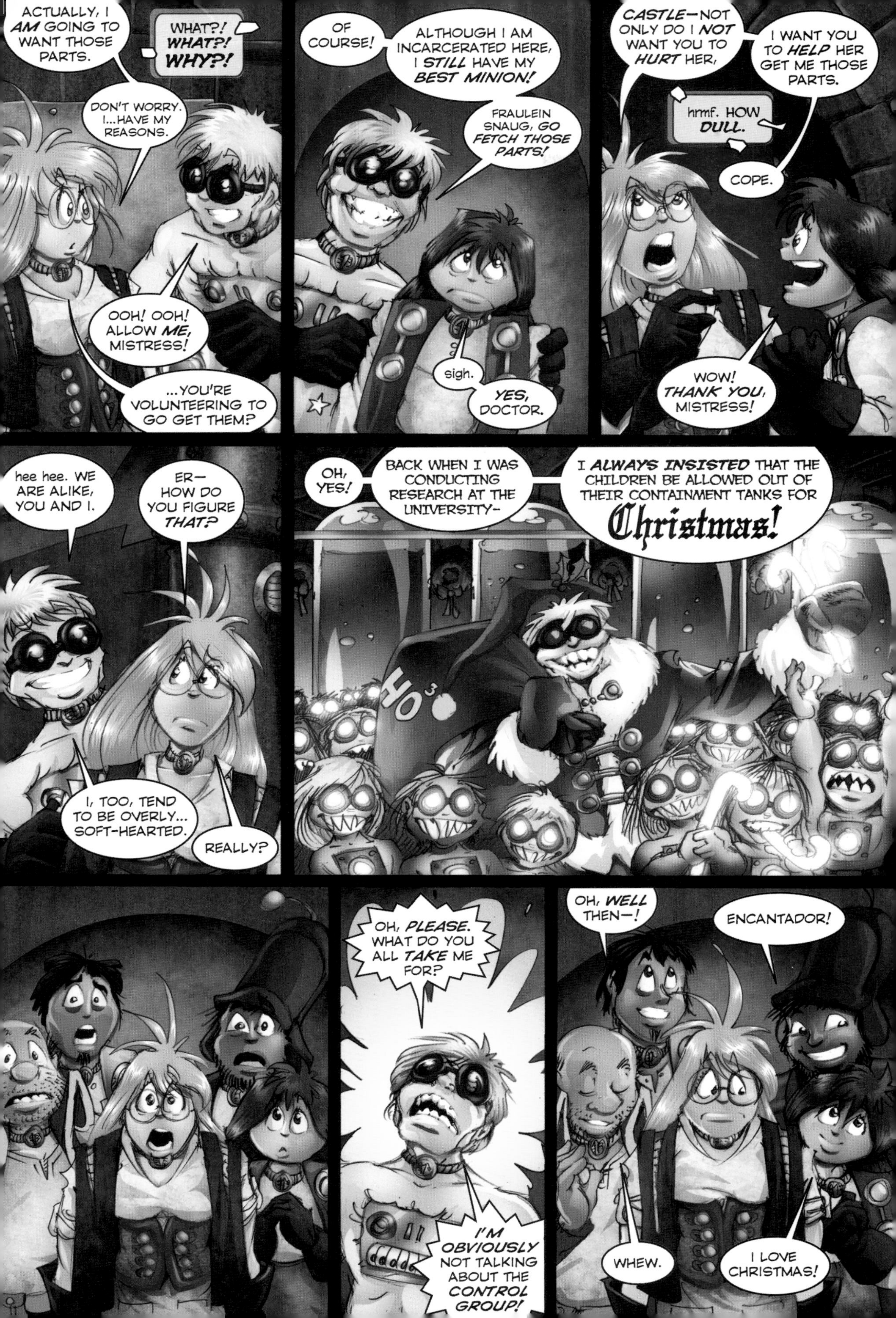
ACTUALLY, I AM GOING TO WANT THOSE PARTS.
WHAT?! WHAT?! WHY?!
DON'T WORRY. I...HAVE MY REASONS.
OOH! OOH! ALLOW ME, MISTRESS!
...YOU'RE VOLUNTEERING TO GO GET THEM?
OF COURSE!
ALTHOUGH I AM INCARCERATED HERE, I STILL HAVE MY BEST MINION!
FRAULEIN SNAUG, GO FETCH THOSE PARTS!
sigh.
YES, DOCTOR.
CASTLE—NOT ONLY DO I NOT WANT YOU TO HURT HER,
I WANT YOU TO HELP HER GET ME THOSE PARTS.
hrmf. HOW DULL.
COPE.
WOW! THANK YOU, MISTRESS!
hee hee. WE ARE ALIKE, YOU AND I.
ER— HOW DO YOU FIGURE THAT?
I, TOO, TEND TO BE OVERLY... SOFT-HEARTED.
REALLY?
OH, YES!
BACK WHEN I WAS CONDUCTING RESEARCH AT THE UNIVERSITY-
I ALWAYS INSISTED THAT THE CHILDREN BE ALLOWED OUT OF THEIR CONTAINMENT TANKS FOR Christmas!
HO³
OH, PLEASE. WHAT DO YOU ALL TAKE ME FOR?
I'M OBVIOUSLY NOT TALKING ABOUT THE CONTROL GROUP!
OH, WELL THEN—!
ENCANTADOR!
WHEW.
I LOVE CHRISTMAS!

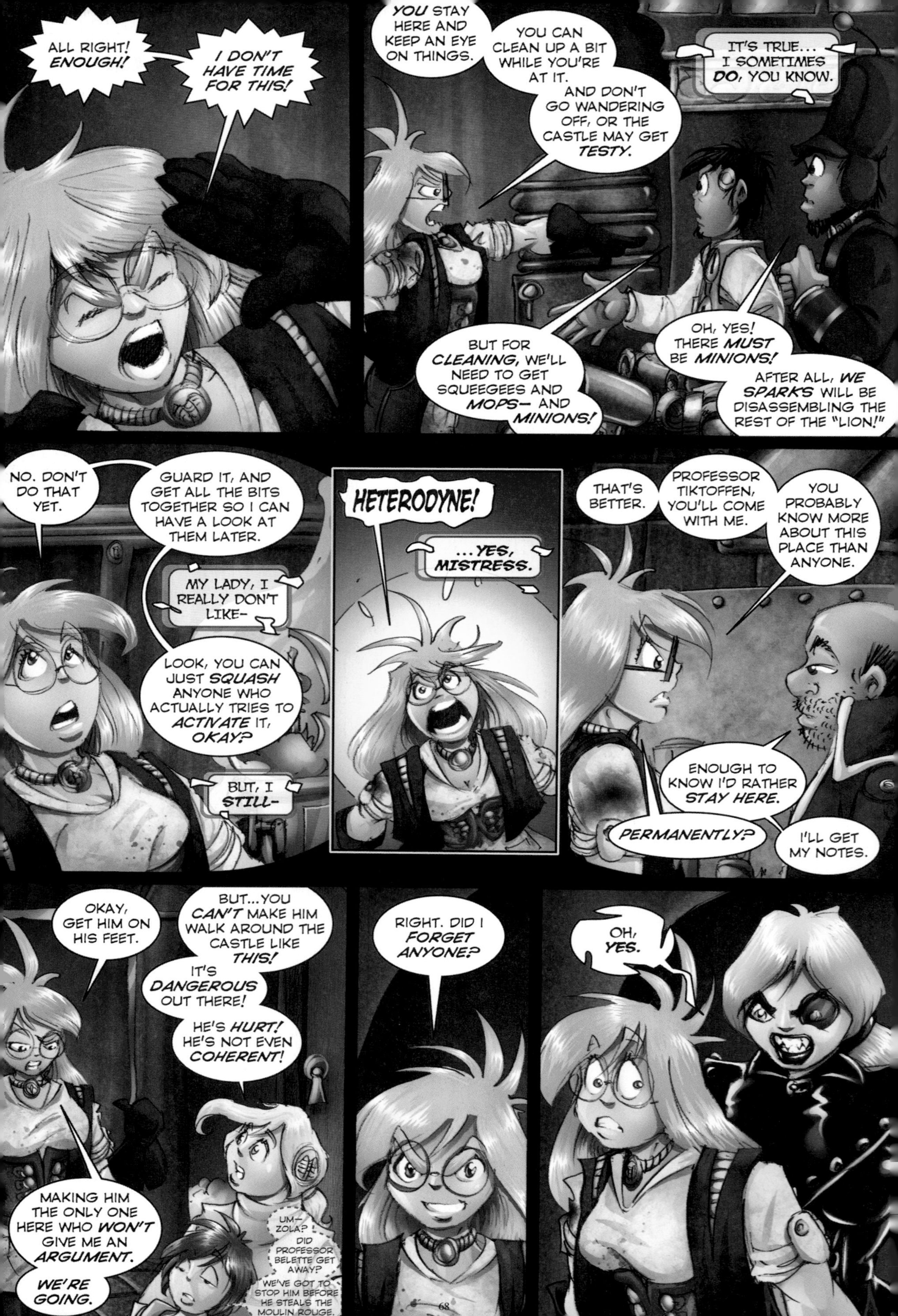

ALL RIGHT! *ENOUGH!*
I DON'T HAVE TIME FOR THIS!
YOU STAY HERE AND KEEP AN EYE ON THINGS.
YOU CAN CLEAN UP A BIT WHILE YOU'RE AT IT.
AND DON'T GO WANDERING OFF, OR THE CASTLE MAY GET *TESTY*.
IT'S TRUE... I SOMETIMES *DO*, YOU KNOW.
BUT FOR *CLEANING*, WE'LL NEED TO GET SQUEEGEES AND *MOPS*— AND *MINIONS!*
OH, YES! THERE *MUST* BE *MINIONS!*
AFTER ALL, *WE SPARKS* WILL BE DISASSEMBLING THE REST OF THE "LION!"
NO. DON'T DO THAT YET.
GUARD IT, AND GET ALL THE BITS TOGETHER SO I CAN HAVE A LOOK AT THEM LATER.
MY LADY, I REALLY DON'T LIKE-
LOOK, YOU CAN JUST *SQUASH* ANYONE WHO ACTUALLY TRIES TO *ACTIVATE* IT, *OKAY?*
BUT, I *STILL-*
HETERODYNE!
...*YES, MISTRESS.*
THAT'S BETTER.
PROFESSOR TIKTOFFEN, YOU'LL COME WITH ME.
YOU PROBABLY KNOW MORE ABOUT THIS PLACE THAN ANYONE.
ENOUGH TO KNOW I'D RATHER *STAY HERE*.
PERMANENTLY?
I'LL GET MY NOTES.
OKAY, GET HIM ON HIS FEET.
BUT...YOU *CAN'T* MAKE HIM WALK AROUND THE CASTLE LIKE *THIS!*
IT'S *DANGEROUS* OUT THERE!
HE'S *HURT!* HE'S NOT EVEN *COHERENT!*
MAKING HIM THE ONLY ONE HERE WHO *WON'T* GIVE ME AN *ARGUMENT*.
WE'RE GOING.
UM- ZOLA? DID PROFESSOR BELETTE GET AWAY? WE'VE GOT TO STOP HIM BEFORE HE STEALS THE MOULIN ROUGE.
RIGHT. DID I *FORGET ANYONE?*
OH, *YES.*

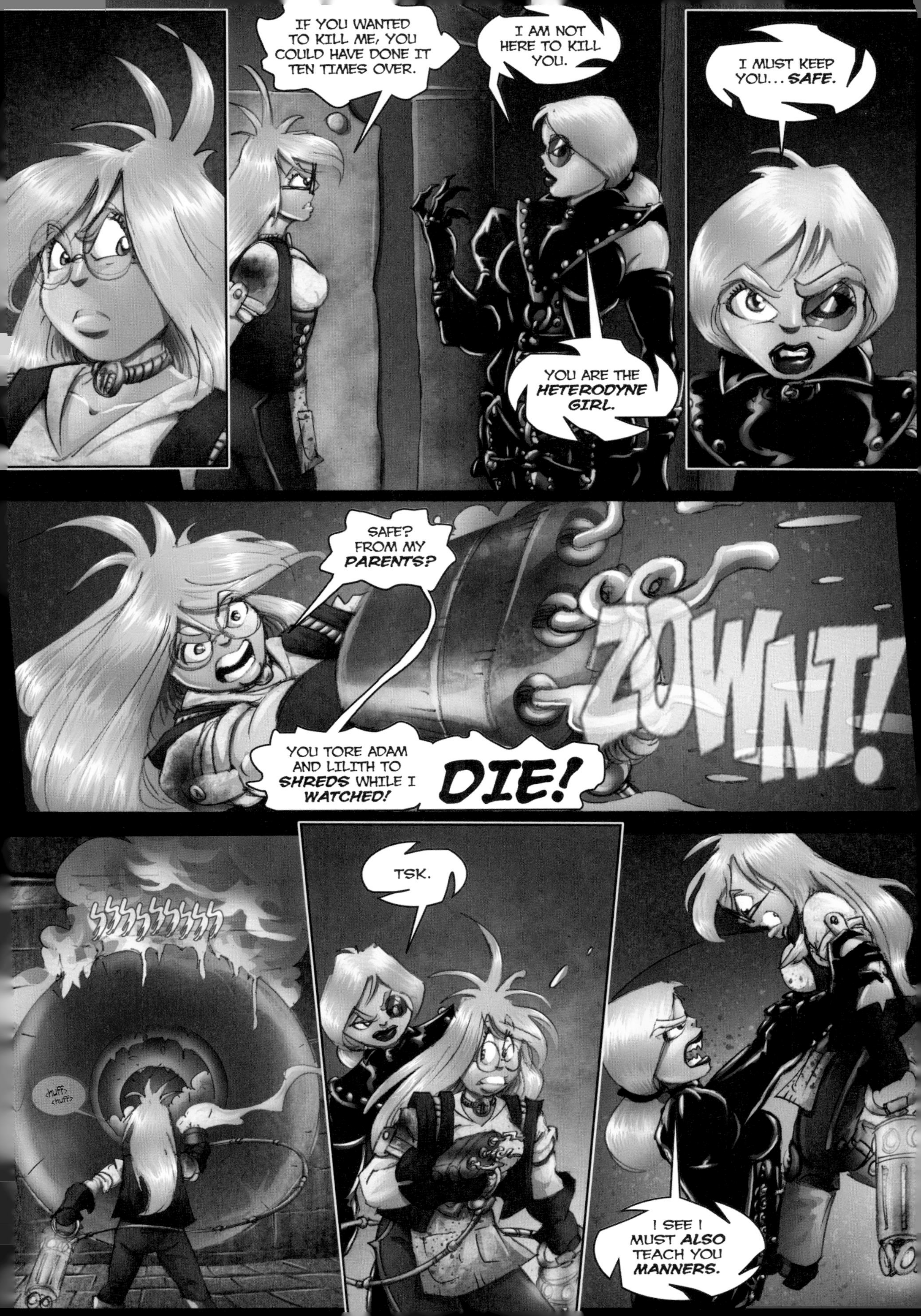

IF YOU WANTED TO KILL ME, YOU COULD HAVE DONE IT TEN TIMES OVER.
I AM NOT HERE TO KILL YOU.
YOU ARE THE HETERODYNE GIRL.
I MUST KEEP YOU... SAFE.
SAFE? FROM MY PARENTS?
YOU TORE ADAM AND LILITH TO SHREDS WHILE I WATCHED!
DIE!
ZOWNT!
TSK.
I SEE I MUST ALSO TEACH YOU MANNERS.

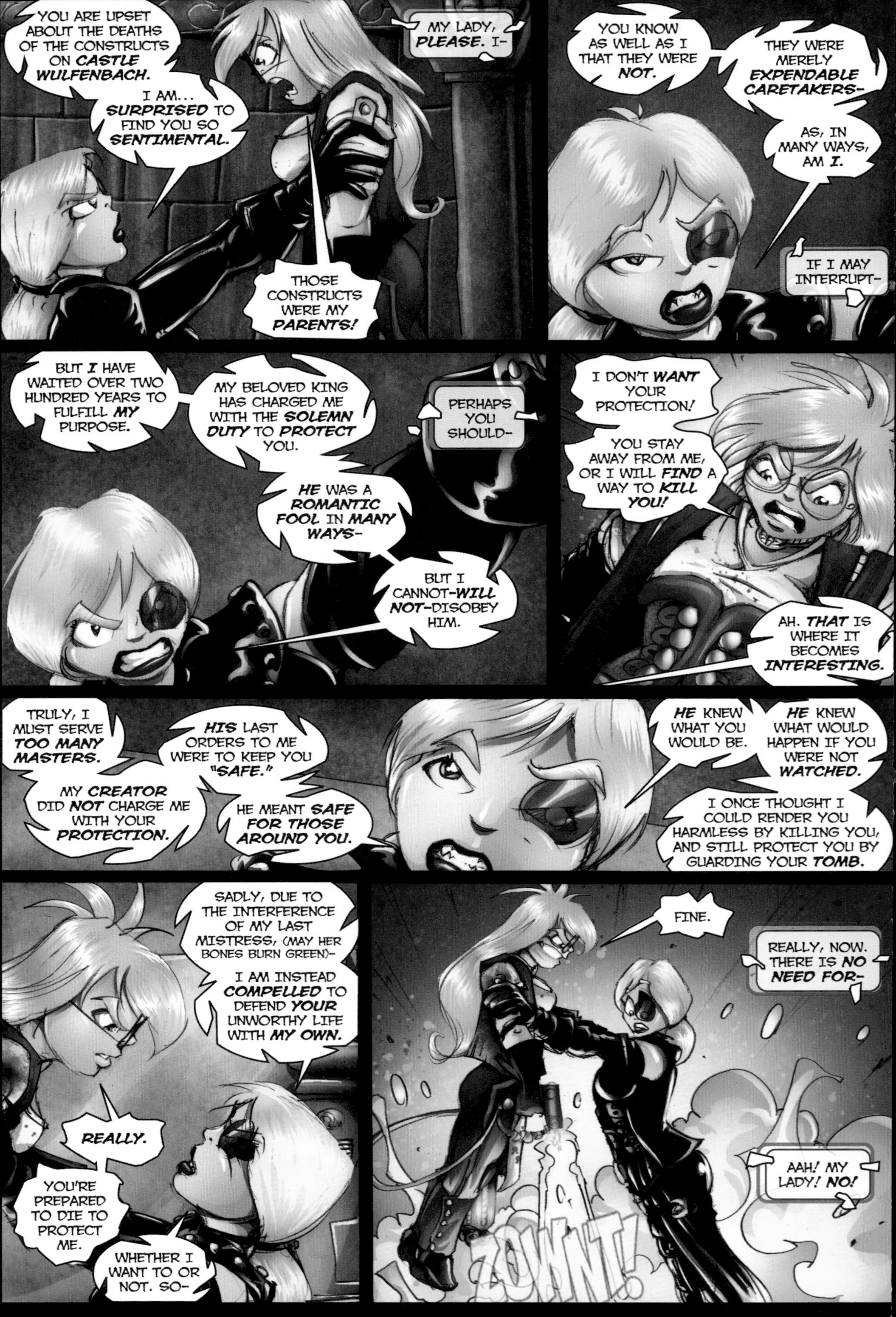

YOU ARE UPSET ABOUT THE DEATHS OF THE CONSTRUCTS ON CASTLE WULFENBACH.
I AM... SURPRISED TO FIND YOU SO SENTIMENTAL.
THOSE CONSTRUCTS WERE MY PARENTS!
MY LADY, PLEASE. I-
YOU KNOW AS WELL AS I THAT THEY WERE NOT.
THEY WERE MERELY EXPENDABLE CARETAKERS-
AS, IN MANY WAYS, AM I.
IF I MAY INTERRUPT-
BUT I HAVE WAITED OVER TWO HUNDRED YEARS TO FULFILL MY PURPOSE.
MY BELOVED KING HAS CHARGED ME WITH THE SOLEMN DUTY TO PROTECT YOU.
PERHAPS YOU SHOULD-
HE WAS A ROMANTIC FOOL IN MANY WAYS-
BUT I CANNOT-WILL NOT-DISOBEY HIM.
I DON'T WANT YOUR PROTECTION!
YOU STAY AWAY FROM ME, OR I WILL FIND A WAY TO KILL YOU!
AH. THAT IS WHERE IT BECOMES INTERESTING.
TRULY, I MUST SERVE TOO MANY MASTERS.
MY CREATOR DID NOT CHARGE ME WITH YOUR PROTECTION.
HIS LAST ORDERS TO ME WERE TO KEEP YOU "SAFE."
HE MEANT SAFE FOR THOSE AROUND YOU.
HE KNEW WHAT YOU WOULD BE.
HE KNEW WHAT WOULD HAPPEN IF YOU WERE NOT WATCHED.
I ONCE THOUGHT I COULD RENDER YOU HARMLESS BY KILLING YOU, AND STILL PROTECT YOU BY GUARDING YOUR TOMB.
SADLY, DUE TO THE INTERFERENCE OF MY LAST MISTRESS, (MAY HER BONES BURN GREEN)-
I AM INSTEAD COMPELLED TO DEFEND YOUR UNWORTHY LIFE WITH MY OWN.
REALLY.
YOU'RE PREPARED TO DIE TO PROTECT ME.
WHETHER I WANT TO OR NOT. SO-
FINE.
REALLY, NOW. THERE IS NO NEED FOR-
AAH! MY LADY! NO!
ZONNT!

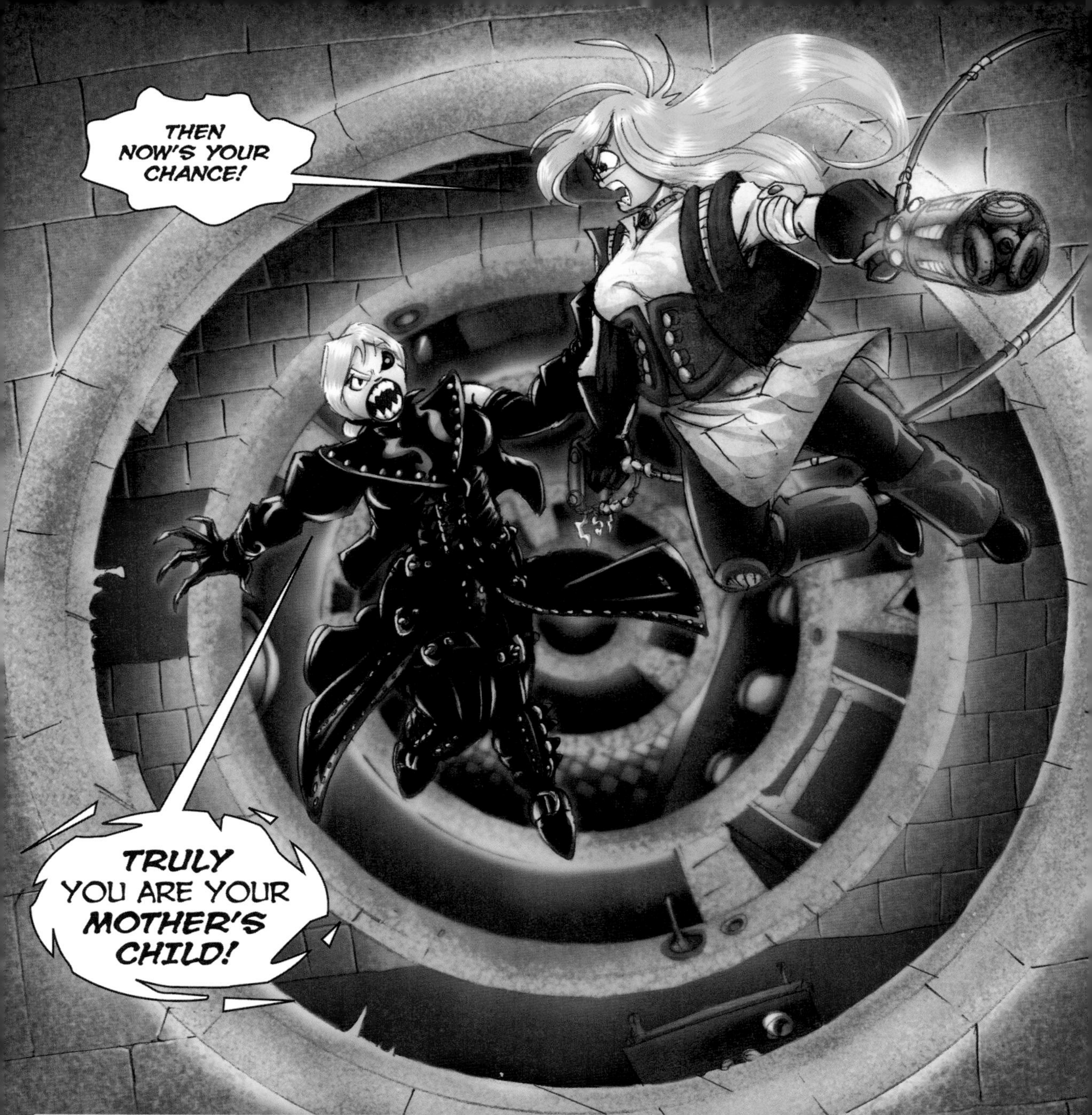
THEN NOW'S YOUR CHANCE!
TRULY YOU ARE YOUR MOTHER'S CHILD!

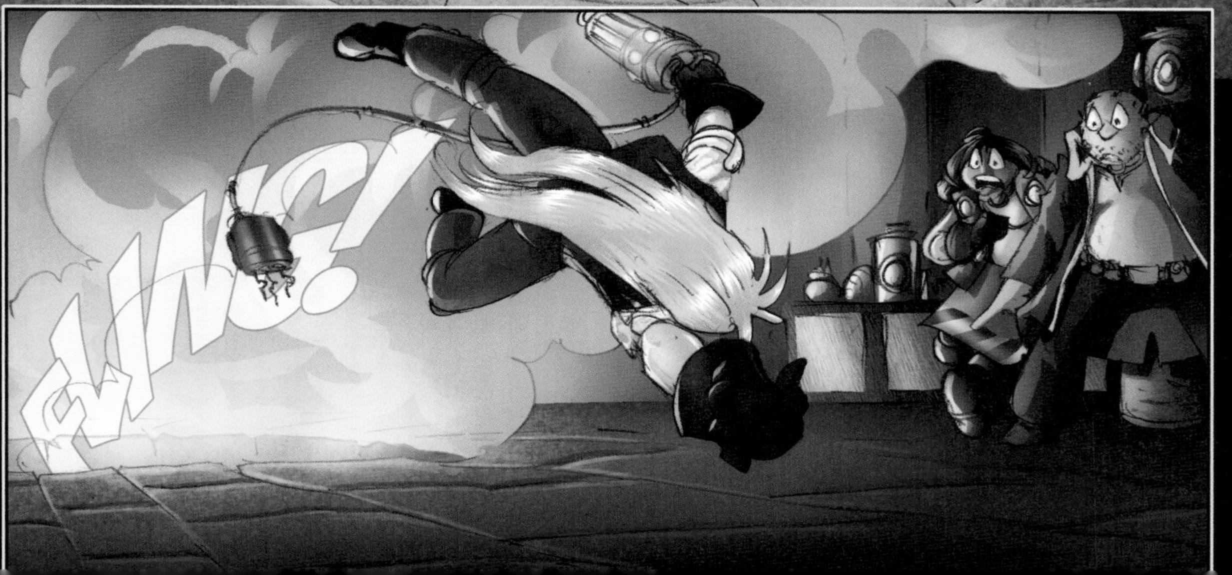
FLING!

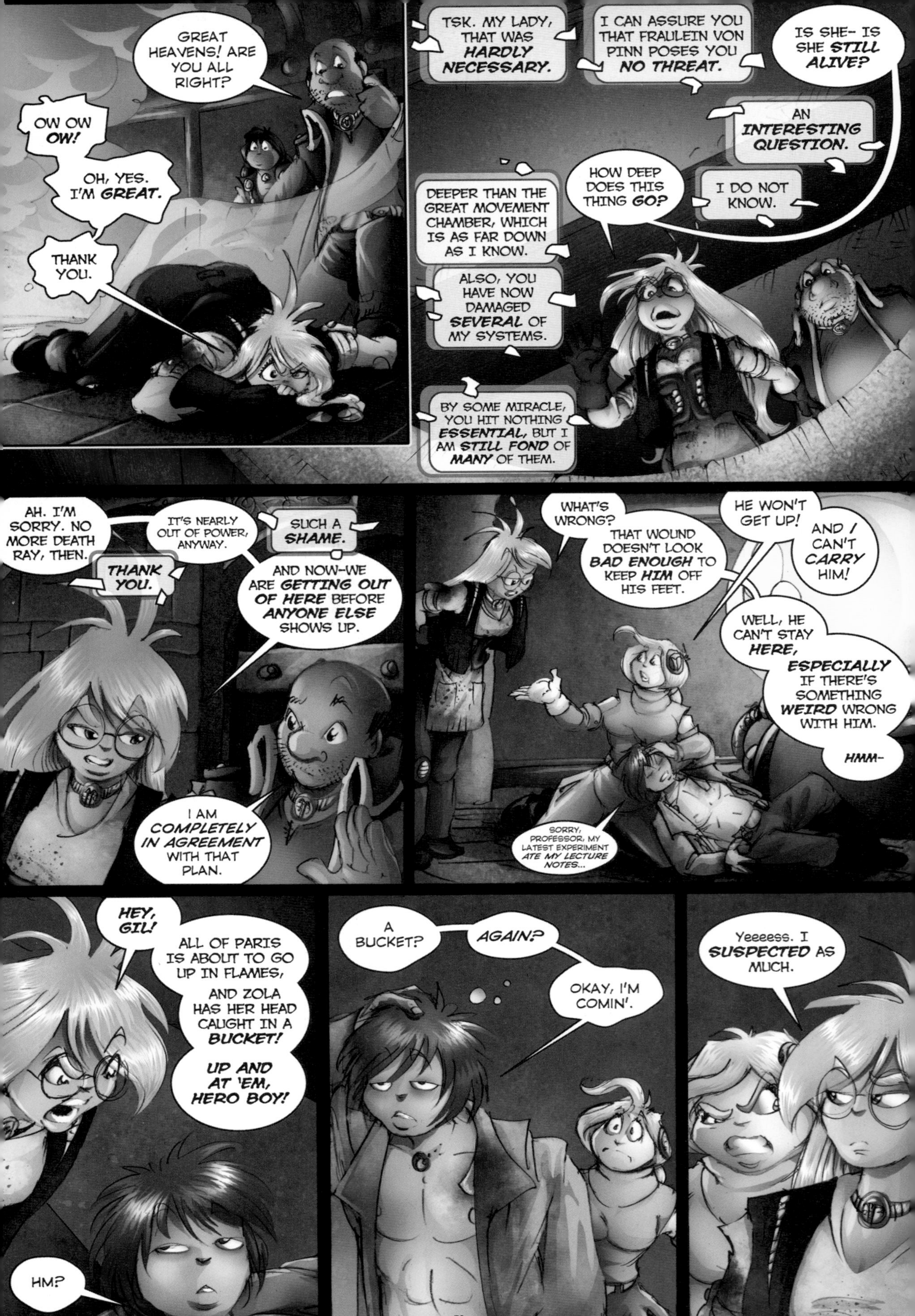
GREAT HEAVENS! ARE YOU ALL RIGHT?
OW OW OW!
OH, YES. I'M GREAT.
THANK YOU.
TSK. MY LADY, THAT WAS HARDLY NECESSARY.
I CAN ASSURE YOU THAT FRAULEIN VON PINN POSES YOU NO THREAT.
IS SHE- IS SHE STILL ALIVE?
AN INTERESTING QUESTION.
I DO NOT KNOW.
HOW DEEP DOES THIS THING GO?
DEEPER THAN THE GREAT MOVEMENT CHAMBER, WHICH IS AS FAR DOWN AS I KNOW.
ALSO, YOU HAVE NOW DAMAGED SEVERAL OF MY SYSTEMS.
BY SOME MIRACLE, YOU HIT NOTHING ESSENTIAL, BUT I AM STILL FOND OF MANY OF THEM.
AH. I'M SORRY. NO MORE DEATH RAY, THEN.
IT'S NEARLY OUT OF POWER, ANYWAY.
SUCH A SHAME.
THANK YOU.
AND NOW–WE ARE GETTING OUT OF HERE BEFORE ANYONE ELSE SHOWS UP.
I AM COMPLETELY IN AGREEMENT WITH THAT PLAN.
WHAT'S WRONG?
THAT WOUND DOESN'T LOOK BAD ENOUGH TO KEEP HIM OFF HIS FEET.
HE WON'T GET UP!
AND I CAN'T CARRY HIM!
WELL, HE CAN'T STAY HERE,
ESPECIALLY IF THERE'S SOMETHING WEIRD WRONG WITH HIM.
HMM-
SORRY, PROFESSOR, MY LATEST EXPERIMENT ATE MY LECTURE NOTES...
HEY, GIL!
ALL OF PARIS IS ABOUT TO GO UP IN FLAMES,
AND ZOLA HAS HER HEAD CAUGHT IN A BUCKET!
UP AND AT 'EM, HERO BOY!
HM?
A BUCKET?
AGAIN?
OKAY, I'M COMIN'.
Yeeeess. I SUSPECTED AS MUCH.

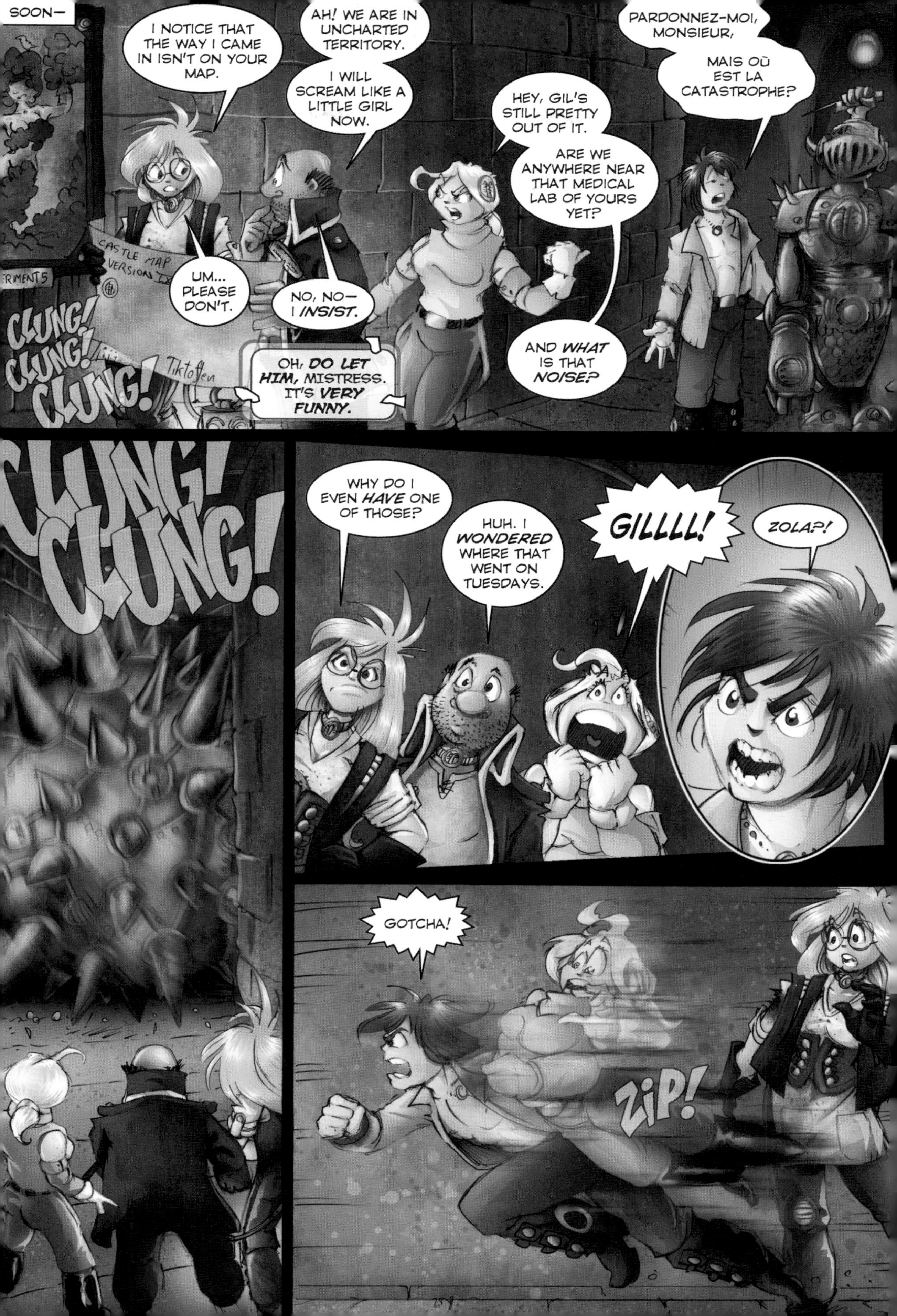

SOON—
I NOTICE THAT THE WAY I CAME IN ISN'T ON YOUR MAP.
AH! WE ARE IN UNCHARTED TERRITORY.
I WILL SCREAM LIKE A LITTLE GIRL NOW.
UM... PLEASE DON'T.
NO, NO— I *INSIST*.
OH, *DO LET HIM*, MISTRESS. IT'S *VERY FUNNY*.
CASTLE MAP VERSION IX
HEY, GIL'S STILL PRETTY OUT OF IT.
ARE WE ANYWHERE NEAR THAT MEDICAL LAB OF YOURS YET?
AND *WHAT* IS THAT *NOISE*?
PARDONNEZ-MOI, MONSIEUR,
MAIS OÙ EST LA CATASTROPHE?
CLUNG! CLUNG! CLUNG!
CLUNG! CLUNG!
WHY DO I EVEN *HAVE* ONE OF THOSE?
HUH. I *WONDERED* WHERE THAT WENT ON TUESDAYS.
GILLLL!
ZOLA?!
GOTCHA!
ZIP!

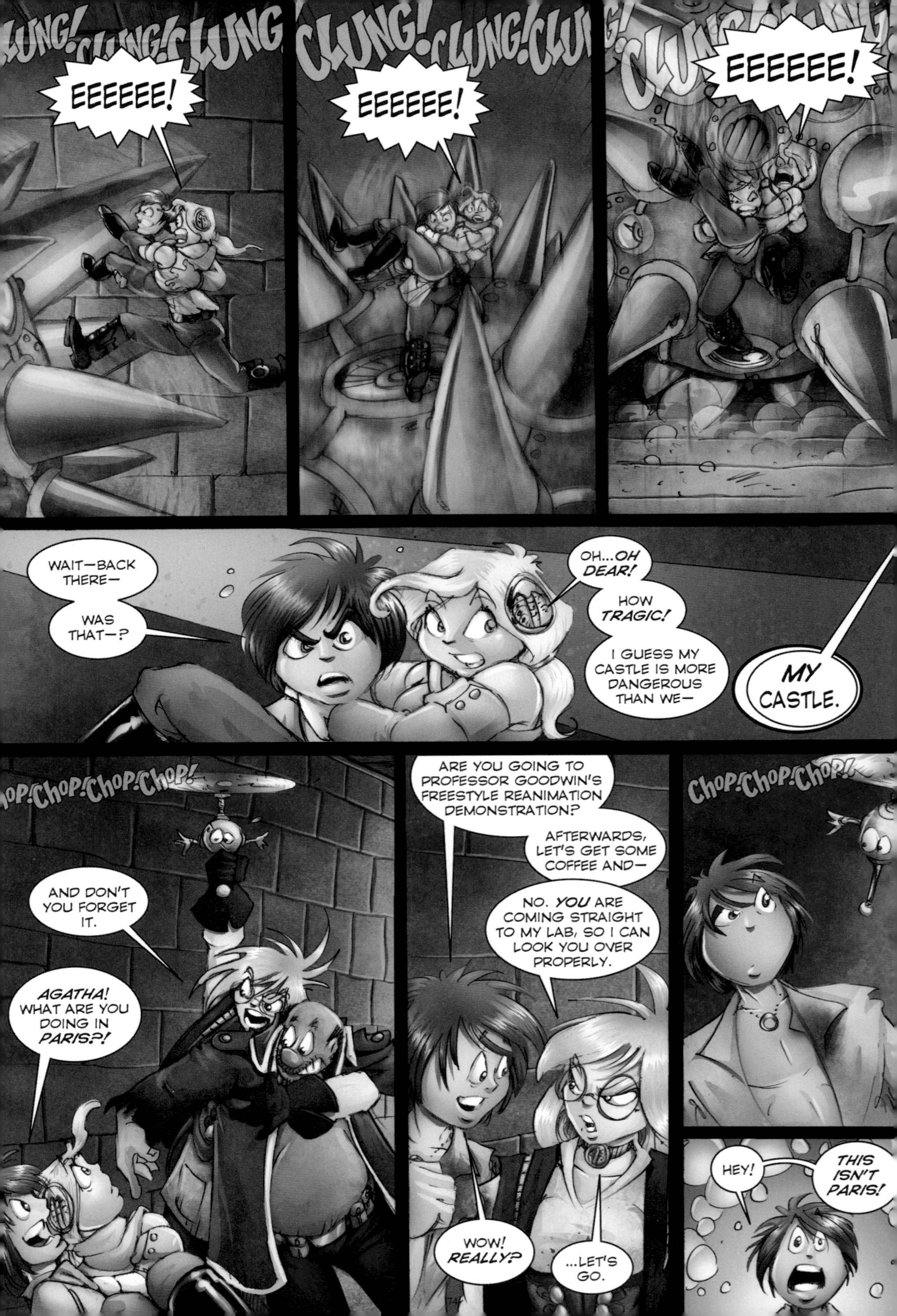

CLUNG! CLUNG! CLUNG!
EEEEEE!
CLUNG! CLUNG! CLUNG!
EEEEEE!
EEEEEE!
WAIT—BACK THERE—
WAS THAT—?
OH...OH DEAR!
HOW TRAGIC!
I GUESS MY CASTLE IS MORE DANGEROUS THAN WE—
MY CASTLE.
CHOP! CHOP! CHOP! CHOP!
AND DON'T YOU FORGET IT.
AGATHA! WHAT ARE YOU DOING IN PARIS?!
ARE YOU GOING TO PROFESSOR GOODWIN'S FREESTYLE REANIMATION DEMONSTRATION?
AFTERWARDS, LET'S GET SOME COFFEE AND—
NO. YOU ARE COMING STRAIGHT TO MY LAB, SO I CAN LOOK YOU OVER PROPERLY.
WOW! REALLY?
...LET'S GO.
CHOP! CHOP! CHOP!
HEY!
THIS ISN'T PARIS!

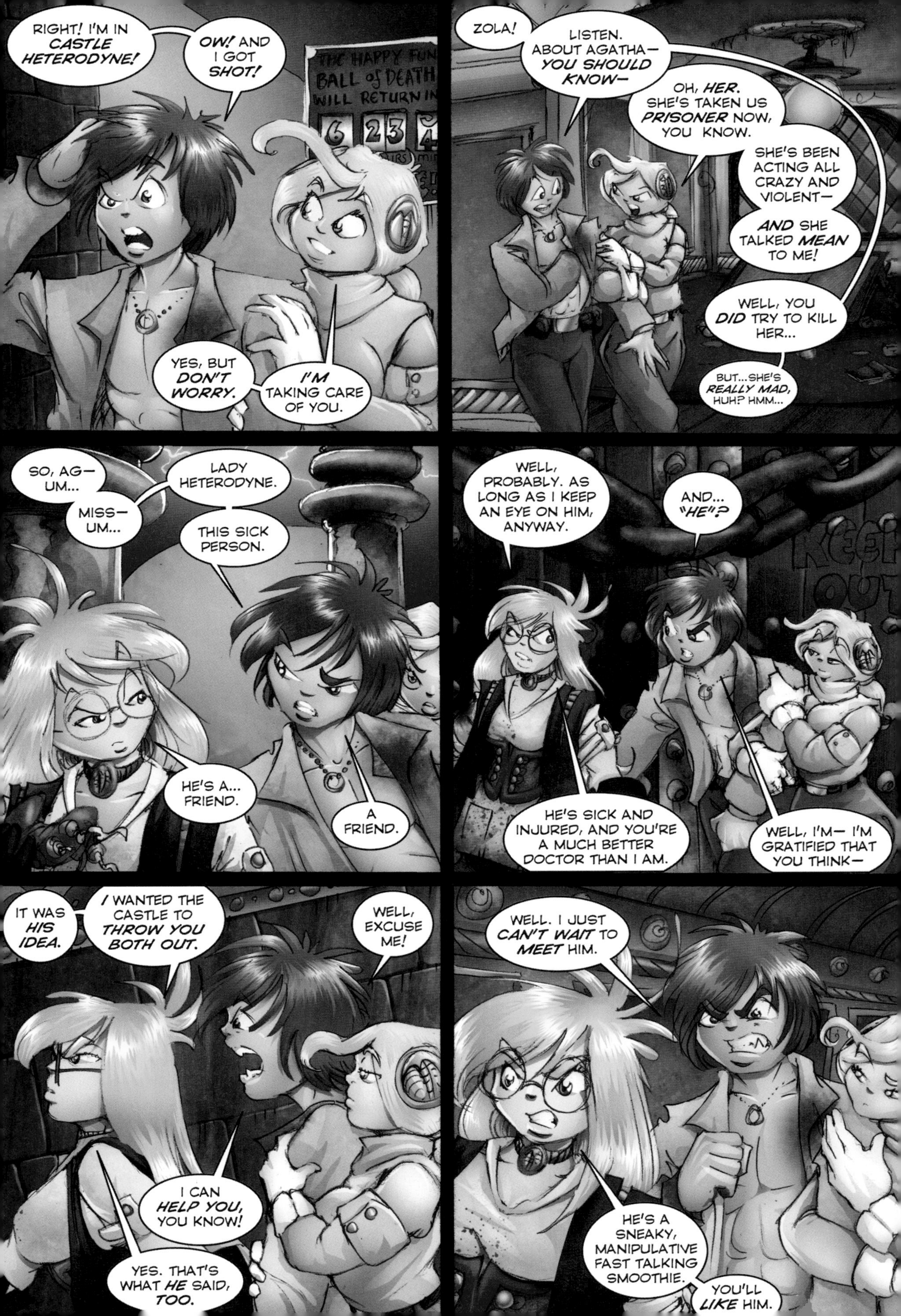
RIGHT! I'M IN CASTLE HETERODYNE!
OW! AND I GOT SHOT!
THE HAPPY FUN BALL of DEATH WILL RETURN IN
YES, BUT DON'T WORRY.
I'M TAKING CARE OF YOU.
ZOLA!
LISTEN. ABOUT AGATHA— YOU SHOULD KNOW—
OH, HER. SHE'S TAKEN US PRISONER NOW, YOU KNOW.
SHE'S BEEN ACTING ALL CRAZY AND VIOLENT—
AND SHE TALKED MEAN TO ME!
WELL, YOU DID TRY TO KILL HER...
BUT...SHE'S REALLY MAD, HUH? HMM...
SO, AG— UM...
MISS— UM...
LADY HETERODYNE.
THIS SICK PERSON.
HE'S A... FRIEND.
A FRIEND.
WELL, PROBABLY. AS LONG AS I KEEP AN EYE ON HIM, ANYWAY.
AND... "HE"?
HE'S SICK AND INJURED, AND YOU'RE A MUCH BETTER DOCTOR THAN I AM.
WELL, I'M— I'M GRATIFIED THAT YOU THINK—
IT WAS HIS IDEA.
I WANTED THE CASTLE TO THROW YOU BOTH OUT.
WELL, EXCUSE ME!
I CAN HELP YOU, YOU KNOW!
YES. THAT'S WHAT HE SAID, TOO.
WELL. I JUST CAN'T WAIT TO MEET HIM.
HE'S A SNEAKY, MANIPULATIVE FAST TALKING SMOOTHIE.
YOU'LL LIKE HIM.

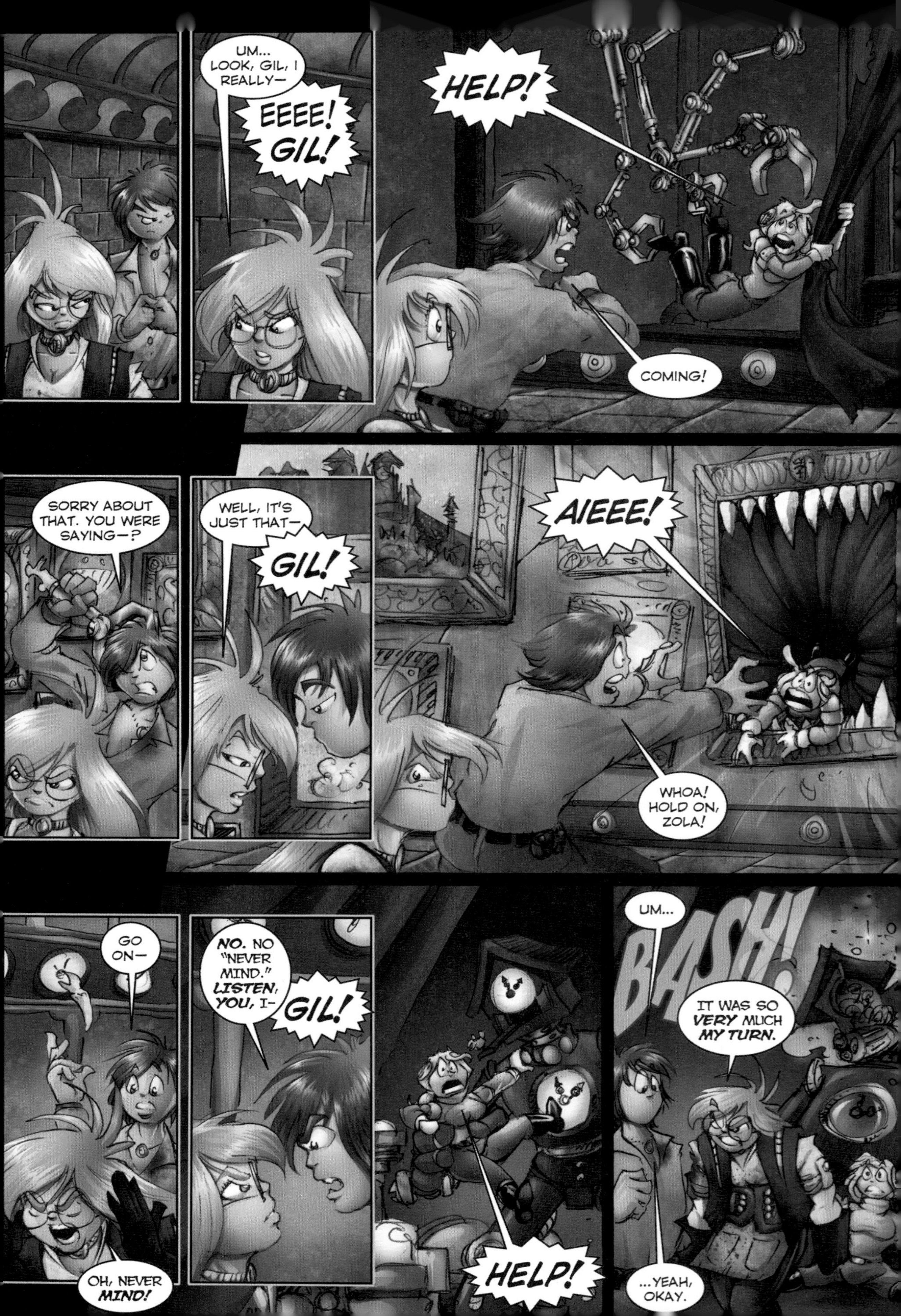
UM... LOOK, GIL, I REALLY—
EEEE! GIL!
HELP!
COMING!
SORRY ABOUT THAT. YOU WERE SAYING—?
WELL, IT'S JUST THAT—
GIL!
AIEEE!
WHOA! HOLD ON, ZOLA!
GO ON—
OH, NEVER MIND!
NO. NO "NEVER MIND." LISTEN, YOU, I-
GIL!
HELP!
UM...
BASH!
IT WAS SO VERY MUCH MY TURN.
...YEAH, OKAY.

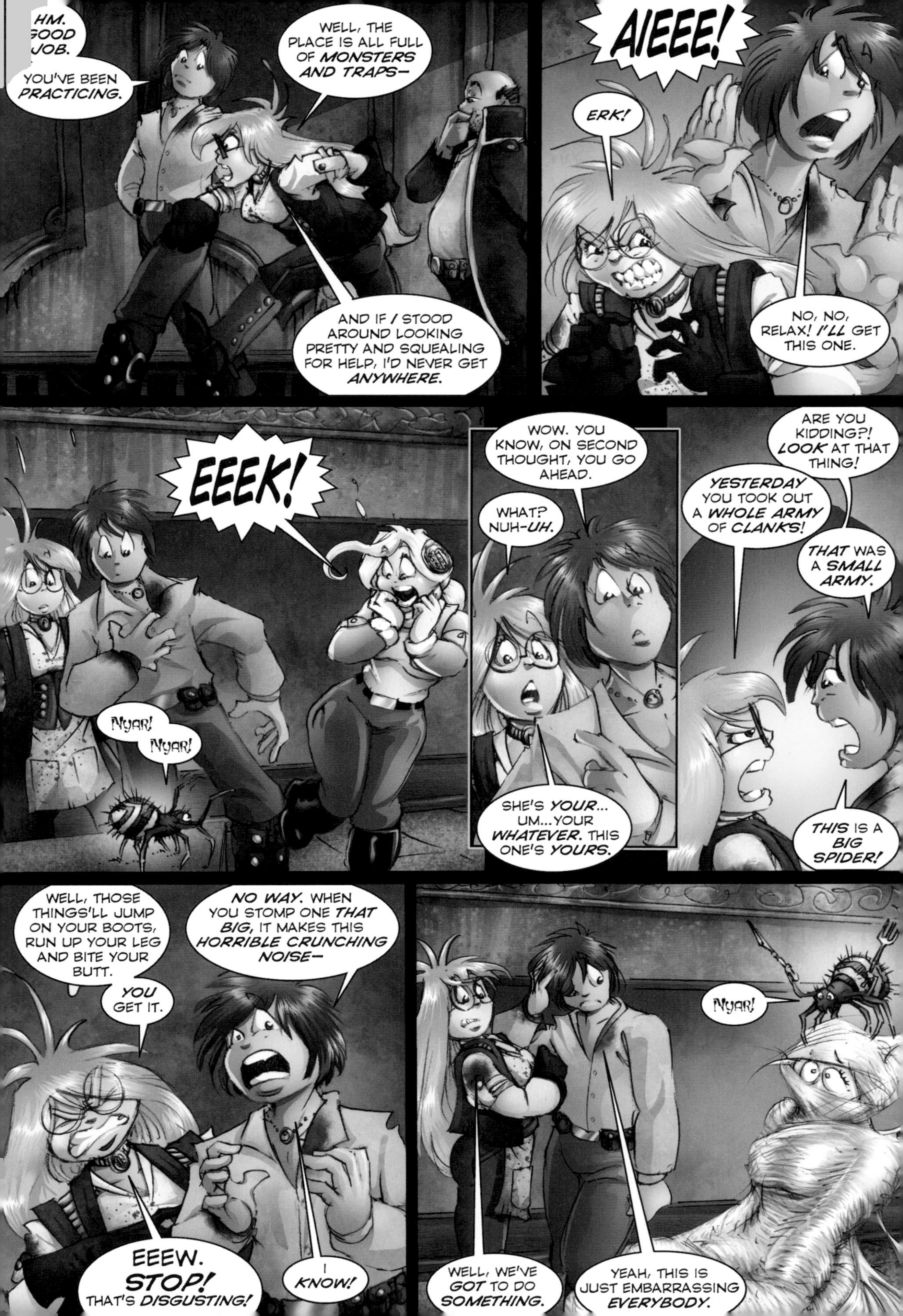

HM. GOOD JOB.
YOU'VE BEEN PRACTICING.
WELL, THE PLACE IS ALL FULL OF MONSTERS AND TRAPS—
AND IF I STOOD AROUND LOOKING PRETTY AND SQUEALING FOR HELP, I'D NEVER GET ANYWHERE.
AIEEE!
ERK!
NO, NO, RELAX! I'LL GET THIS ONE.
EEEK!
NYAR! NYAR!
WOW. YOU KNOW, ON SECOND THOUGHT, YOU GO AHEAD.
WHAT? NUH-UH.
SHE'S YOUR... UM...YOUR WHATEVER. THIS ONE'S YOURS.
ARE YOU KIDDING?! LOOK AT THAT THING!
YESTERDAY YOU TOOK OUT A WHOLE ARMY OF CLANKS!
THAT WAS A SMALL ARMY.
THIS IS A BIG SPIDER!
WELL, THOSE THINGS'LL JUMP ON YOUR BOOTS, RUN UP YOUR LEG AND BITE YOUR BUTT.
YOU GET IT.
NO WAY. WHEN YOU STOMP ONE THAT BIG, IT MAKES THIS HORRIBLE CRUNCHING NOISE—
EEEW. STOP! THAT'S DISGUSTING!
I KNOW!
NYAR!
WELL, WE'VE GOT TO DO SOMETHING.
YEAH, THIS IS JUST EMBARRASSING EVERYBODY.

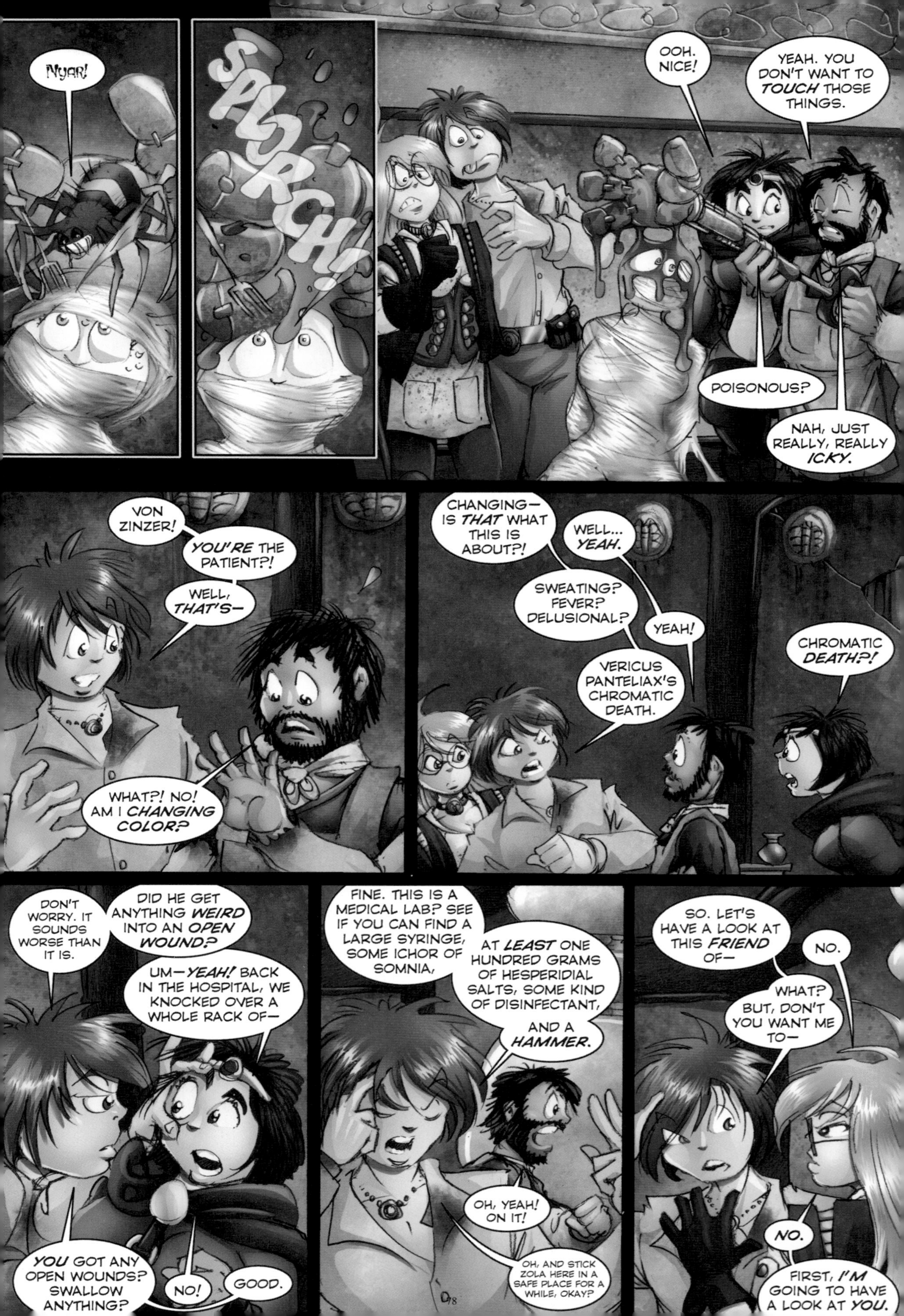

NYAR!
SPLORCH!
OOH. NICE!
YEAH. YOU DON'T WANT TO *TOUCH* THOSE THINGS.
POISONOUS?
NAH, JUST REALLY, REALLY *ICKY.*
VON ZINZER!
YOU'RE THE PATIENT?!
WELL, *THAT'S*—
WHAT?! NO! AM I *CHANGING COLOR?*
CHANGING— IS *THAT* WHAT THIS IS ABOUT?!
WELL... *YEAH.*
SWEATING? FEVER? DELUSIONAL?
YEAH!
VERICUS PANTELIAX'S CHROMATIC DEATH.
CHROMATIC *DEATH?!*
DON'T WORRY. IT SOUNDS WORSE THAN IT IS.
DID HE GET ANYTHING *WEIRD* INTO AN *OPEN WOUND?*
UM—*YEAH!* BACK IN THE HOSPITAL, WE KNOCKED OVER A WHOLE RACK OF—
YOU GOT ANY OPEN WOUNDS? SWALLOW ANYTHING?
NO!
GOOD.
FINE. THIS IS A MEDICAL LAB? SEE IF YOU CAN FIND A LARGE SYRINGE, SOME ICHOR OF SOMNIA,
AT *LEAST* ONE HUNDRED GRAMS OF HESPERIDIAL SALTS, SOME KIND OF DISINFECTANT,
AND A *HAMMER.*
OH, YEAH! ON IT!
OH, AND STICK ZOLA HERE IN A SAFE PLACE FOR A WHILE, OKAY?
SO. LET'S HAVE A LOOK AT THIS *FRIEND* OF—
NO.
WHAT? BUT, DON'T YOU WANT ME TO—
NO.
FIRST, *I'M* GOING TO HAVE A LOOK AT *YOU.*

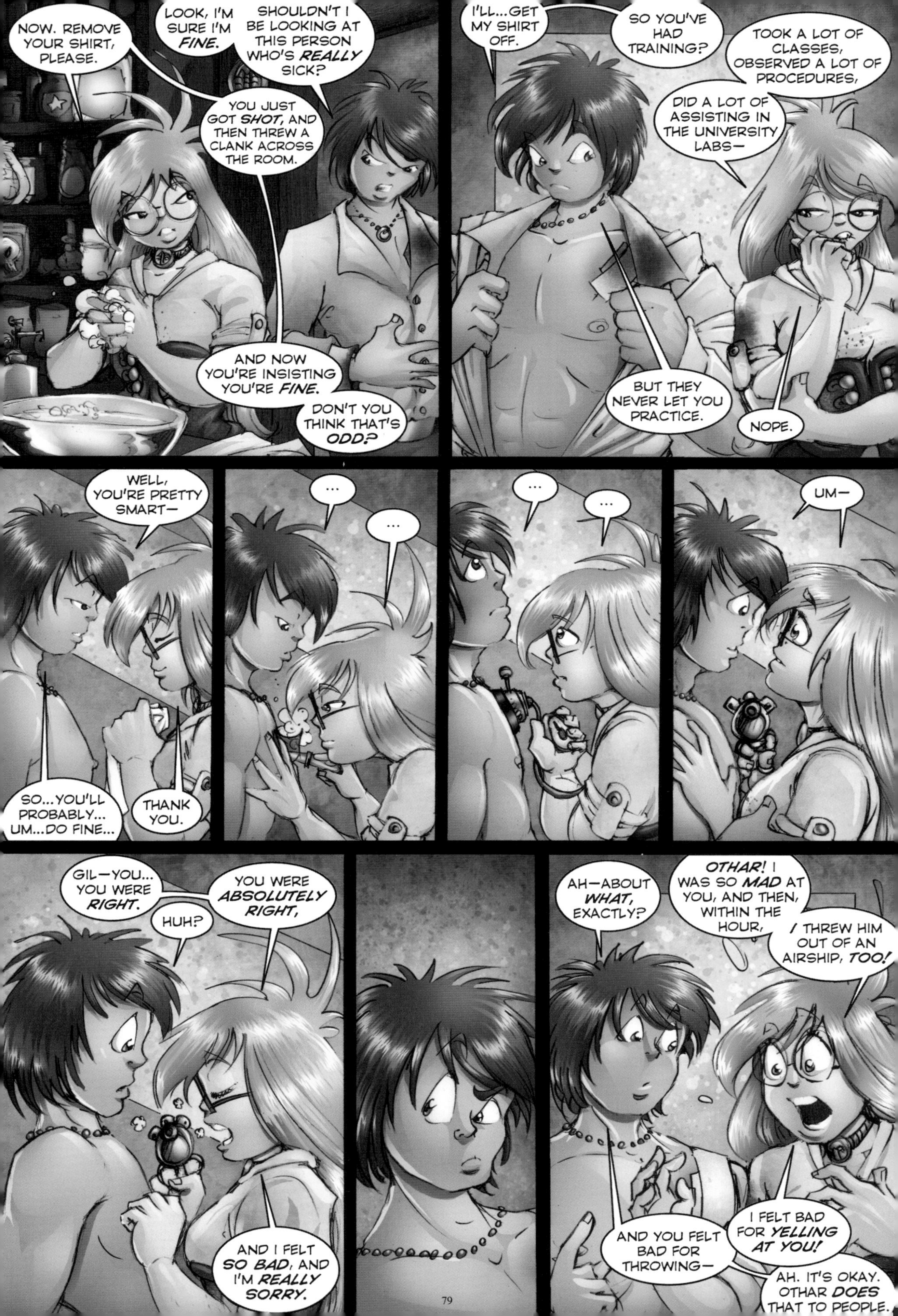

NOW. REMOVE YOUR SHIRT, PLEASE.
LOOK, I'M SURE I'M *FINE*.
SHOULDN'T I BE LOOKING AT THIS PERSON WHO'S *REALLY* SICK?
YOU JUST GOT *SHOT*, AND THEN THREW A CLANK ACROSS THE ROOM.
AND NOW YOU'RE INSISTING YOU'RE *FINE*.
DON'T YOU THINK THAT'S *ODD?*
I'LL...GET MY SHIRT OFF.
SO YOU'VE HAD TRAINING?
TOOK A LOT OF CLASSES, OBSERVED A LOT OF PROCEDURES,
DID A LOT OF ASSISTING IN THE UNIVERSITY LABS—
BUT THEY NEVER LET YOU PRACTICE.
NOPE.
WELL, YOU'RE PRETTY SMART—
SO...YOU'LL PROBABLY... UM...DO FINE...
THANK YOU.
...
...
...
...
UM—
GIL—YOU... YOU WERE *RIGHT*.
HUH?
YOU WERE *ABSOLUTELY RIGHT*,
AND I FELT *SO BAD*, AND I'M *REALLY SORRY*.
AH—ABOUT *WHAT*, EXACTLY?
OTHAR! I WAS SO *MAD* AT YOU, AND THEN, WITHIN THE HOUR,
I THREW HIM OUT OF AN AIRSHIP, *TOO!*
AND YOU FELT BAD FOR THROWING—
I FELT BAD FOR *YELLING AT YOU!*
AH. IT'S OKAY. OTHAR *DOES* THAT TO PEOPLE.

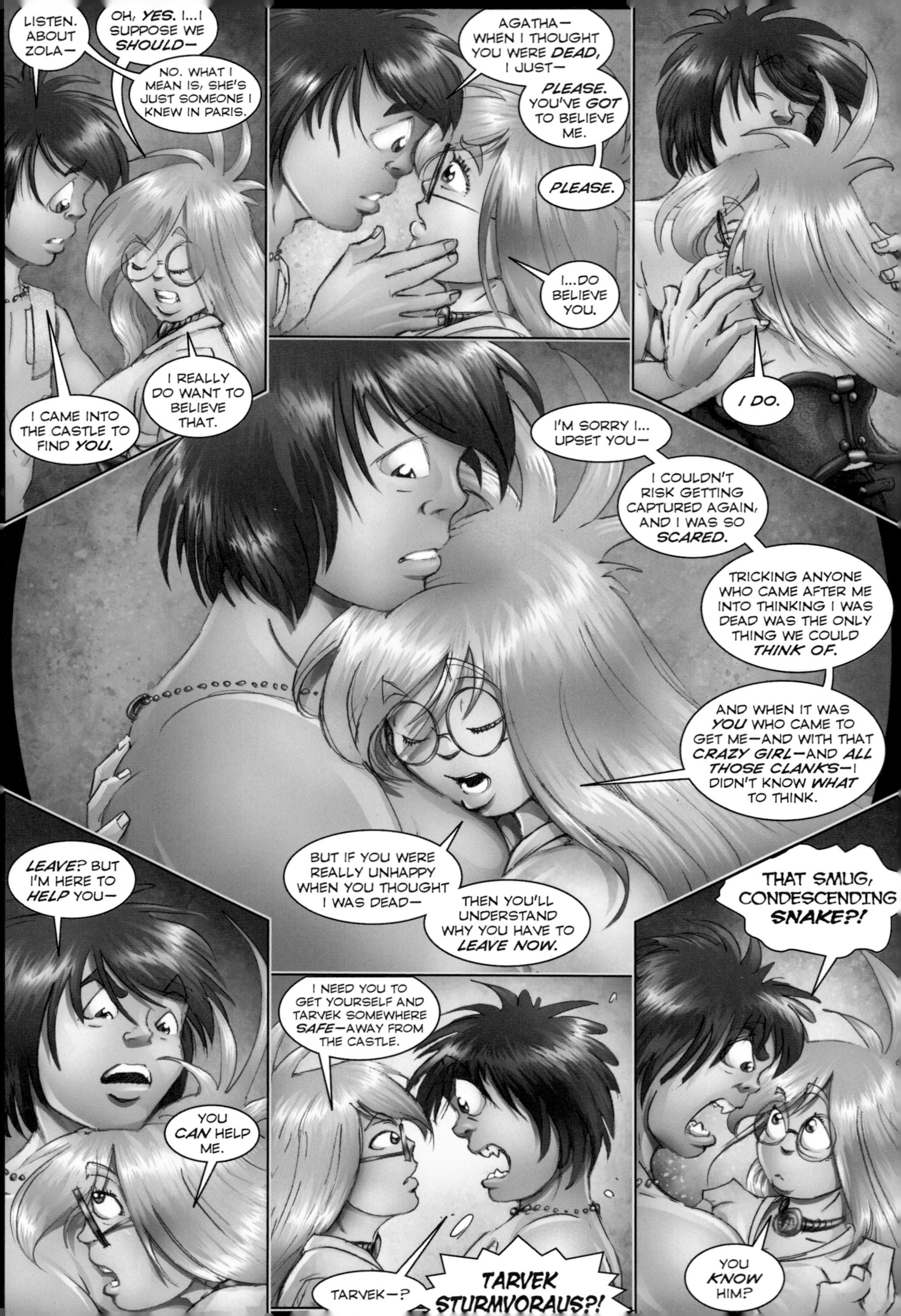
LISTEN. ABOUT ZOLA—
OH, YES. I...I SUPPOSE WE SHOULD—
NO. WHAT I MEAN IS, SHE'S JUST SOMEONE I KNEW IN PARIS.
I CAME INTO THE CASTLE TO FIND YOU.
I REALLY DO WANT TO BELIEVE THAT.
AGATHA— WHEN I THOUGHT YOU WERE DEAD, I JUST—
PLEASE. YOU'VE GOT TO BELIEVE ME.
PLEASE.
I...DO BELIEVE YOU.
I DO.
I'M SORRY I... UPSET YOU—
I COULDN'T RISK GETTING CAPTURED AGAIN, AND I WAS SO SCARED.
TRICKING ANYONE WHO CAME AFTER ME INTO THINKING I WAS DEAD WAS THE ONLY THING WE COULD THINK OF.
AND WHEN IT WAS YOU WHO CAME TO GET ME—AND WITH THAT CRAZY GIRL—AND ALL THOSE CLANKS—I DIDN'T KNOW WHAT TO THINK.
BUT IF YOU WERE REALLY UNHAPPY WHEN YOU THOUGHT I WAS DEAD—
THEN YOU'LL UNDERSTAND WHY YOU HAVE TO LEAVE NOW.
LEAVE? BUT I'M HERE TO HELP YOU—
YOU CAN HELP ME.
I NEED YOU TO GET YOURSELF AND TARVEK SOMEWHERE SAFE—AWAY FROM THE CASTLE.
TARVEK—?
TARVEK STURMVORAUS?!
THAT SMUG, CONDESCENDING SNAKE?!
YOU KNOW HIM?

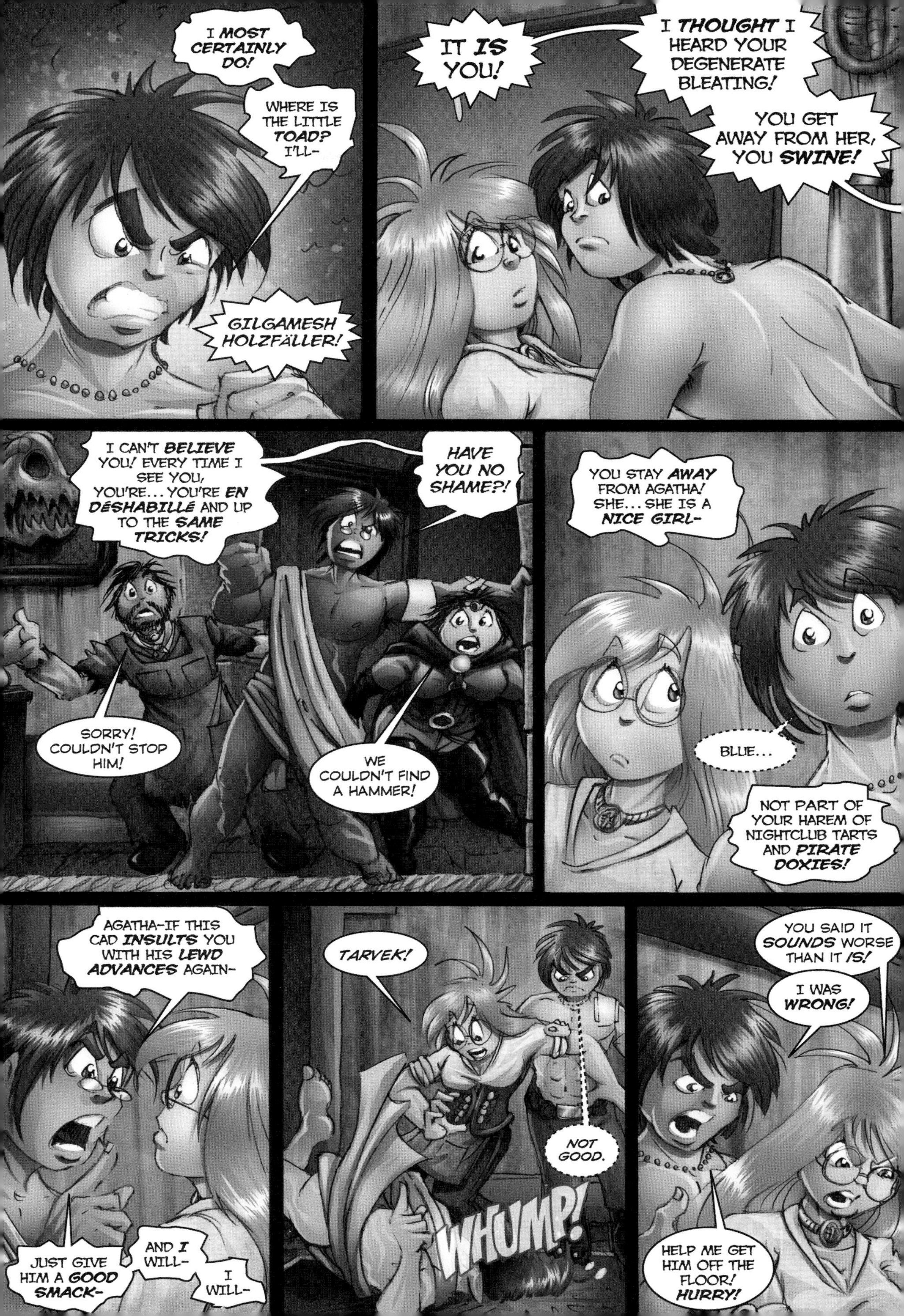

I MOST CERTAINLY DO!
WHERE IS THE LITTLE TOAD? I'LL-
GILGAMESH HOLZFÄLLER!
IT IS YOU!
I THOUGHT I HEARD YOUR DEGENERATE BLEATING!
YOU GET AWAY FROM HER, YOU SWINE!
I CAN'T BELIEVE YOU! EVERY TIME I SEE YOU, YOU'RE... YOU'RE EN DÉSHABILLÉ AND UP TO THE SAME TRICKS!
HAVE YOU NO SHAME?!
SORRY! COULDN'T STOP HIM!
WE COULDN'T FIND A HAMMER!
YOU STAY AWAY FROM AGATHA! SHE... SHE IS A NICE GIRL-
BLUE...
NOT PART OF YOUR HAREM OF NIGHTCLUB TARTS AND PIRATE DOXIES!
AGATHA-IF THIS CAD INSULTS YOU WITH HIS LEWD ADVANCES AGAIN-
JUST GIVE HIM A GOOD SMACK-
AND I WILL-
I WILL-
TARVEK!
NOT GOOD.
WHUMP!
YOU SAID IT SOUNDS WORSE THAN IT IS!
I WAS WRONG!
HELP ME GET HIM OFF THE FLOOR! HURRY!

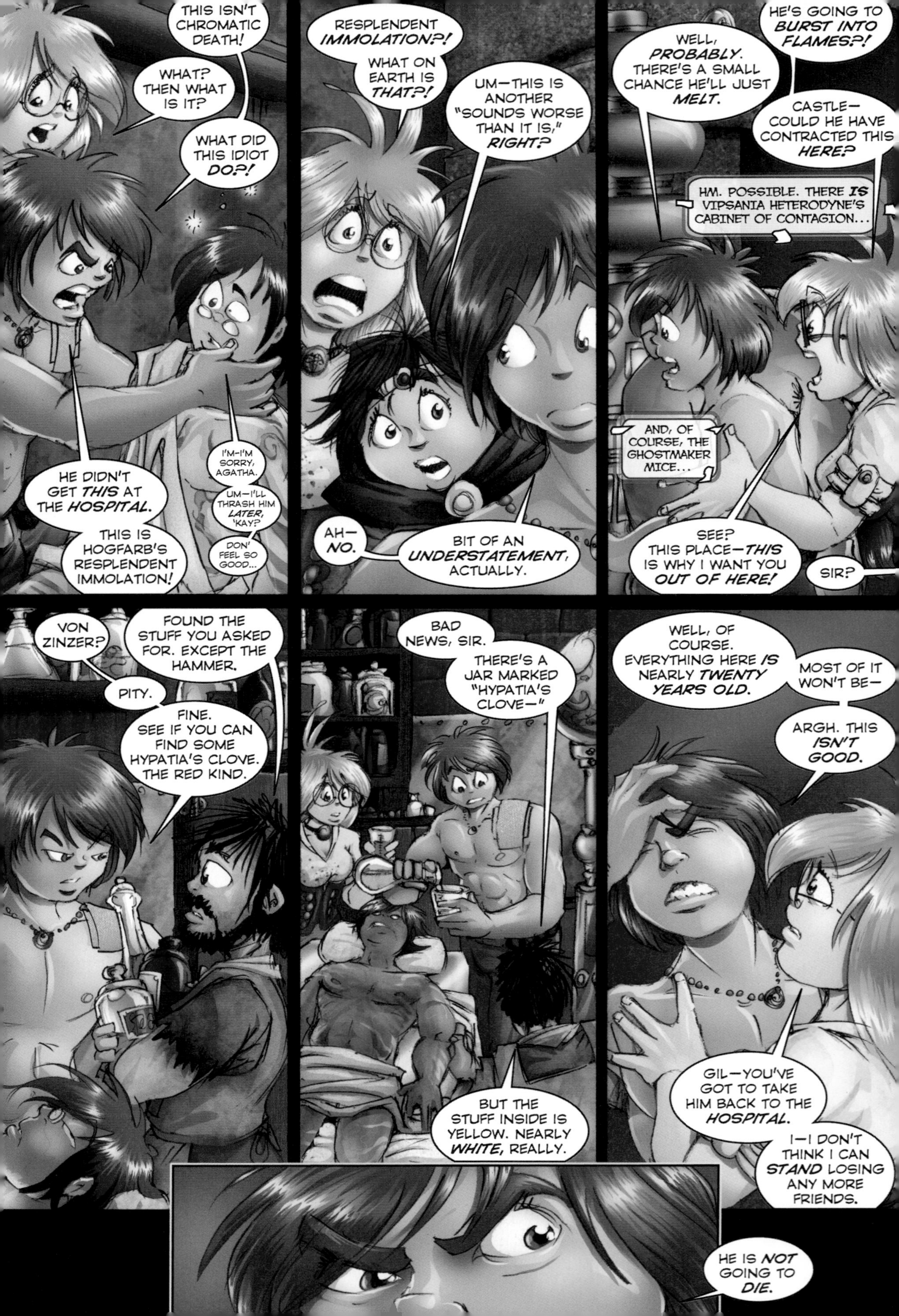
THIS ISN'T CHROMATIC DEATH!
WHAT? THEN WHAT IS IT?
WHAT DID THIS IDIOT DO?!
HE DIDN'T GET THIS AT THE HOSPITAL.
THIS IS HOGFARB'S RESPLENDENT IMMOLATION!
I'M-I'M SORRY, AGATHA.
UM—I'LL THRASH HIM LATER, 'KAY?
DON' FEEL SO GOOD...
RESPLENDENT IMMOLATION?!
WHAT ON EARTH IS THAT?!
UM—THIS IS ANOTHER "SOUNDS WORSE THAN IT IS," RIGHT?
AH—NO.
BIT OF AN UNDERSTATEMENT, ACTUALLY.
WELL, PROBABLY. THERE'S A SMALL CHANCE HE'LL JUST MELT.
HE'S GOING TO BURST INTO FLAMES?!
CASTLE—COULD HE HAVE CONTRACTED THIS HERE?
HM. POSSIBLE. THERE IS VIPSANIA HETERODYNE'S CABINET OF CONTAGION...
AND, OF COURSE, THE GHOSTMAKER MICE...
SEE? THIS PLACE—THIS IS WHY I WANT YOU OUT OF HERE!
SIR?
VON ZINZER?
FOUND THE STUFF YOU ASKED FOR. EXCEPT THE HAMMER.
PITY.
FINE. SEE IF YOU CAN FIND SOME HYPATIA'S CLOVE. THE RED KIND.
BAD NEWS, SIR.
THERE'S A JAR MARKED "HYPATIA'S CLOVE—"
BUT THE STUFF INSIDE IS YELLOW. NEARLY WHITE, REALLY.
WELL, OF COURSE. EVERYTHING HERE IS NEARLY TWENTY YEARS OLD.
MOST OF IT WON'T BE—
ARGH. THIS ISN'T GOOD.
GIL—YOU'VE GOT TO TAKE HIM BACK TO THE HOSPITAL.
I—I DON'T THINK I CAN STAND LOSING ANY MORE FRIENDS.
HE IS NOT GOING TO DIE.

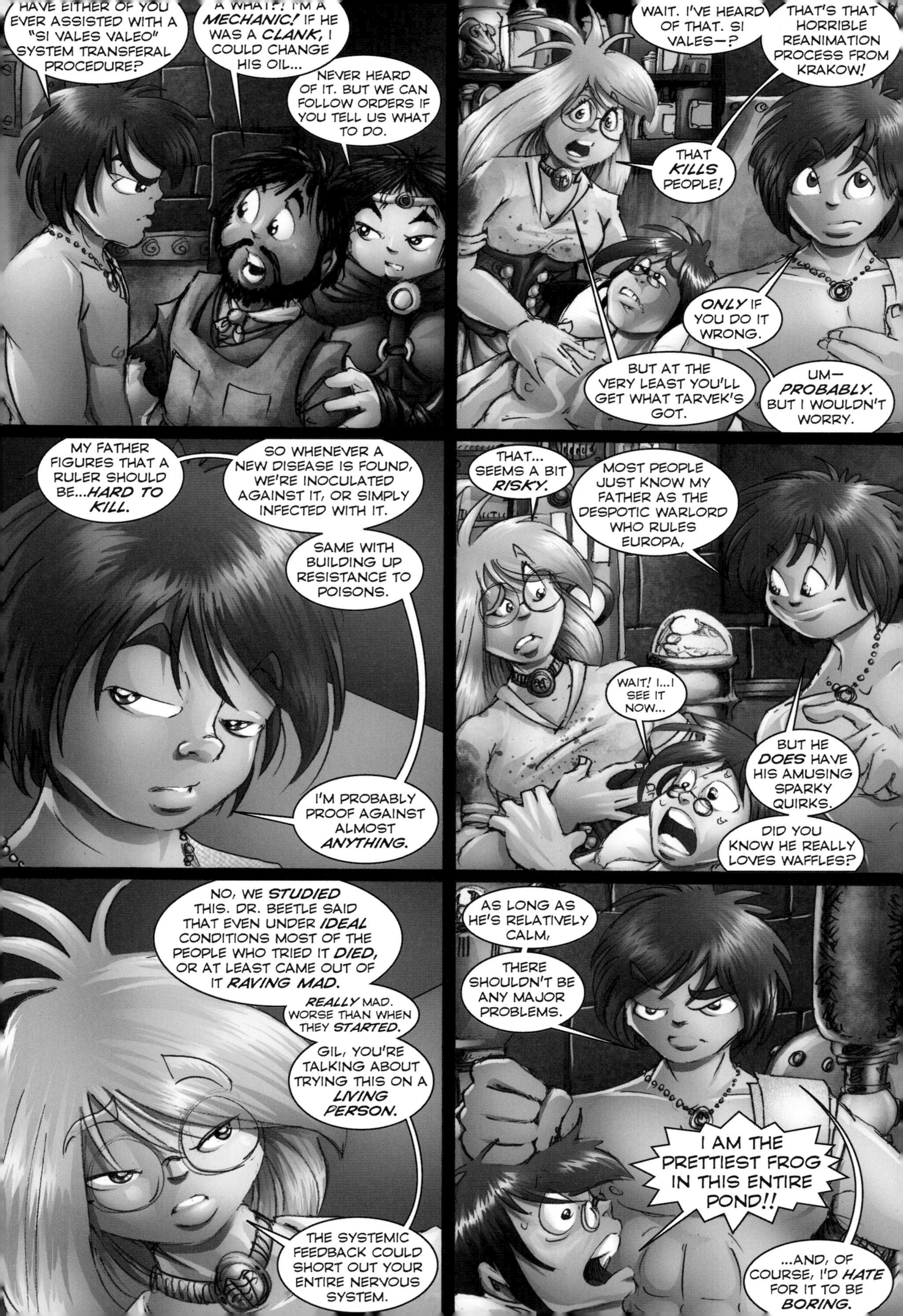
HAVE EITHER OF YOU EVER ASSISTED WITH A "SI VALES VALEO" SYSTEM TRANSFERAL PROCEDURE?
A WHAT!? I'M A *MECHANIC!* IF HE WAS A *CLANK,* I COULD CHANGE HIS OIL...
NEVER HEARD OF IT. BUT WE CAN FOLLOW ORDERS IF YOU TELL US WHAT TO DO.
WAIT. I'VE HEARD OF THAT. SI VALES—?
THAT'S THAT HORRIBLE REANIMATION PROCESS FROM KRAKOW!
THAT *KILLS* PEOPLE!
ONLY IF YOU DO IT WRONG.
BUT AT THE VERY LEAST YOU'LL GET WHAT TARVEK'S GOT.
UM— *PROBABLY.* BUT I WOULDN'T WORRY.
MY FATHER FIGURES THAT A RULER SHOULD BE...*HARD TO KILL.*
SO WHENEVER A NEW DISEASE IS FOUND, WE'RE INOCULATED AGAINST IT, OR SIMPLY INFECTED WITH IT.
SAME WITH BUILDING UP RESISTANCE TO POISONS.
I'M PROBABLY PROOF AGAINST ALMOST *ANYTHING.*
THAT... SEEMS A BIT *RISKY.*
MOST PEOPLE JUST KNOW MY FATHER AS THE DESPOTIC WARLORD WHO RULES EUROPA,
WAIT! I...I SEE IT NOW...
BUT HE *DOES* HAVE HIS AMUSING SPARKY QUIRKS.
DID YOU KNOW HE REALLY LOVES WAFFLES?
NO, WE *STUDIED* THIS. DR. BEETLE SAID THAT EVEN UNDER *IDEAL* CONDITIONS MOST OF THE PEOPLE WHO TRIED IT *DIED,* OR AT LEAST CAME OUT OF IT *RAVING MAD.*
REALLY MAD. WORSE THAN WHEN THEY *STARTED.*
GIL, YOU'RE TALKING ABOUT TRYING THIS ON A *LIVING PERSON.*
THE SYSTEMIC FEEDBACK COULD SHORT OUT YOUR ENTIRE NERVOUS SYSTEM.
AS LONG AS HE'S RELATIVELY CALM,
THERE SHOULDN'T BE ANY MAJOR PROBLEMS.
I AM THE PRETTIEST FROG IN THIS ENTIRE POND!!
...AND, OF COURSE, I'D *HATE* FOR IT TO BE *BORING.*

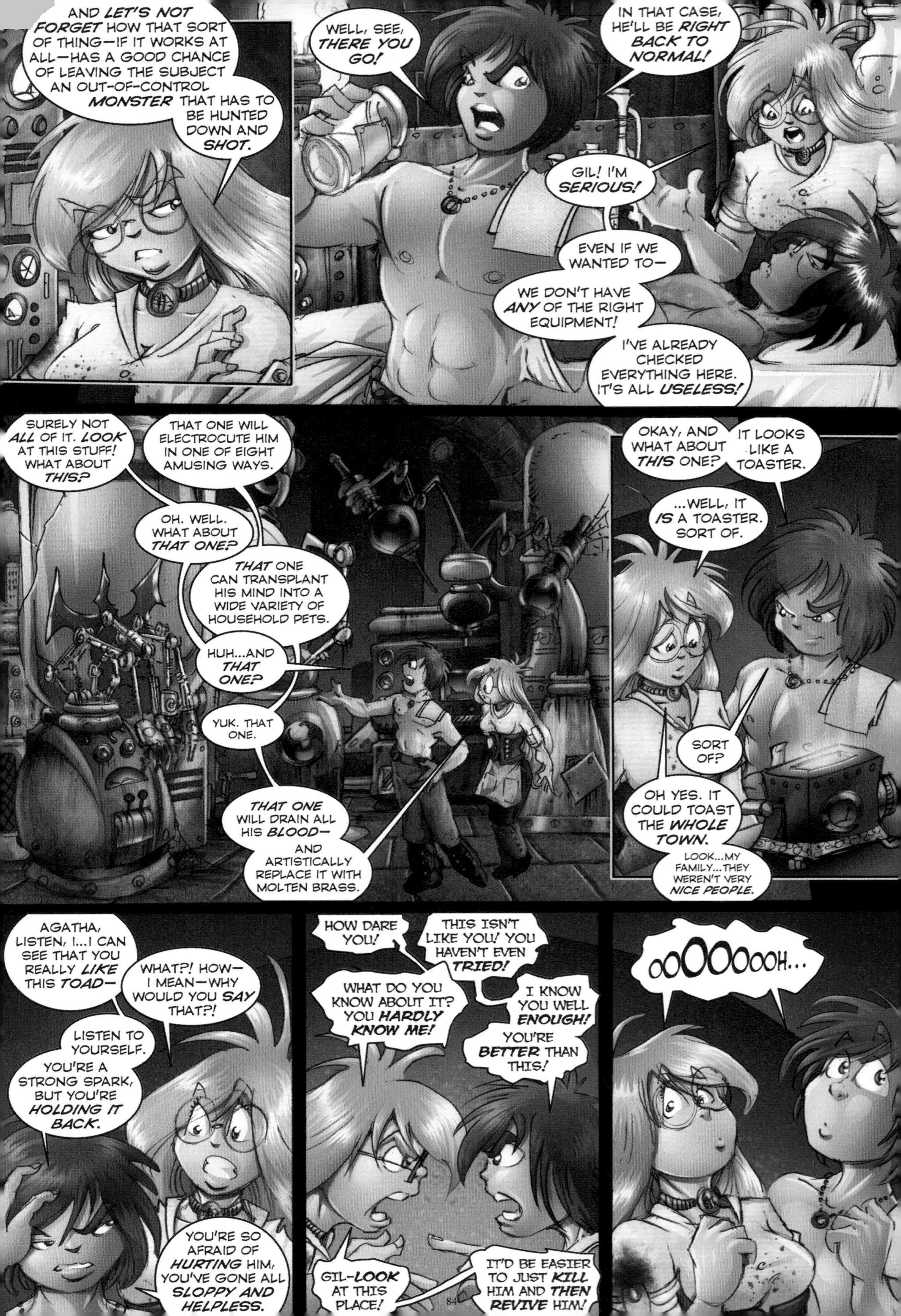
AND LET'S NOT FORGET HOW THAT SORT OF THING—IF IT WORKS AT ALL—HAS A GOOD CHANCE OF LEAVING THE SUBJECT AN OUT-OF-CONTROL MONSTER THAT HAS TO BE HUNTED DOWN AND SHOT.
WELL, SEE, THERE YOU GO!
IN THAT CASE, HE'LL BE RIGHT BACK TO NORMAL!
GIL! I'M SERIOUS!
EVEN IF WE WANTED TO—
WE DON'T HAVE ANY OF THE RIGHT EQUIPMENT!
I'VE ALREADY CHECKED EVERYTHING HERE. IT'S ALL USELESS!
SURELY NOT ALL OF IT. LOOK AT THIS STUFF! WHAT ABOUT THIS?
THAT ONE WILL ELECTROCUTE HIM IN ONE OF EIGHT AMUSING WAYS.
OH. WELL. WHAT ABOUT THAT ONE?
THAT ONE CAN TRANSPLANT HIS MIND INTO A WIDE VARIETY OF HOUSEHOLD PETS.
HUH...AND THAT ONE?
YUK. THAT ONE.
THAT ONE WILL DRAIN ALL HIS BLOOD—
AND ARTISTICALLY REPLACE IT WITH MOLTEN BRASS.
OKAY, AND WHAT ABOUT THIS ONE?
IT LOOKS LIKE A TOASTER.
...WELL, IT IS A TOASTER. SORT OF.
SORT OF?
OH YES. IT COULD TOAST THE WHOLE TOWN.
LOOK...MY FAMILY...THEY WEREN'T VERY NICE PEOPLE.
AGATHA, LISTEN, I...I CAN SEE THAT YOU REALLY LIKE THIS TOAD—
WHAT?! HOW—I MEAN—WHY WOULD YOU SAY THAT?!
LISTEN TO YOURSELF.
YOU'RE A STRONG SPARK, BUT YOU'RE HOLDING IT BACK.
YOU'RE SO AFRAID OF HURTING HIM, YOU'VE GONE ALL SLOPPY AND HELPLESS.
HOW DARE YOU!
THIS ISN'T LIKE YOU! YOU HAVEN'T EVEN TRIED!
WHAT DO YOU KNOW ABOUT IT? YOU HARDLY KNOW ME!
I KNOW YOU WELL ENOUGH!
YOU'RE BETTER THAN THIS!
GIL—LOOK AT THIS PLACE!
IT'D BE EASIER TO JUST KILL HIM AND THEN REVIVE HIM!
oOOOOooH...

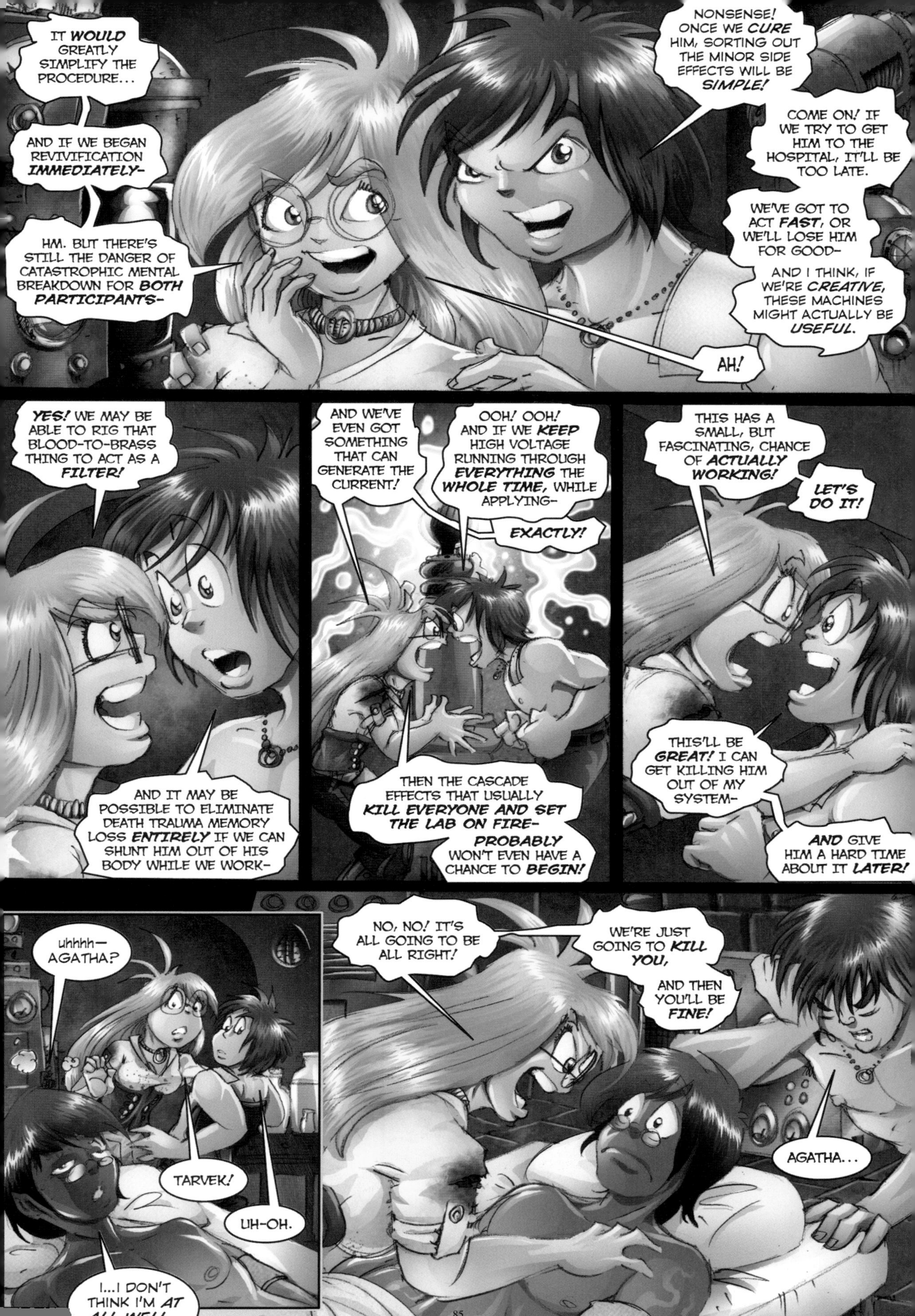
IT WOULD GREATLY SIMPLIFY THE PROCEDURE...
AND IF WE BEGAN REVIVIFICATION IMMEDIATELY-
HM. BUT THERE'S STILL THE DANGER OF CATASTROPHIC MENTAL BREAKDOWN FOR BOTH PARTICIPANTS-
NONSENSE! ONCE WE CURE HIM, SORTING OUT THE MINOR SIDE EFFECTS WILL BE SIMPLE!
COME ON! IF WE TRY TO GET HIM TO THE HOSPITAL, IT'LL BE TOO LATE.
WE'VE GOT TO ACT FAST, OR WE'LL LOSE HIM FOR GOOD-
AND I THINK, IF WE'RE CREATIVE, THESE MACHINES MIGHT ACTUALLY BE USEFUL.
AH!
YES! WE MAY BE ABLE TO RIG THAT BLOOD-TO-BRASS THING TO ACT AS A FILTER!
AND IT MAY BE POSSIBLE TO ELIMINATE DEATH TRAUMA MEMORY LOSS ENTIRELY IF WE CAN SHUNT HIM OUT OF HIS BODY WHILE WE WORK-
AND WE'VE EVEN GOT SOMETHING THAT CAN GENERATE THE CURRENT!
OOH! OOH! AND IF WE KEEP HIGH VOLTAGE RUNNING THROUGH EVERYTHING THE WHOLE TIME, WHILE APPLYING-
EXACTLY!
THEN THE CASCADE EFFECTS THAT USUALLY KILL EVERYONE AND SET THE LAB ON FIRE-
PROBABLY WON'T EVEN HAVE A CHANCE TO BEGIN!
THIS HAS A SMALL, BUT FASCINATING, CHANCE OF ACTUALLY WORKING!
LET'S DO IT!
THIS'LL BE GREAT! I CAN GET KILLING HIM OUT OF MY SYSTEM-
AND GIVE HIM A HARD TIME ABOUT IT LATER!
uhhhh— AGATHA?
TARVEK!
UH-OH.
I...I DON'T THINK I'M AT ALL WELL...
NO, NO! IT'S ALL GOING TO BE ALL RIGHT!
WE'RE JUST GOING TO KILL YOU,
AND THEN YOU'LL BE FINE!
AGATHA...

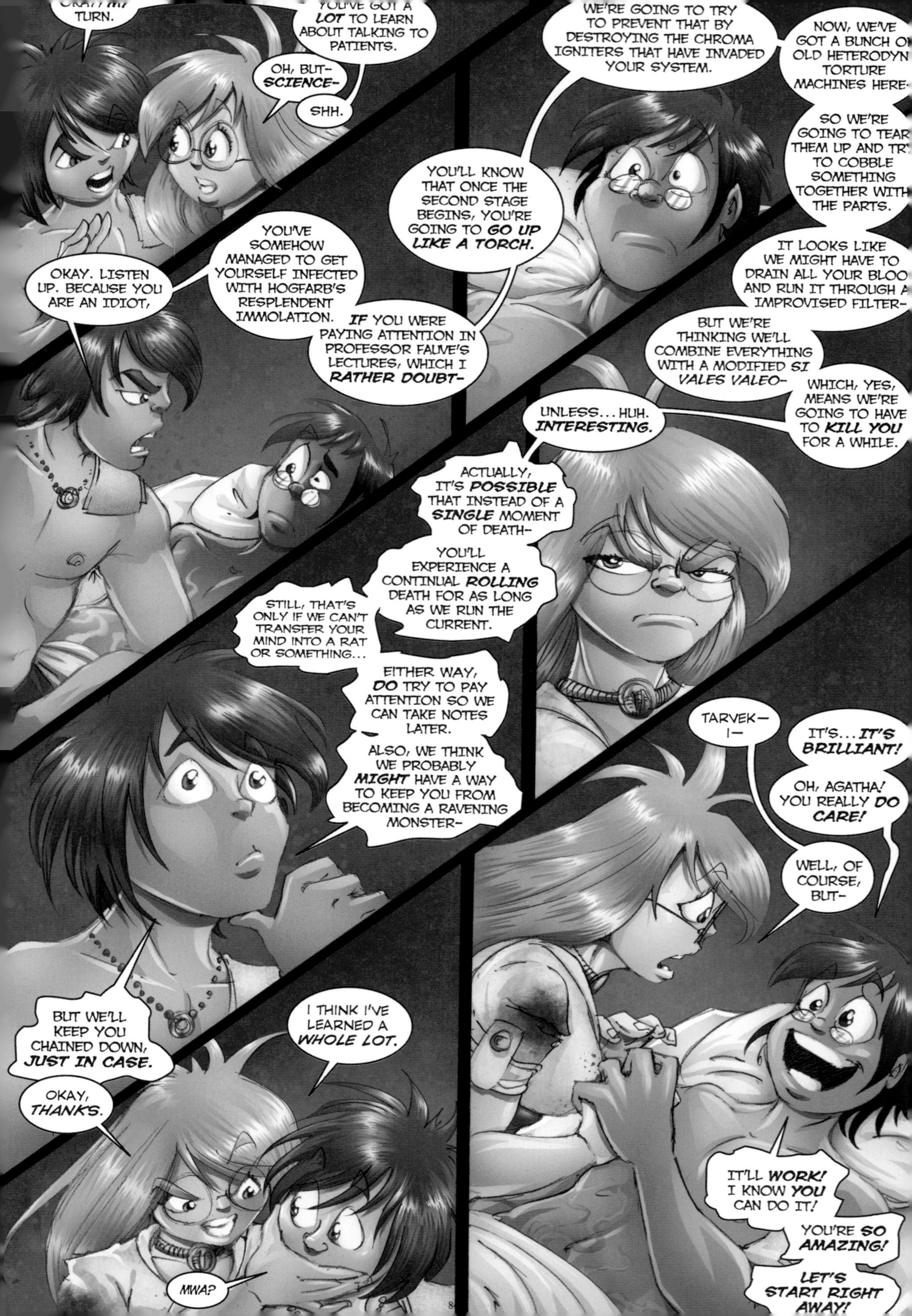

TURN.
YOU'VE GOT A LOT TO LEARN ABOUT TALKING TO PATIENTS.
OH, BUT- SCIENCE-
SHH.
OKAY. LISTEN UP. BECAUSE YOU ARE AN IDIOT,
YOU'VE SOMEHOW MANAGED TO GET YOURSELF INFECTED WITH HOGFARB'S RESPLENDENT IMMOLATION.
IF YOU WERE PAYING ATTENTION IN PROFESSOR FAUVE'S LECTURES, WHICH I RATHER DOUBT-
YOU'LL KNOW THAT ONCE THE SECOND STAGE BEGINS, YOU'RE GOING TO GO UP LIKE A TORCH.
WE'RE GOING TO TRY TO PREVENT THAT BY DESTROYING THE CHROMA IGNITERS THAT HAVE INVADED YOUR SYSTEM.
NOW, WE'VE GOT A BUNCH O OLD HETERODYN TORTURE MACHINES HERE-
SO WE'RE GOING TO TEAR THEM UP AND TR TO COBBLE SOMETHING TOGETHER WITH THE PARTS.
IT LOOKS LIKE WE MIGHT HAVE TO DRAIN ALL YOUR BLOO AND RUN IT THROUGH A IMPROVISED FILTER-
BUT WE'RE THINKING WE'LL COMBINE EVERYTHING WITH A MODIFIED SI VALES VALEO-
WHICH, YES, MEANS WE'RE GOING TO HAVE TO KILL YOU FOR A WHILE.
UNLESS... HUH. INTERESTING.
ACTUALLY, IT'S POSSIBLE THAT INSTEAD OF A SINGLE MOMENT OF DEATH-
YOU'LL EXPERIENCE A CONTINUAL ROLLING DEATH FOR AS LONG AS WE RUN THE CURRENT.
STILL, THAT'S ONLY IF WE CAN'T TRANSFER YOUR MIND INTO A RAT OR SOMETHING...
EITHER WAY, DO TRY TO PAY ATTENTION SO WE CAN TAKE NOTES LATER.
ALSO, WE THINK WE PROBABLY MIGHT HAVE A WAY TO KEEP YOU FROM BECOMING A RAVENING MONSTER-
BUT WE'LL KEEP YOU CHAINED DOWN, JUST IN CASE.
OKAY, THANKS.
I THINK I'VE LEARNED A WHOLE LOT.
MWA?
TARVEK- I-
IT'S... IT'S BRILLIANT!
OH, AGATHA! YOU REALLY DO CARE!
WELL, OF COURSE, BUT-
IT'LL WORK! I KNOW YOU CAN DO IT!
YOU'RE SO AMAZING!
LET'S START RIGHT AWAY!

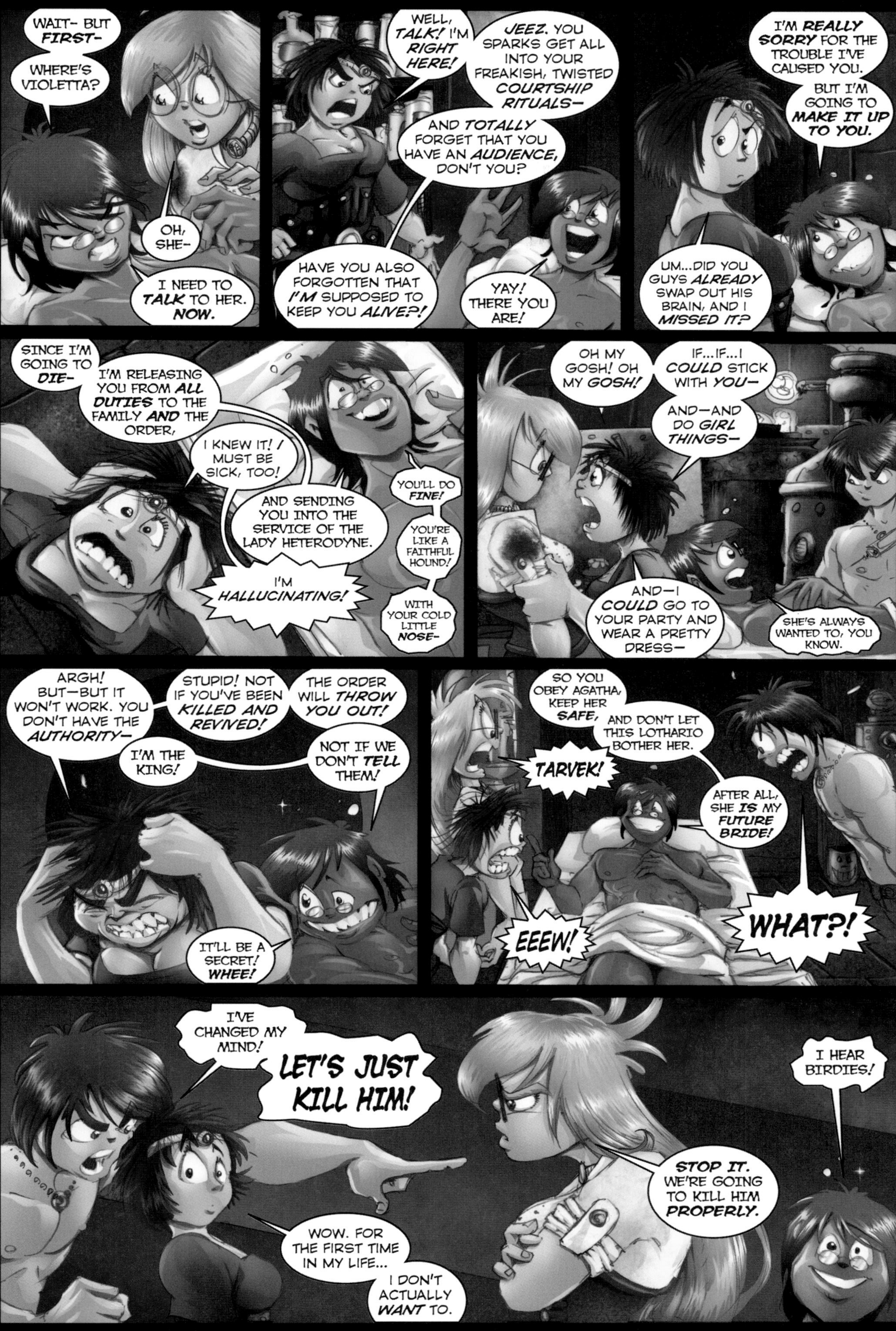

WAIT- BUT FIRST-
WHERE'S VIOLETTA?
OH, SHE-
I NEED TO TALK TO HER. NOW.
WELL, TALK! I'M RIGHT HERE!
JEEZ. YOU SPARKS GET ALL INTO YOUR FREAKISH, TWISTED COURTSHIP RITUALS—
AND TOTALLY FORGET THAT YOU HAVE AN AUDIENCE, DON'T YOU?
HAVE YOU ALSO FORGOTTEN THAT I'M SUPPOSED TO KEEP YOU ALIVE?!
YAY! THERE YOU ARE!
I'M REALLY SORRY FOR THE TROUBLE I'VE CAUSED YOU.
BUT I'M GOING TO MAKE IT UP TO YOU.
UM...DID YOU GUYS ALREADY SWAP OUT HIS BRAIN, AND I MISSED IT?
SINCE I'M GOING TO DIE-
I'M RELEASING YOU FROM ALL DUTIES TO THE FAMILY AND THE ORDER,
I KNEW IT! I MUST BE SICK, TOO!
AND SENDING YOU INTO THE SERVICE OF THE LADY HETERODYNE.
I'M HALLUCINATING!
YOU'LL DO FINE!
YOU'RE LIKE A FAITHFUL HOUND!
WITH YOUR COLD LITTLE NOSE-
OH MY GOSH! OH MY GOSH!
IF...IF...I COULD STICK WITH YOU—
AND—AND DO GIRL THINGS—
AND—I COULD GO TO YOUR PARTY AND WEAR A PRETTY DRESS—
SHE'S ALWAYS WANTED TO, YOU KNOW.
ARGH! BUT—BUT IT WON'T WORK. YOU DON'T HAVE THE AUTHORITY—
I'M THE KING!
STUPID! NOT IF YOU'VE BEEN KILLED AND REVIVED!
THE ORDER WILL THROW YOU OUT!
NOT IF WE DON'T TELL THEM!
IT'LL BE A SECRET! WHEE!
SO YOU OBEY AGATHA, KEEP HER SAFE,
AND DON'T LET THIS LOTHARIO BOTHER HER.
TARVEK!
AFTER ALL, SHE IS MY FUTURE BRIDE!
EEEW!
WHAT?!
I'VE CHANGED MY MIND!
LET'S JUST KILL HIM!
WOW. FOR THE FIRST TIME IN MY LIFE...
I DON'T ACTUALLY WANT TO.
STOP IT. WE'RE GOING TO KILL HIM PROPERLY.
I HEAR BIRDIES!

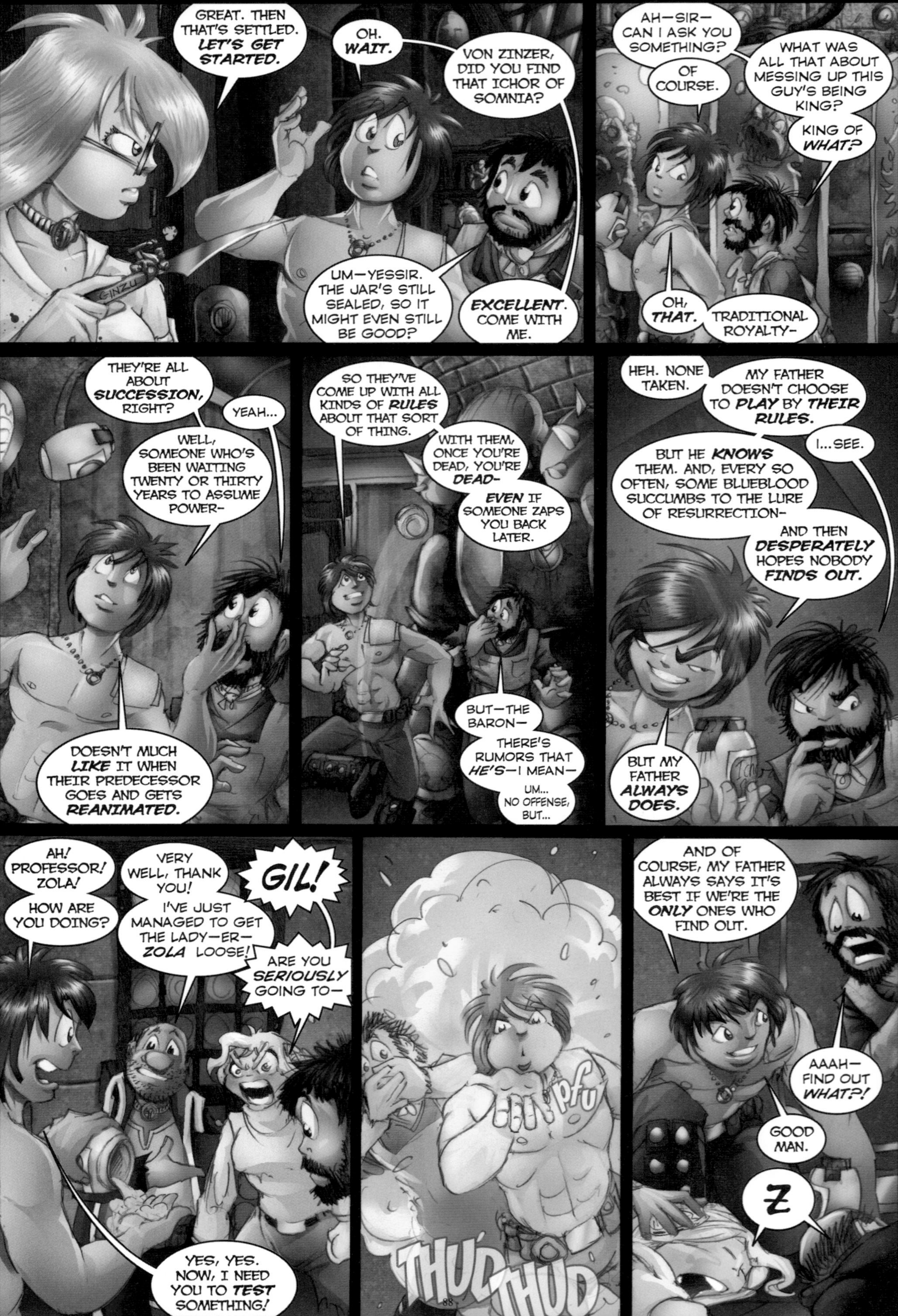
GREAT. THEN THAT'S SETTLED. LET'S GET STARTED.
GINZU
OH. WAIT.
VON ZINZER, DID YOU FIND THAT ICHOR OF SOMNIA?
UM—YESSIR. THE JAR'S STILL SEALED, SO IT MIGHT EVEN STILL BE GOOD?
EXCELLENT. COME WITH ME.
AH—SIR—CAN I ASK YOU SOMETHING?
OF COURSE.
WHAT WAS ALL THAT ABOUT MESSING UP THIS GUY'S BEING KING?
KING OF WHAT?
OH, THAT.
TRADITIONAL ROYALTY-
THEY'RE ALL ABOUT SUCCESSION, RIGHT?
YEAH...
WELL, SOMEONE WHO'S BEEN WAITING TWENTY OR THIRTY YEARS TO ASSUME POWER-
DOESN'T MUCH LIKE IT WHEN THEIR PREDECESSOR GOES AND GETS REANIMATED.
SO THEY'VE COME UP WITH ALL KINDS OF RULES ABOUT THAT SORT OF THING.
WITH THEM, ONCE YOU'RE DEAD, YOU'RE DEAD-
EVEN IF SOMEONE ZAPS YOU BACK LATER.
BUT—THE BARON—
THERE'S RUMORS THAT HE'S—I MEAN—
UM... NO OFFENSE, BUT...
HEH. NONE TAKEN.
MY FATHER DOESN'T CHOOSE TO PLAY BY THEIR RULES.
I...SEE.
BUT HE KNOWS THEM. AND, EVERY SO OFTEN, SOME BLUEBLOOD SUCCUMBS TO THE LURE OF RESURRECTION-
AND THEN DESPERATELY HOPES NOBODY FINDS OUT.
BUT MY FATHER ALWAYS DOES.
AH! PROFESSOR! ZOLA!
HOW ARE YOU DOING?
VERY WELL, THANK YOU!
I'VE JUST MANAGED TO GET THE LADY—ER—ZOLA LOOSE!
GIL!
ARE YOU SERIOUSLY GOING TO—
YES, YES. NOW, I NEED YOU TO TEST SOMETHING!
pfu
THUD THUD
AND OF COURSE, MY FATHER ALWAYS SAYS IT'S BEST IF WE'RE THE ONLY ONES WHO FIND OUT.
AAAH—FIND OUT WHAT?!
GOOD MAN.
Z

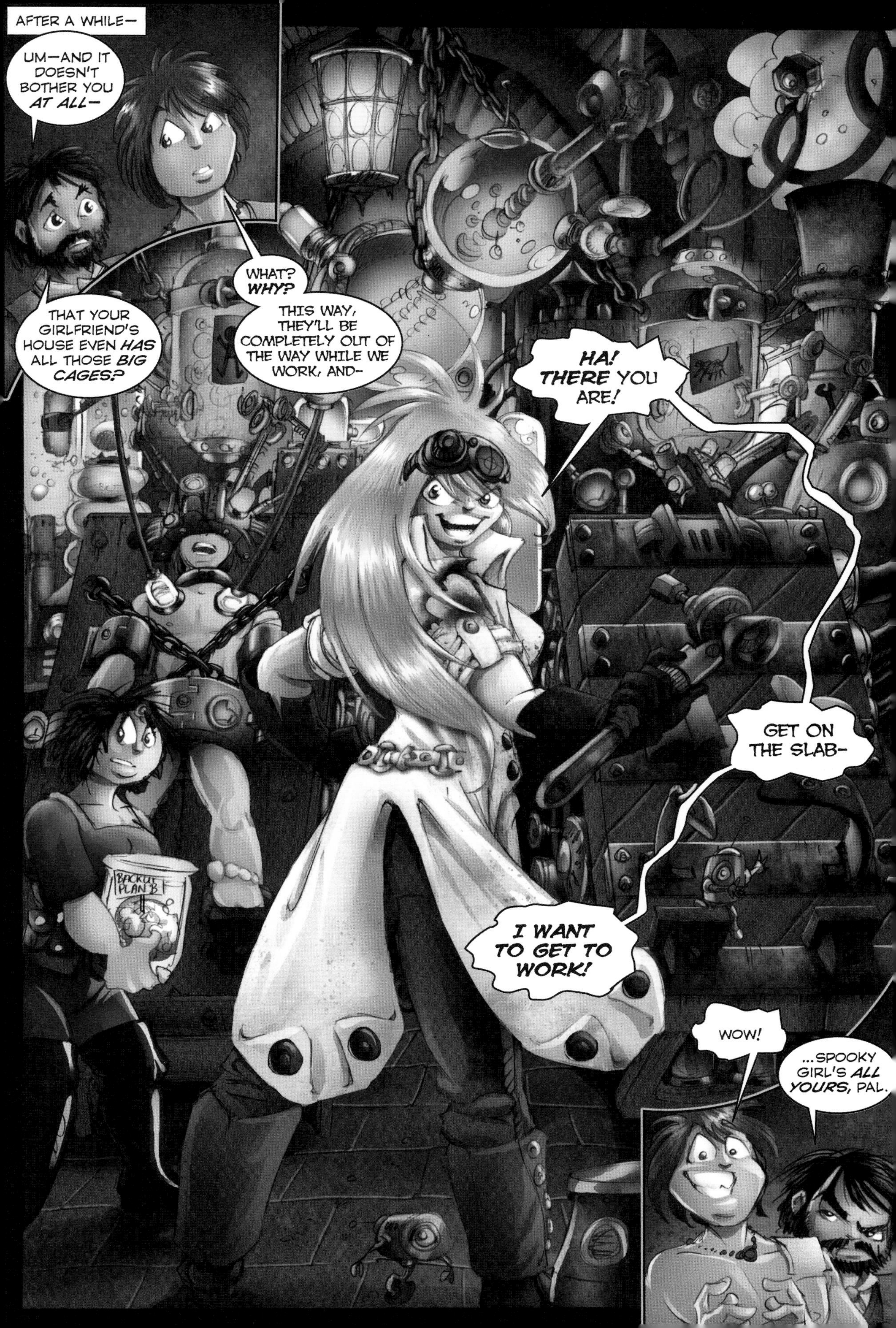
AFTER A WHILE—
UM—AND IT DOESN'T BOTHER YOU *AT ALL*—
THAT YOUR GIRLFRIEND'S HOUSE EVEN *HAS* ALL THOSE *BIG* CAGES?
WHAT? *WHY?*
THIS WAY, THEY'LL BE COMPLETELY OUT OF THE WAY WHILE WE WORK, AND-
HA! THERE YOU ARE!
GET ON THE SLAB-
I WANT TO GET TO WORK!
WOW!
...SPOOKY GIRL'S *ALL YOURS*, PAL.

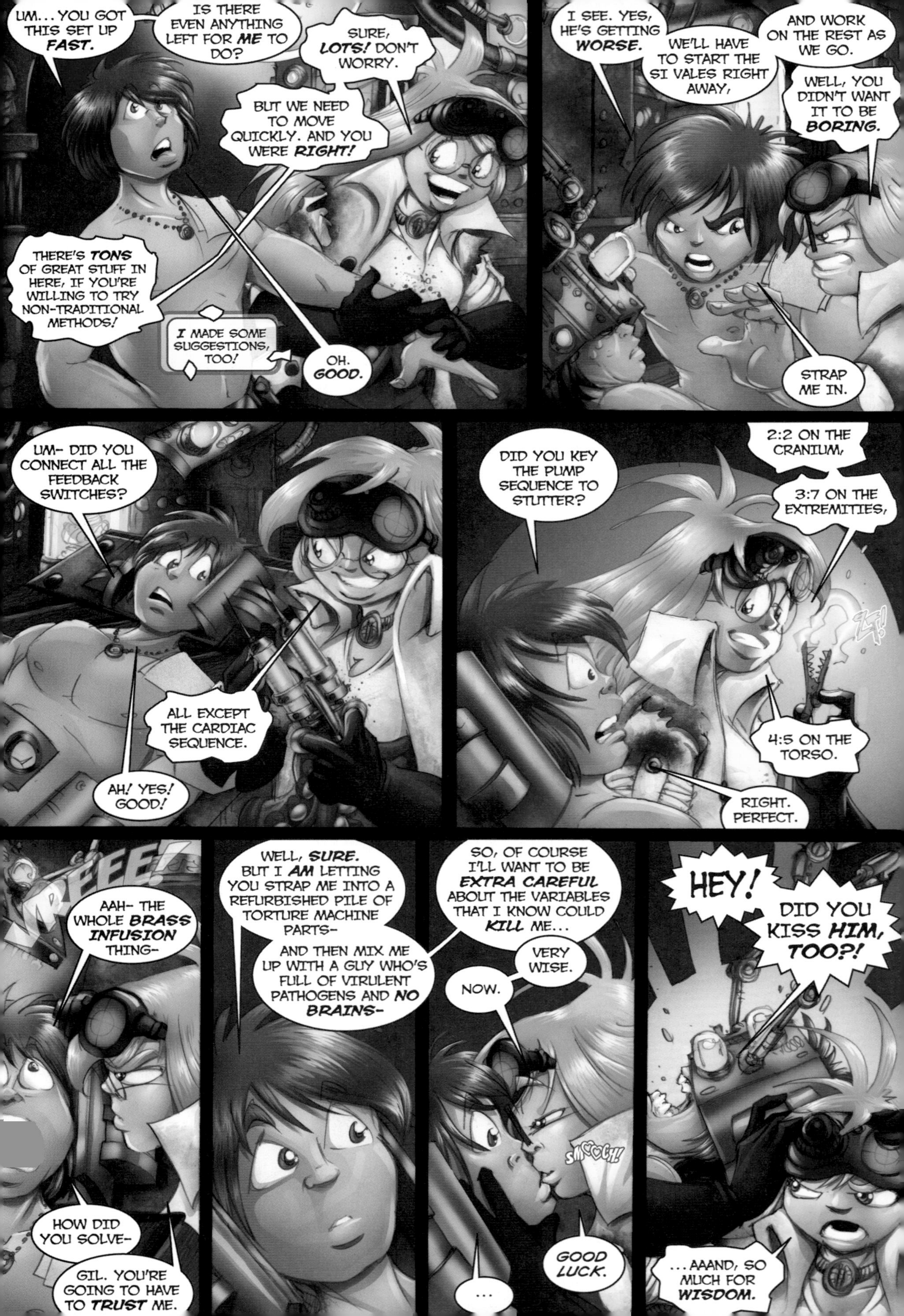
UM... YOU GOT THIS SET UP FAST.
IS THERE EVEN ANYTHING LEFT FOR ME TO DO?
SURE, LOTS! DON'T WORRY.
BUT WE NEED TO MOVE QUICKLY. AND YOU WERE RIGHT!
THERE'S TONS OF GREAT STUFF IN HERE, IF YOU'RE WILLING TO TRY NON-TRADITIONAL METHODS!
I MADE SOME SUGGESTIONS, TOO!
OH. GOOD.
I SEE. YES, HE'S GETTING WORSE.
WE'LL HAVE TO START THE SI VALES RIGHT AWAY,
AND WORK ON THE REST AS WE GO.
WELL, YOU DIDN'T WANT IT TO BE BORING.
STRAP ME IN.
UM- DID YOU CONNECT ALL THE FEEDBACK SWITCHES?
ALL EXCEPT THE CARDIAC SEQUENCE.
AH! YES! GOOD!
DID YOU KEY THE PUMP SEQUENCE TO STUTTER?
2:2 ON THE CRANIUM,
3:7 ON THE EXTREMITIES,
4:5 ON THE TORSO.
RIGHT. PERFECT.
AAH- THE WHOLE BRASS INFUSION THING-
HOW DID YOU SOLVE-
GIL. YOU'RE GOING TO HAVE TO TRUST ME.
WELL, SURE. BUT I AM LETTING YOU STRAP ME INTO A REFURBISHED PILE OF TORTURE MACHINE PARTS-
AND THEN MIX ME UP WITH A GUY WHO'S FULL OF VIRULENT PATHOGENS AND NO BRAINS-
SO, OF COURSE I'LL WANT TO BE EXTRA CAREFUL ABOUT THE VARIABLES THAT I KNOW COULD KILL ME...
VERY WISE.
NOW.
SMOOCH!
GOOD LUCK.
...
HEY!
DID YOU KISS HIM, TOO?!
...AAAND, SO MUCH FOR WISDOM.

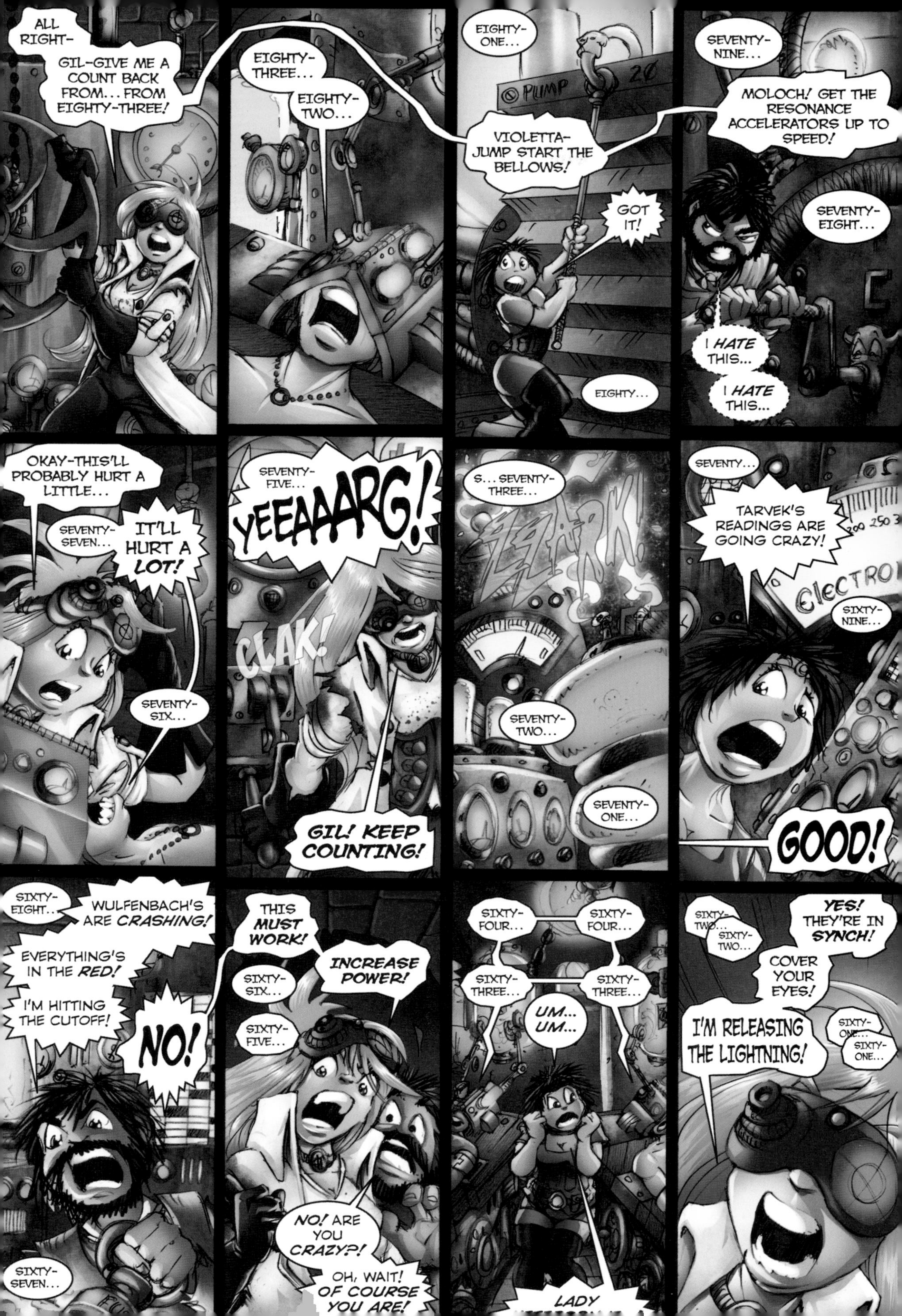

ALL RIGHT-
GIL-GIVE ME A COUNT BACK FROM... FROM EIGHTY-THREE!
EIGHTY-THREE...
EIGHTY-TWO...
EIGHTY-ONE...
VIOLETTA-JUMP START THE BELLOWS!
PUMP 20
GOT IT!
EIGHTY...
SEVENTY-NINE...
MOLOCH! GET THE RESONANCE ACCELERATORS UP TO SPEED!
SEVENTY-EIGHT...
I HATE THIS...
I HATE THIS...
OKAY-THIS'LL PROBABLY HURT A LITTLE...
SEVENTY-SEVEN...
IT'LL HURT A LOT!
SEVENTY-SIX...
SEVENTY-FIVE...
YEEAAARG!
CLAK!
GIL! KEEP COUNTING!
S... SEVENTY-THREE...
ZZAARK!
SEVENTY-TWO...
SEVENTY-ONE...
SEVENTY...
TARVEK'S READINGS ARE GOING CRAZY!
SIXTY-NINE...
GOOD!
SIXTY-EIGHT...
WULFENBACH'S ARE CRASHING!
EVERYTHING'S IN THE RED!
I'M HITTING THE CUTOFF!
NO!
SIXTY-SEVEN...
THIS MUST WORK!
INCREASE POWER!
SIXTY-SIX...
SIXTY-FIVE...
NO! ARE YOU CRAZY?!
OH, WAIT! OF COURSE YOU ARE!
SIXTY-FOUR...
SIXTY-FOUR...
SIXTY-THREE...
SIXTY-THREE...
UM... UM...
LADY
SIXTY-TWO...
SIXTY-TWO...
YES! THEY'RE IN SYNCH!
COVER YOUR EYES!
I'M RELEASING THE LIGHTNING!
SIXTY-ONE...
SIXTY-ONE...

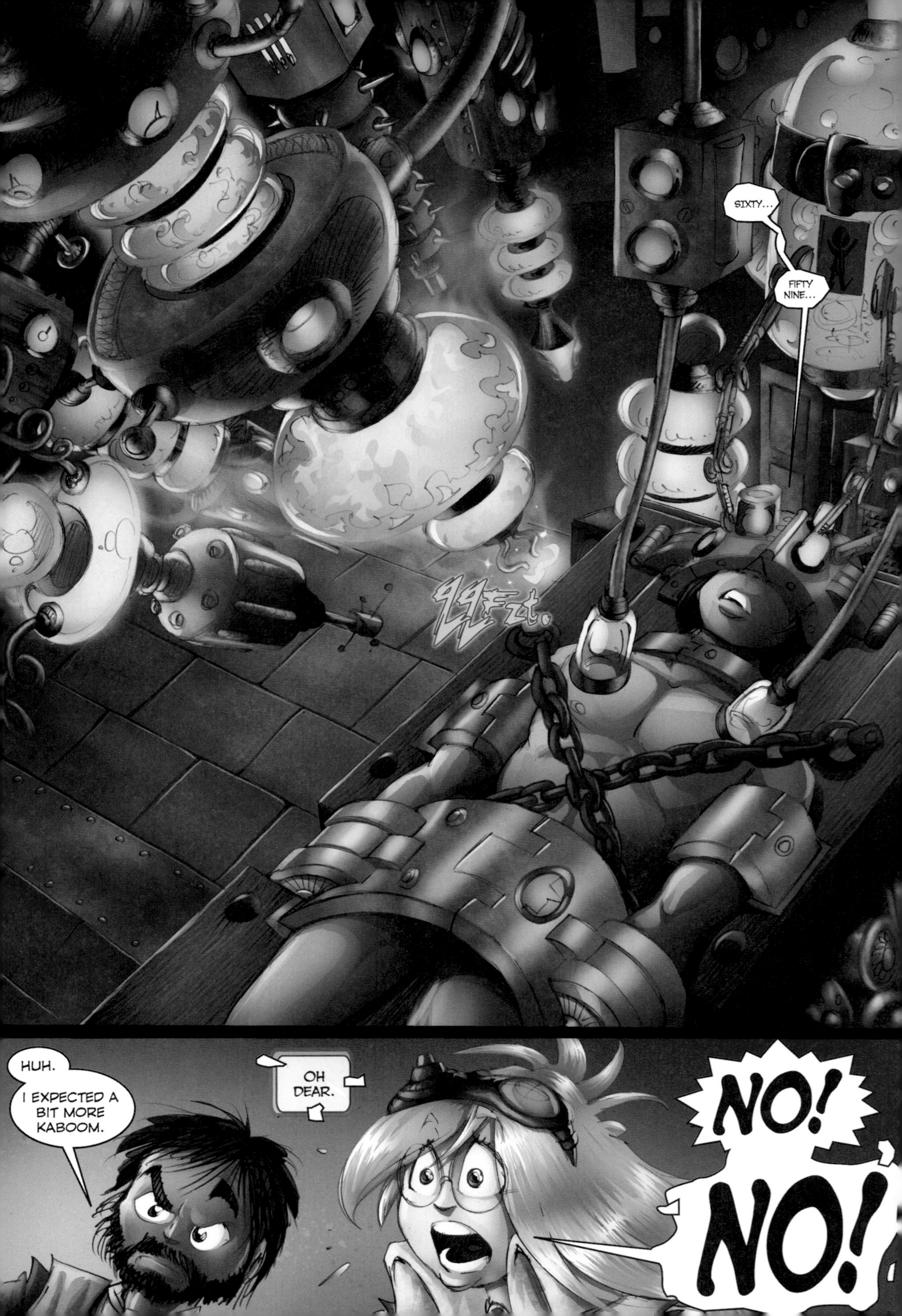
SIXTY...
FIFTY NINE...
ZZFzt.
HUH. I EXPECTED A BIT MORE KABOOM.
OH DEAR.
NO!
NO!
NO!

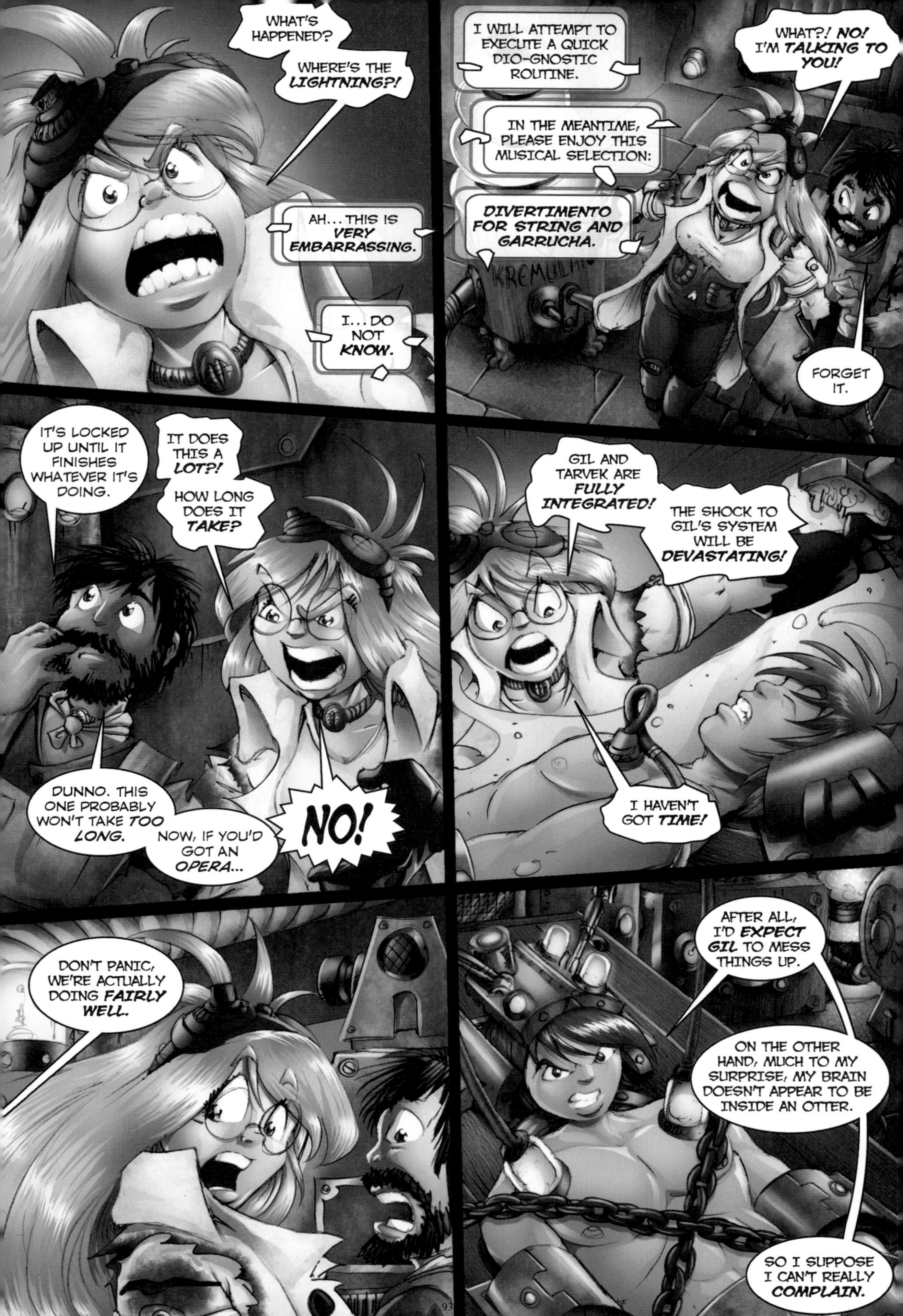
WHAT'S HAPPENED?
WHERE'S THE LIGHTNING?!
AH... THIS IS VERY EMBARRASSING.
I... DO NOT KNOW.
I WILL ATTEMPT TO EXECUTE A QUICK DIO-GNOSTIC ROUTINE.
IN THE MEANTIME, PLEASE ENJOY THIS MUSICAL SELECTION:
DIVERTIMENTO FOR STRING AND GARRUCHA.
KREMULAH
WHAT?! NO! I'M TALKING TO YOU!
FORGET IT.
IT'S LOCKED UP UNTIL IT FINISHES WHATEVER IT'S DOING.
IT DOES THIS A LOT?!
HOW LONG DOES IT TAKE?
DUNNO. THIS ONE PROBABLY WON'T TAKE TOO LONG.
NOW, IF YOU'D GOT AN OPERA...
NO!
GIL AND TARVEK ARE FULLY INTEGRATED!
THE SHOCK TO GIL'S SYSTEM WILL BE DEVASTATING!
I HAVEN'T GOT TIME!
DON'T PANIC, WE'RE ACTUALLY DOING FAIRLY WELL.
AFTER ALL, I'D EXPECT GIL TO MESS THINGS UP.
ON THE OTHER HAND, MUCH TO MY SURPRISE, MY BRAIN DOESN'T APPEAR TO BE INSIDE AN OTTER.
SO I SUPPOSE I CAN'T REALLY COMPLAIN.

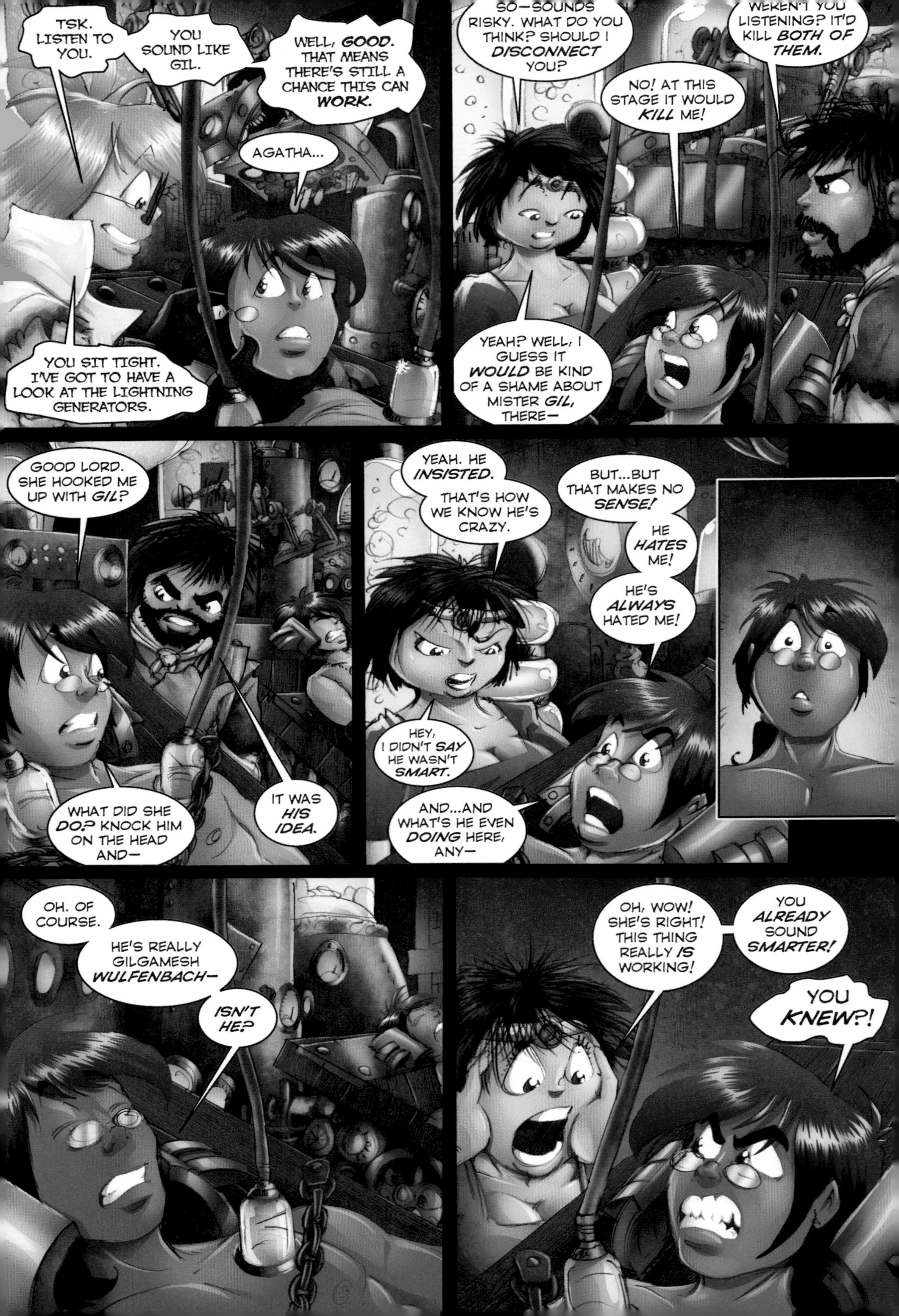
TSK. LISTEN TO YOU.
YOU SOUND LIKE GIL.
WELL, GOOD. THAT MEANS THERE'S STILL A CHANCE THIS CAN WORK.
AGATHA...
YOU SIT TIGHT. I'VE GOT TO HAVE A LOOK AT THE LIGHTNING GENERATORS.
SO—SOUNDS RISKY. WHAT DO YOU THINK? SHOULD I DISCONNECT YOU?
NO! AT THIS STAGE IT WOULD KILL ME!
WEREN'T YOU LISTENING? IT'D KILL BOTH OF THEM.
YEAH? WELL, I GUESS IT WOULD BE KIND OF A SHAME ABOUT MISTER GIL, THERE—
GOOD LORD. SHE HOOKED ME UP WITH GIL?
WHAT DID SHE DO? KNOCK HIM ON THE HEAD AND—
IT WAS HIS IDEA.
YEAH. HE INSISTED.
THAT'S HOW WE KNOW HE'S CRAZY.
BUT...BUT THAT MAKES NO SENSE!
HE HATES ME!
HE'S ALWAYS HATED ME!
HEY, I DIDN'T SAY HE WASN'T SMART.
AND...AND WHAT'S HE EVEN DOING HERE, ANY—
OH. OF COURSE.
HE'S REALLY GILGAMESH WULFENBACH—
ISN'T HE?
OH, WOW! SHE'S RIGHT! THIS THING REALLY IS WORKING!
YOU ALREADY SOUND SMARTER!
YOU KNEW?!

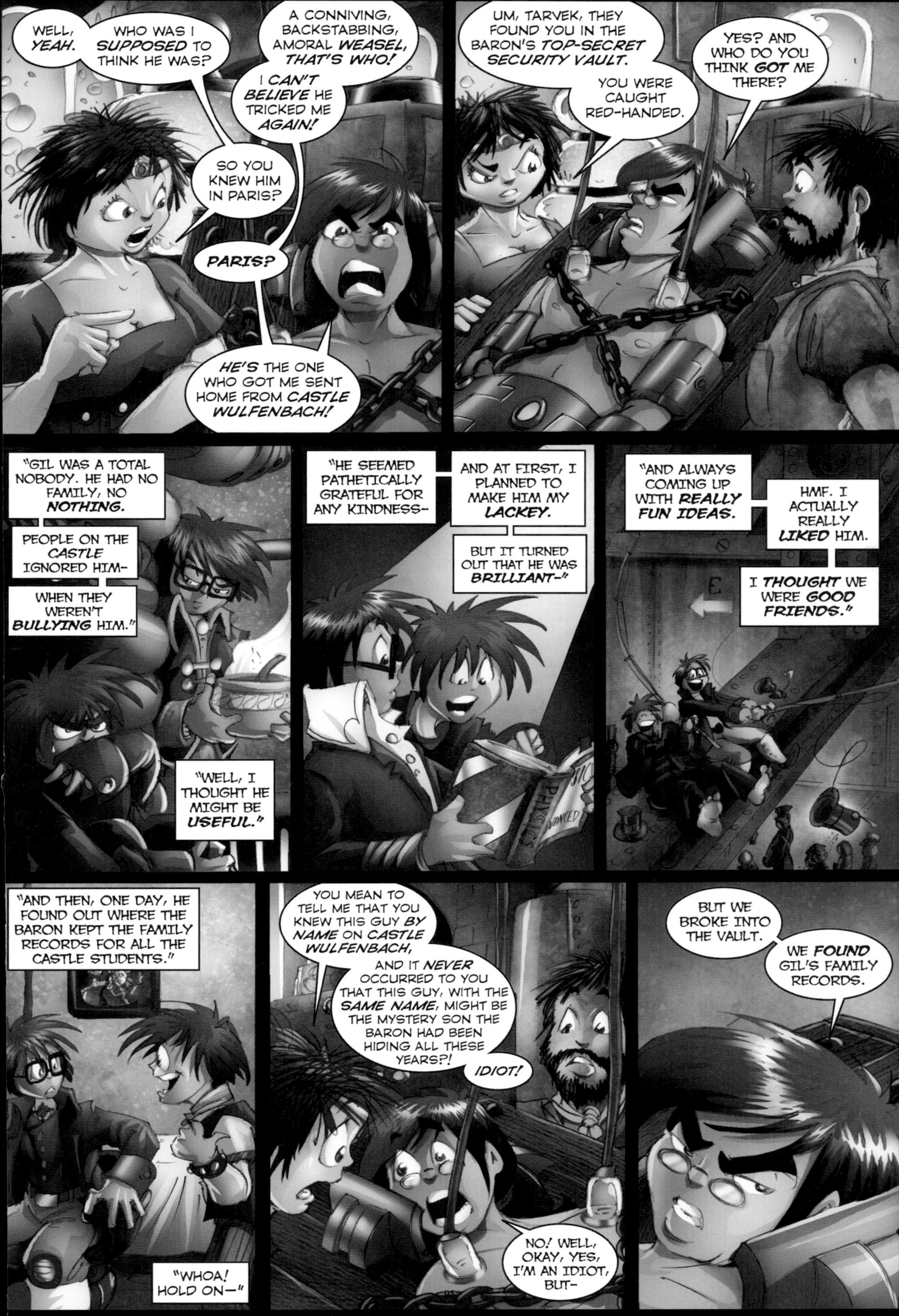

WELL, YEAH.
WHO WAS I SUPPOSED TO THINK HE WAS?
A CONNIVING, BACKSTABBING, AMORAL WEASEL, THAT'S WHO!
I CAN'T BELIEVE HE TRICKED ME AGAIN!
SO YOU KNEW HIM IN PARIS?
PARIS?
HE'S THE ONE WHO GOT ME SENT HOME FROM CASTLE WULFENBACH!
UM, TARVEK, THEY FOUND YOU IN THE BARON'S TOP-SECRET SECURITY VAULT.
YOU WERE CAUGHT RED-HANDED.
YES? AND WHO DO YOU THINK GOT ME THERE?
"GIL WAS A TOTAL NOBODY. HE HAD NO FAMILY, NO NOTHING.
PEOPLE ON THE CASTLE IGNORED HIM-
WHEN THEY WEREN'T BULLYING HIM."
"WELL, I THOUGHT HE MIGHT BE USEFUL."
"HE SEEMED PATHETICALLY GRATEFUL FOR ANY KINDNESS-
AND AT FIRST, I PLANNED TO MAKE HIM MY LACKEY.
BUT IT TURNED OUT THAT HE WAS BRILLIANT-"
"AND ALWAYS COMING UP WITH REALLY FUN IDEAS.
HMF. I ACTUALLY REALLY LIKED HIM.
I THOUGHT WE WERE GOOD FRIENDS."
"AND THEN, ONE DAY, HE FOUND OUT WHERE THE BARON KEPT THE FAMILY RECORDS FOR ALL THE CASTLE STUDENTS."
"WHOA! HOLD ON—"
YOU MEAN TO TELL ME THAT YOU KNEW THIS GUY BY NAME ON CASTLE WULFENBACH,
AND IT NEVER OCCURRED TO YOU THAT THIS GUY, WITH THE SAME NAME, MIGHT BE THE MYSTERY SON THE BARON HAD BEEN HIDING ALL THESE YEARS?!
IDIOT!
NO! WELL, OKAY, YES, I'M AN IDIOT, BUT-
BUT WE BROKE INTO THE VAULT.
WE FOUND GIL'S FAMILY RECORDS.

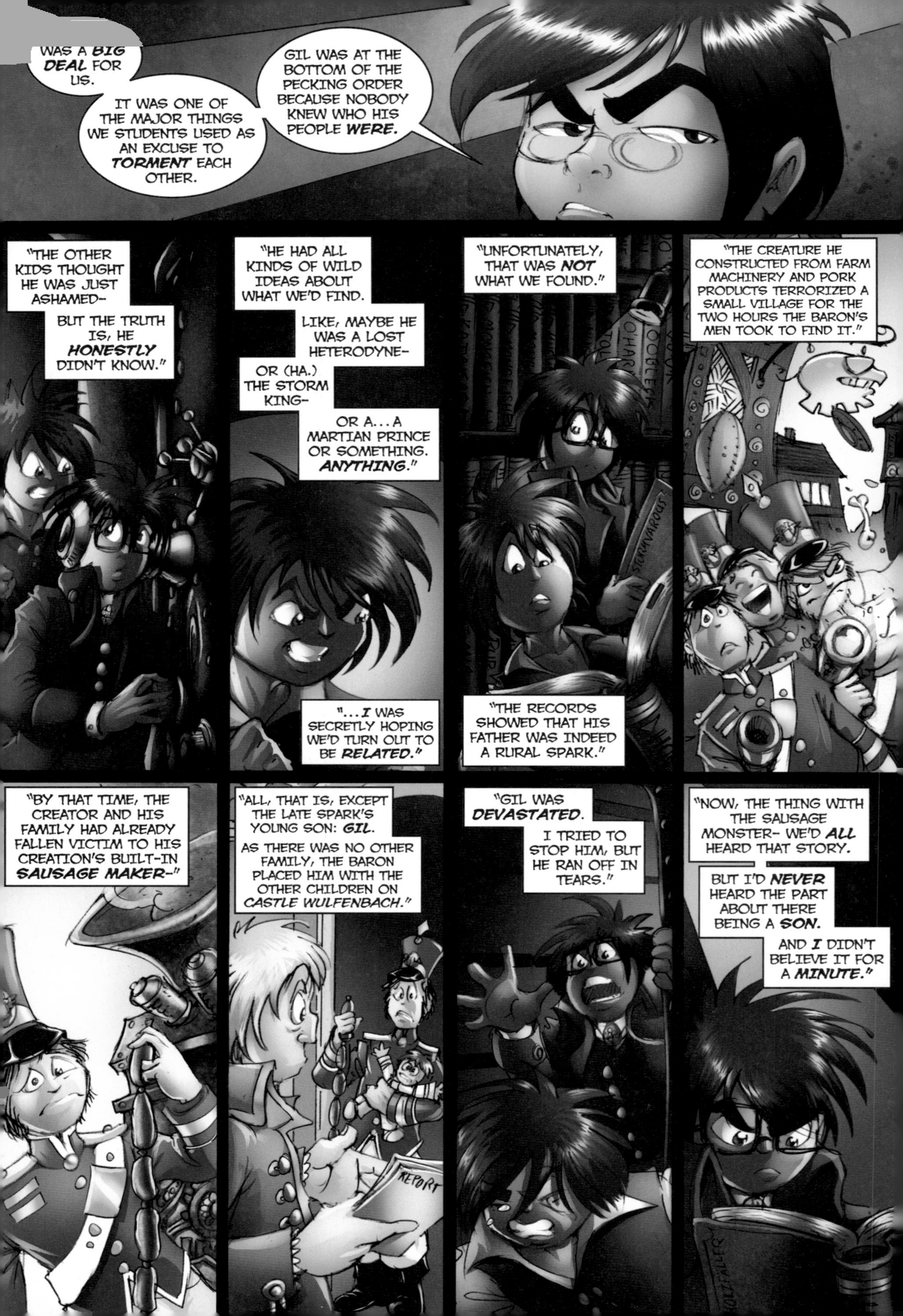

WAS A BIG DEAL FOR US.
IT WAS ONE OF THE MAJOR THINGS WE STUDENTS USED AS AN EXCUSE TO TORMENT EACH OTHER.
GIL WAS AT THE BOTTOM OF THE PECKING ORDER BECAUSE NOBODY KNEW WHO HIS PEOPLE WERE.
"THE OTHER KIDS THOUGHT HE WAS JUST ASHAMED-
BUT THE TRUTH IS, HE HONESTLY DIDN'T KNOW."
"HE HAD ALL KINDS OF WILD IDEAS ABOUT WHAT WE'D FIND.
LIKE, MAYBE HE WAS A LOST HETERODYNE-
OR (HA.) THE STORM KING-
OR A... A MARTIAN PRINCE OR SOMETHING. ANYTHING."
"...I WAS SECRETLY HOPING WE'D TURN OUT TO BE RELATED."
"UNFORTUNATELY, THAT WAS NOT WHAT WE FOUND."
"THE RECORDS SHOWED THAT HIS FATHER WAS INDEED A RURAL SPARK."
"THE CREATURE HE CONSTRUCTED FROM FARM MACHINERY AND PORK PRODUCTS TERRORIZED A SMALL VILLAGE FOR THE TWO HOURS THE BARON'S MEN TOOK TO FIND IT."
"BY THAT TIME, THE CREATOR AND HIS FAMILY HAD ALREADY FALLEN VICTIM TO HIS CREATION'S BUILT-IN SAUSAGE MAKER-"
"ALL, THAT IS, EXCEPT THE LATE SPARK'S YOUNG SON: GIL.
AS THERE WAS NO OTHER FAMILY, THE BARON PLACED HIM WITH THE OTHER CHILDREN ON CASTLE WULFENBACH."
REPORT
"GIL WAS DEVASTATED.
I TRIED TO STOP HIM, BUT HE RAN OFF IN TEARS."
"NOW, THE THING WITH THE SAUSAGE MONSTER- WE'D ALL HEARD THAT STORY.
BUT I'D NEVER HEARD THE PART ABOUT THERE BEING A SON.
AND I DIDN'T BELIEVE IT FOR A MINUTE."

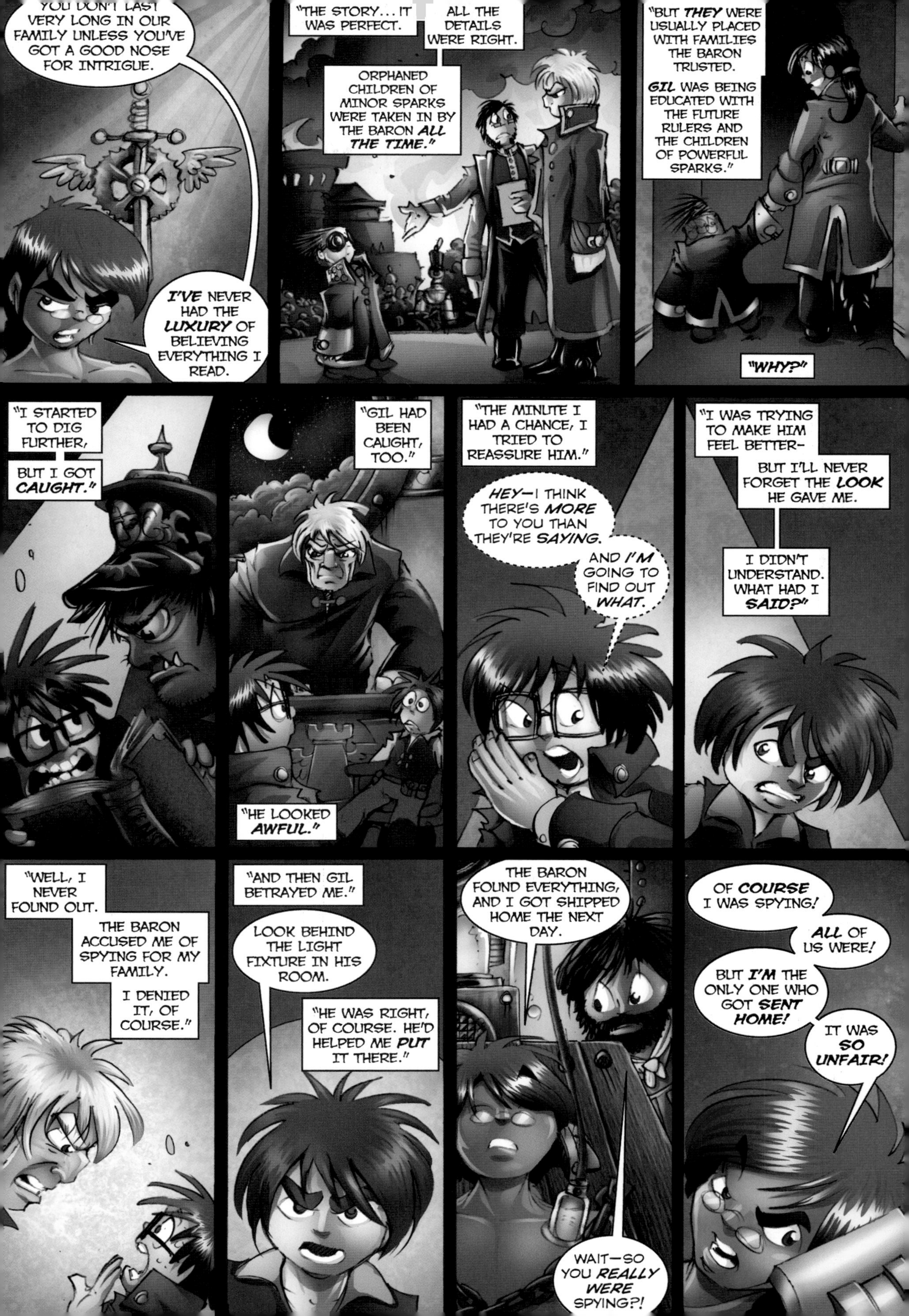
YOU DON'T LAST VERY LONG IN OUR FAMILY UNLESS YOU'VE GOT A GOOD NOSE FOR INTRIGUE.
I'VE NEVER HAD THE LUXURY OF BELIEVING EVERYTHING I READ.
"THE STORY... IT WAS PERFECT.
ALL THE DETAILS WERE RIGHT.
ORPHANED CHILDREN OF MINOR SPARKS WERE TAKEN IN BY THE BARON ALL THE TIME."
"BUT THEY WERE USUALLY PLACED WITH FAMILIES THE BARON TRUSTED.
GIL WAS BEING EDUCATED WITH THE FUTURE RULERS AND THE CHILDREN OF POWERFUL SPARKS."
"WHY?"
"I STARTED TO DIG FURTHER,
BUT I GOT CAUGHT."
"GIL HAD BEEN CAUGHT, TOO."
"HE LOOKED AWFUL."
"THE MINUTE I HAD A CHANCE, I TRIED TO REASSURE HIM."
HEY—I THINK THERE'S MORE TO YOU THAN THEY'RE SAYING.
AND I'M GOING TO FIND OUT WHAT.
"I WAS TRYING TO MAKE HIM FEEL BETTER-
BUT I'LL NEVER FORGET THE LOOK HE GAVE ME.
I DIDN'T UNDERSTAND. WHAT HAD I SAID?"
"WELL, I NEVER FOUND OUT.
THE BARON ACCUSED ME OF SPYING FOR MY FAMILY.
I DENIED IT, OF COURSE."
"AND THEN GIL BETRAYED ME."
LOOK BEHIND THE LIGHT FIXTURE IN HIS ROOM.
"HE WAS RIGHT, OF COURSE. HE'D HELPED ME PUT IT THERE."
THE BARON FOUND EVERYTHING, AND I GOT SHIPPED HOME THE NEXT DAY.
WAIT—SO YOU REALLY WERE SPYING?!
OF COURSE I WAS SPYING!
ALL OF US WERE!
BUT I'M THE ONLY ONE WHO GOT SENT HOME!
IT WAS SO UNFAIR!

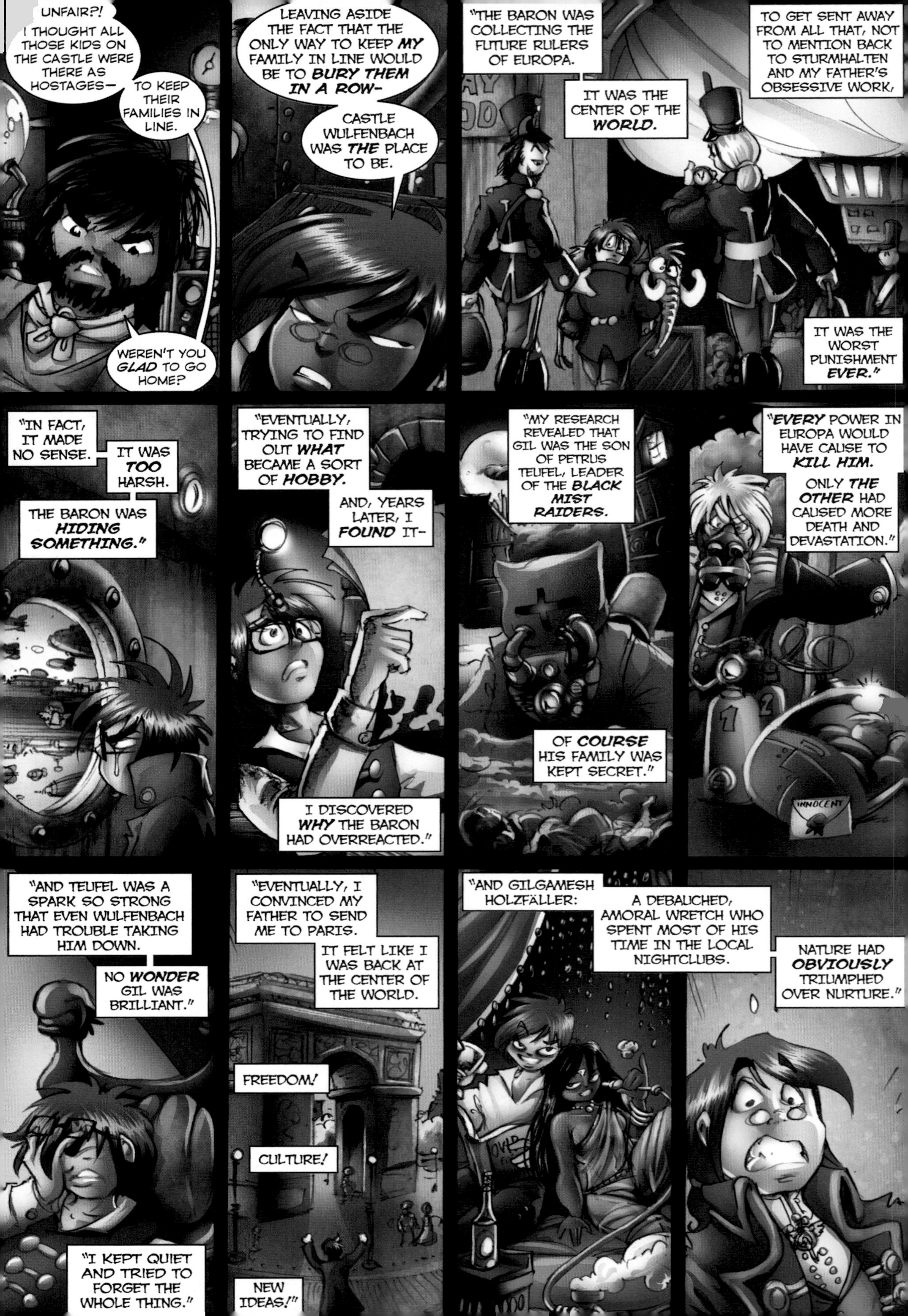
UNFAIR?!
I THOUGHT ALL THOSE KIDS ON THE CASTLE WERE THERE AS HOSTAGES—
TO KEEP THEIR FAMILIES IN LINE.
WEREN'T YOU GLAD TO GO HOME?
LEAVING ASIDE THE FACT THAT THE ONLY WAY TO KEEP MY FAMILY IN LINE WOULD BE TO BURY THEM IN A ROW-
CASTLE WULFENBACH WAS THE PLACE TO BE.
"THE BARON WAS COLLECTING THE FUTURE RULERS OF EUROPA.
IT WAS THE CENTER OF THE WORLD.
TO GET SENT AWAY FROM ALL THAT, NOT TO MENTION BACK TO STURMHALTEN AND MY FATHER'S OBSESSIVE WORK,
IT WAS THE WORST PUNISHMENT EVER."
"IN FACT, IT MADE NO SENSE.
IT WAS TOO HARSH.
THE BARON WAS HIDING SOMETHING."
"EVENTUALLY, TRYING TO FIND OUT WHAT BECAME A SORT OF HOBBY.
AND, YEARS LATER, I FOUND IT-
I DISCOVERED WHY THE BARON HAD OVERREACTED."
"MY RESEARCH REVEALED THAT GIL WAS THE SON OF PETRUS TEUFEL, LEADER OF THE BLACK MIST RAIDERS.
OF COURSE HIS FAMILY WAS KEPT SECRET."
"EVERY POWER IN EUROPA WOULD HAVE CAUSE TO KILL HIM.
ONLY THE OTHER HAD CAUSED MORE DEATH AND DEVASTATION."
INNOCENT
"AND TEUFEL WAS A SPARK SO STRONG THAT EVEN WULFENBACH HAD TROUBLE TAKING HIM DOWN.
NO WONDER GIL WAS BRILLIANT."
"I KEPT QUIET AND TRIED TO FORGET THE WHOLE THING."
"EVENTUALLY, I CONVINCED MY FATHER TO SEND ME TO PARIS.
IT FELT LIKE I WAS BACK AT THE CENTER OF THE WORLD.
FREEDOM!
CULTURE!
NEW IDEAS!"
"AND GILGAMESH HOLZFÄLLER:
A DEBAUCHED, AMORAL WRETCH WHO SPENT MOST OF HIS TIME IN THE LOCAL NIGHTCLUBS.
NATURE HAD OBVIOUSLY TRIUMPHED OVER NURTURE."

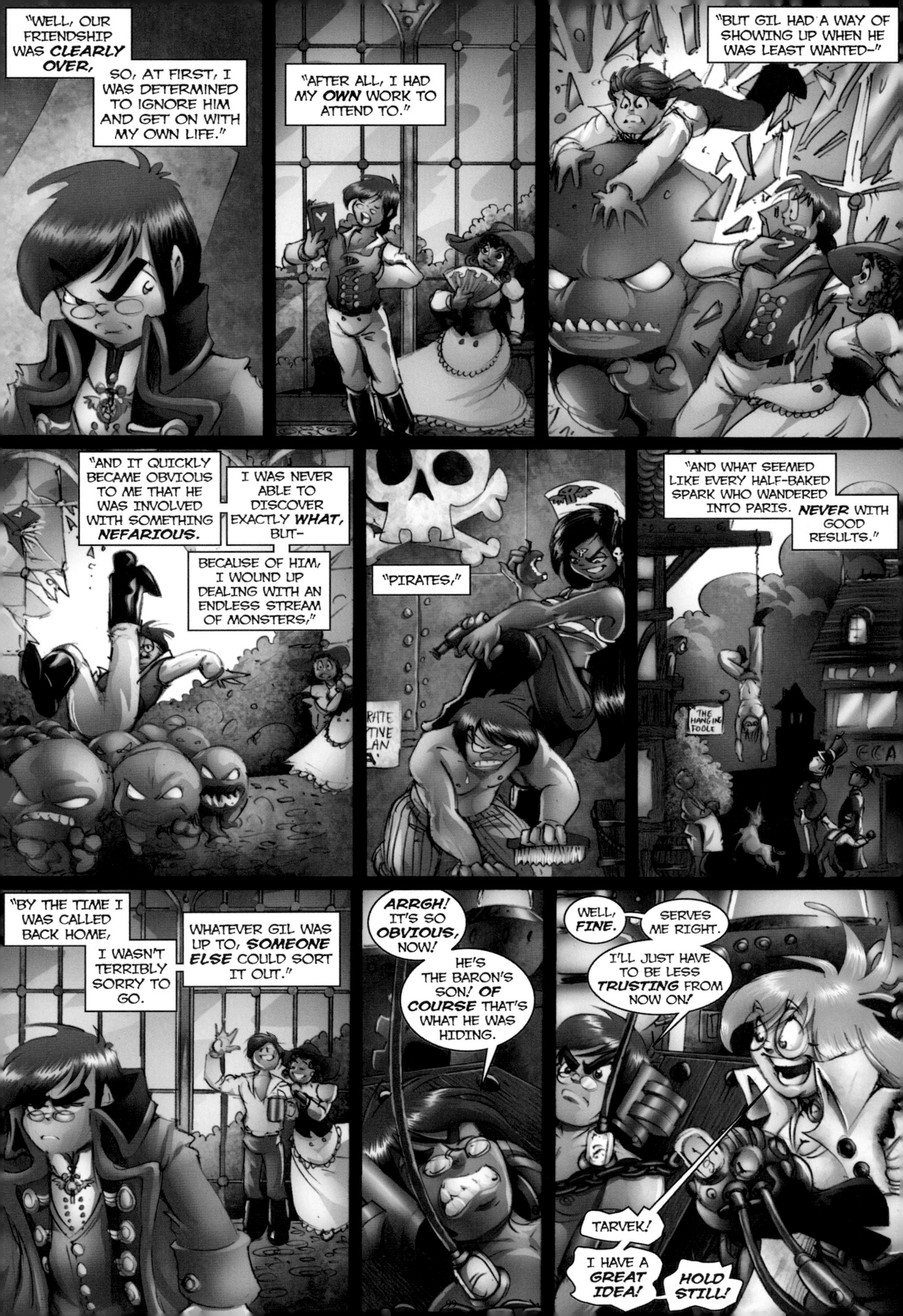

"WELL, OUR FRIENDSHIP WAS **CLEARLY OVER,**
SO, AT FIRST, I WAS DETERMINED TO IGNORE HIM AND GET ON WITH MY OWN LIFE."
"AFTER ALL, I HAD MY **OWN** WORK TO ATTEND TO."
"BUT GIL HAD A WAY OF SHOWING UP WHEN HE WAS LEAST WANTED–"
"AND IT QUICKLY BECAME OBVIOUS TO ME THAT HE WAS INVOLVED WITH SOMETHING **NEFARIOUS.**
I WAS NEVER ABLE TO DISCOVER EXACTLY **WHAT,** BUT–
BECAUSE OF HIM, I WOUND UP DEALING WITH AN ENDLESS STREAM OF MONSTERS,"
"PIRATES,"
"AND WHAT SEEMED LIKE EVERY HALF-BAKED SPARK WHO WANDERED INTO PARIS. **NEVER** WITH GOOD RESULTS."
THE HANGING FOOLE
"BY THE TIME I WAS CALLED BACK HOME,
I WASN'T TERRIBLY SORRY TO GO.
WHATEVER GIL WAS UP TO, **SOMEONE ELSE** COULD SORT IT OUT."
ARRGH! IT'S SO **OBVIOUS,** NOW!
HE'S THE BARON'S SON! **OF COURSE** THAT'S WHAT HE WAS HIDING.
WELL, **FINE.**
SERVES ME RIGHT.
I'LL JUST HAVE TO BE LESS **TRUSTING** FROM NOW ON!
TARVEK!
I HAVE A **GREAT IDEA!**
HOLD STILL!

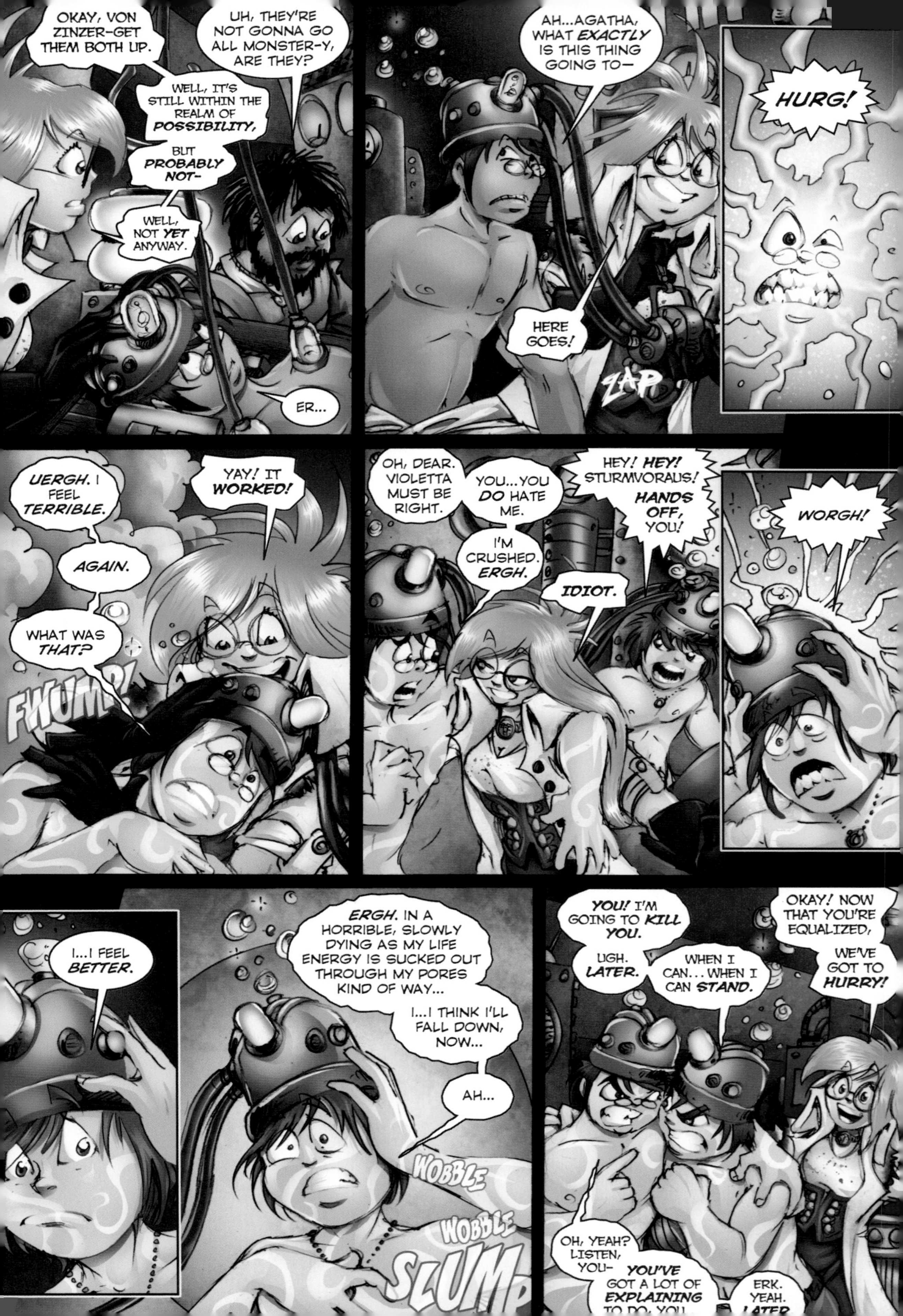

OKAY, VON ZINZER–GET THEM BOTH UP.
UH, THEY'RE NOT GONNA GO ALL MONSTER-Y, ARE THEY?
WELL, IT'S STILL WITHIN THE REALM OF POSSIBILITY,
BUT PROBABLY NOT–
WELL, NOT YET ANYWAY.
ER...
AH...AGATHA, WHAT EXACTLY IS THIS THING GOING TO–
HERE GOES!
ZAP
HURG!
UERGH. I FEEL TERRIBLE.
AGAIN.
WHAT WAS THAT?
YAY! IT WORKED!
FWUMP!
OH, DEAR. VIOLETTA MUST BE RIGHT.
YOU...YOU DO HATE ME.
I'M CRUSHED. ERGH.
HEY! HEY! STURMVORAUS! HANDS OFF, YOU!
IDIOT.
WORGH!
I...I FEEL BETTER.
ERGH. IN A HORRIBLE, SLOWLY DYING AS MY LIFE ENERGY IS SUCKED OUT THROUGH MY PORES KIND OF WAY...
I...I THINK I'LL FALL DOWN, NOW...
AH...
WOBBLE
WOBBLE
SLUMP
YOU! I'M GOING TO KILL YOU.
UGH. LATER.
WHEN I CAN... WHEN I CAN STAND.
OKAY! NOW THAT YOU'RE EQUALIZED,
WE'VE GOT TO HURRY!
OH, YEAH? LISTEN, YOU–
YOU'VE GOT A LOT OF EXPLAINING TO DO, YOU
ERK. YEAH. LATER

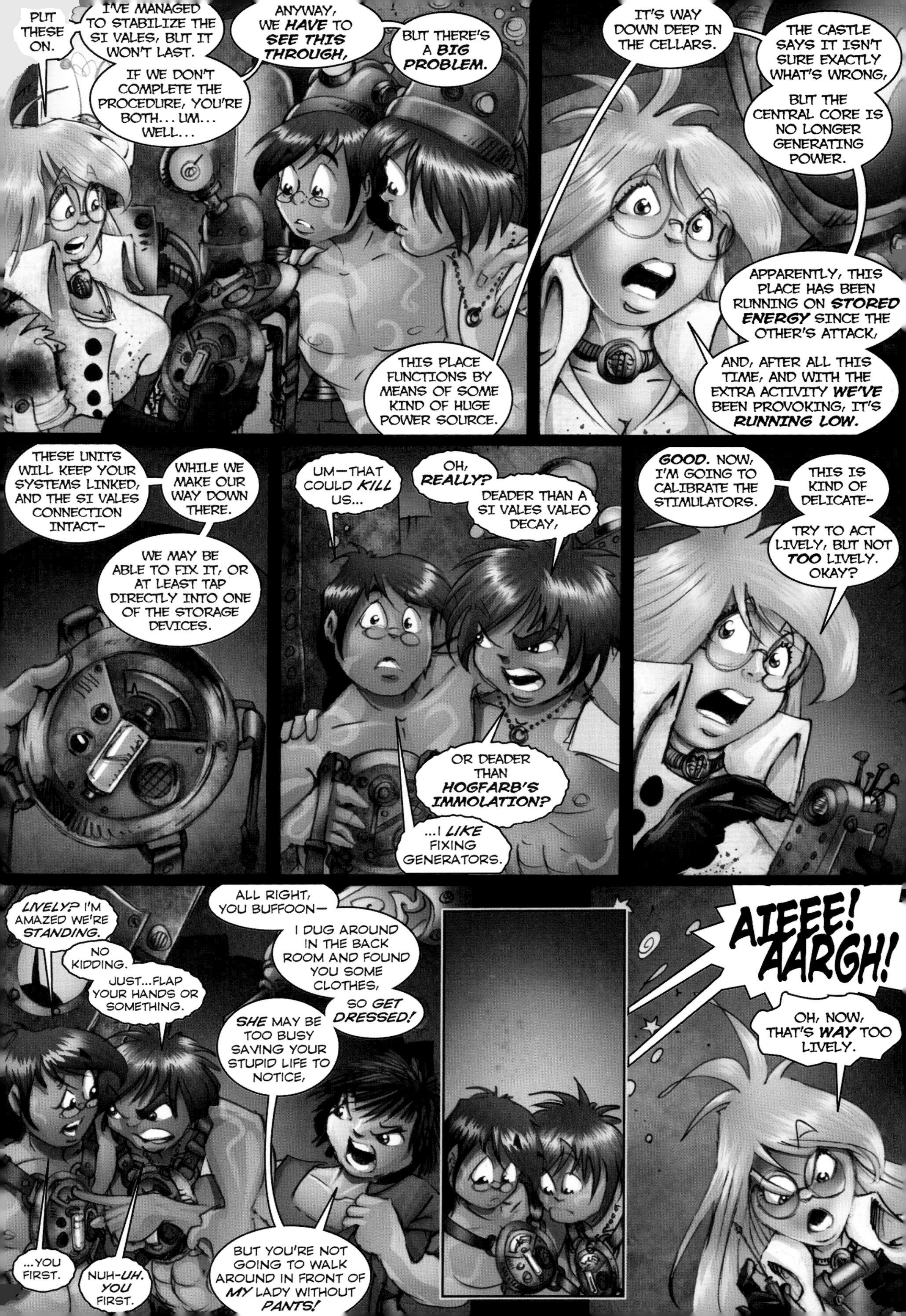

PUT THESE ON.
I'VE MANAGED TO STABILIZE THE SI VALES, BUT IT WON'T LAST.
IF WE DON'T COMPLETE THE PROCEDURE, YOU'RE BOTH... UM... WELL...
ANYWAY, WE HAVE TO SEE THIS THROUGH,
BUT THERE'S A BIG PROBLEM.
THIS PLACE FUNCTIONS BY MEANS OF SOME KIND OF HUGE POWER SOURCE.
IT'S WAY DOWN DEEP IN THE CELLARS.
THE CASTLE SAYS IT ISN'T SURE EXACTLY WHAT'S WRONG,
BUT THE CENTRAL CORE IS NO LONGER GENERATING POWER.
APPARENTLY, THIS PLACE HAS BEEN RUNNING ON STORED ENERGY SINCE THE OTHER'S ATTACK,
AND, AFTER ALL THIS TIME, AND WITH THE EXTRA ACTIVITY WE'VE BEEN PROVOKING, IT'S RUNNING LOW.
THESE UNITS WILL KEEP YOUR SYSTEMS LINKED, AND THE SI VALES CONNECTION INTACT-
WHILE WE MAKE OUR WAY DOWN THERE.
WE MAY BE ABLE TO FIX IT, OR AT LEAST TAP DIRECTLY INTO ONE OF THE STORAGE DEVICES.
UM—THAT COULD KILL US...
OH, REALLY?
DEADER THAN A SI VALES VALEO DECAY,
OR DEADER THAN HOGFARB'S IMMOLATION?
...I LIKE FIXING GENERATORS.
GOOD. NOW, I'M GOING TO CALIBRATE THE STIMULATORS.
THIS IS KIND OF DELICATE-
TRY TO ACT LIVELY, BUT NOT TOO LIVELY. OKAY?
LIVELY? I'M AMAZED WE'RE STANDING.
NO KIDDING.
JUST...FLAP YOUR HANDS OR SOMETHING.
...YOU FIRST.
NUH-UH. YOU FIRST.
ALL RIGHT, YOU BUFFOON—
I DUG AROUND IN THE BACK ROOM AND FOUND YOU SOME CLOTHES,
SO GET DRESSED!
SHE MAY BE TOO BUSY SAVING YOUR STUPID LIFE TO NOTICE,
BUT YOU'RE NOT GOING TO WALK AROUND IN FRONT OF MY LADY WITHOUT PANTS!
AIEEE! AARGH!
OH, NOW, THAT'S WAY TOO LIVELY.

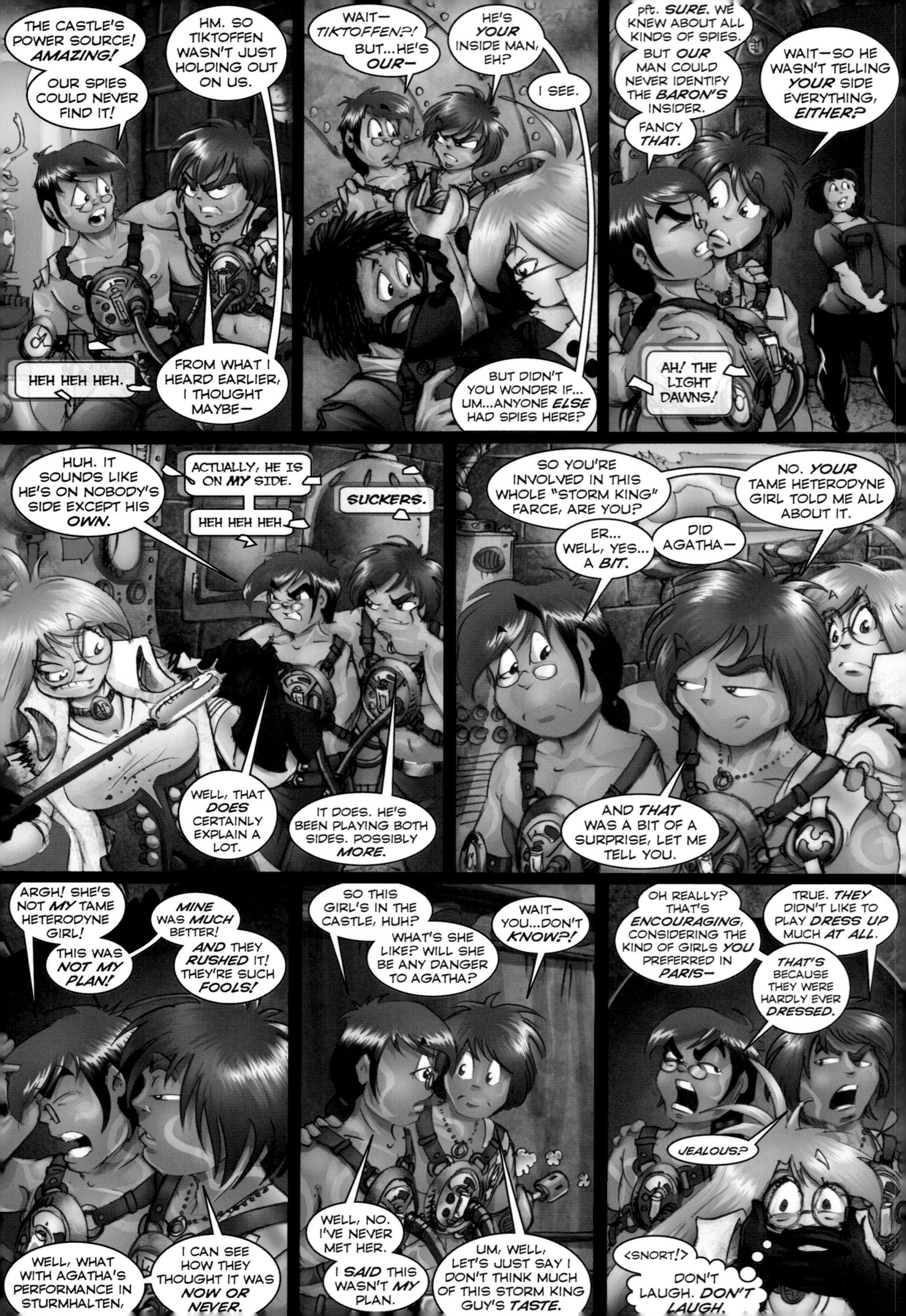
THE CASTLE'S POWER SOURCE! AMAZING!
OUR SPIES COULD NEVER FIND IT!
HM. SO TIKTOFFEN WASN'T JUST HOLDING OUT ON US.
HEH HEH HEH.
FROM WHAT I HEARD EARLIER, I THOUGHT MAYBE—
WAIT— TIKTOFFEN?! BUT...HE'S OUR—
HE'S YOUR INSIDE MAN, EH?
I SEE.
BUT DIDN'T YOU WONDER IF... UM...ANYONE ELSE HAD SPIES HERE?
pft. SURE. WE KNEW ABOUT ALL KINDS OF SPIES.
BUT OUR MAN COULD NEVER IDENTIFY THE BARON'S INSIDER.
FANCY THAT.
WAIT—SO HE WASN'T TELLING YOUR SIDE EVERYTHING, EITHER?
AH! THE LIGHT DAWNS!
HUH. IT SOUNDS LIKE HE'S ON NOBODY'S SIDE EXCEPT HIS OWN.
ACTUALLY, HE IS ON MY SIDE.
HEH HEH HEH.
SUCKERS.
WELL, THAT DOES CERTAINLY EXPLAIN A LOT.
IT DOES. HE'S BEEN PLAYING BOTH SIDES. POSSIBLY MORE.
SO YOU'RE INVOLVED IN THIS WHOLE "STORM KING" FARCE, ARE YOU?
ER... WELL, YES... A BIT.
NO. YOUR TAME HETERODYNE GIRL TOLD ME ALL ABOUT IT.
DID AGATHA—
AND THAT WAS A BIT OF A SURPRISE, LET ME TELL YOU.
ARGH! SHE'S NOT MY TAME HETERODYNE GIRL!
THIS WAS NOT MY PLAN!
MINE WAS MUCH BETTER!
AND THEY RUSHED IT! THEY'RE SUCH FOOLS!
WELL, WHAT WITH AGATHA'S PERFORMANCE IN STURMHALTEN,
I CAN SEE HOW THEY THOUGHT IT WAS NOW OR NEVER.
SO THIS GIRL'S IN THE CASTLE, HUH?
WHAT'S SHE LIKE? WILL SHE BE ANY DANGER TO AGATHA?
WAIT— YOU...DON'T KNOW?!
WELL, NO. I'VE NEVER MET HER.
I SAID THIS WASN'T MY PLAN.
UM, WELL, LET'S JUST SAY I DON'T THINK MUCH OF THIS STORM KING GUY'S TASTE.
OH REALLY? THAT'S ENCOURAGING, CONSIDERING THE KIND OF GIRLS YOU PREFERRED IN PARIS—
TRUE. THEY DIDN'T LIKE TO PLAY DRESS UP MUCH AT ALL.
THAT'S BECAUSE THEY WERE HARDLY EVER DRESSED.
JEALOUS?
<SNORT!>
DON'T LAUGH. DON'T LAUGH.

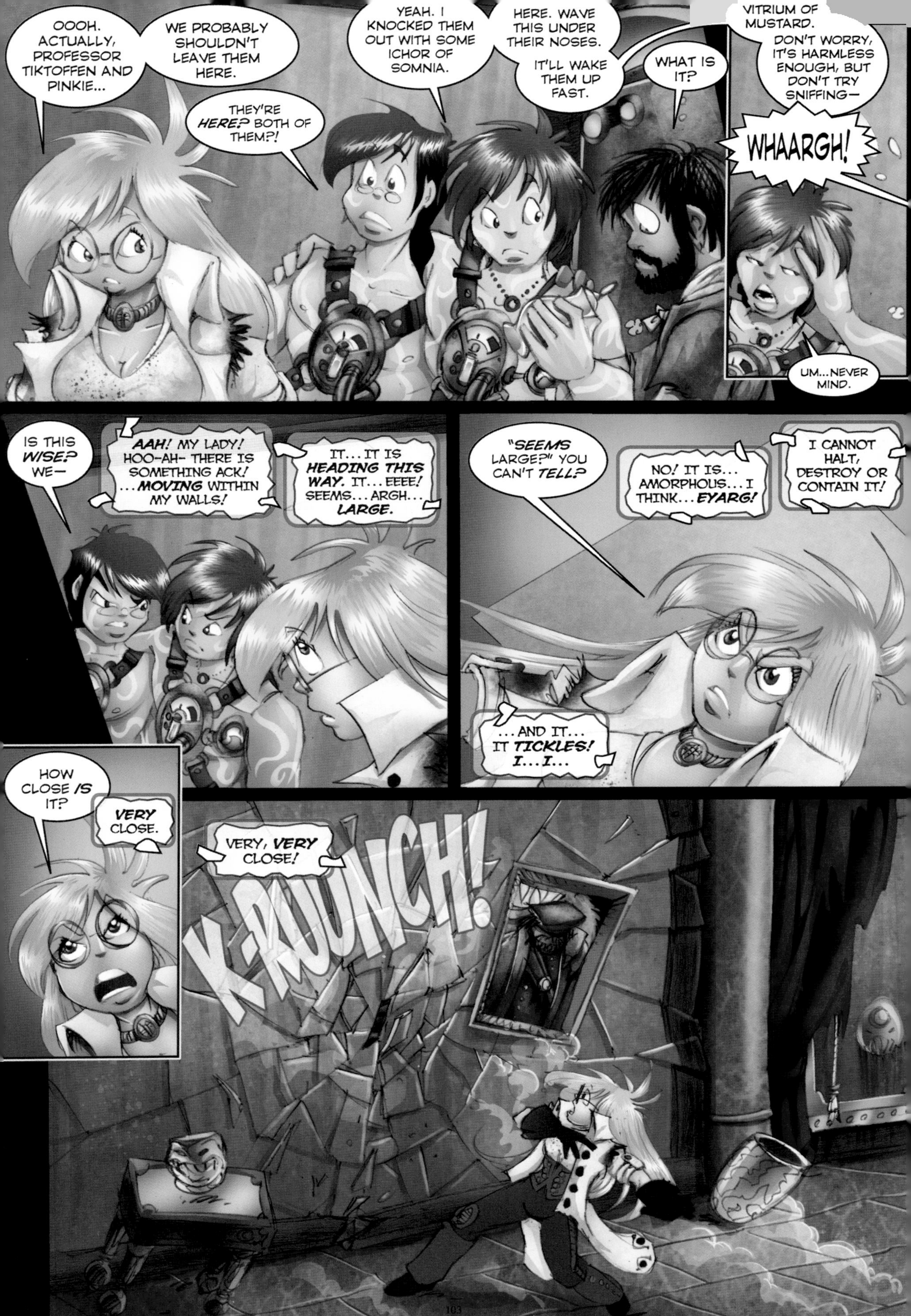
OOOH. ACTUALLY, PROFESSOR TIKTOFFEN AND PINKIE...
WE PROBABLY SHOULDN'T LEAVE THEM HERE.
THEY'RE *HERE?* BOTH OF THEM?!
YEAH. I KNOCKED THEM OUT WITH SOME ICHOR OF SOMNIA.
HERE. WAVE THIS UNDER THEIR NOSES.
IT'LL WAKE THEM UP FAST.
WHAT IS IT?
VITRIUM OF MUSTARD.
DON'T WORRY, IT'S HARMLESS ENOUGH, BUT DON'T TRY SNIFFING—
WHAARGH!
UM...NEVER MIND.
IS THIS *WISE?* WE—
AAH! MY LADY! HOO-AH- THERE IS SOMETHING ACK! ...*MOVING* WITHIN MY WALLS!
IT... IT IS *HEADING THIS WAY.* IT... EEEE! SEEMS... ARGH... *LARGE.*
"*SEEMS* LARGE?" YOU CAN'T *TELL?*
NO! IT IS... AMORPHOUS... I THINK... *EYARG!*
I CANNOT HALT, DESTROY OR CONTAIN IT!
...AND IT... IT *TICKLES! I... I...*
HOW CLOSE *IS* IT?
VERY CLOSE.
VERY, *VERY* CLOSE!
K-RUUNCH!

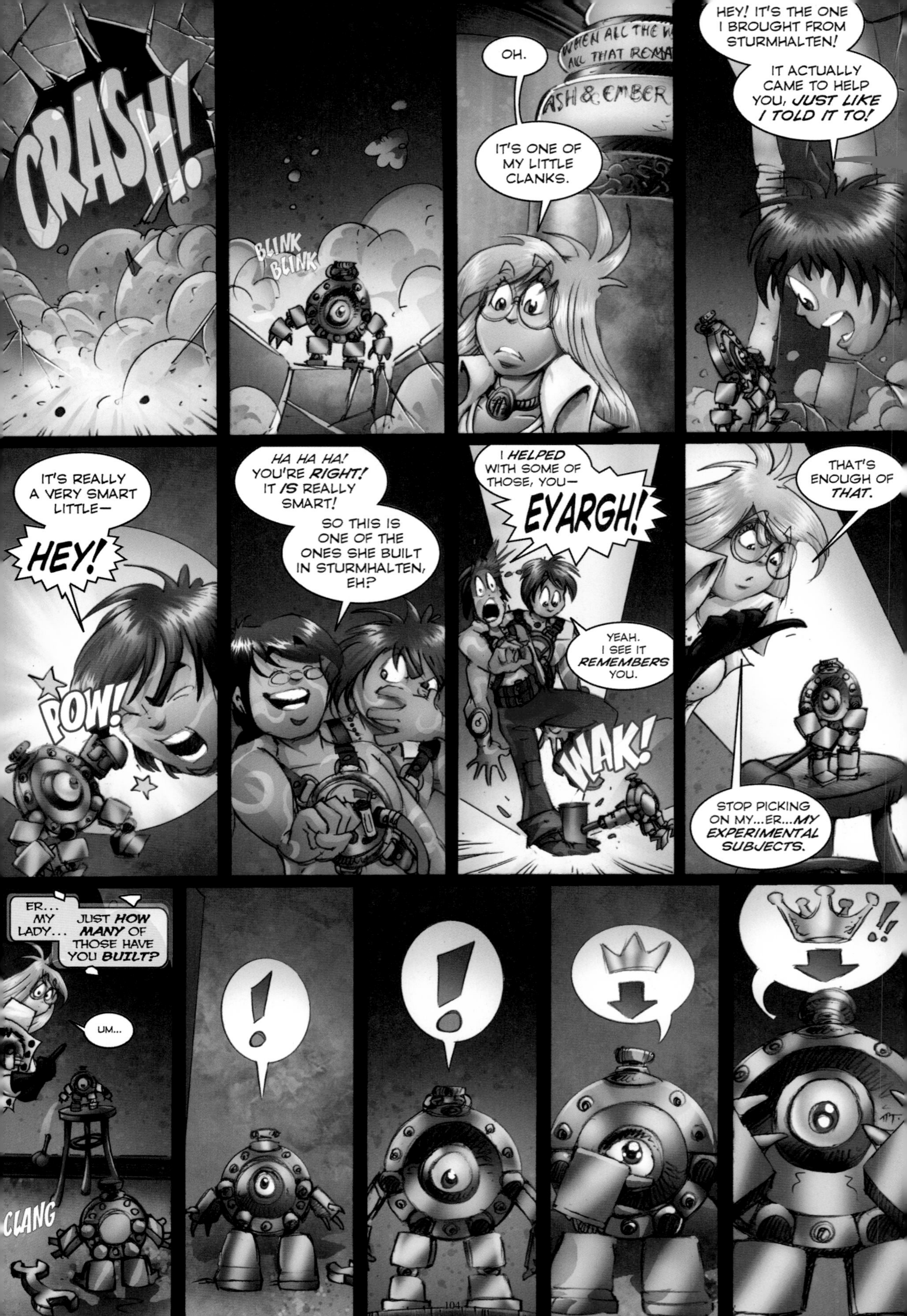

CRASH!
BLINK BLINK
OH.
IT'S ONE OF MY LITTLE CLANKS.
HEY! IT'S THE ONE I BROUGHT FROM STURMHALTEN!
IT ACTUALLY CAME TO HELP YOU, JUST LIKE I TOLD IT TO!
IT'S REALLY A VERY SMART LITTLE—
HEY!
POW!
HA HA HA! YOU'RE RIGHT! IT IS REALLY SMART!
SO THIS IS ONE OF THE ONES SHE BUILT IN STURMHALTEN, EH?
I HELPED WITH SOME OF THOSE, YOU—
EYARGH!
YEAH. I SEE IT REMEMBERS YOU.
WAK!
THAT'S ENOUGH OF THAT.
STOP PICKING ON MY...ER...MY EXPERIMENTAL SUBJECTS.
ER... MY LADY...
JUST HOW MANY OF THOSE HAVE YOU BUILT?
UM...
CLANG
!
!
!!

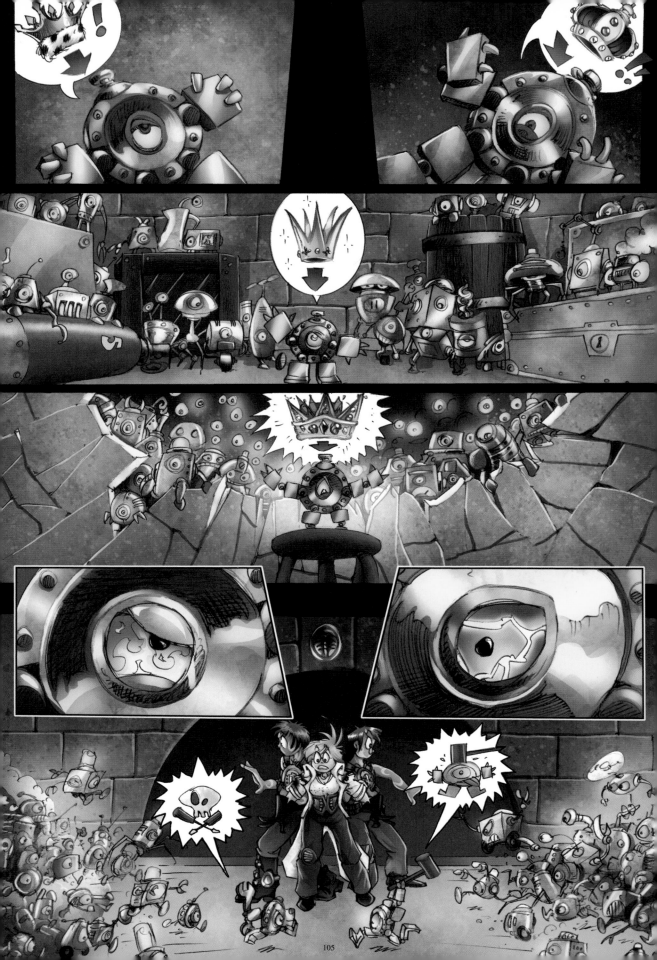

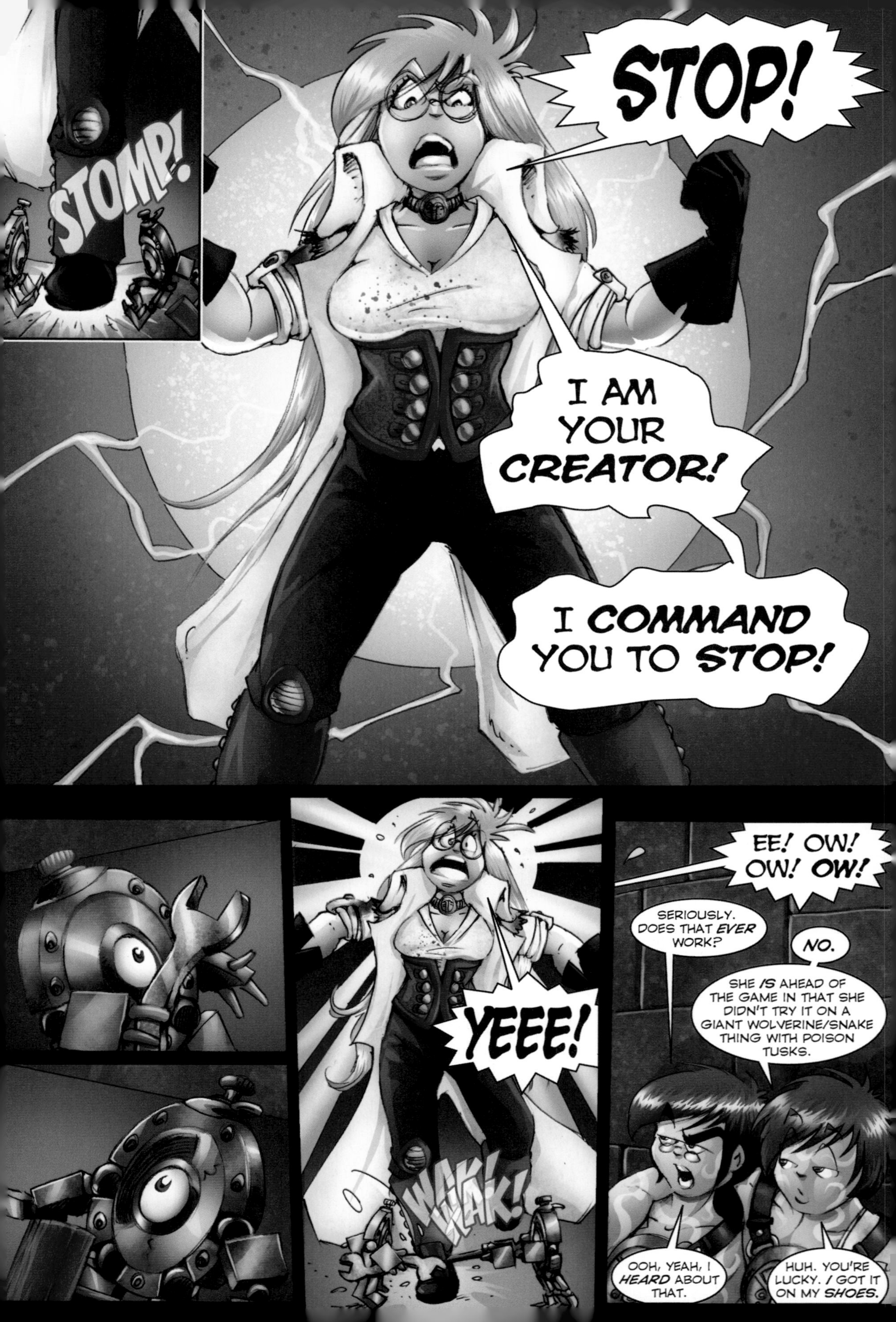
STOMP!
STOP!
I AM YOUR CREATOR!
I COMMAND YOU TO STOP!
YEEE!
WHAK!
EE! OW! OW! OW!
SERIOUSLY. DOES THAT EVER WORK?
NO.
SHE IS AHEAD OF THE GAME IN THAT SHE DIDN'T TRY IT ON A GIANT WOLVERINE/SNAKE THING WITH POISON TUSKS.
OOH, YEAH, I HEARD ABOUT THAT.
HUH. YOU'RE LUCKY. I GOT IT ON MY SHOES.

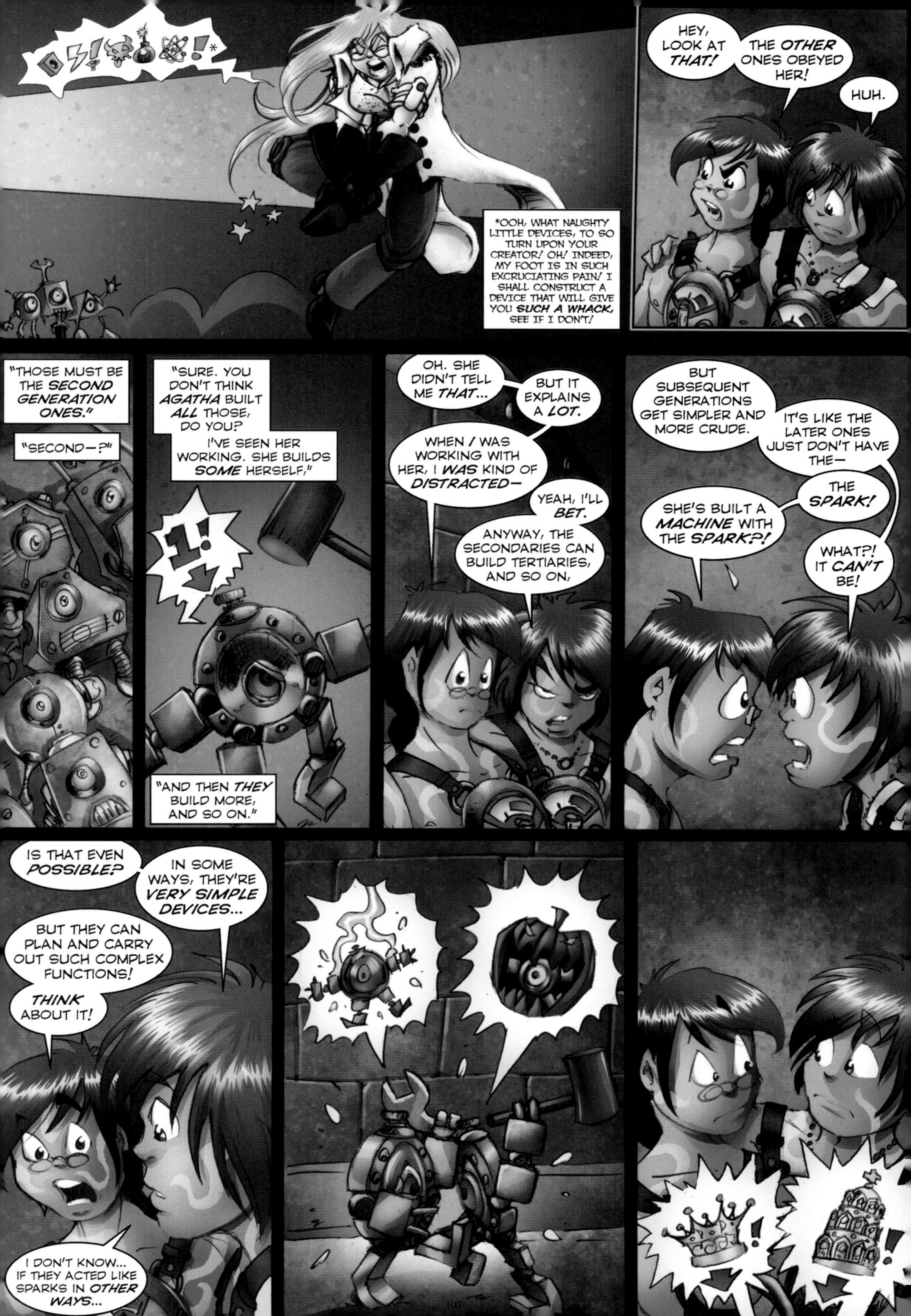
!*
*OOH, WHAT NAUGHTY LITTLE DEVICES, TO SO TURN UPON YOUR CREATOR! OH! INDEED, MY FOOT IS IN SUCH EXCRUCIATING PAIN! I SHALL CONSTRUCT A DEVICE THAT WILL GIVE YOU SUCH A WHACK, SEE IF I DON'T!
HEY, LOOK AT THAT!
THE OTHER ONES OBEYED HER!
HUH.
"THOSE MUST BE THE SECOND GENERATION ONES."
"SECOND—?"
"SURE. YOU DON'T THINK AGATHA BUILT ALL THOSE, DO YOU?
I'VE SEEN HER WORKING. SHE BUILDS SOME HERSELF,"
1!
"AND THEN THEY BUILD MORE, AND SO ON."
OH. SHE DIDN'T TELL ME THAT...
BUT IT EXPLAINS A LOT.
WHEN I WAS WORKING WITH HER, I WAS KIND OF DISTRACTED—
YEAH, I'LL BET.
ANYWAY, THE SECONDARIES CAN BUILD TERTIARIES, AND SO ON,
BUT SUBSEQUENT GENERATIONS GET SIMPLER AND MORE CRUDE.
IT'S LIKE THE LATER ONES JUST DON'T HAVE THE—
THE SPARK!
SHE'S BUILT A MACHINE WITH THE SPARK?!
WHAT?! IT CAN'T BE!
IS THAT EVEN POSSIBLE?
IN SOME WAYS, THEY'RE VERY SIMPLE DEVICES...
BUT THEY CAN PLAN AND CARRY OUT SUCH COMPLEX FUNCTIONS!
THINK ABOUT IT!
I DON'T KNOW... IF THEY ACTED LIKE SPARKS IN OTHER WAYS...
!
!

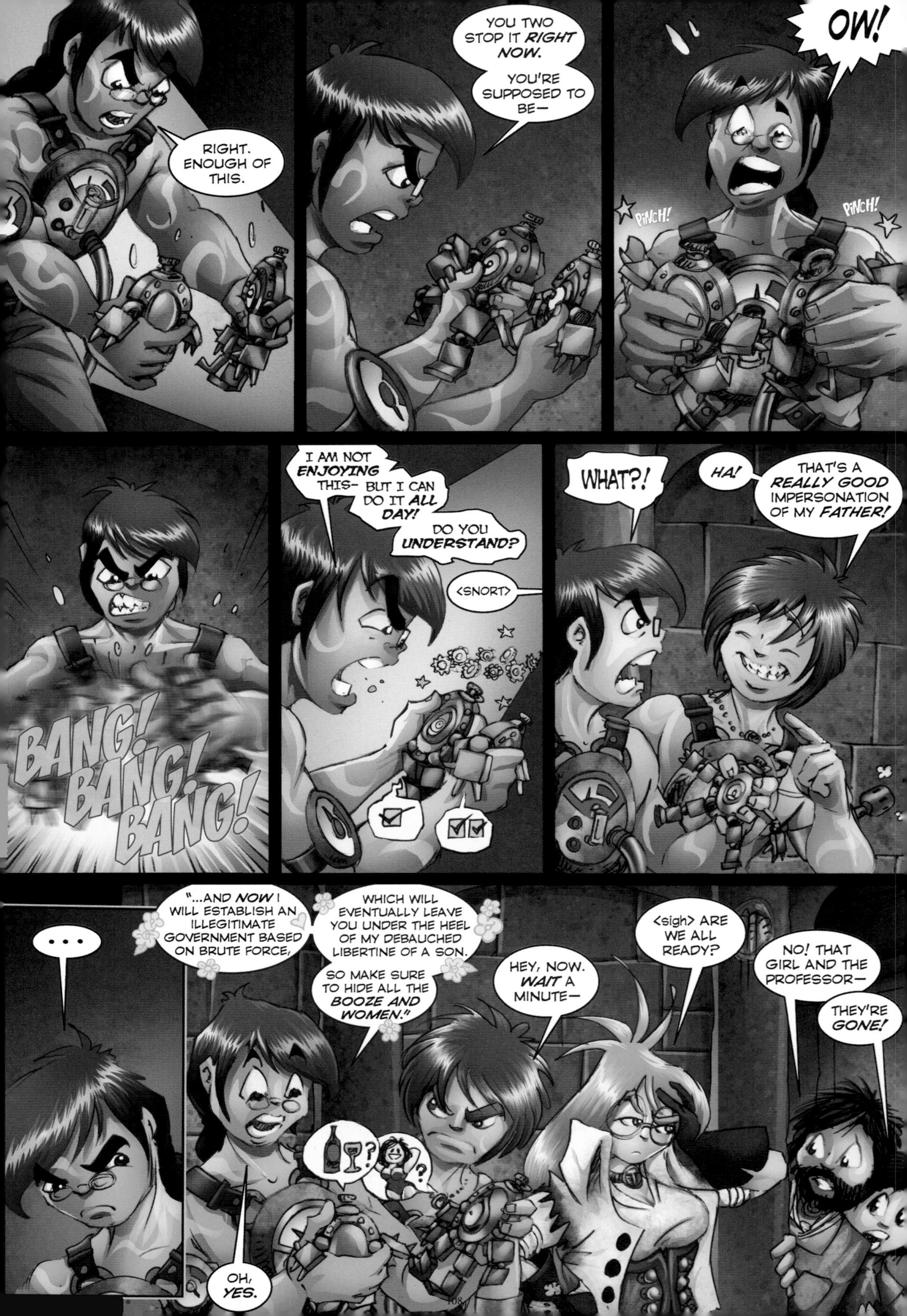
RIGHT. ENOUGH OF THIS.
YOU TWO STOP IT RIGHT NOW.
YOU'RE SUPPOSED TO BE—
OW!
PINCH!
PINCH!
BANG! BANG! BANG!
I AM NOT ENJOYING THIS-
BUT I CAN DO IT ALL DAY!
DO YOU UNDERSTAND?
<SNORT>
WHAT?!
HA!
THAT'S A REALLY GOOD IMPERSONATION OF MY FATHER!
. . .
"...AND NOW I WILL ESTABLISH AN ILLEGITIMATE GOVERNMENT BASED ON BRUTE FORCE,
WHICH WILL EVENTUALLY LEAVE YOU UNDER THE HEEL OF MY DEBAUCHED LIBERTINE OF A SON.
SO MAKE SURE TO HIDE ALL THE BOOZE AND WOMEN."
OH, YES.
HEY, NOW. WAIT A MINUTE—
<sigh> ARE WE ALL READY?
NO! THAT GIRL AND THE PROFESSOR—
THEY'RE GONE!

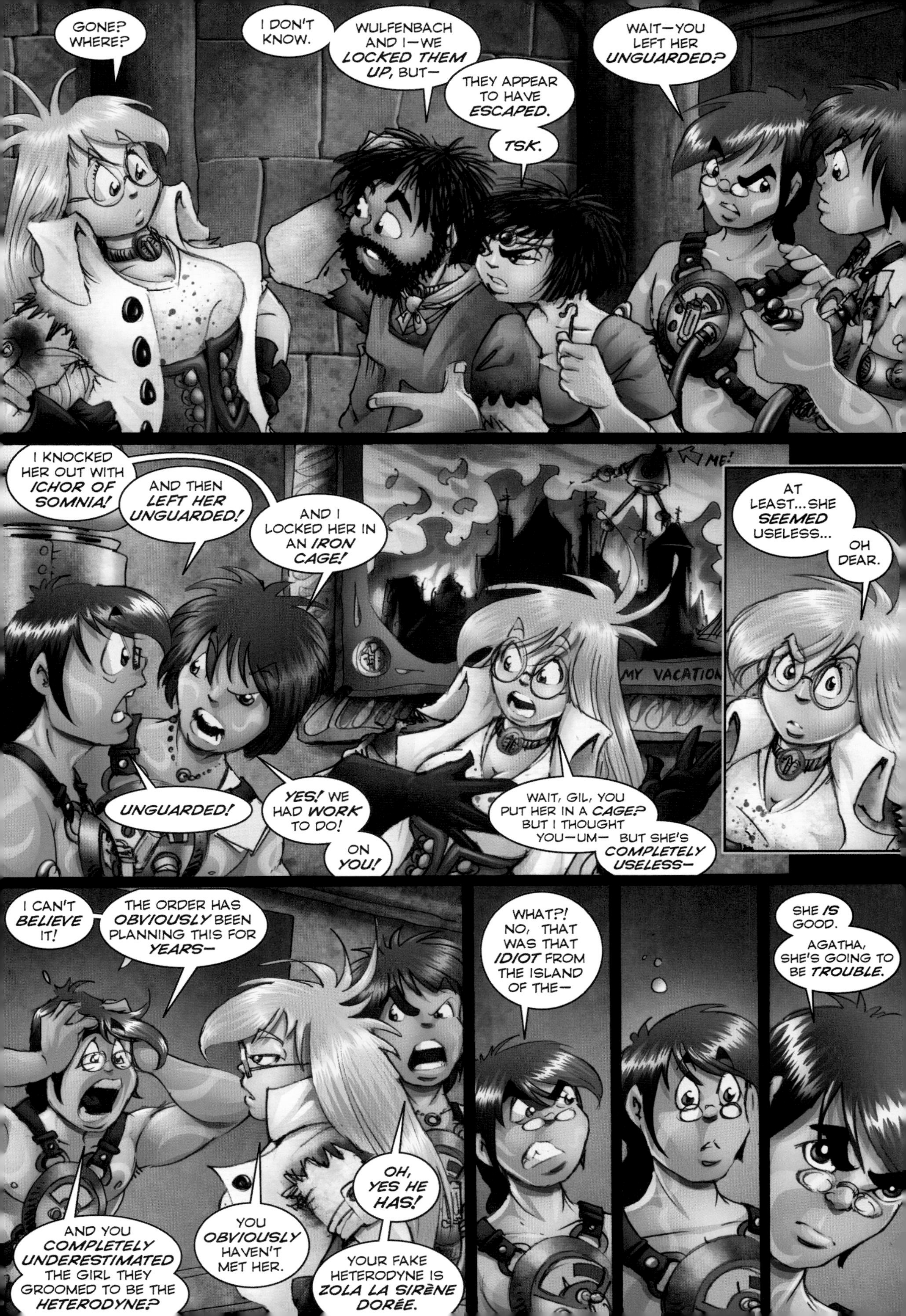
GONE? WHERE?
I DON'T KNOW.
WULFENBACH AND I—WE LOCKED THEM UP, BUT—
THEY APPEAR TO HAVE ESCAPED.
TSK.
WAIT—YOU LEFT HER UNGUARDED?
I KNOCKED HER OUT WITH ICHOR OF SOMNIA!
AND THEN LEFT HER UNGUARDED!
AND I LOCKED HER IN AN IRON CAGE!
ME!
MY VACATION
UNGUARDED!
YES! WE HAD WORK TO DO!
ON YOU!
WAIT, GIL, YOU PUT HER IN A CAGE? BUT I THOUGHT YOU—UM— BUT SHE'S COMPLETELY USELESS—
AT LEAST...SHE SEEMED USELESS...
OH DEAR.
I CAN'T BELIEVE IT!
THE ORDER HAS OBVIOUSLY BEEN PLANNING THIS FOR YEARS—
AND YOU COMPLETELY UNDERESTIMATED THE GIRL THEY GROOMED TO BE THE HETERODYNE?
YOU OBVIOUSLY HAVEN'T MET HER.
OH, YES HE HAS!
YOUR FAKE HETERODYNE IS ZOLA LA SIRÈNE DORÉE.
WHAT?! NO, THAT WAS THAT IDIOT FROM THE ISLAND OF THE—
SHE IS GOOD.
AGATHA, SHE'S GOING TO BE TROUBLE.

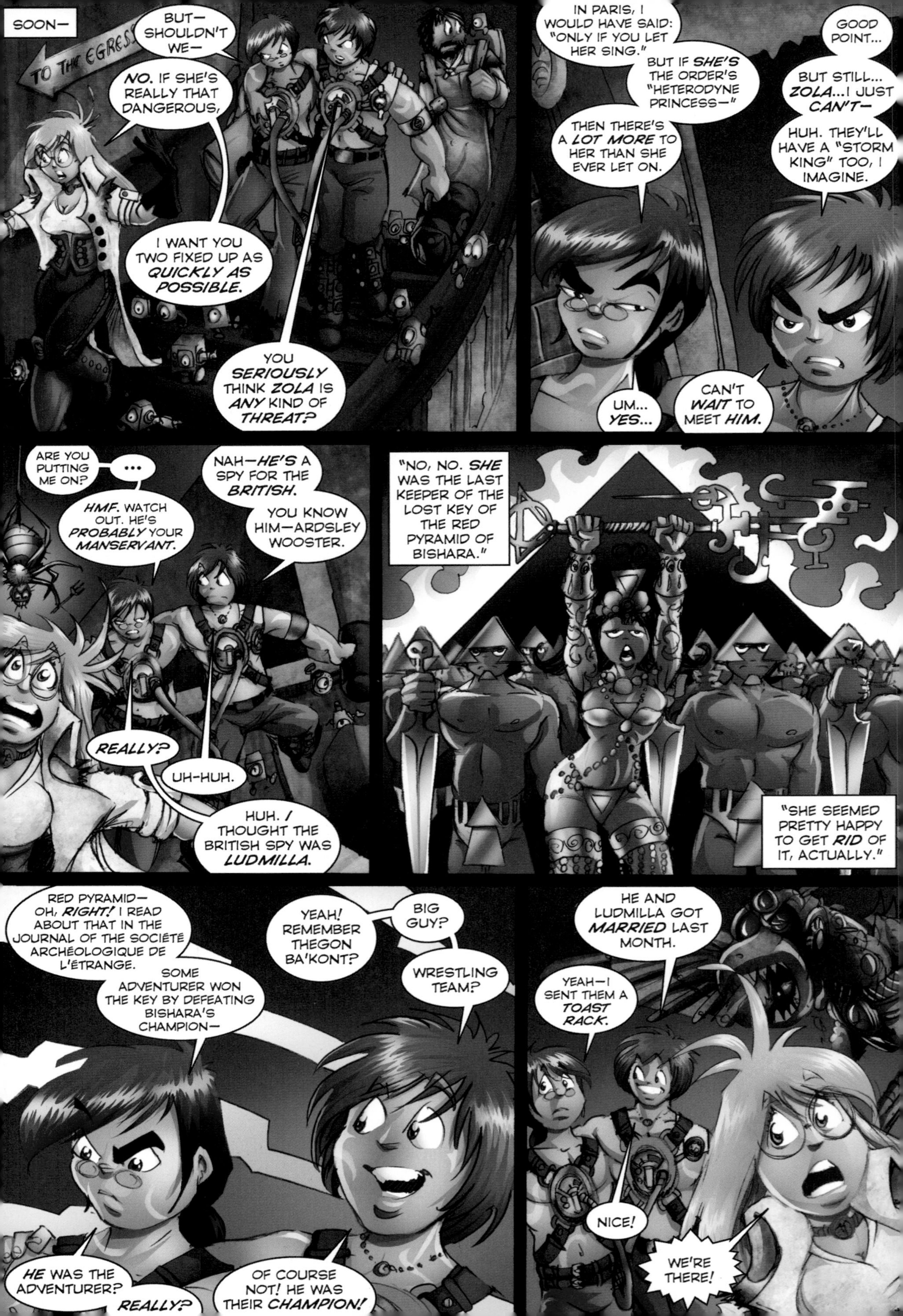
SOON—
TO THE EGRESS
BUT— SHOULDN'T WE—
NO. IF SHE'S REALLY THAT DANGEROUS,
I WANT YOU TWO FIXED UP AS QUICKLY AS POSSIBLE.
YOU SERIOUSLY THINK ZOLA IS ANY KIND OF THREAT?
UM... YES...
IN PARIS, I WOULD HAVE SAID: "ONLY IF YOU LET HER SING."
BUT IF SHE'S THE ORDER'S "HETERODYNE PRINCESS—"
THEN THERE'S A LOT MORE TO HER THAN SHE EVER LET ON.
GOOD POINT...
BUT STILL... ZOLA...I JUST CAN'T—
HUH. THEY'LL HAVE A "STORM KING" TOO, I IMAGINE.
CAN'T WAIT TO MEET HIM.
ARE YOU PUTTING ME ON?
...
HMF. WATCH OUT. HE'S PROBABLY YOUR MANSERVANT.
NAH—HE'S A SPY FOR THE BRITISH.
YOU KNOW HIM—ARDSLEY WOOSTER.
REALLY?
UH-HUH.
HUH. I THOUGHT THE BRITISH SPY WAS LUDMILLA.
"NO, NO. SHE WAS THE LAST KEEPER OF THE LOST KEY OF THE RED PYRAMID OF BISHARA."
"SHE SEEMED PRETTY HAPPY TO GET RID OF IT, ACTUALLY."
RED PYRAMID— OH, RIGHT! I READ ABOUT THAT IN THE JOURNAL OF THE SOCIÉTÉ ARCHÉOLOGIQUE DE L'ÉTRANGE.
SOME ADVENTURER WON THE KEY BY DEFEATING BISHARA'S CHAMPION—
YEAH! REMEMBER THEGON BA'KONT?
BIG GUY?
WRESTLING TEAM?
HE WAS THE ADVENTURER? REALLY?
OF COURSE NOT! HE WAS THEIR CHAMPION!
HE AND LUDMILLA GOT MARRIED LAST MONTH.
YEAH—I SENT THEM A TOAST RACK.
NICE!
WE'RE THERE!

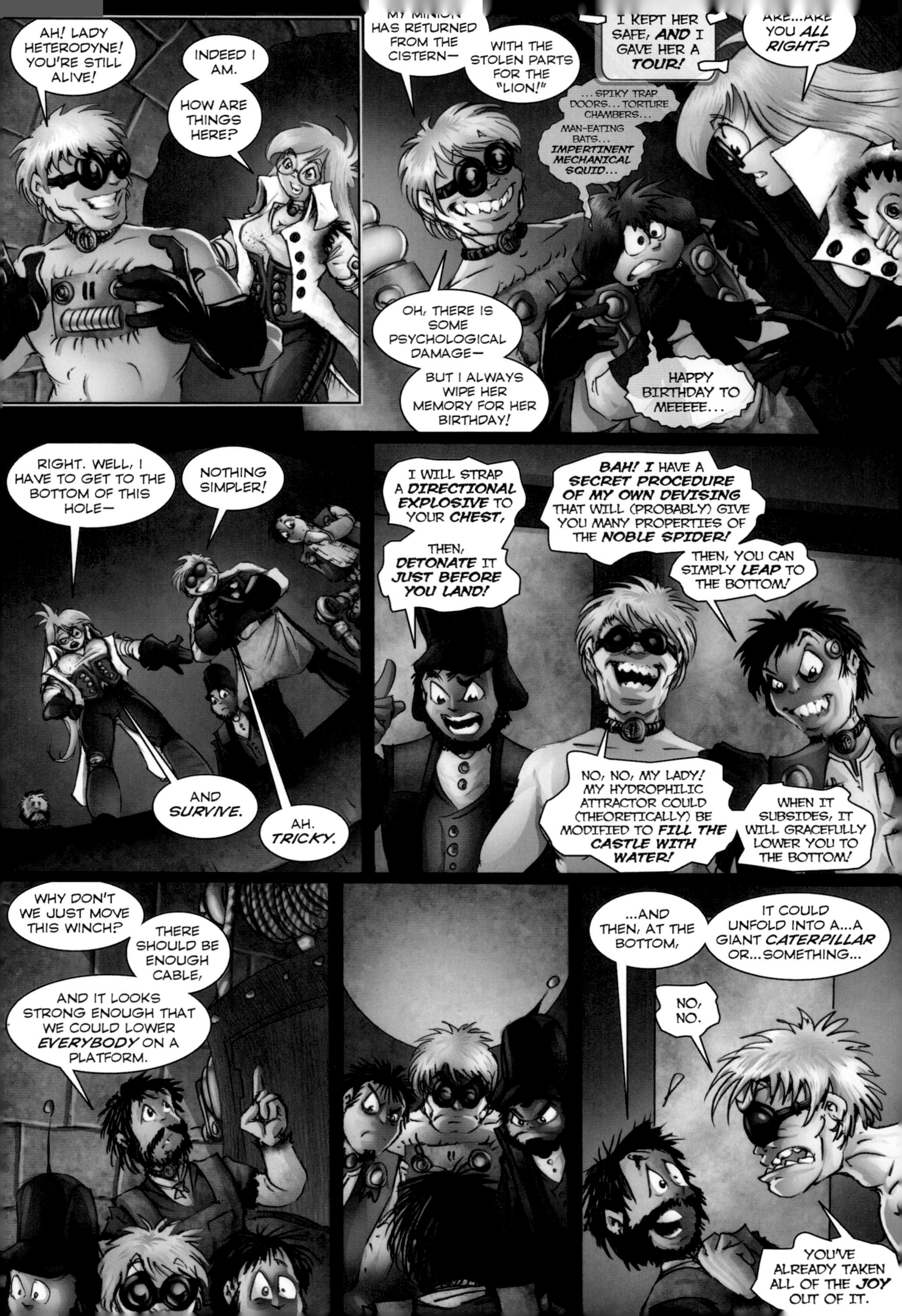
AH! LADY HETERODYNE! YOU'RE STILL ALIVE!
INDEED I AM.
HOW ARE THINGS HERE?
MY MINION HAS RETURNED FROM THE CISTERN—
WITH THE STOLEN PARTS FOR THE "LION!"
OH, THERE IS SOME PSYCHOLOGICAL DAMAGE—
BUT I ALWAYS WIPE HER MEMORY FOR HER BIRTHDAY!
I KEPT HER SAFE, AND I GAVE HER A TOUR!
...SPIKY TRAP DOORS... TORTURE CHAMBERS...
MAN-EATING BATS...
IMPERTINENT MECHANICAL SQUID...
ARE...ARE YOU ALL RIGHT?
HAPPY BIRTHDAY TO MEEEEE...
RIGHT. WELL, I HAVE TO GET TO THE BOTTOM OF THIS HOLE—
NOTHING SIMPLER!
AND SURVIVE.
AH. TRICKY.
I WILL STRAP A DIRECTIONAL EXPLOSIVE TO YOUR CHEST,
THEN, DETONATE IT JUST BEFORE YOU LAND!
BAH! I HAVE A SECRET PROCEDURE OF MY OWN DEVISING THAT WILL (PROBABLY) GIVE YOU MANY PROPERTIES OF THE NOBLE SPIDER!
THEN, YOU CAN SIMPLY LEAP TO THE BOTTOM!
NO, NO, MY LADY! MY HYDROPHILIC ATTRACTOR COULD (THEORETICALLY) BE MODIFIED TO FILL THE CASTLE WITH WATER!
WHEN IT SUBSIDES, IT WILL GRACEFULLY LOWER YOU TO THE BOTTOM!
WHY DON'T WE JUST MOVE THIS WINCH?
THERE SHOULD BE ENOUGH CABLE,
AND IT LOOKS STRONG ENOUGH THAT WE COULD LOWER EVERYBODY ON A PLATFORM.
...AND THEN, AT THE BOTTOM,
IT COULD UNFOLD INTO A...A GIANT CATERPILLAR OR...SOMETHING...
NO, NO.
YOU'VE ALREADY TAKEN ALL OF THE JOY OUT OF IT.

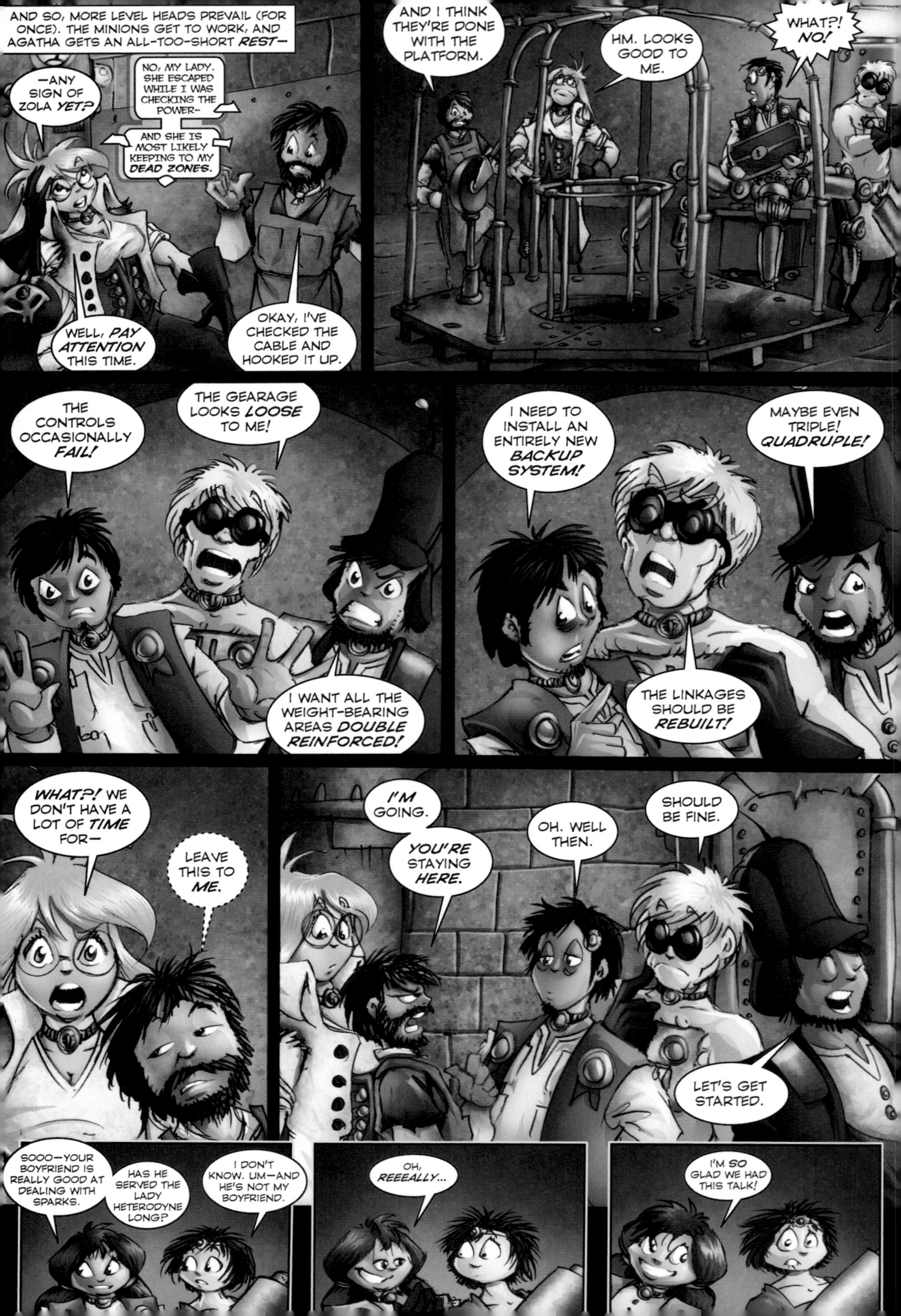
AND SO, MORE LEVEL HEADS PREVAIL (FOR ONCE). THE MINIONS GET TO WORK, AND AGATHA GETS AN ALL-TOO-SHORT REST—
—ANY SIGN OF ZOLA YET?
NO, MY LADY. SHE ESCAPED WHILE I WAS CHECKING THE POWER-
AND SHE IS MOST LIKELY KEEPING TO MY DEAD ZONES.
WELL, PAY ATTENTION THIS TIME.
OKAY, I'VE CHECKED THE CABLE AND HOOKED IT UP.
AND I THINK THEY'RE DONE WITH THE PLATFORM.
HM. LOOKS GOOD TO ME.
WHAT?! NO!
THE CONTROLS OCCASIONALLY FAIL!
THE GEARAGE LOOKS LOOSE TO ME!
I WANT ALL THE WEIGHT-BEARING AREAS DOUBLE REINFORCED!
I NEED TO INSTALL AN ENTIRELY NEW BACKUP SYSTEM!
MAYBE EVEN TRIPLE! QUADRUPLE!
THE LINKAGES SHOULD BE REBUILT!
WHAT?! WE DON'T HAVE A LOT OF TIME FOR—
LEAVE THIS TO ME.
I'M GOING.
YOU'RE STAYING HERE.
OH. WELL THEN.
SHOULD BE FINE.
LET'S GET STARTED.
SOOO—YOUR BOYFRIEND IS REALLY GOOD AT DEALING WITH SPARKS.
HAS HE SERVED THE LADY HETERODYNE LONG?
I DON'T KNOW. UM—AND HE'S NOT MY BOYFRIEND.
OH, REEEALLY...
I'M SO GLAD WE HAD THIS TALK!

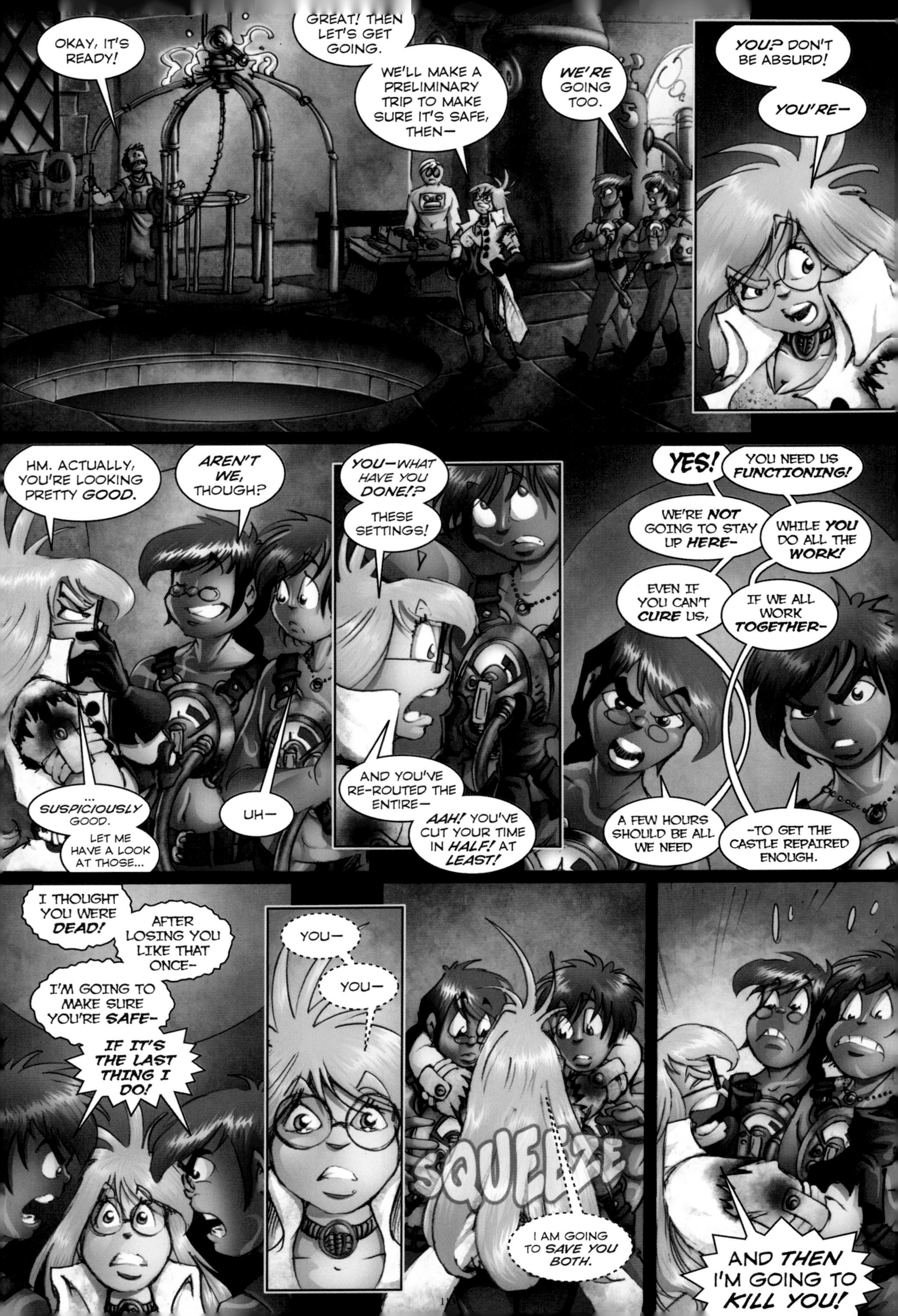

OKAY, IT'S READY!
GREAT! THEN LET'S GET GOING.
WE'LL MAKE A PRELIMINARY TRIP TO MAKE SURE IT'S SAFE, THEN—
WE'RE GOING TOO.
YOU? DON'T BE ABSURD!
YOU'RE—
HM. ACTUALLY, YOU'RE LOOKING PRETTY GOOD.
AREN'T WE, THOUGH?
... SUSPICIOUSLY GOOD.
LET ME HAVE A LOOK AT THOSE...
UH—
YOU—WHAT HAVE YOU DONE!?
THESE SETTINGS!
AND YOU'VE RE-ROUTED THE ENTIRE—
AAH! YOU'VE CUT YOUR TIME IN HALF! AT LEAST!
YES!
YOU NEED US FUNCTIONING!
WE'RE NOT GOING TO STAY UP HERE-
WHILE YOU DO ALL THE WORK!
EVEN IF YOU CAN'T CURE US,
IF WE ALL WORK TOGETHER-
A FEW HOURS SHOULD BE ALL WE NEED
-TO GET THE CASTLE REPAIRED ENOUGH.
I THOUGHT YOU WERE DEAD!
AFTER LOSING YOU LIKE THAT ONCE-
I'M GOING TO MAKE SURE YOU'RE SAFE-
IF IT'S THE LAST THING I DO!
YOU—
YOU—
SQUEEZE
I AM GOING TO SAVE YOU BOTH.
AND THEN I'M GOING TO KILL YOU!

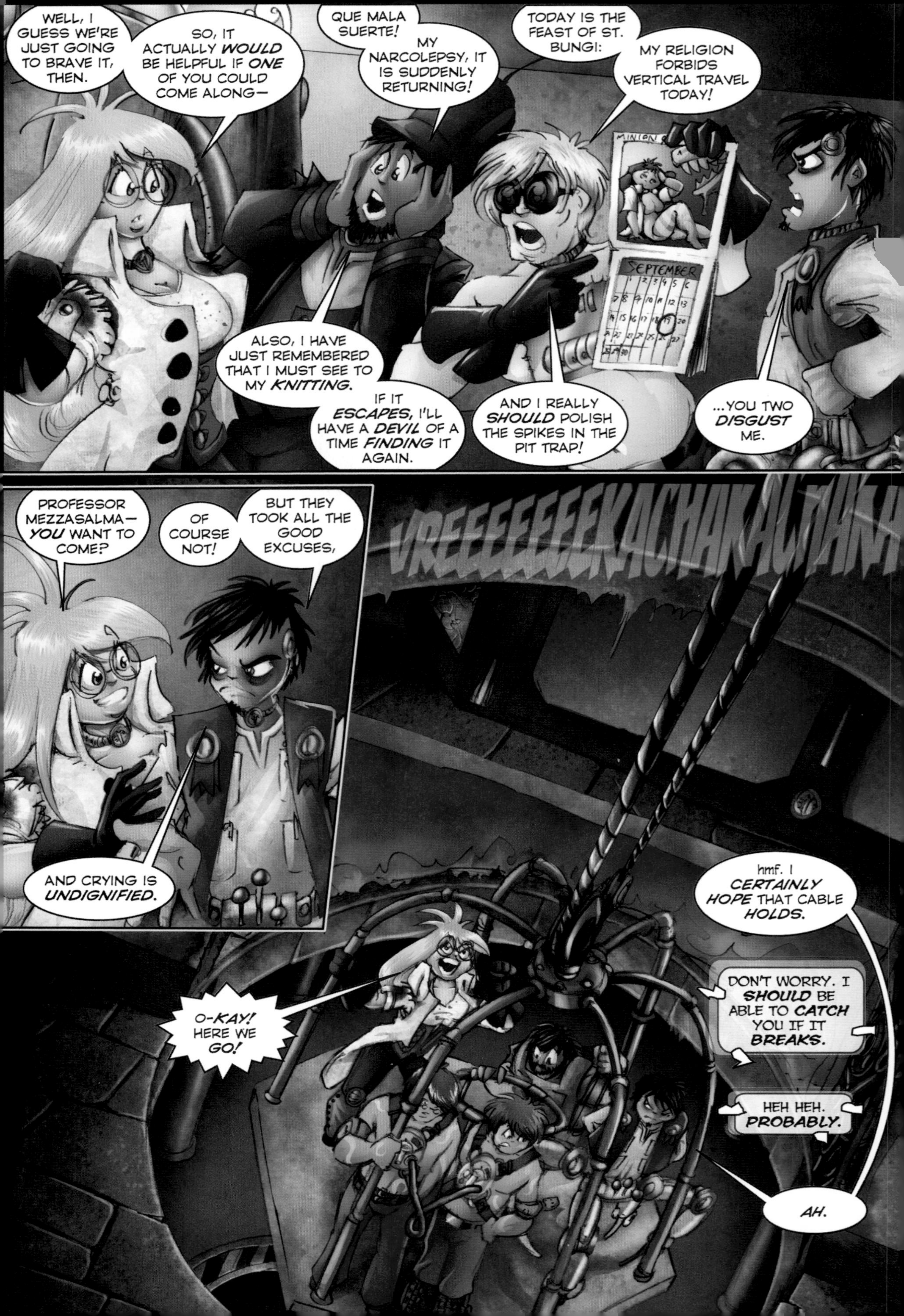
WELL, I GUESS WE'RE JUST GOING TO BRAVE IT, THEN.
SO, IT ACTUALLY *WOULD* BE HELPFUL IF *ONE* OF YOU COULD COME ALONG—
QUE MALA SUERTE!
MY NARCOLEPSY, IT IS SUDDENLY RETURNING!
TODAY IS THE FEAST OF ST. BUNGI:
MY RELIGION FORBIDS VERTICAL TRAVEL TODAY!
MINION
SEPTEMBER
ALSO, I HAVE JUST REMEMBERED THAT I MUST SEE TO MY *KNITTING*.
IF IT *ESCAPES*, I'LL HAVE A *DEVIL* OF A TIME *FINDING* IT AGAIN.
AND I REALLY *SHOULD* POLISH THE SPIKES IN THE PIT TRAP!
...YOU TWO *DISGUST* ME.
PROFESSOR MEZZASALMA— *YOU* WANT TO COME?
OF COURSE NOT!
BUT THEY TOOK ALL THE GOOD EXCUSES,
AND CRYING IS *UNDIGNIFIED.*
VREEEEEEEKACHAKACHAKA
O-*KAY!* HERE WE *GO!*
hmf. I *CERTAINLY HOPE* THAT CABLE *HOLDS*.
DON'T WORRY. I *SHOULD* BE ABLE TO *CATCH* YOU IF IT *BREAKS.*
HEH HEH. *PROBABLY.*
AH.

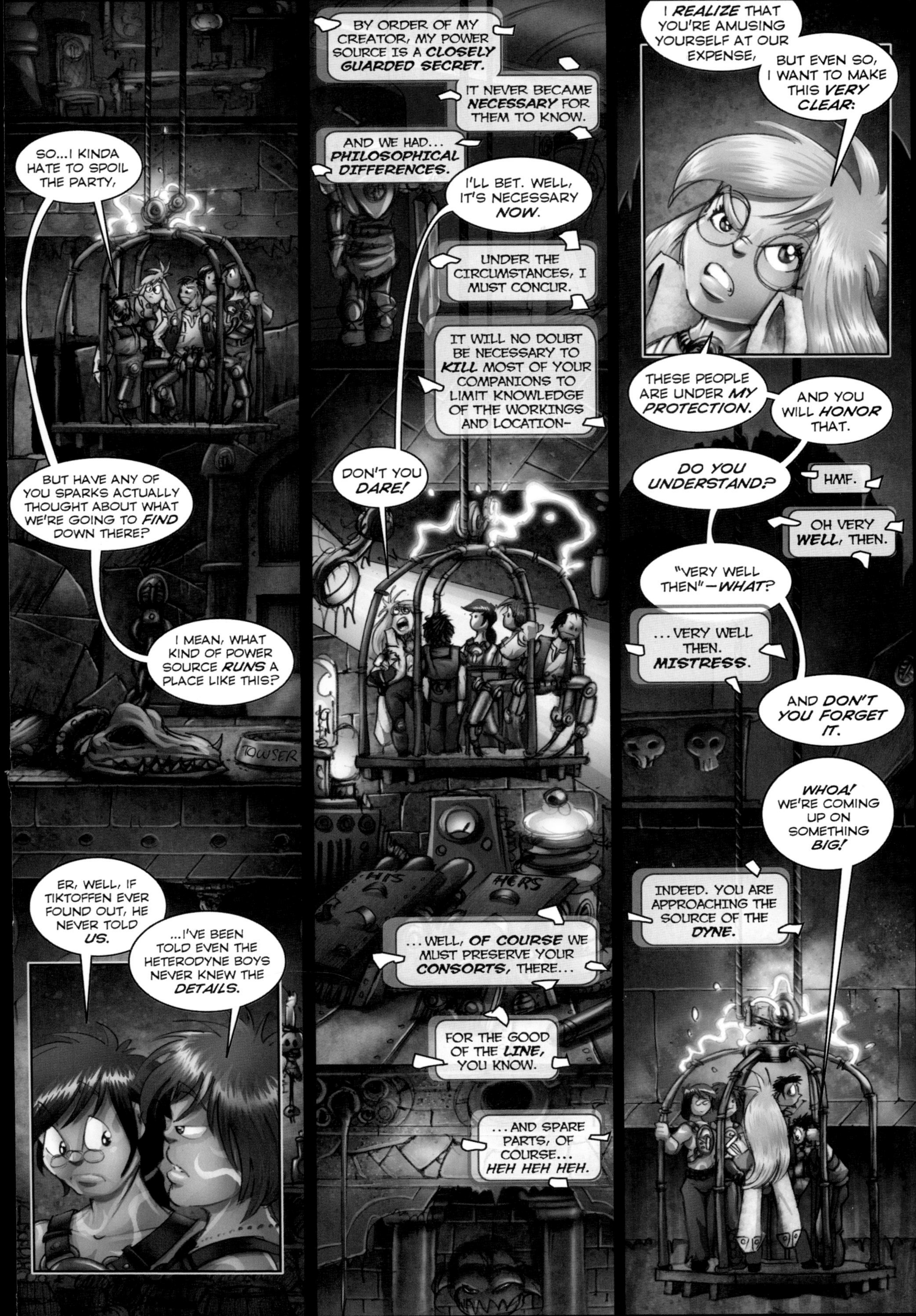

SO...I KINDA HATE TO SPOIL THE PARTY,
BUT HAVE ANY OF YOU SPARKS ACTUALLY THOUGHT ABOUT WHAT WE'RE GOING TO FIND DOWN THERE?
I MEAN, WHAT KIND OF POWER SOURCE RUNS A PLACE LIKE THIS?
TOWSER
ER, WELL, IF TIKTOFFEN EVER FOUND OUT, HE NEVER TOLD US.
...I'VE BEEN TOLD EVEN THE HETERODYNE BOYS NEVER KNEW THE DETAILS.
BY ORDER OF MY CREATOR, MY POWER SOURCE IS A CLOSELY GUARDED SECRET.
IT NEVER BECAME NECESSARY FOR THEM TO KNOW.
AND WE HAD... PHILOSOPHICAL DIFFERENCES.
I'LL BET. WELL, IT'S NECESSARY NOW.
UNDER THE CIRCUMSTANCES, I MUST CONCUR.
IT WILL NO DOUBT BE NECESSARY TO KILL MOST OF YOUR COMPANIONS TO LIMIT KNOWLEDGE OF THE WORKINGS AND LOCATION-
DON'T YOU DARE!
HIS
HERS
...WELL, OF COURSE WE MUST PRESERVE YOUR CONSORTS, THERE...
FOR THE GOOD OF THE LINE, YOU KNOW.
...AND SPARE PARTS, OF COURSE... HEH HEH HEH.
I REALIZE THAT YOU'RE AMUSING YOURSELF AT OUR EXPENSE,
BUT EVEN SO, I WANT TO MAKE THIS VERY CLEAR:
THESE PEOPLE ARE UNDER MY PROTECTION.
AND YOU WILL HONOR THAT.
DO YOU UNDERSTAND?
HMF.
OH VERY WELL, THEN.
"VERY WELL THEN"—WHAT?
...VERY WELL THEN. MISTRESS.
AND DON'T YOU FORGET IT.
WHOA! WE'RE COMING UP ON SOMETHING BIG!
INDEED. YOU ARE APPROACHING THE SOURCE OF THE DYNE.

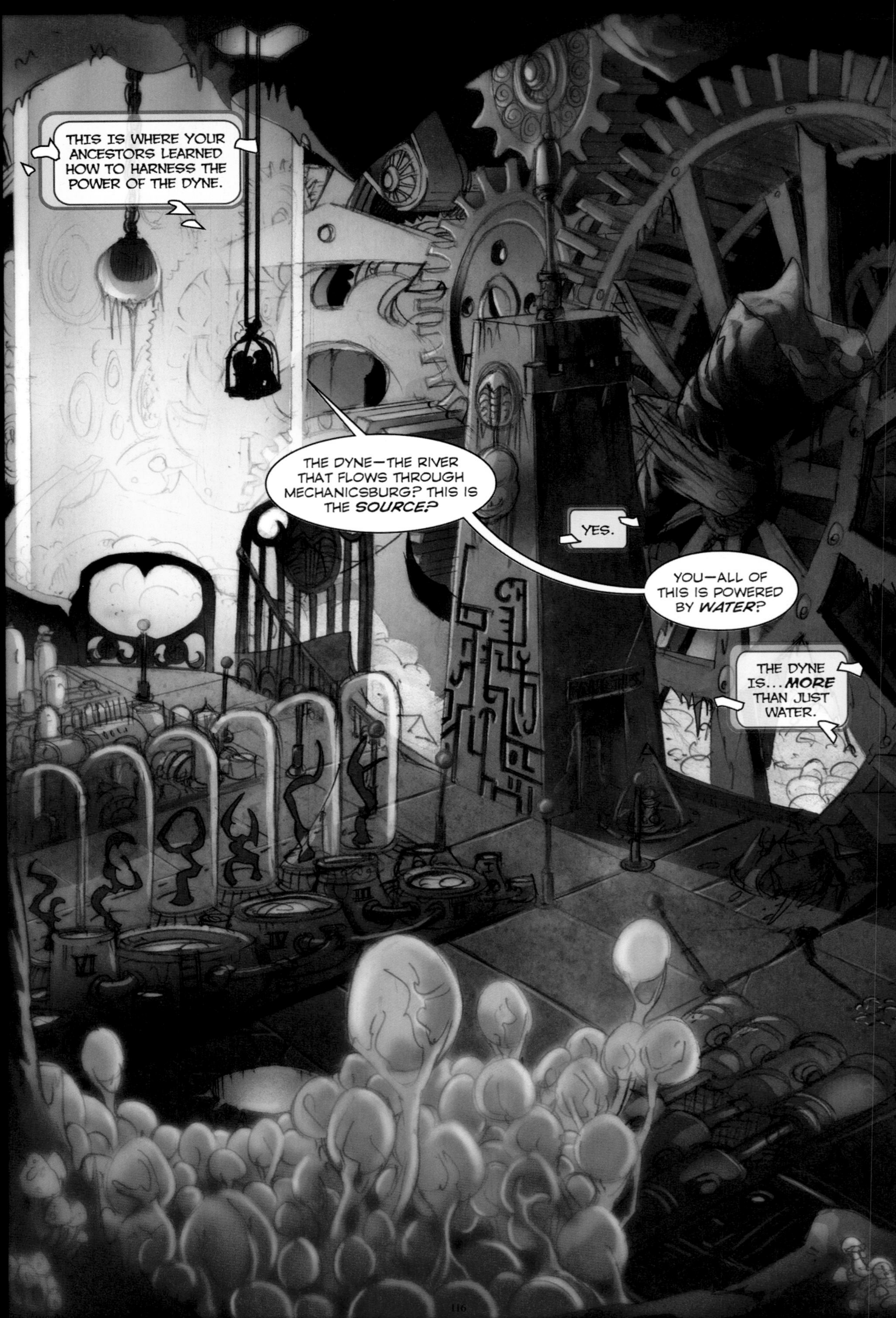
THIS IS WHERE YOUR ANCESTORS LEARNED HOW TO HARNESS THE POWER OF THE DYNE.
THE DYNE—THE RIVER THAT FLOWS THROUGH MECHANICSBURG? THIS IS THE *SOURCE?*
YES.
YOU—ALL OF THIS IS POWERED BY *WATER*?
THE DYNE IS... ***MORE*** THAN JUST WATER.

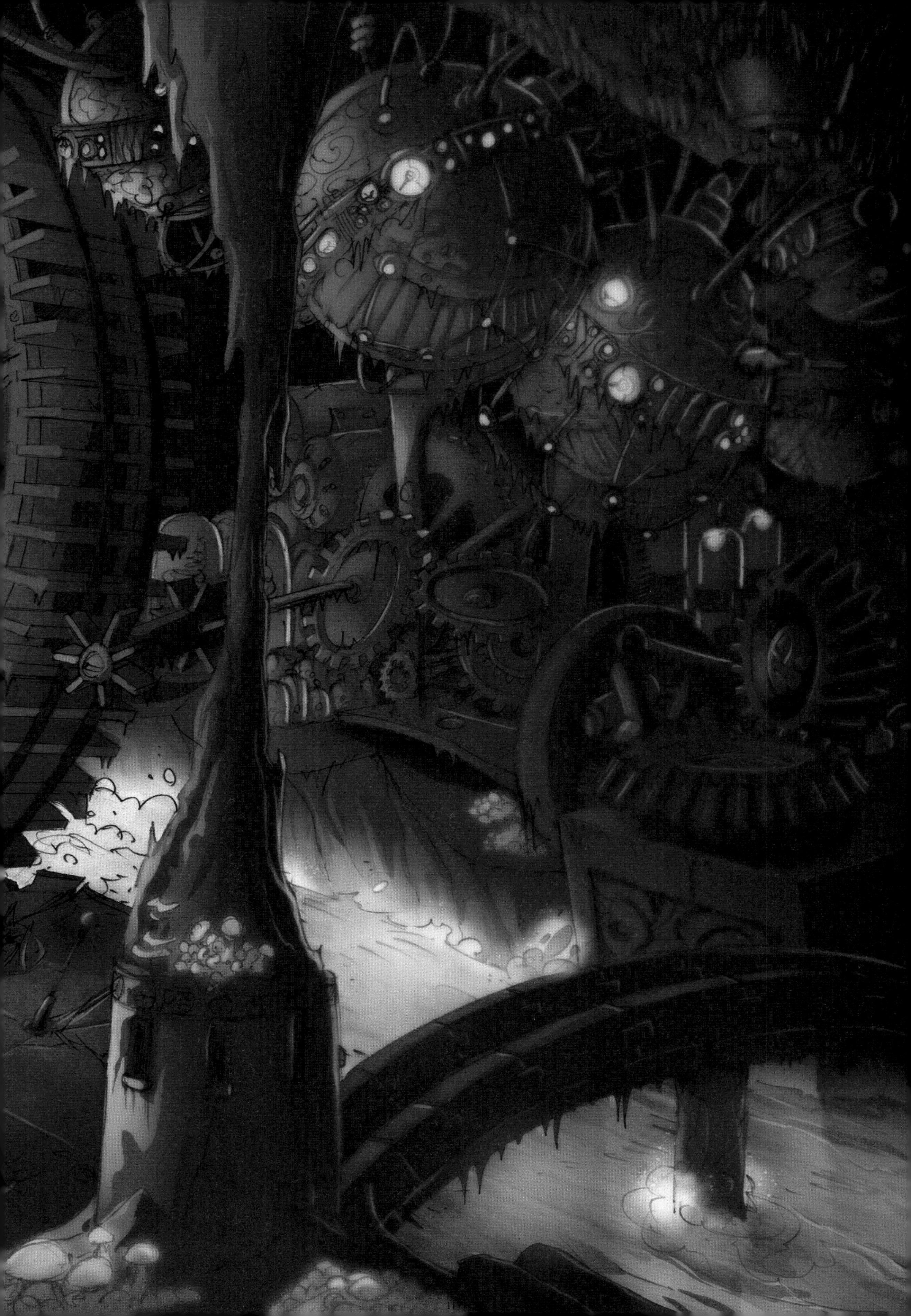

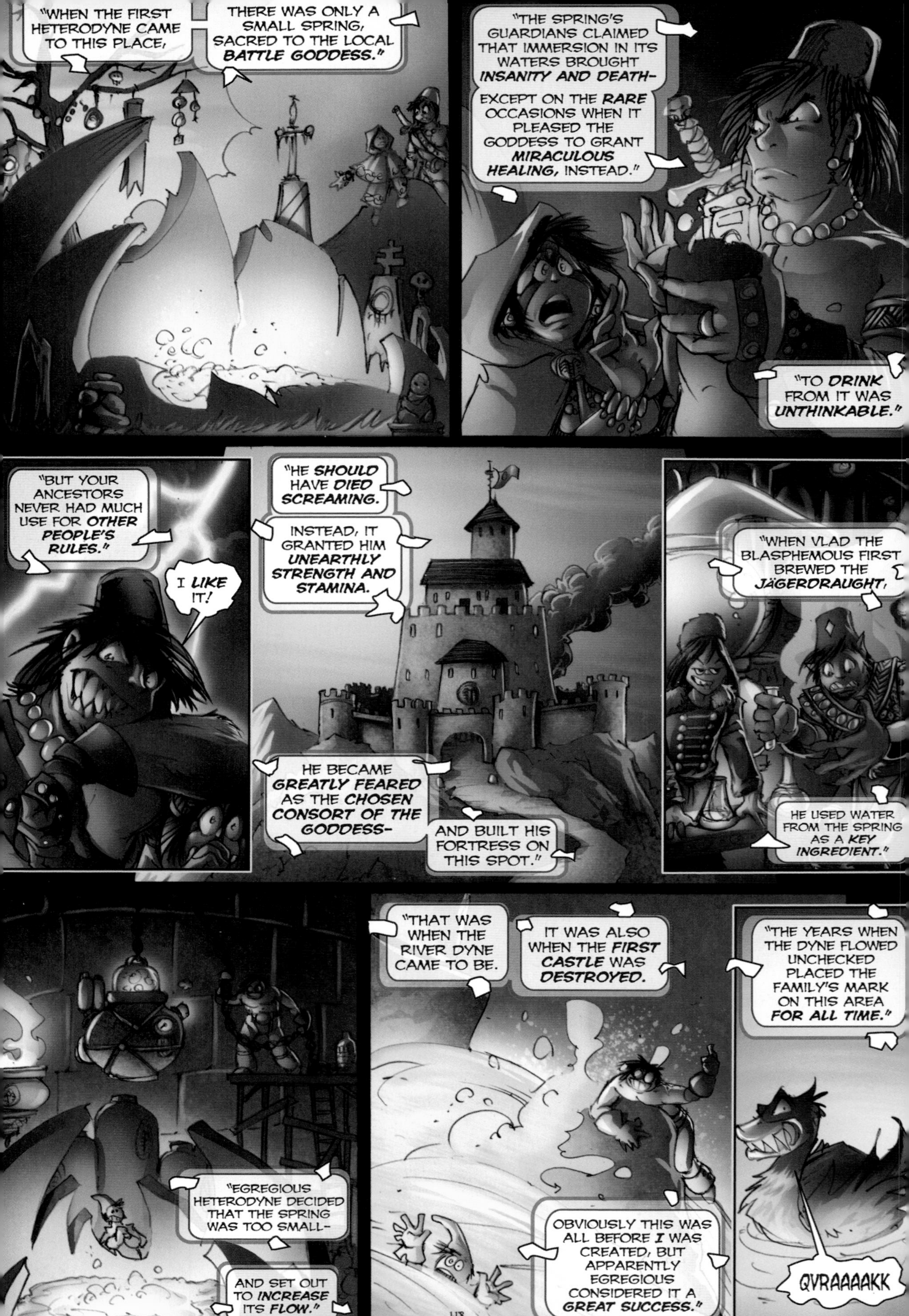

"WHEN THE FIRST HETERODYNE CAME TO THIS PLACE,
THERE WAS ONLY A SMALL SPRING, SACRED TO THE LOCAL BATTLE GODDESS."
"THE SPRING'S GUARDIANS CLAIMED THAT IMMERSION IN ITS WATERS BROUGHT INSANITY AND DEATH-
EXCEPT ON THE RARE OCCASIONS WHEN IT PLEASED THE GODDESS TO GRANT MIRACULOUS HEALING, INSTEAD."
"TO DRINK FROM IT WAS UNTHINKABLE."
"BUT YOUR ANCESTORS NEVER HAD MUCH USE FOR OTHER PEOPLE'S RULES."
I LIKE IT!
"HE SHOULD HAVE DIED SCREAMING.
INSTEAD, IT GRANTED HIM UNEARTHLY STRENGTH AND STAMINA.
HE BECAME GREATLY FEARED AS THE CHOSEN CONSORT OF THE GODDESS-
AND BUILT HIS FORTRESS ON THIS SPOT."
"WHEN VLAD THE BLASPHEMOUS FIRST BREWED THE JÄGERDRAUGHT,
HE USED WATER FROM THE SPRING AS A KEY INGREDIENT."
"EGREGIOUS HETERODYNE DECIDED THAT THE SPRING WAS TOO SMALL-
AND SET OUT TO INCREASE ITS FLOW."
"THAT WAS WHEN THE RIVER DYNE CAME TO BE.
IT WAS ALSO WHEN THE FIRST CASTLE WAS DESTROYED.
OBVIOUSLY THIS WAS ALL BEFORE I WAS CREATED, BUT APPARENTLY EGREGIOUS CONSIDERED IT A GREAT SUCCESS."
"THE YEARS WHEN THE DYNE FLOWED UNCHECKED PLACED THE FAMILY'S MARK ON THIS AREA FOR ALL TIME."
QVRAAAAKK

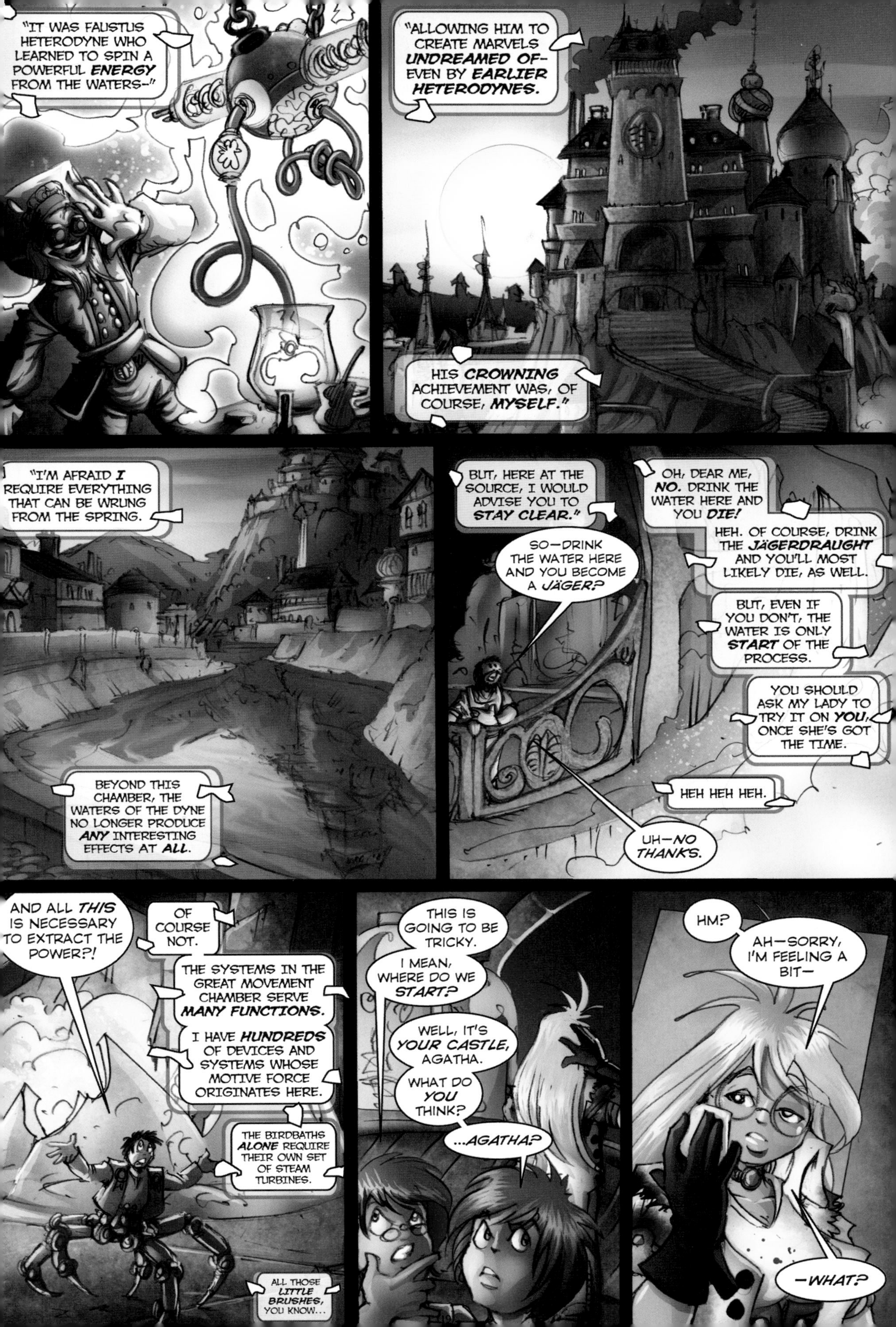
"IT WAS FAUSTUS HETERODYNE WHO LEARNED TO SPIN A POWERFUL ENERGY FROM THE WATERS-"
"ALLOWING HIM TO CREATE MARVELS UNDREAMED OF- EVEN BY EARLIER HETERODYNES.
HIS CROWNING ACHIEVEMENT WAS, OF COURSE, MYSELF."
"I'M AFRAID I REQUIRE EVERYTHING THAT CAN BE WRUNG FROM THE SPRING.
BEYOND THIS CHAMBER, THE WATERS OF THE DYNE NO LONGER PRODUCE ANY INTERESTING EFFECTS AT ALL.
BUT, HERE AT THE SOURCE, I WOULD ADVISE YOU TO STAY CLEAR."
SO—DRINK THE WATER HERE AND YOU BECOME A JÄGER?
OH, DEAR ME, NO. DRINK THE WATER HERE AND YOU DIE!
HEH. OF COURSE, DRINK THE JÄGERDRAUGHT AND YOU'LL MOST LIKELY DIE, AS WELL.
BUT, EVEN IF YOU DON'T, THE WATER IS ONLY START OF THE PROCESS.
YOU SHOULD ASK MY LADY TO TRY IT ON YOU, ONCE SHE'S GOT THE TIME.
HEH HEH HEH.
UH—NO THANKS.
AND ALL THIS IS NECESSARY TO EXTRACT THE POWER?!
OF COURSE NOT.
THE SYSTEMS IN THE GREAT MOVEMENT CHAMBER SERVE MANY FUNCTIONS.
I HAVE HUNDREDS OF DEVICES AND SYSTEMS WHOSE MOTIVE FORCE ORIGINATES HERE.
THE BIRDBATHS ALONE REQUIRE THEIR OWN SET OF STEAM TURBINES.
ALL THOSE LITTLE BRUSHES, YOU KNOW...
THIS IS GOING TO BE TRICKY.
I MEAN, WHERE DO WE START?
WELL, IT'S YOUR CASTLE, AGATHA.
WHAT DO YOU THINK?
...AGATHA?
HM?
AH—SORRY, I'M FEELING A BIT—
—WHAT?

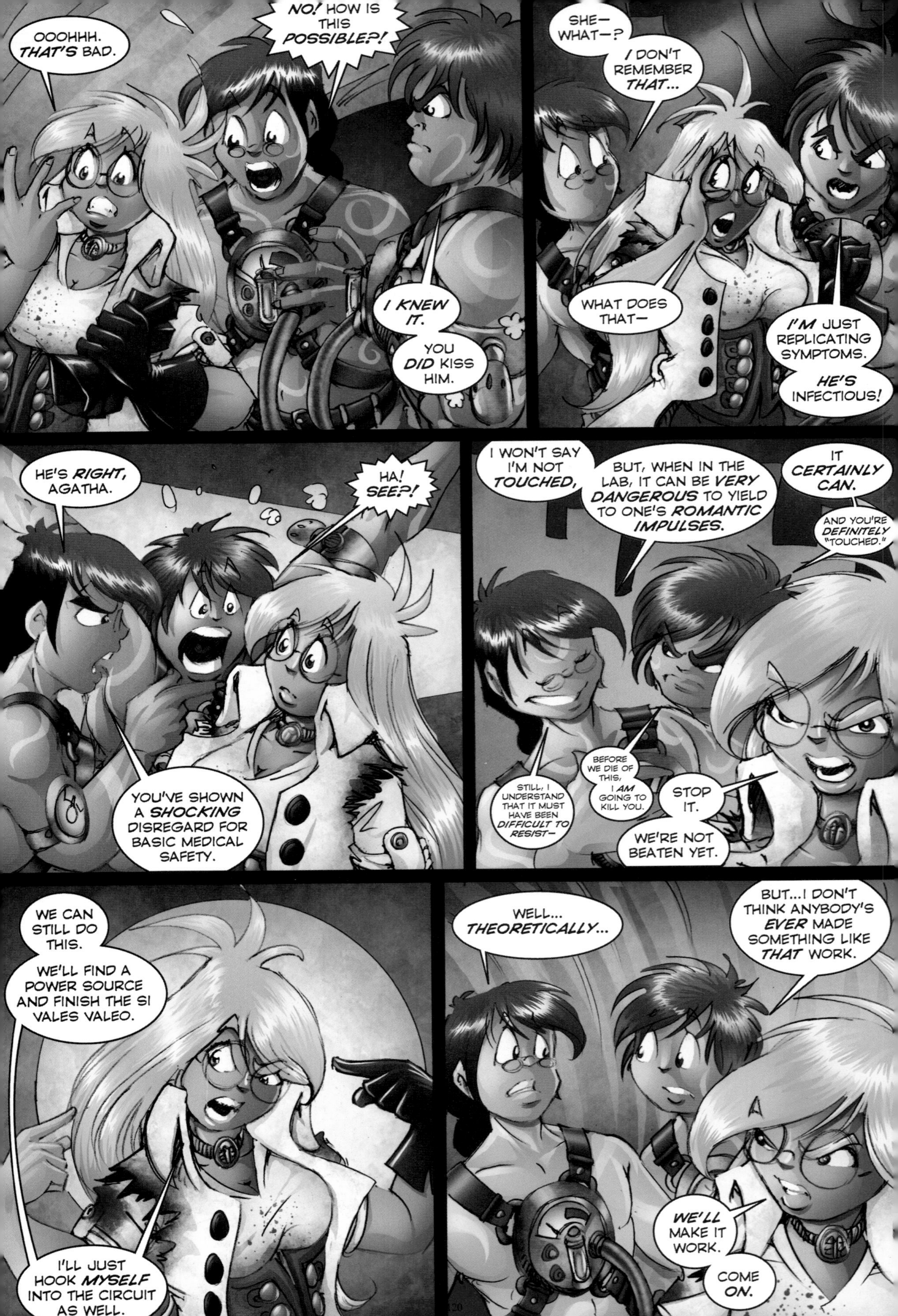
OOOHHH. *THAT'S* BAD.
NO! HOW IS THIS *POSSIBLE?!*
I KNEW IT.
YOU *DID* KISS HIM.
SHE— WHAT—?
I DON'T REMEMBER *THAT*...
WHAT DOES THAT—
I'M JUST REPLICATING SYMPTOMS.
HE'S INFECTIOUS!
HE'S *RIGHT,* AGATHA.
HA! *SEE?!*
YOU'VE SHOWN A *SHOCKING* DISREGARD FOR BASIC MEDICAL SAFETY.
I WON'T SAY I'M NOT *TOUCHED,*
BUT, WHEN IN THE LAB, IT CAN BE *VERY DANGEROUS* TO YIELD TO ONE'S *ROMANTIC IMPULSES.*
IT *CERTAINLY CAN.*
AND YOU'RE *DEFINITELY* "TOUCHED."
STILL, I UNDERSTAND THAT IT MUST HAVE BEEN *DIFFICULT TO RESIST—*
BEFORE WE DIE OF THIS, I *AM* GOING TO KILL YOU.
STOP IT.
WE'RE NOT BEATEN YET.
WE CAN STILL DO THIS.
WE'LL FIND A POWER SOURCE AND FINISH THE SI VALES VALEO.
I'LL JUST HOOK *MYSELF* INTO THE CIRCUIT AS WELL.
WELL... *THEORETICALLY...*
BUT...I DON'T THINK ANYBODY'S *EVER* MADE SOMETHING LIKE *THAT* WORK.
WE'LL MAKE IT WORK.
COME *ON.*

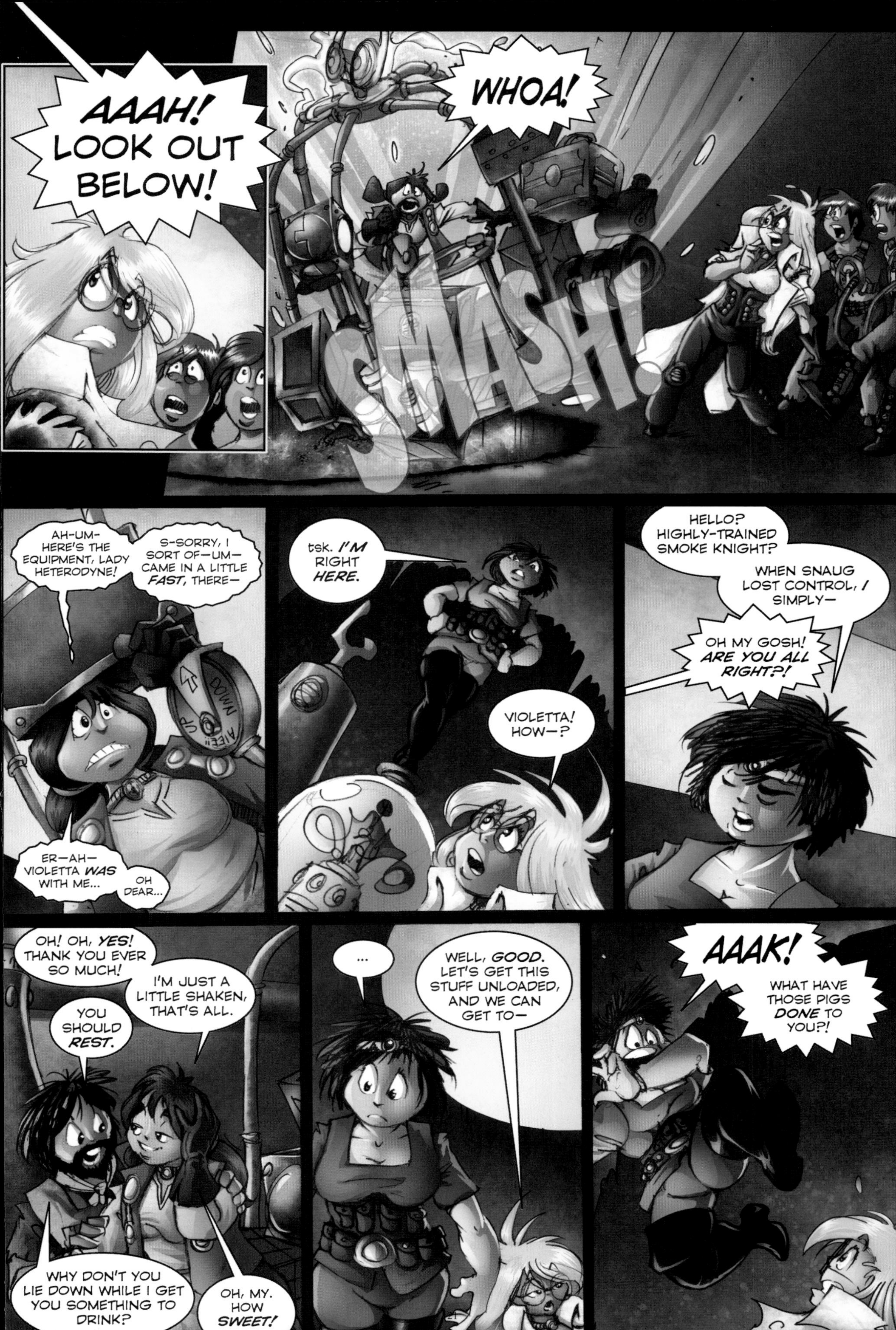
AAAH! LOOK OUT BELOW!
WHOA!
SMASH!
AH-UM- HERE'S THE EQUIPMENT, LADY HETERODYNE!
S-SORRY, I SORT OF—UM— CAME IN A LITTLE FAST, THERE—
UP
DOWN
AIEE!!
ER—AH— VIOLETTA WAS WITH ME...
OH DEAR...
tsk. I'M RIGHT HERE.
VIOLETTA! HOW—?
HELLO? HIGHLY-TRAINED SMOKE KNIGHT?
WHEN SNAUG LOST CONTROL, I SIMPLY—
OH MY GOSH! ARE YOU ALL RIGHT?!
OH! OH, YES! THANK YOU EVER SO MUCH!
I'M JUST A LITTLE SHAKEN, THAT'S ALL.
YOU SHOULD REST.
WHY DON'T YOU LIE DOWN WHILE I GET YOU SOMETHING TO DRINK?
OH, MY. HOW SWEET!
...
WELL, GOOD. LET'S GET THIS STUFF UNLOADED, AND WE CAN GET TO—
AAAK!
WHAT HAVE THOSE PIGS DONE TO YOU?!

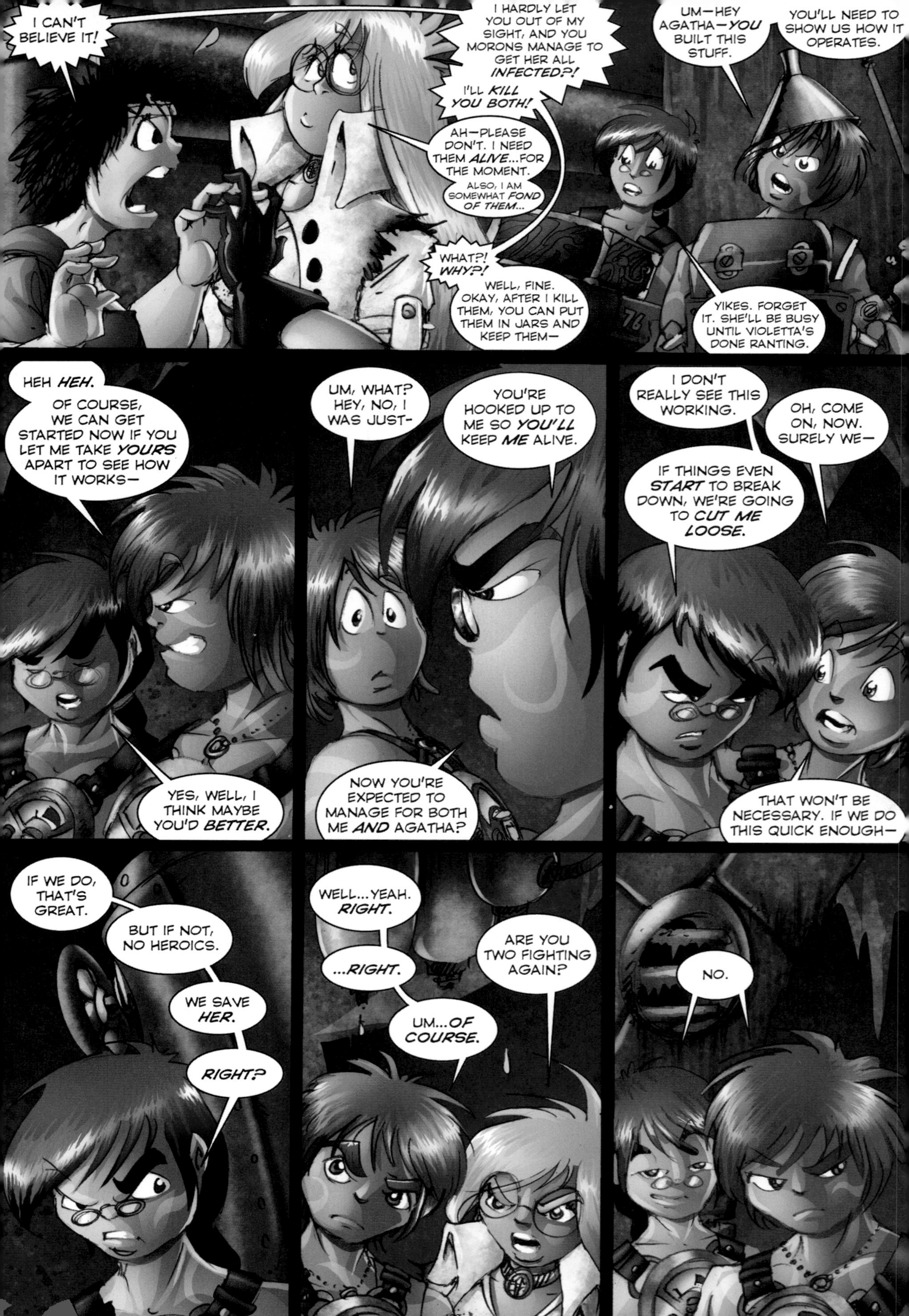
I CAN'T BELIEVE IT!
I HARDLY LET YOU OUT OF MY SIGHT, AND YOU MORONS MANAGE TO GET HER ALL *INFECTED?!*
I'LL *KILL YOU BOTH!*
AH—PLEASE DON'T. I NEED THEM *ALIVE*...FOR THE MOMENT.
ALSO, I AM SOMEWHAT *FOND OF THEM*...
WHAT?! *WHY?!*
WELL, FINE. OKAY, AFTER I KILL THEM, YOU CAN PUT THEM IN JARS AND KEEP THEM—
UM—HEY AGATHA—*YOU* BUILT THIS STUFF.
YOU'LL NEED TO SHOW US HOW IT OPERATES.
YIKES. FORGET IT. SHE'LL BE BUSY UNTIL VIOLETTA'S DONE RANTING.
HEH *HEH*.
OF COURSE, WE CAN GET STARTED NOW IF YOU LET ME TAKE *YOURS* APART TO SEE HOW IT WORKS—
YES, WELL, I THINK MAYBE YOU'D *BETTER*.
UM, WHAT? HEY, NO, I WAS JUST-
YOU'RE HOOKED UP TO ME SO *YOU'LL* KEEP *ME* ALIVE.
NOW YOU'RE EXPECTED TO MANAGE FOR BOTH ME *AND* AGATHA?
I DON'T REALLY SEE THIS WORKING.
OH, COME ON, NOW. SURELY WE—
IF THINGS EVEN *START* TO BREAK DOWN, WE'RE GOING TO *CUT ME LOOSE*.
THAT WON'T BE NECESSARY. IF WE DO THIS QUICK ENOUGH—
IF WE DO, THAT'S GREAT.
BUT IF NOT, NO HEROICS.
WE SAVE *HER*.
RIGHT?
WELL...YEAH. *RIGHT*.
...*RIGHT*.
UM...*OF COURSE*.
ARE YOU TWO FIGHTING AGAIN?
NO.

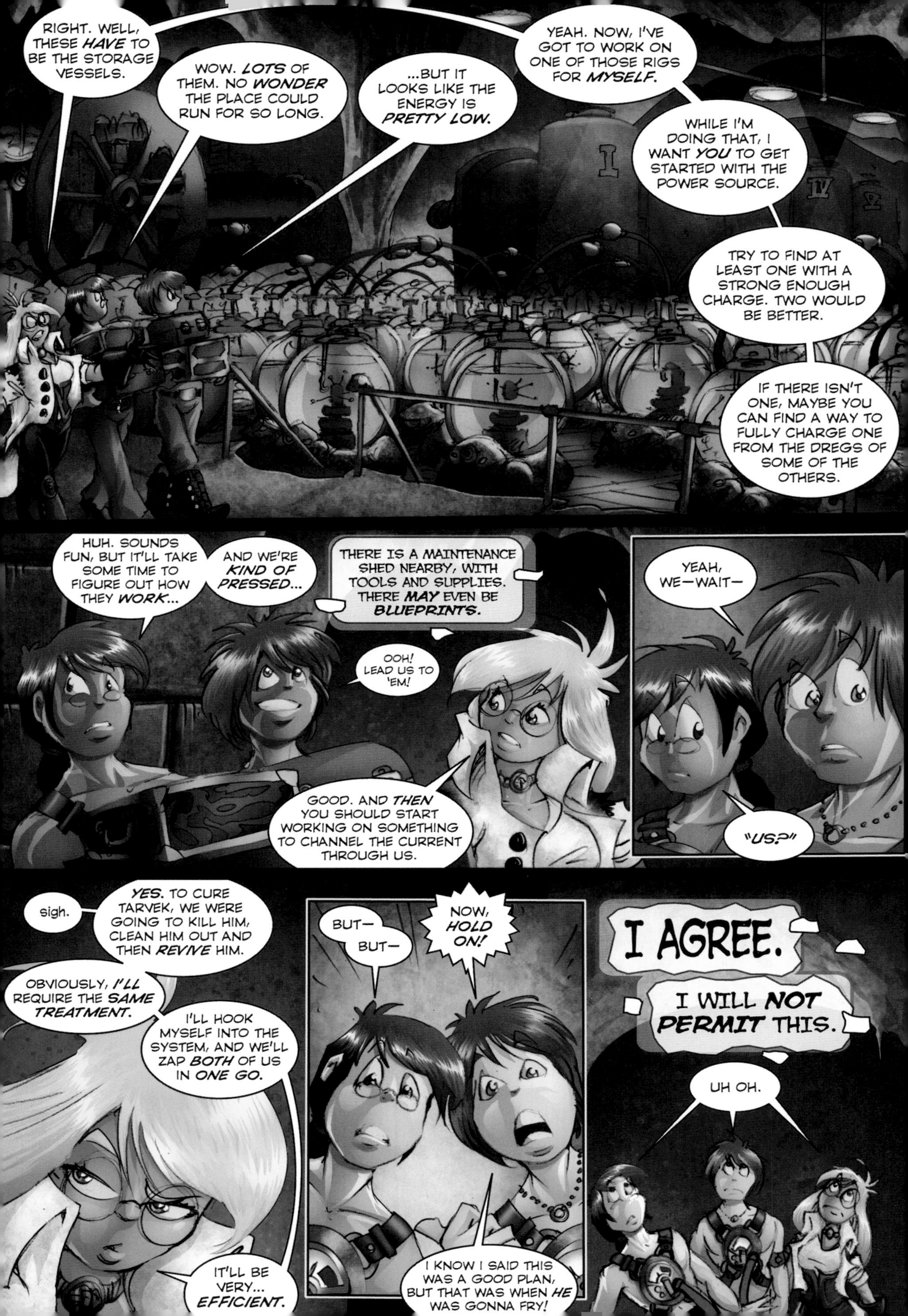
RIGHT. WELL, THESE HAVE TO BE THE STORAGE VESSELS.
WOW. LOTS OF THEM. NO WONDER THE PLACE COULD RUN FOR SO LONG.
...BUT IT LOOKS LIKE THE ENERGY IS PRETTY LOW.
YEAH. NOW, I'VE GOT TO WORK ON ONE OF THOSE RIGS FOR MYSELF.
WHILE I'M DOING THAT, I WANT YOU TO GET STARTED WITH THE POWER SOURCE.
TRY TO FIND AT LEAST ONE WITH A STRONG ENOUGH CHARGE. TWO WOULD BE BETTER.
IF THERE ISN'T ONE, MAYBE YOU CAN FIND A WAY TO FULLY CHARGE ONE FROM THE DREGS OF SOME OF THE OTHERS.
HUH. SOUNDS FUN, BUT IT'LL TAKE SOME TIME TO FIGURE OUT HOW THEY WORK...
AND WE'RE KIND OF PRESSED...
THERE IS A MAINTENANCE SHED NEARBY, WITH TOOLS AND SUPPLIES. THERE MAY EVEN BE BLUEPRINTS.
OOH! LEAD US TO 'EM!
GOOD. AND THEN YOU SHOULD START WORKING ON SOMETHING TO CHANNEL THE CURRENT THROUGH US.
YEAH, WE—WAIT—
"US?"
sigh.
YES. TO CURE TARVEK, WE WERE GOING TO KILL HIM, CLEAN HIM OUT AND THEN REVIVE HIM.
OBVIOUSLY, I'LL REQUIRE THE SAME TREATMENT.
I'LL HOOK MYSELF INTO THE SYSTEM, AND WE'LL ZAP BOTH OF US IN ONE GO.
IT'LL BE VERY... EFFICIENT.
BUT— BUT—
NOW, HOLD ON!
I KNOW I SAID THIS WAS A GOOD PLAN, BUT THAT WAS WHEN HE WAS GONNA FRY!
I AGREE.
I WILL NOT PERMIT THIS.
UH OH.

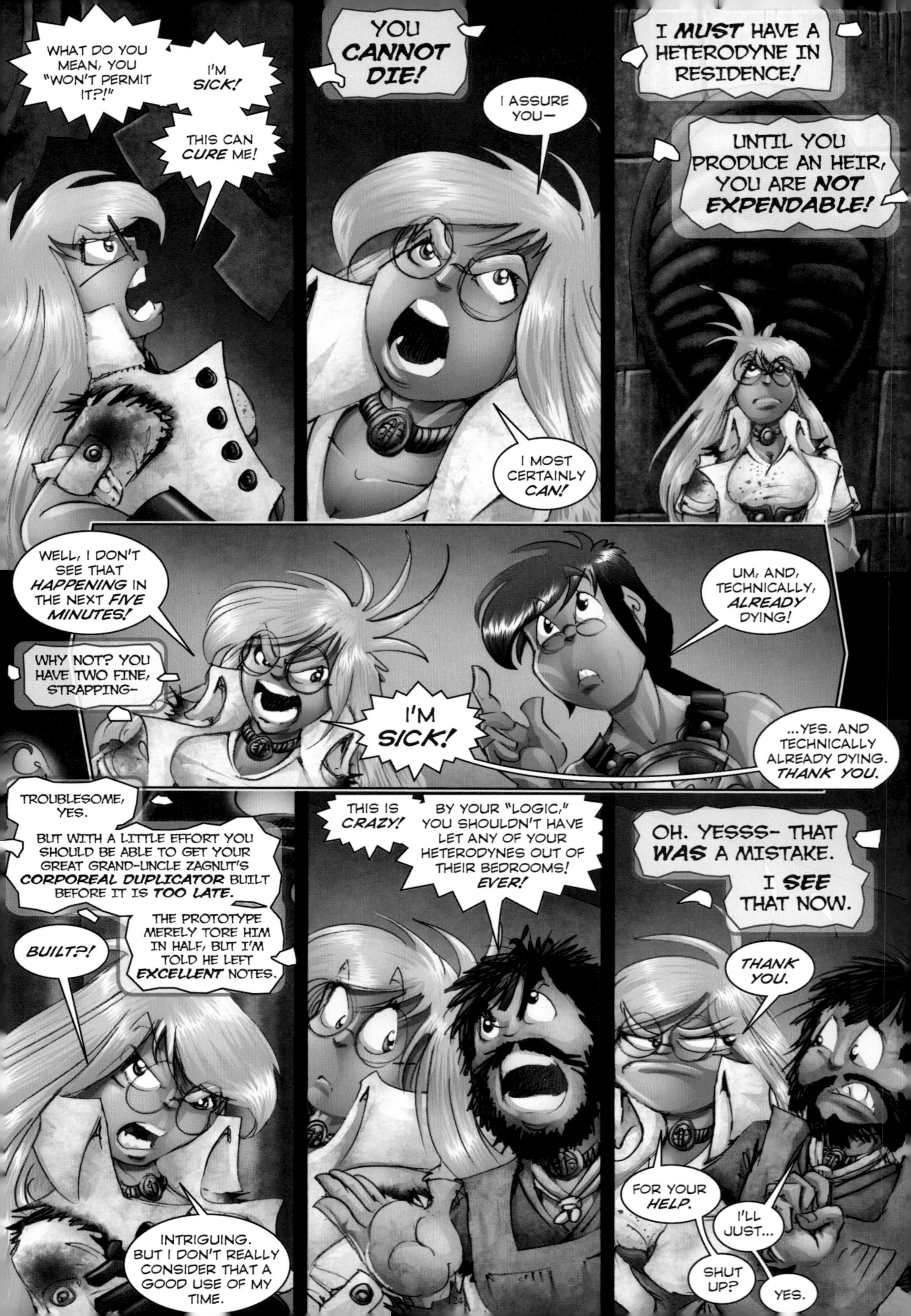

WHAT DO YOU MEAN, YOU "WON'T PERMIT IT?!"
I'M SICK!
THIS CAN CURE ME!
YOU CANNOT DIE!
I ASSURE YOU—
I MOST CERTAINLY CAN!
I MUST HAVE A HETERODYNE IN RESIDENCE!
UNTIL YOU PRODUCE AN HEIR, YOU ARE NOT EXPENDABLE!
WELL, I DON'T SEE THAT HAPPENING IN THE NEXT FIVE MINUTES!
WHY NOT? YOU HAVE TWO FINE, STRAPPING-
I'M SICK!
UM, AND, TECHNICALLY, ALREADY DYING!
...YES. AND TECHNICALLY ALREADY DYING. THANK YOU.
TROUBLESOME, YES.
BUT WITH A LITTLE EFFORT YOU SHOULD BE ABLE TO GET YOUR GREAT GRAND-UNCLE ZAGNUT'S CORPOREAL DUPLICATOR BUILT BEFORE IT IS TOO LATE.
THE PROTOTYPE MERELY TORE HIM IN HALF, BUT I'M TOLD HE LEFT EXCELLENT NOTES.
BUILT?!
INTRIGUING. BUT I DON'T REALLY CONSIDER THAT A GOOD USE OF MY TIME.
THIS IS CRAZY!
BY YOUR "LOGIC," YOU SHOULDN'T HAVE LET ANY OF YOUR HETERODYNES OUT OF THEIR BEDROOMS! EVER!
OH. YESSS- THAT WAS A MISTAKE.
I SEE THAT NOW.
THANK YOU.
FOR YOUR HELP.
I'LL JUST...
SHUT UP?
YES.

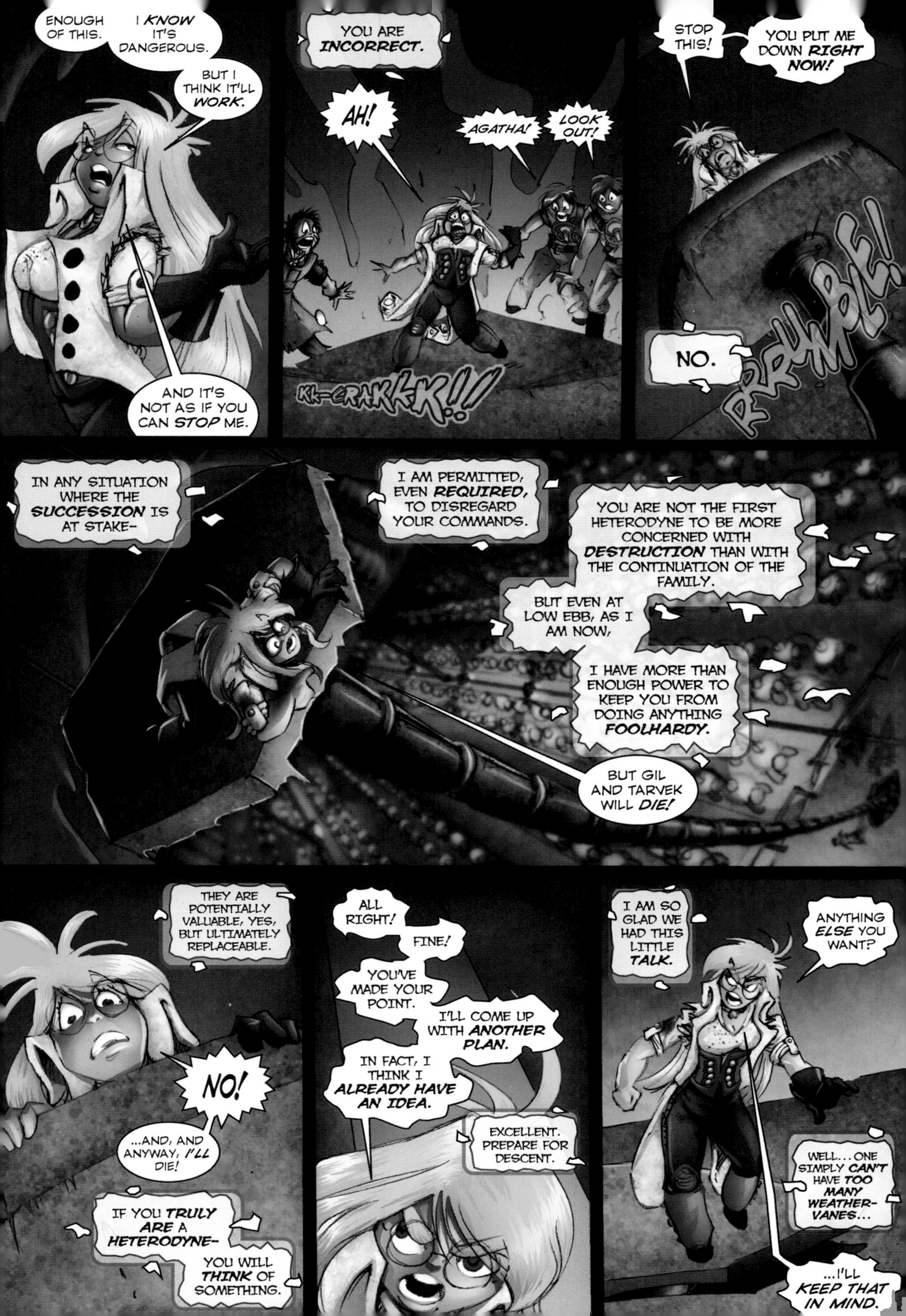

ENOUGH OF THIS.
I KNOW IT'S DANGEROUS.
BUT I THINK IT'LL WORK.
AND IT'S NOT AS IF YOU CAN STOP ME.
YOU ARE INCORRECT.
AH!
AGATHA!
LOOK OUT!
KK-CRAKKKK!!!
STOP THIS!
YOU PUT ME DOWN RIGHT NOW!
NO.
RRRUMBLE!
IN ANY SITUATION WHERE THE SUCCESSION IS AT STAKE-
I AM PERMITTED, EVEN REQUIRED, TO DISREGARD YOUR COMMANDS.
YOU ARE NOT THE FIRST HETERODYNE TO BE MORE CONCERNED WITH DESTRUCTION THAN WITH THE CONTINUATION OF THE FAMILY.
BUT EVEN AT LOW EBB, AS I AM NOW,
I HAVE MORE THAN ENOUGH POWER TO KEEP YOU FROM DOING ANYTHING FOOLHARDY.
BUT GIL AND TARVEK WILL DIE!
THEY ARE POTENTIALLY VALUABLE, YES, BUT ULTIMATELY REPLACEABLE.
NO!
...AND, AND ANYWAY, I'LL DIE!
IF YOU TRULY ARE A HETERODYNE-
YOU WILL THINK OF SOMETHING.
ALL RIGHT!
FINE!
YOU'VE MADE YOUR POINT.
I'LL COME UP WITH ANOTHER PLAN.
IN FACT, I THINK I ALREADY HAVE AN IDEA.
EXCELLENT. PREPARE FOR DESCENT.
I AM SO GLAD WE HAD THIS LITTLE TALK.
ANYTHING ELSE YOU WANT?
WELL... ONE SIMPLY CAN'T HAVE TOO MANY WEATHER-VANES...
...I'LL KEEP THAT IN MIND.

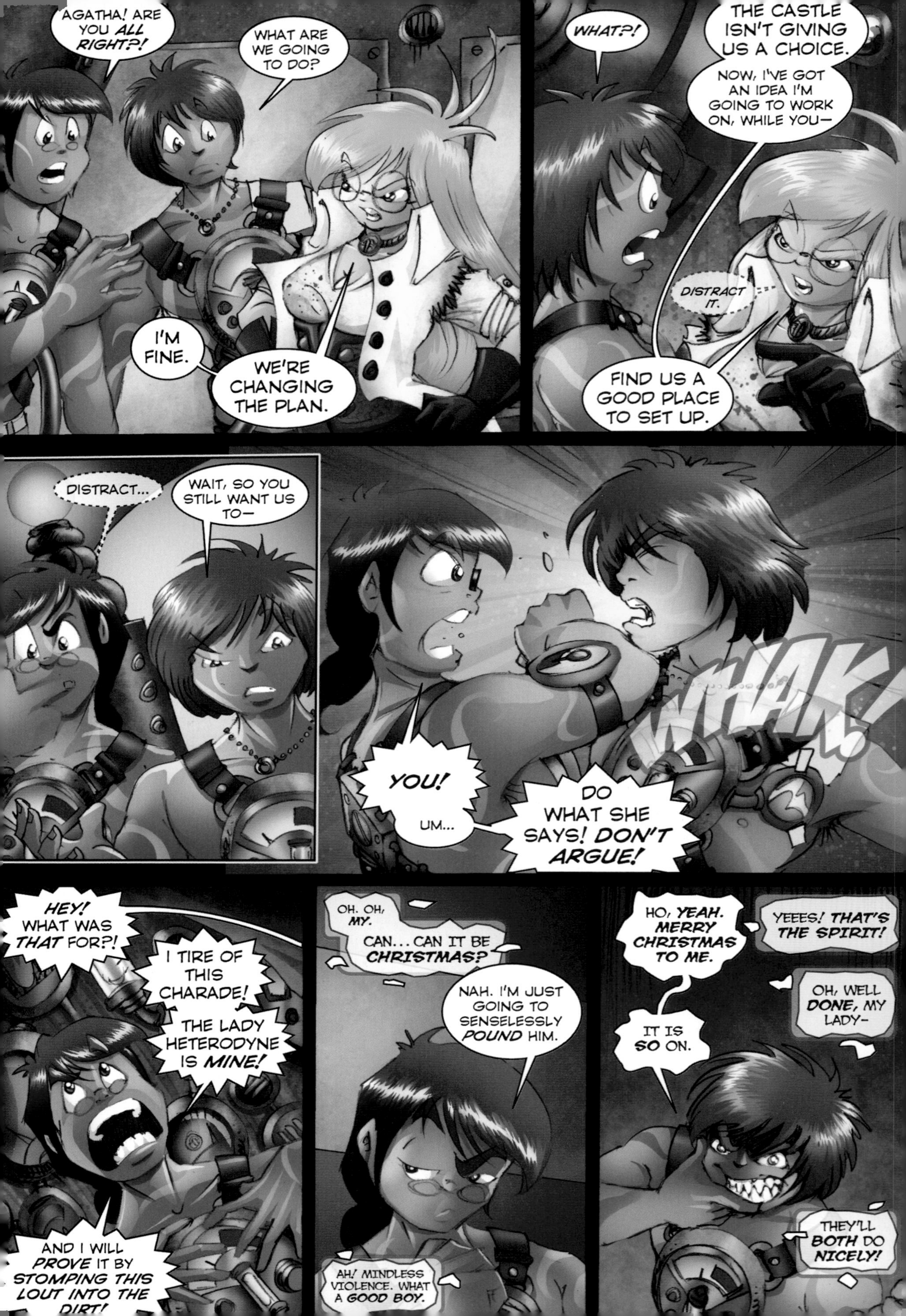

AGATHA! ARE YOU ALL RIGHT?!
WHAT ARE WE GOING TO DO?
I'M FINE.
WE'RE CHANGING THE PLAN.
WHAT?!
THE CASTLE ISN'T GIVING US A CHOICE.
NOW, I'VE GOT AN IDEA I'M GOING TO WORK ON, WHILE YOU—
DISTRACT IT.
FIND US A GOOD PLACE TO SET UP.
DISTRACT...
WAIT, SO YOU STILL WANT US TO—
YOU!
UM...
DO WHAT SHE SAYS! DON'T ARGUE!
WHAK!
HEY! WHAT WAS THAT FOR?!
I TIRE OF THIS CHARADE!
THE LADY HETERODYNE IS MINE!
AND I WILL PROVE IT BY STOMPING THIS LOUT INTO THE DIRT!
OH. OH, MY.
CAN... CAN IT BE CHRISTMAS?
NAH. I'M JUST GOING TO SENSELESSLY POUND HIM.
AH! MINDLESS VIOLENCE. WHAT A GOOD BOY.
HO, YEAH. MERRY CHRISTMAS TO ME.
IT IS SO ON.
YEEES! THAT'S THE SPIRIT!
OH, WELL DONE, MY LADY—
THEY'LL BOTH DO NICELY!

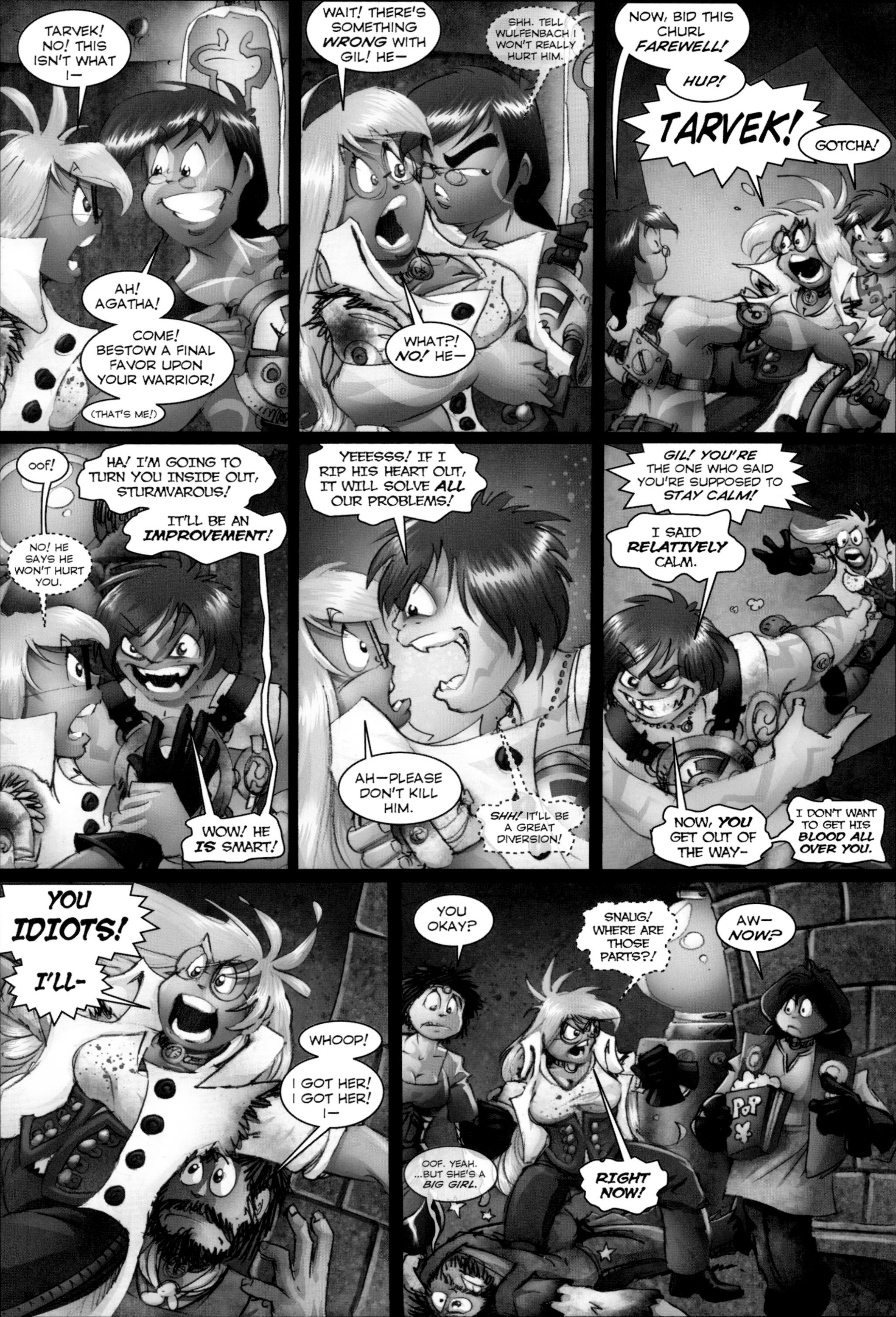
TARVEK! NO! THIS ISN'T WHAT I—
AH! AGATHA!
COME! BESTOW A FINAL FAVOR UPON YOUR WARRIOR!
(THAT'S ME!)
WAIT! THERE'S SOMETHING WRONG WITH GIL! HE—
SHH. TELL WULFENBACH I WON'T REALLY HURT HIM.
WHAT?! NO! HE—
NOW, BID THIS CHURL FAREWELL!
HUP!
TARVEK!
GOTCHA!
oof!
HA! I'M GOING TO TURN YOU INSIDE OUT, STURMVAROUS!
NO! HE SAYS HE WON'T HURT YOU.
IT'LL BE AN IMPROVEMENT!
WOW! HE IS SMART!
YEEESSS! IF I RIP HIS HEART OUT, IT WILL SOLVE ALL OUR PROBLEMS!
AH—PLEASE DON'T KILL HIM.
SHH! IT'LL BE A GREAT DIVERSION!
GIL! YOU'RE THE ONE WHO SAID YOU'RE SUPPOSED TO STAY CALM!
I SAID RELATIVELY CALM.
NOW, YOU GET OUT OF THE WAY-
I DON'T WANT TO GET HIS BLOOD ALL OVER YOU.
YOU IDIOTS!
I'LL-
WHOOP!
I GOT HER! I GOT HER! I—
YOU OKAY?
OOF. YEAH. ...BUT SHE'S A BIG GIRL.
SNAUG! WHERE ARE THOSE PARTS?!
RIGHT NOW!
AW— NOW?
POP

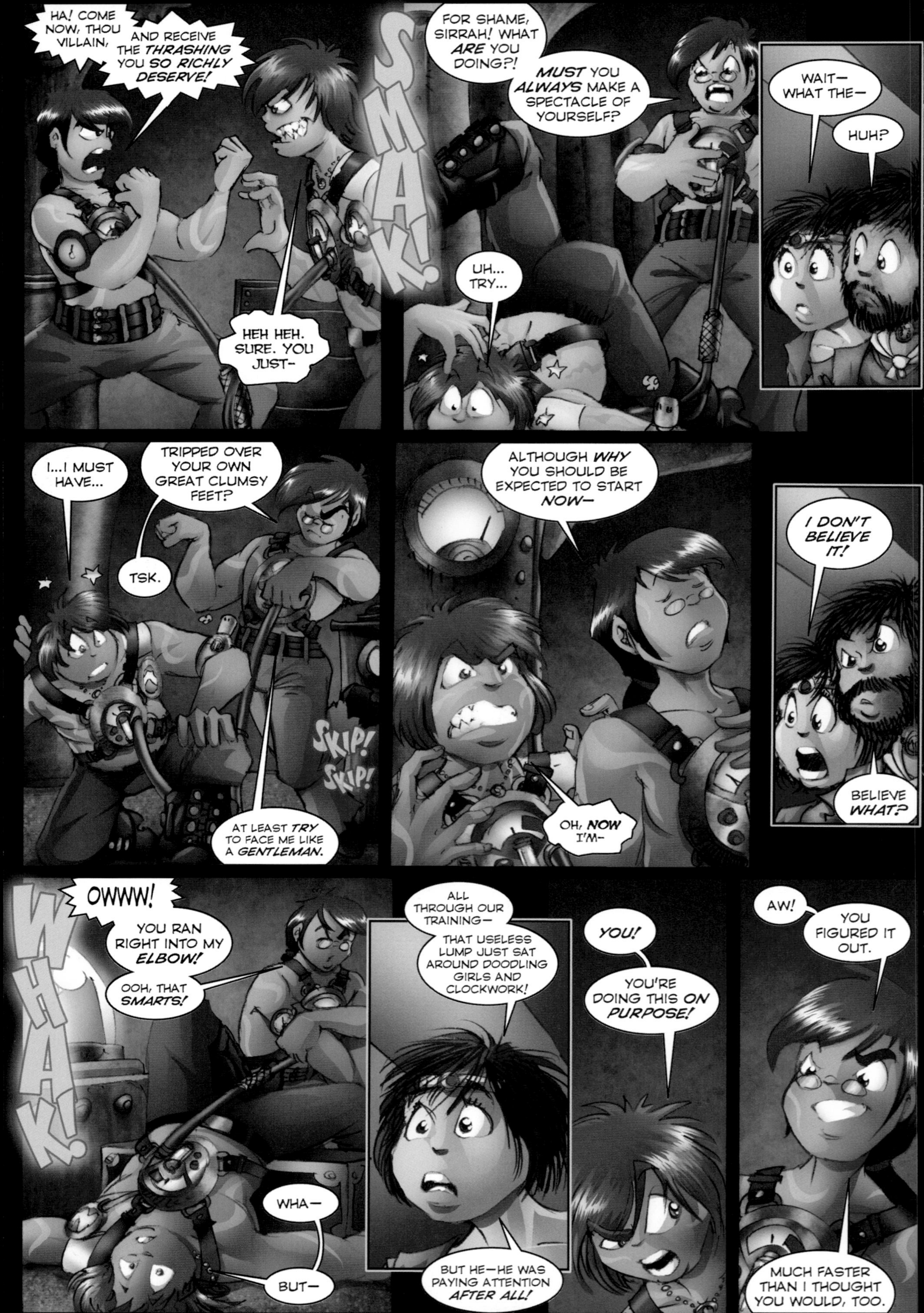
HA! COME NOW, THOU VILLAIN,
AND RECEIVE THE THRASHING YOU SO RICHLY DESERVE!
HEH HEH. SURE. YOU JUST-
SMAK!
FOR SHAME, SIRRAH! WHAT ARE YOU DOING?!
MUST YOU ALWAYS MAKE A SPECTACLE OF YOURSELF?
UH... TRY...
WAIT— WHAT THE—
HUH?
I...I MUST HAVE...
TRIPPED OVER YOUR OWN GREAT CLUMSY FEET?
TSK.
SKIP! SKIP!
AT LEAST TRY TO FACE ME LIKE A GENTLEMAN.
ALTHOUGH WHY YOU SHOULD BE EXPECTED TO START NOW—
OH, NOW I'M-
I DON'T BELIEVE IT!
BELIEVE WHAT?
WHAK!
OWWW!
YOU RAN RIGHT INTO MY ELBOW!
OOH, THAT SMARTS!
WHA—
BUT—
ALL THROUGH OUR TRAINING—
THAT USELESS LUMP JUST SAT AROUND DOODLING GIRLS AND CLOCKWORK!
BUT HE—HE WAS PAYING ATTENTION AFTER ALL!
YOU!
YOU'RE DOING THIS ON PURPOSE!
AW!
YOU FIGURED IT OUT.
MUCH FASTER THAN I THOUGHT YOU WOULD, TOO.

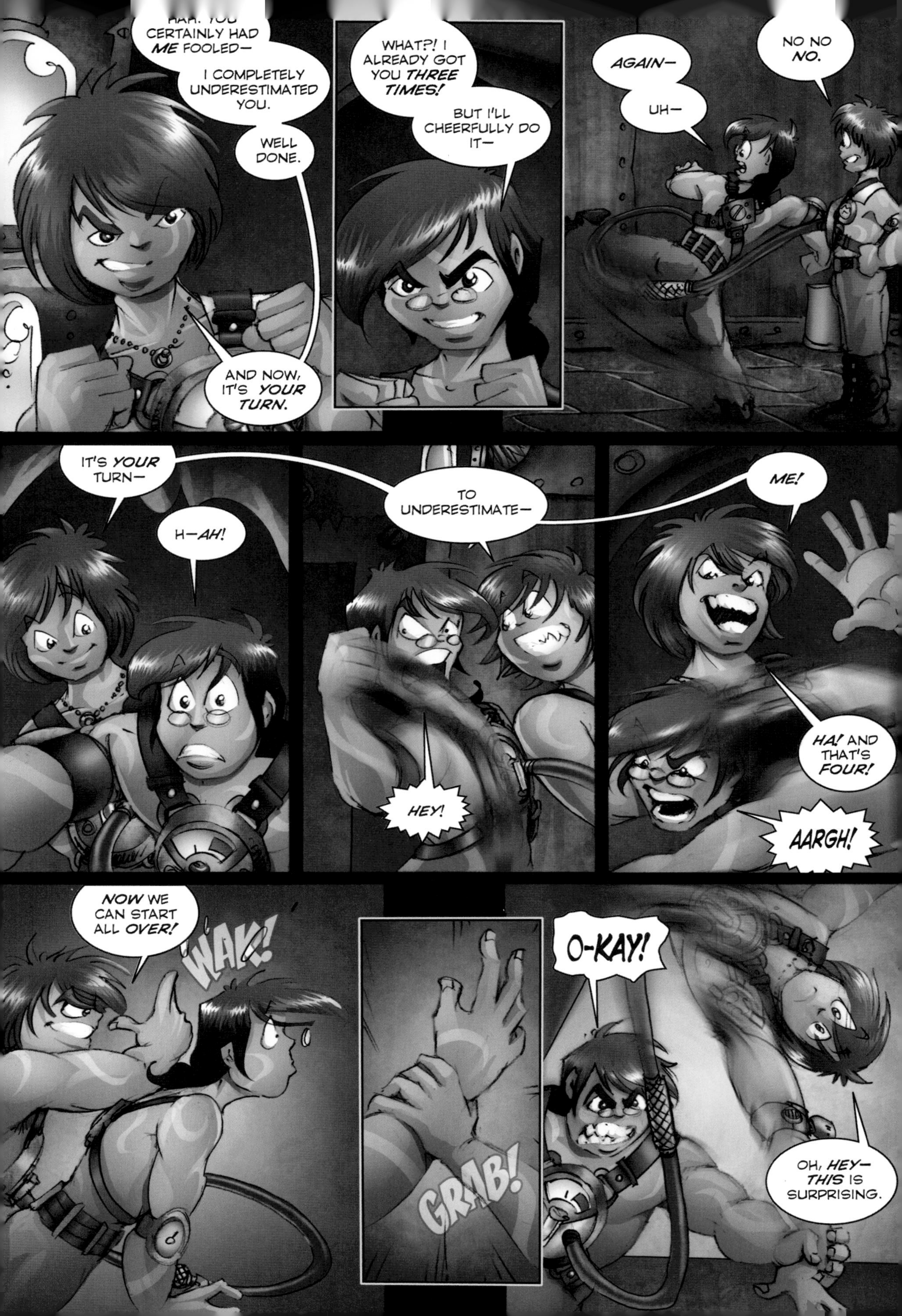
HAH! YOU CERTAINLY HAD ME FOOLED—
I COMPLETELY UNDERESTIMATED YOU.
WELL DONE.
AND NOW, IT'S YOUR TURN.
WHAT?! I ALREADY GOT YOU THREE TIMES!
BUT I'LL CHEERFULLY DO IT—
AGAIN—
UH—
NO NO NO.
IT'S YOUR TURN—
H—AH!
TO UNDERESTIMATE—
HEY!
ME!
HA! AND THAT'S FOUR!
AARGH!
NOW WE CAN START ALL OVER!
WAK!
GRAB!
O-KAY!
OH, HEY— THIS IS SURPRISING.

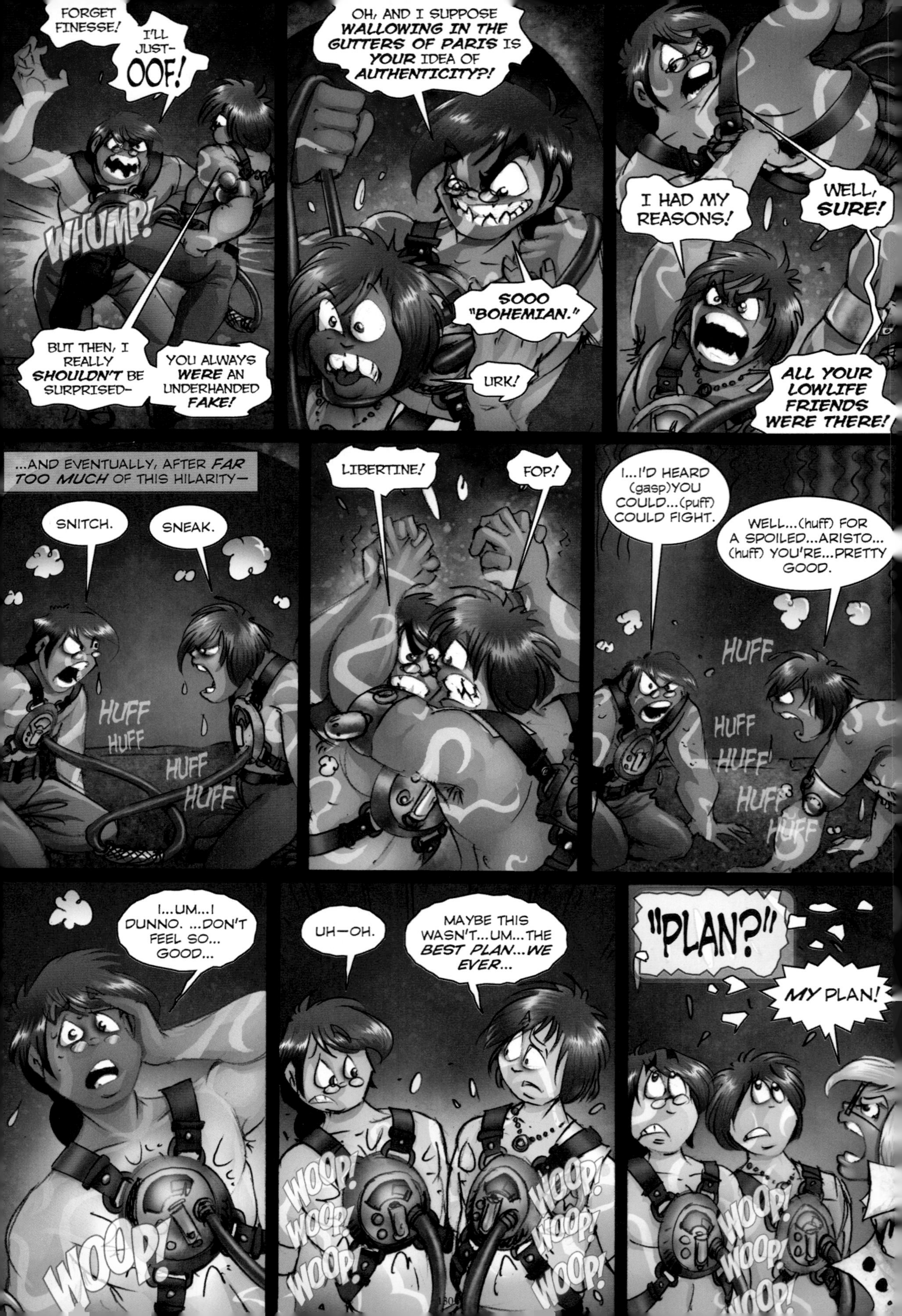

FORGET FINESSE!
I'LL JUST-
OOF!
WHUMP!
BUT THEN, I REALLY SHOULDN'T BE SURPRISED-
YOU ALWAYS WERE AN UNDERHANDED FAKE!
OH, AND I SUPPOSE WALLOWING IN THE GUTTERS OF PARIS IS YOUR IDEA OF AUTHENTICITY?!
SOOO "BOHEMIAN."
URK!
I HAD MY REASONS!
WELL, SURE!
ALL YOUR LOWLIFE FRIENDS WERE THERE!
...AND EVENTUALLY, AFTER FAR TOO MUCH OF THIS HILARITY—
SNITCH.
SNEAK.
HUFF HUFF
HUFF HUFF
LIBERTINE!
FOP!
I...I'D HEARD (gasp) YOU COULD...(puff) COULD FIGHT.
WELL...(huff) FOR A SPOILED...ARISTO... (huff) YOU'RE...PRETTY GOOD.
HUFF
HUFF HUFF HUFF HUFF
I...UM...I DUNNO. ...DON'T FEEL SO... GOOD...
WOOP!
UH—OH.
MAYBE THIS WASN'T...UM...THE BEST PLAN...WE EVER...
WOOP! WOOP! WOOP!
WOOP! WOOP! WOOP!
"PLAN?"
MY PLAN!
WOOP! WOOP! WOOP!

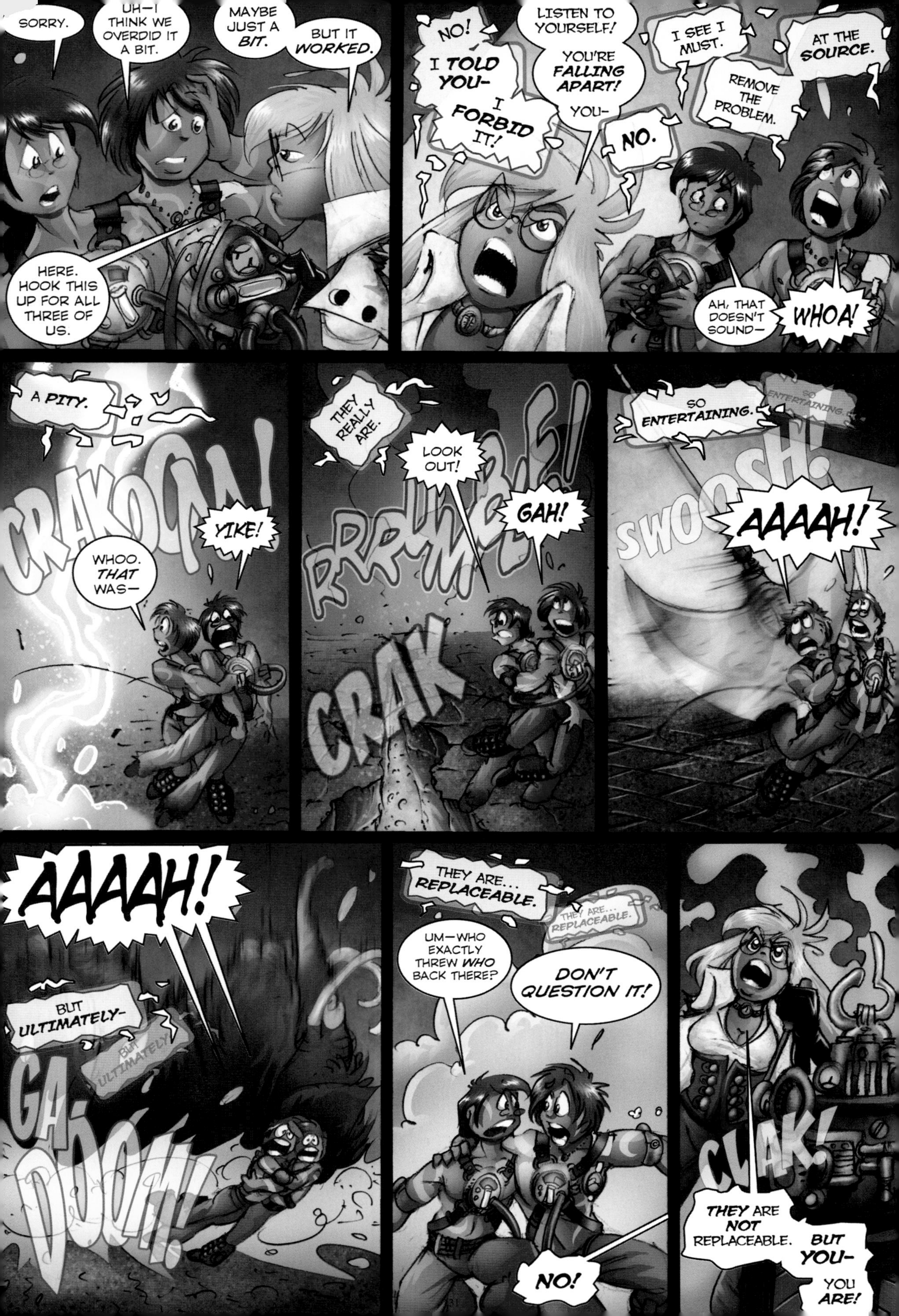

SORRY.
UH—I THINK WE OVERDID IT A BIT.
MAYBE JUST A *BIT*.
BUT IT *WORKED*.
HERE. HOOK THIS UP FOR ALL THREE OF US.
NO!
I *TOLD YOU*-
I *FORBID* IT!
LISTEN TO YOURSELF!
YOU'RE *FALLING APART!*
YOU-
NO.
I SEE I MUST.
REMOVE THE PROBLEM.
AT THE *SOURCE*.
AH, THAT DOESN'T SOUND—
WHOA!
A *PITY*.
CRAKOOM!
YIKE!
WHOO. *THAT* WAS—
THEY REALLY ARE.
LOOK OUT!
BRRUMBLE!
GAH!
CRAK
SO *ENTERTAINING*.
SO ENTERTAINING.
SWOOSH!
AAAAH!
AAAAH!
BUT *ULTIMATELY*-
BUT ULTIMATELY
GA-DOOM!
THEY ARE... *REPLACEABLE*.
THEY ARE... REPLACEABLE.
UM—WHO EXACTLY THREW *WHO* BACK THERE?
DON'T QUESTION IT!
NO!
CLAK!
THEY ARE *NOT* REPLACEABLE.
BUT YOU-
YOU *ARE!*

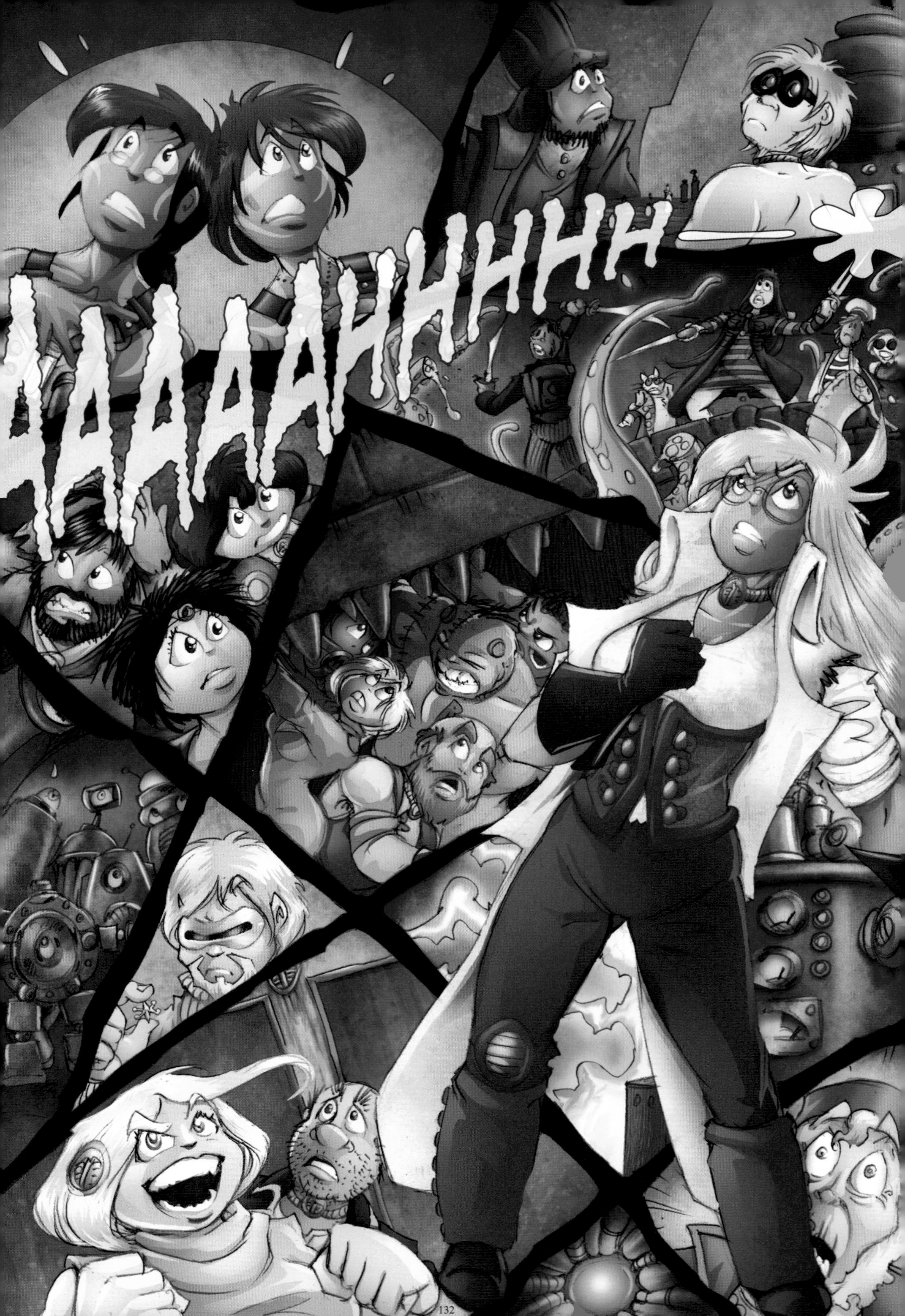
AAAAHHHHHH

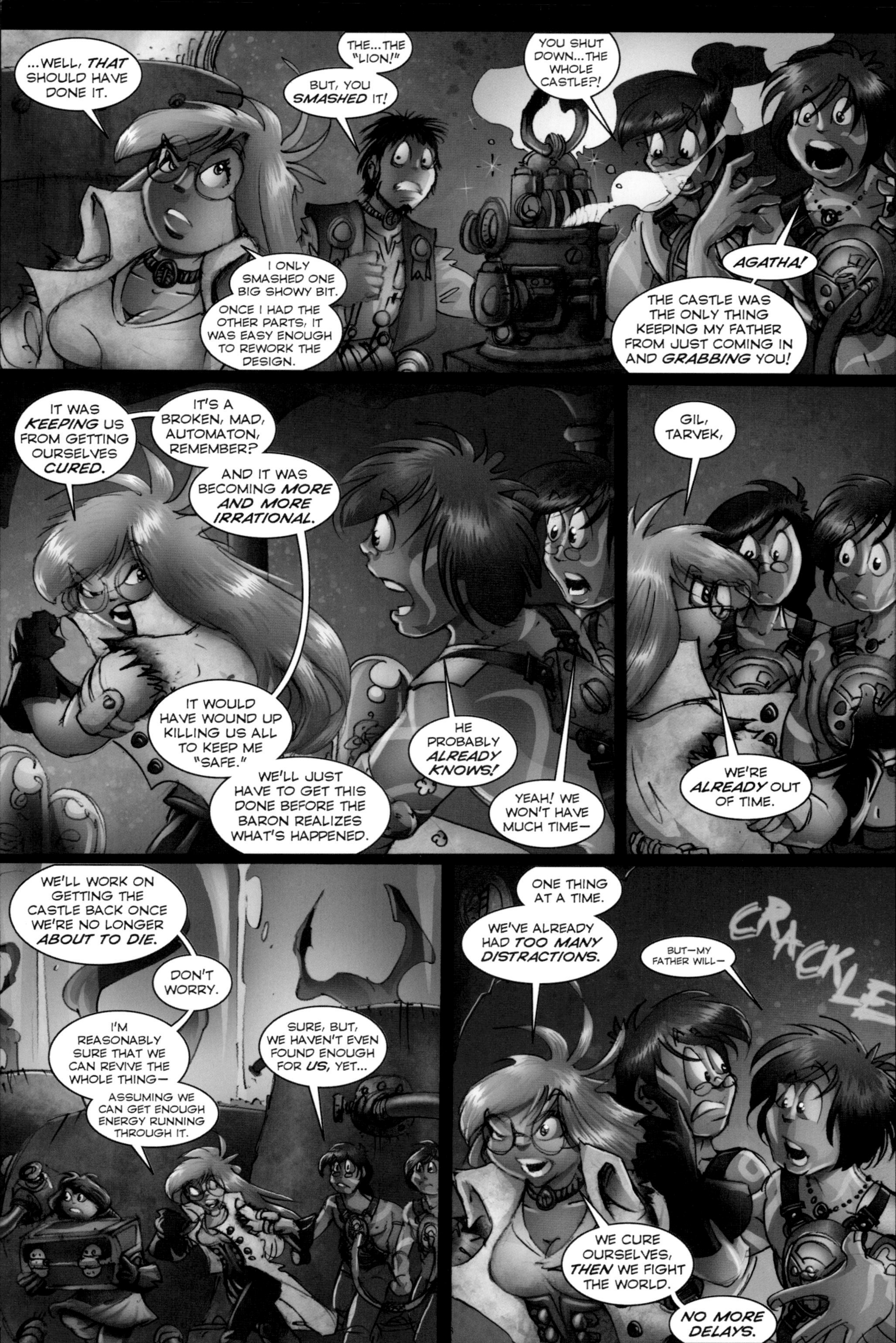
...WELL, *THAT* SHOULD HAVE DONE IT.
THE...THE "LION!"
BUT, YOU *SMASHED* IT!
I ONLY SMASHED ONE BIG SHOWY BIT.
ONCE I HAD THE OTHER PARTS, IT WAS EASY ENOUGH TO REWORK THE DESIGN.
YOU SHUT DOWN...THE WHOLE CASTLE?!
AGATHA!
THE CASTLE WAS THE ONLY THING KEEPING MY FATHER FROM JUST COMING IN AND *GRABBING* YOU!
IT WAS *KEEPING* US FROM GETTING OURSELVES *CURED.*
IT'S A BROKEN, MAD, AUTOMATON, REMEMBER?
AND IT WAS BECOMING *MORE AND MORE IRRATIONAL.*
IT WOULD HAVE WOUND UP KILLING US ALL TO KEEP ME "SAFE."
WE'LL JUST HAVE TO GET THIS DONE BEFORE THE BARON REALIZES WHAT'S HAPPENED.
HE PROBABLY *ALREADY KNOWS!*
YEAH! WE WON'T HAVE MUCH TIME—
GIL, TARVEK,
WE'RE *ALREADY* OUT OF TIME.
WE'LL WORK ON GETTING THE CASTLE BACK ONCE WE'RE NO LONGER *ABOUT TO DIE.*
DON'T WORRY.
I'M REASONABLY SURE THAT WE CAN REVIVE THE WHOLE THING—
ASSUMING WE CAN GET ENOUGH ENERGY RUNNING THROUGH IT.
SURE, BUT, WE HAVEN'T EVEN FOUND ENOUGH FOR *US,* YET...
ONE THING AT A TIME.
WE'VE ALREADY HAD *TOO MANY DISTRACTIONS.*
CRACKLE
BUT—MY FATHER WILL—
WE CURE OURSELVES, *THEN* WE FIGHT THE WORLD.
NO MORE DELAYS.

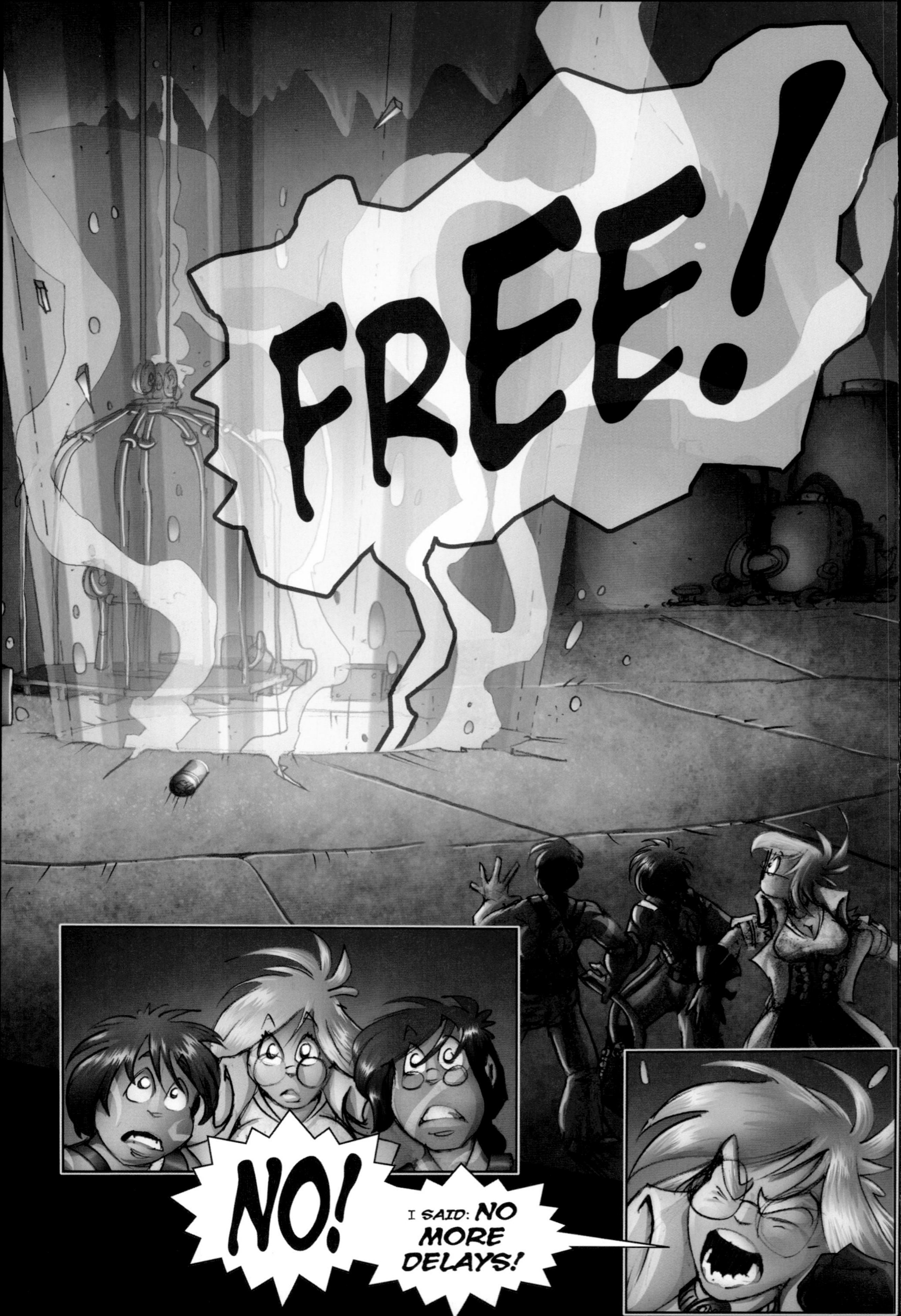
FREE!
NO!
I SAID: NO MORE DELAYS!

TO BE CONTINUED IN:

GIRL GENIUS® Book TEN

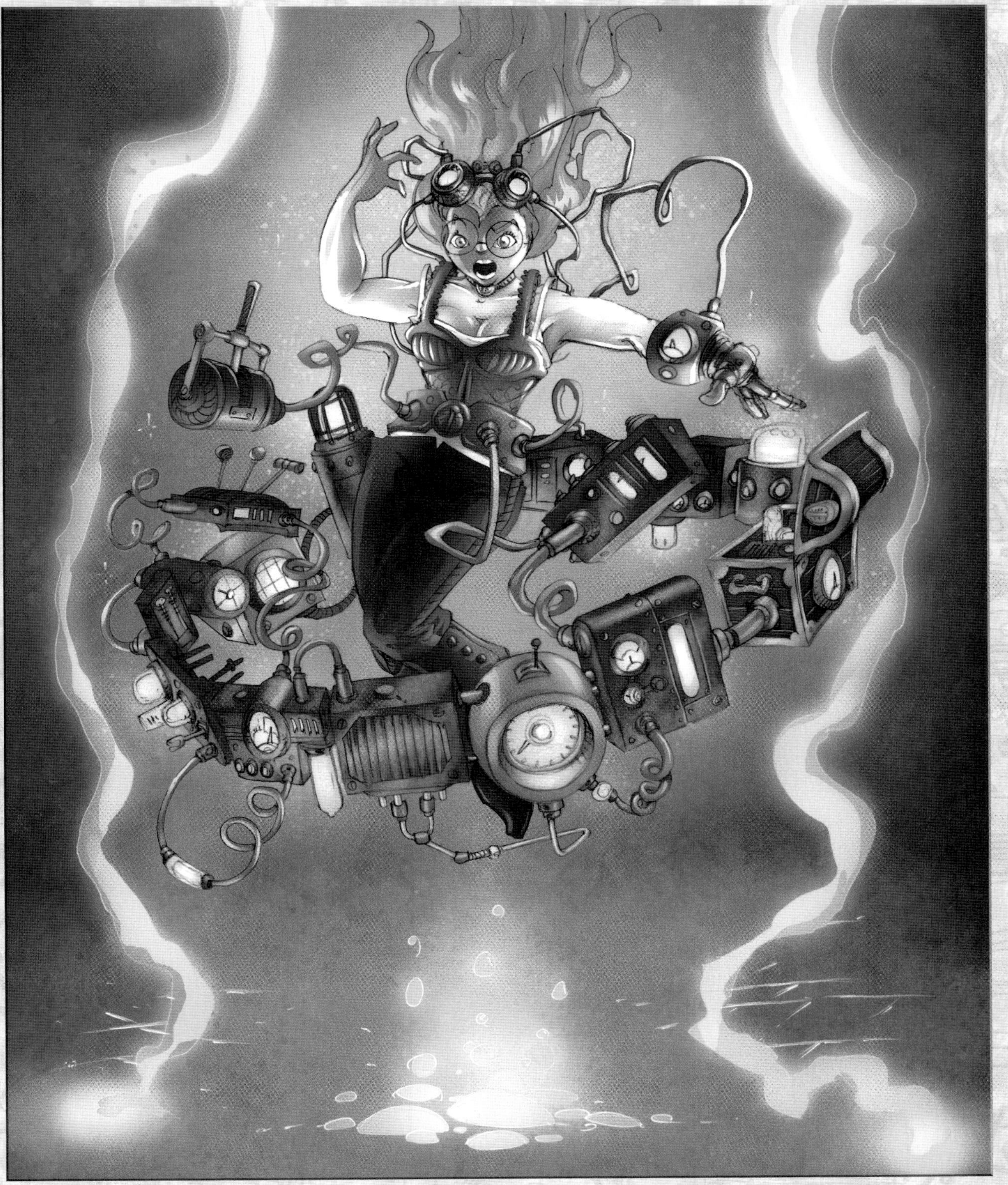

KEEP UP WITH THE STORY! READ NEW COMICS THREE TIMES A WEEK AT:

WWW.GIRLGENIUS.NET

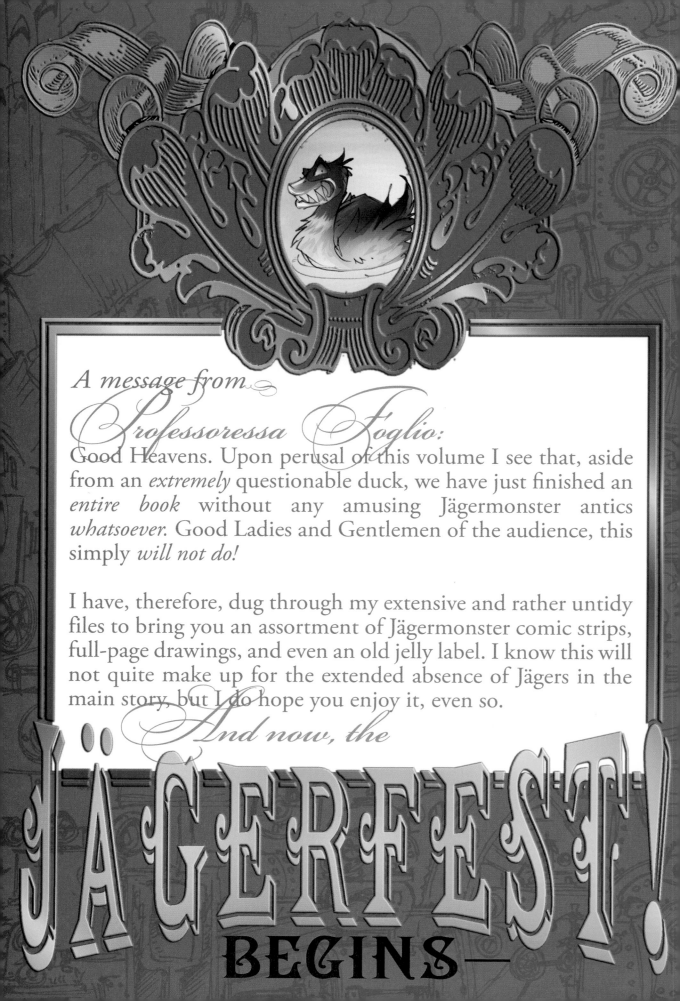

A *message from*

Professoressa Foglio:

Good Heavens. Upon perusal of this volume I see that, aside from an *extremely* questionable duck, we have just finished an *entire book* without any amusing Jägermonster antics *whatsoever*. Good Ladies and Gentlemen of the audience, this simply *will not do!*

I have, therefore, dug through my extensive and rather untidy files to bring you an assortment of Jägermonster comic strips, full-page drawings, and even an old jelly label. I know this will not quite make up for the extended absence of Jägers in the main story, but I do hope you enjoy it, even so.

And now, the

JÄGERFEST!

BEGINS—

I'll begin with our actual first attempt at a webcomic. Yes, long before we took the main Girl Genius story online, we regarded the world of webcomics with envious eyes.

This little comic, entitled *Jägershots,* was our first attempt to join the fun...

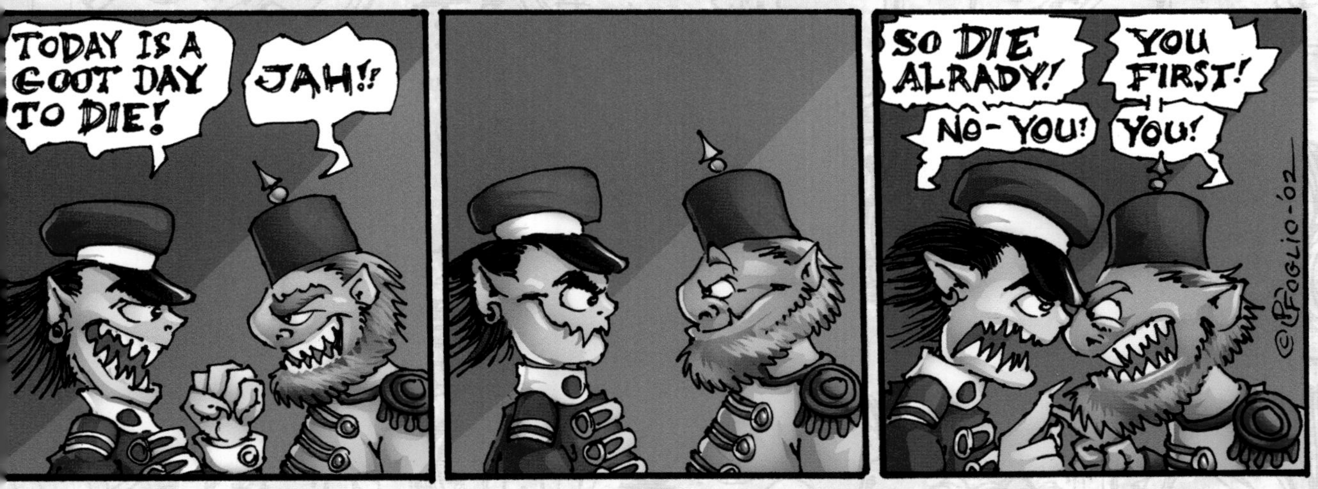
TODAY IS A GOOT DAY TO DIE!
JAH!!
SO DIE ALRADY!
YOU FIRST!
NO-YOU!
YOU!

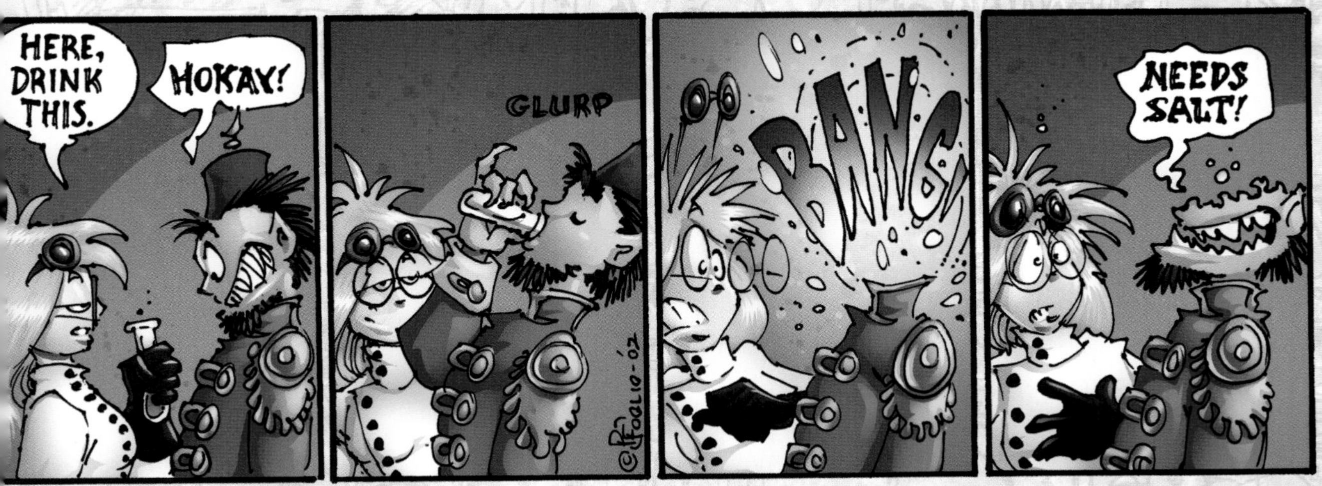
HERE, DRINK THIS.
HOKAY!
GLURP
BANG!
NEEDS SALT!

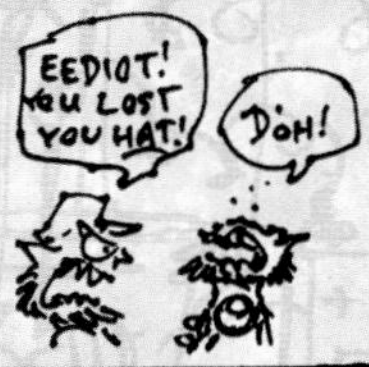
EEDIOT! YOU LOST YOU HAT!
D'OH!

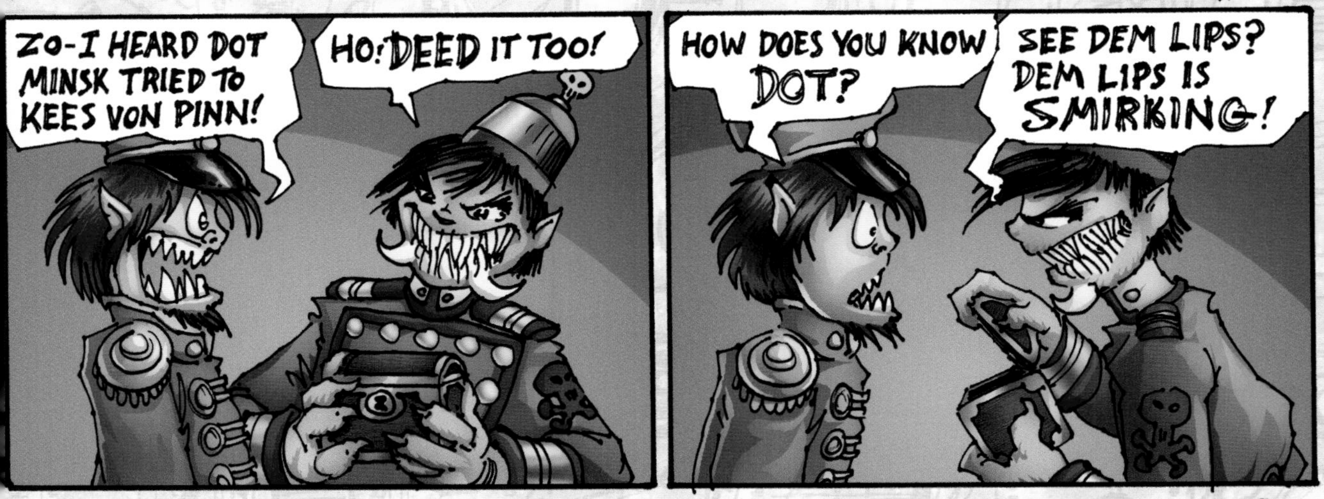
ZO-I HEARD DOT MINSK TRIED TO KEES VON PINN!
HO! DEED IT TOO!
HOW DOES YOU KNOW DOT?
SEE DEM LIPS? DEM LIPS IS SMIRKING!
YEAH BABY!

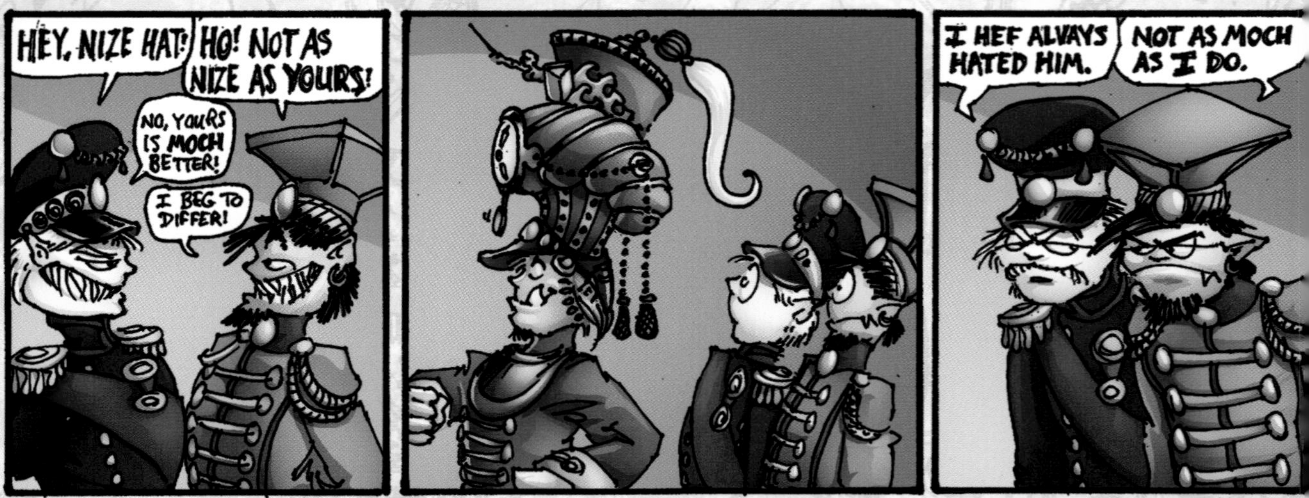
HEY, NIZE HAT!
HO! NOT AS NIZE AS YOURS!
NO, YOURS IS MOCH BETTER!
I BEG TO DIFFER!
I HEF ALWAYS HATED HIM.
NOT AS MOCH AS I DO.

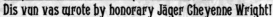

Dis vun vas wrote by honorary Jäger Cheyenne Wright!

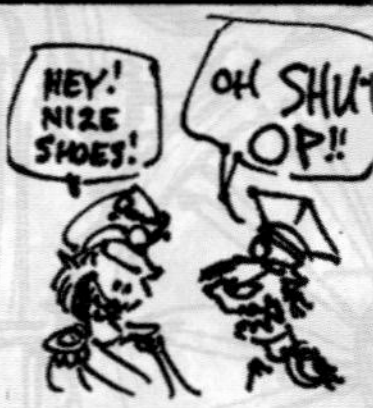
HEY! NIZE SHOES!
OH SHUT OP!!

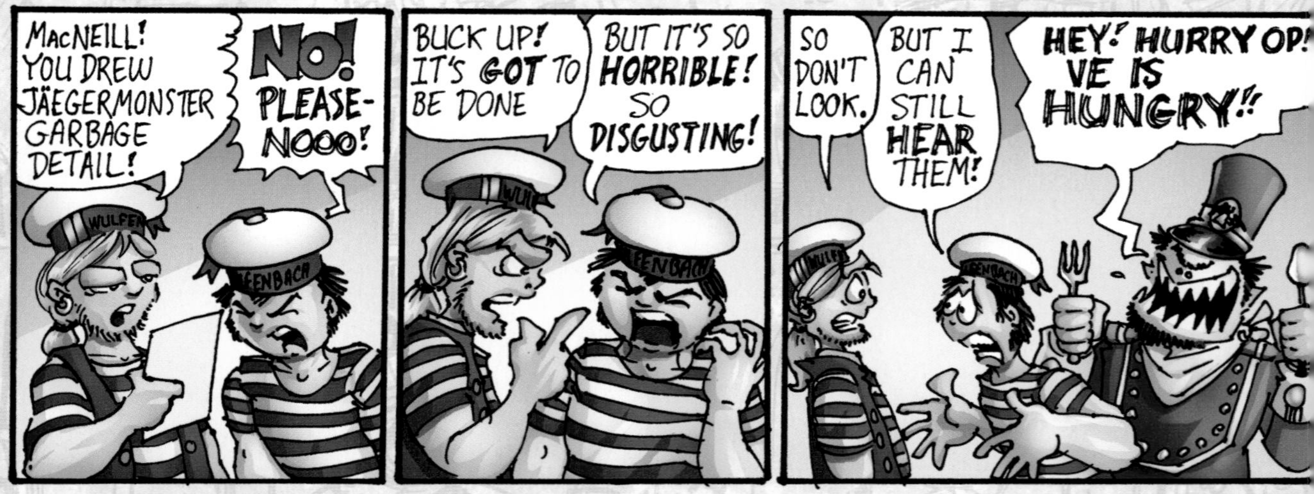
MacNEILL! YOU DREW JÄEGERMONSTER GARBAGE DETAIL!
NO! PLEASE-NOOO!
BUCK UP! IT'S GOT TO BE DONE
BUT IT'S SO HORRIBLE! SO DISGUSTING!
SO DON'T LOOK.
BUT I CAN STILL HEAR THEM!
HEY! HURRY OP! VE IS HUNGRY!!

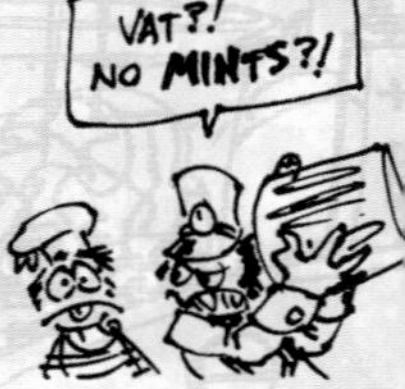
VAT?! NO MINTS?!

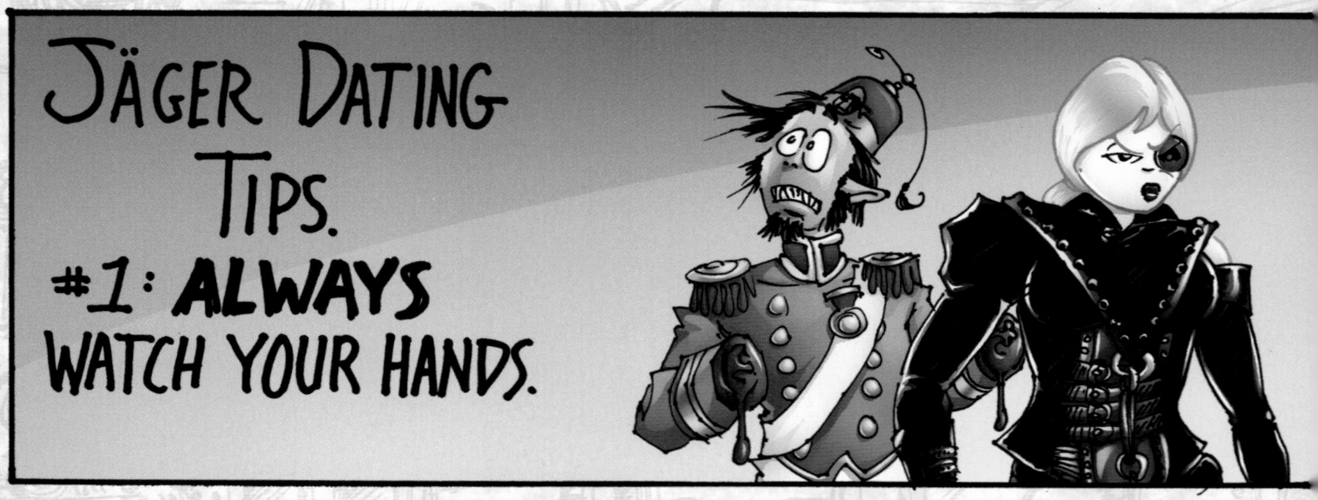
JÄGER DATING TIPS.
#1: ALWAYS WATCH YOUR HANDS.

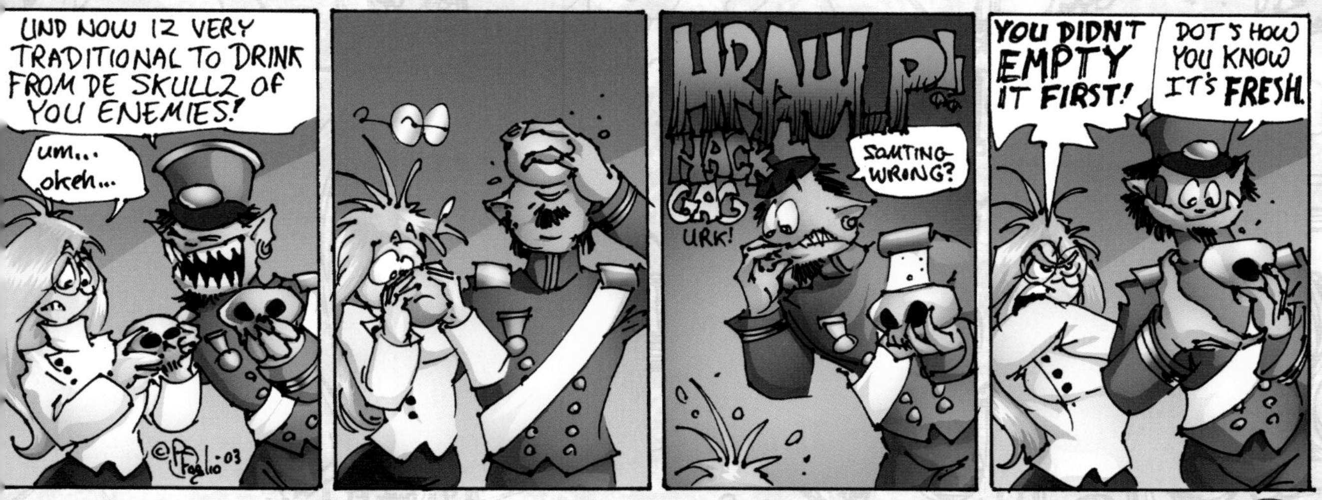
UND NOW IZ VERY TRADITIONAL TO DRINK FROM DE SKULLZ OF YOU ENEMIES!
um... okeh...
HRAULP!
HACK
GAG
URK!
SOMTING WRONG?
YOU DIDN'T EMPTY IT FIRST!
DOT'S HOW YOU KNOW IT'S FRESH.

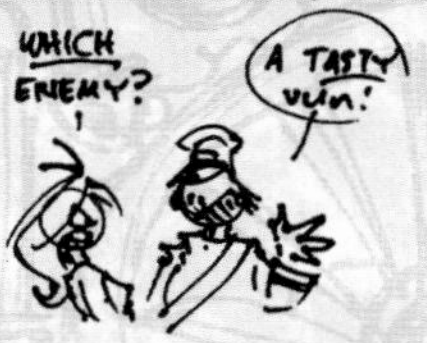
WHICH ENEMY?
A TASTY VUN!

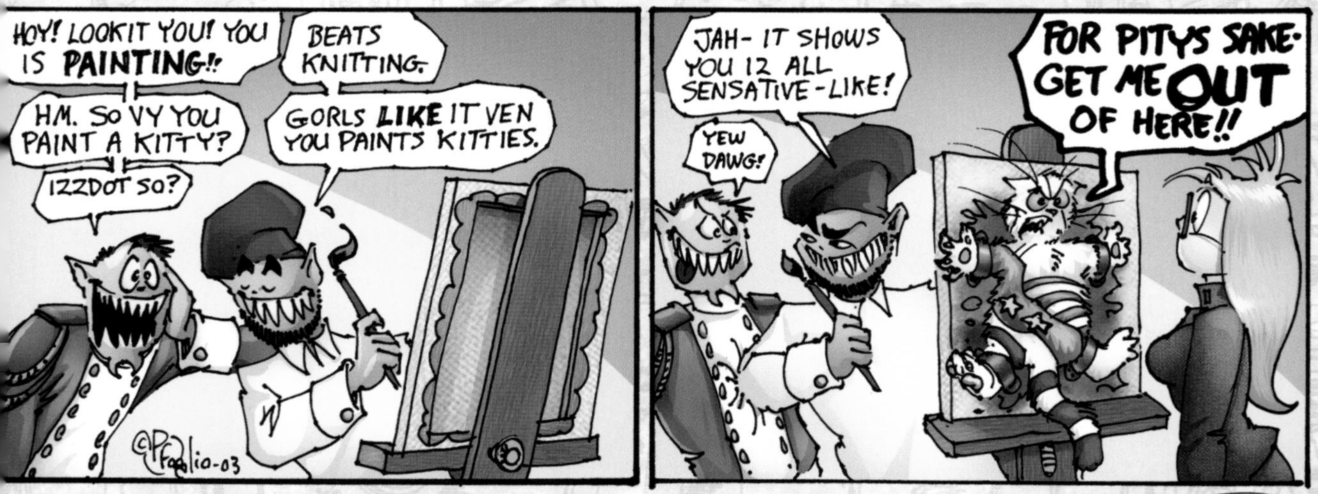
HOY! LOOKIT YOU! YOU IS PAINTING!!
BEATS KNITTING.
HM. SO VY YOU PAINT A KITTY?
GORLS LIKE IT VEN YOU PAINTS KITTIES.
IZZDOT SO?
JAH- IT SHOWS YOU IZ ALL SENSATIVE-LIKE!
YEW DAWG!
FOR PITY'S SAKE- GET ME OUT OF HERE!!

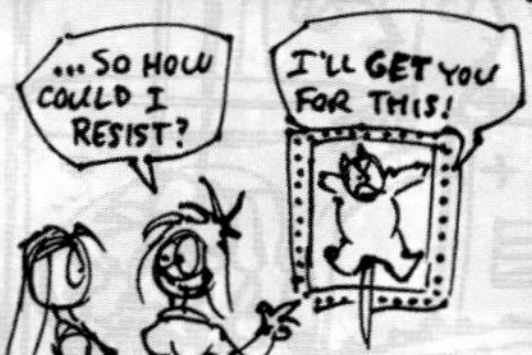
...SO HOW COULD I RESIST?
I'LL GET YOU FOR THIS!

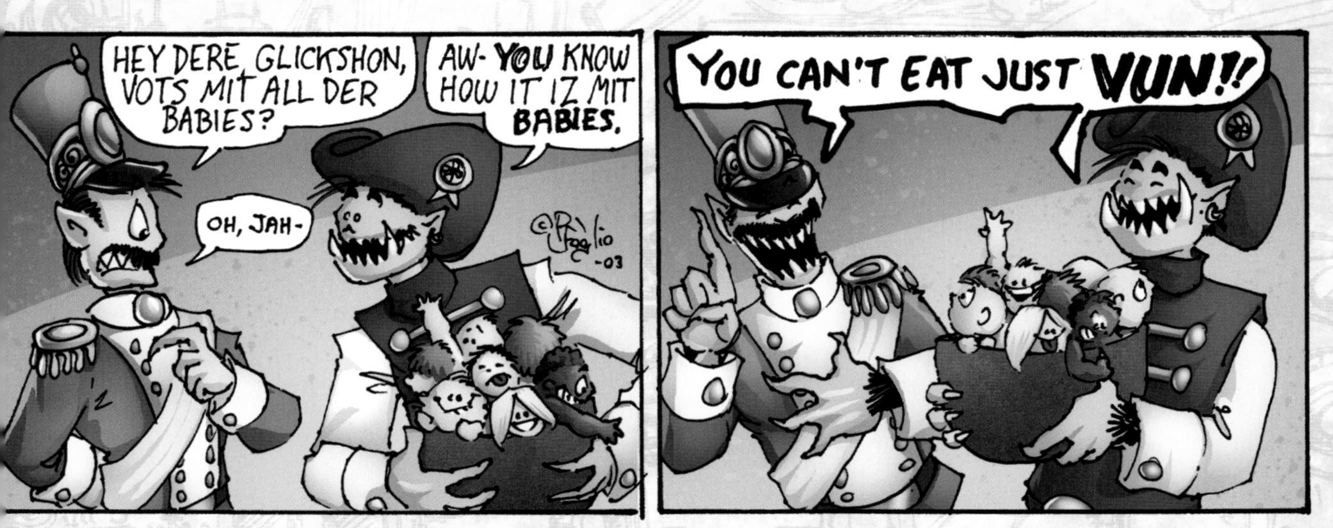
HEY DERE, GLICKSHON, VOTS MIT ALL DER BABIES?
AW- YOU KNOW HOW IT IZ MIT BABIES.
OH, JAH-
YOU CAN'T EAT JUST VUN!!

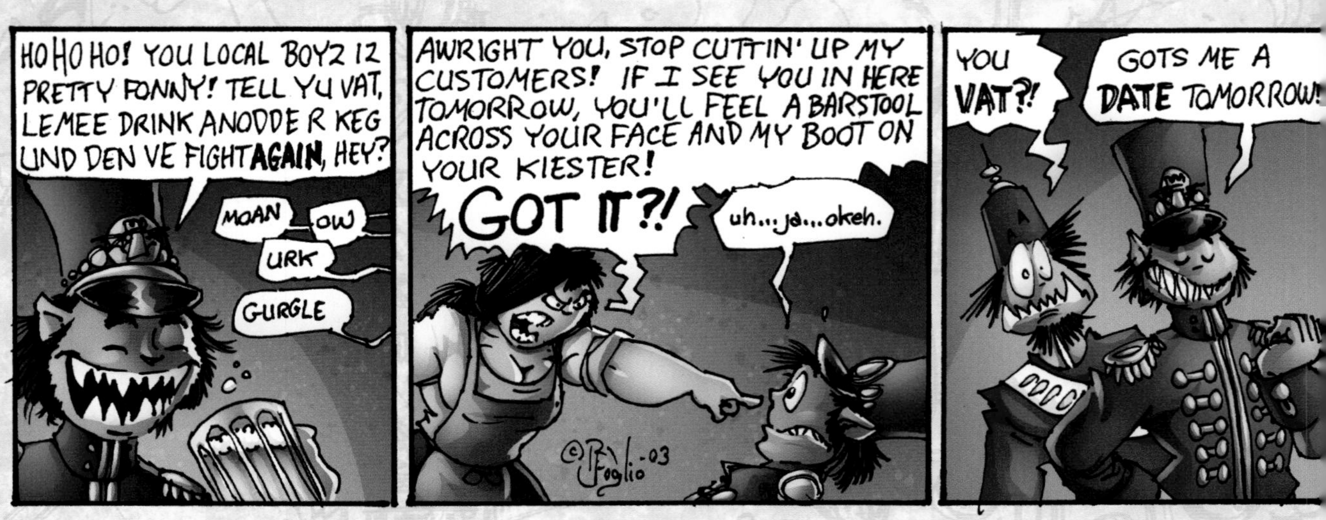
HO HO HO! YOU LOCAL BOYZ IZ PRETTY FONNY! TELL YU VAT, LEMEE DRINK ANODDER KEG UND DEN VE FIGHT AGAIN, HEY?
MOAN
OW
URK
GURGLE
AWRIGHT YOU, STOP CUTTIN' UP MY CUSTOMERS! IF I SEE YOU IN HERE TOMORROW, YOU'LL FEEL A BARSTOOL ACROSS YOUR FACE AND MY BOOT ON YOUR KIESTER!
GOT IT?!
uh...ja...okeh.
YOU VAT?!
GOTS ME A DATE TOMORROW!

...and that's as far as we got. Oh, well. But never fear! I have other Jägerage to share! Below, you'll find the label we used on the last of our homemade grape jelly. We had a lot of grapes that year, and wound up making so much jelly that we had to find a sneaky way to get ric of it all. Brainstorming produced many promising ideas, but the sinister plan we finally settled upon was to stick an amusing label on it and try to convince our friends that we were giving them all a wonderful gift. I'm not sure they bought it (they're a suspicious bunch) but nobody actually "forgot" to take their gifts home, so we counted it as a win. Feel free to try it yourself, in the event that you find yourself with too much jelly and reasonably gullible friends.

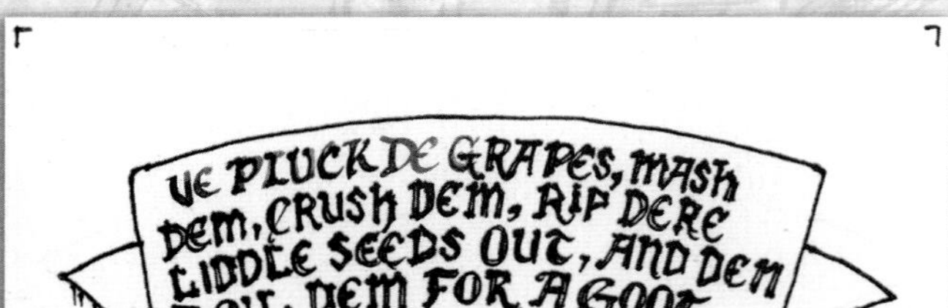
VE PLUCK DE GRAPES, MASH DEM, CRUSH DEM, RIP DERE LIDDLE SEEDS OUT, AND DEN BOIL DEM FOR A GOOT LONG TIME. YOU GETS TO EAT IT.
JÄGERJÄELLY
2002
YOU EAT IT.
NO, YOU EAT IT!
"VE'S ONLY INTERESTED IN DE MASHING!"

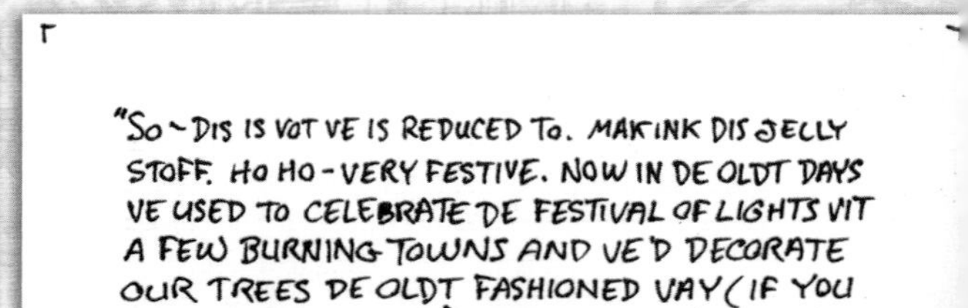
"So~ DIS IS VOT VE IS REDUCED TO. MAKINK DIS JELLY STOFF. HO HO - VERY FESTIVE. NOW IN DE OLDT DAYS VE USED TO CELEBRATE DE FESTIVAL OF LIGHTS VIT A FEW BURNING TOWNS AND VE'D DECORATE OUR TREES DE OLDT FASHIONED VAY (IF YOU KNOW VAT I MEAN) UND NOW VE'S CRUSHING GRAPES. OKAY, SURE, DE **DO** LOOK LIKE LIDDLE HEADS AND CRUSHING DEM **SOUNDS** NIZE, BUT WHOS GOT DE TIME TO DRAW LIDDLE FACES ON ALL OF DEM AND WHERES THE SCREAMING AND BEGGING AND ALL DOT? I MEAN, DIS IS A TIME OF YEAR VEN TRADITIONS IS IMPAWTENT. YOU GETS NOSTOLGIC FOR DE GOOT TIMES MIT YOU FRIENDS AND FAMILY AND VICTEMS. BUT - VAT YOU GONNA DO? DE MASTER SEZ IT'S EXCELLENT 'DISPLACEMENT THERAPY' UND SHE'S THE GENIUS, NOT ME **DOTS** FOR SURE. VELL ANYVAY IT KEEPS US BUSY AND IT TASTES GOOT ON KITTENS AND I SVEAR IT AIN'T GOT NO BUGS IN IT. IT'S A CRYING SHAME, BUT VE VAS OUT."

– OUR MOTTO –

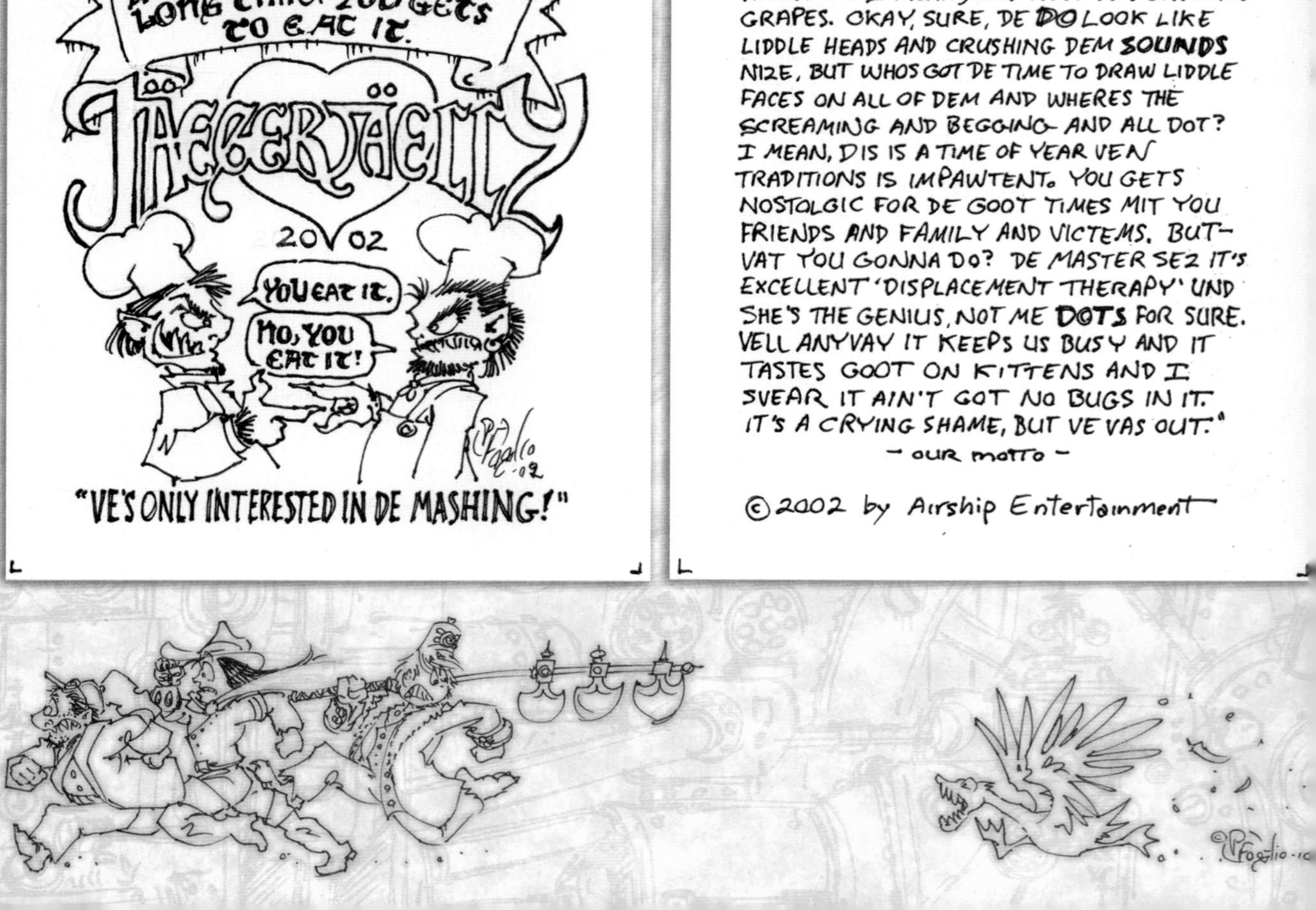

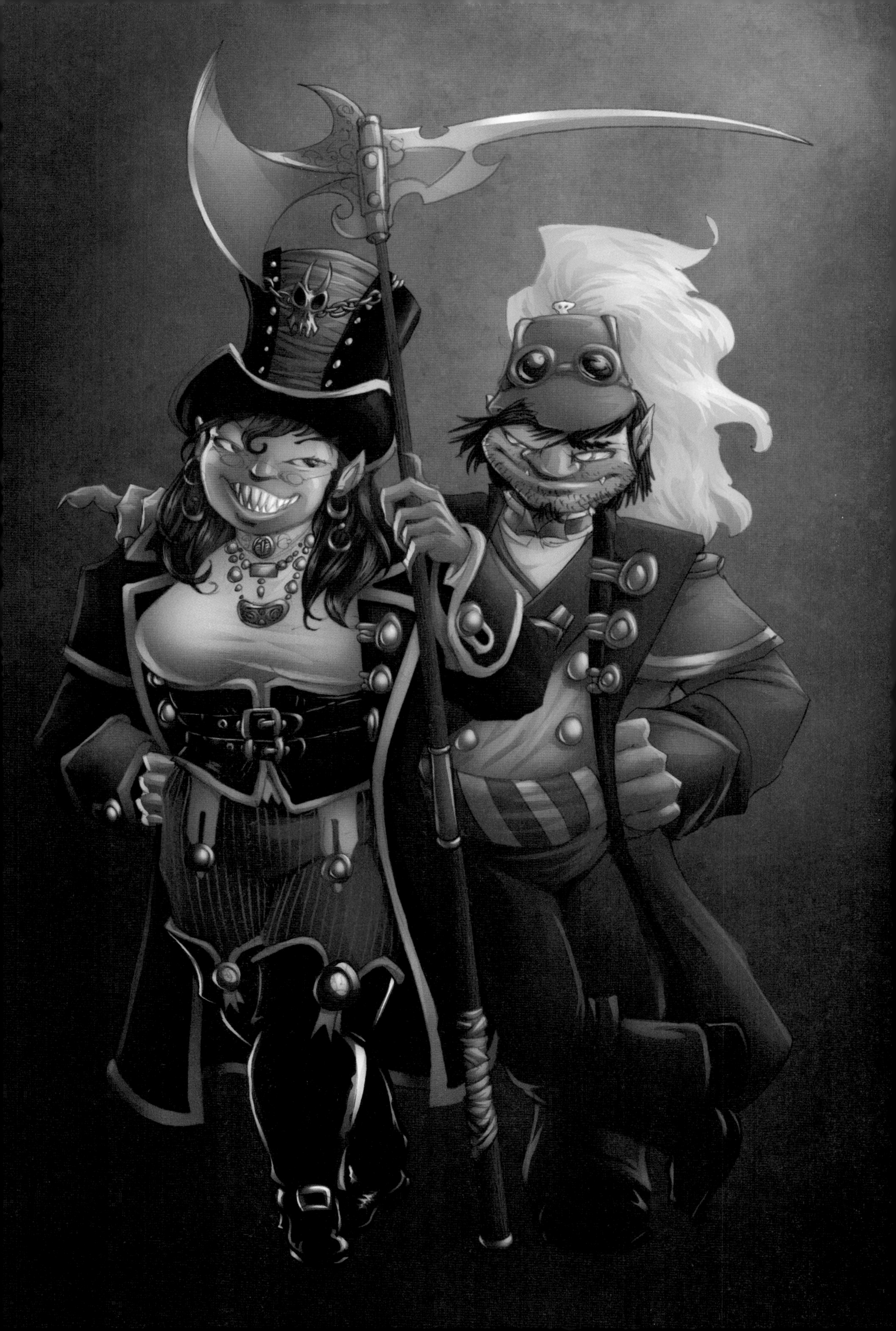

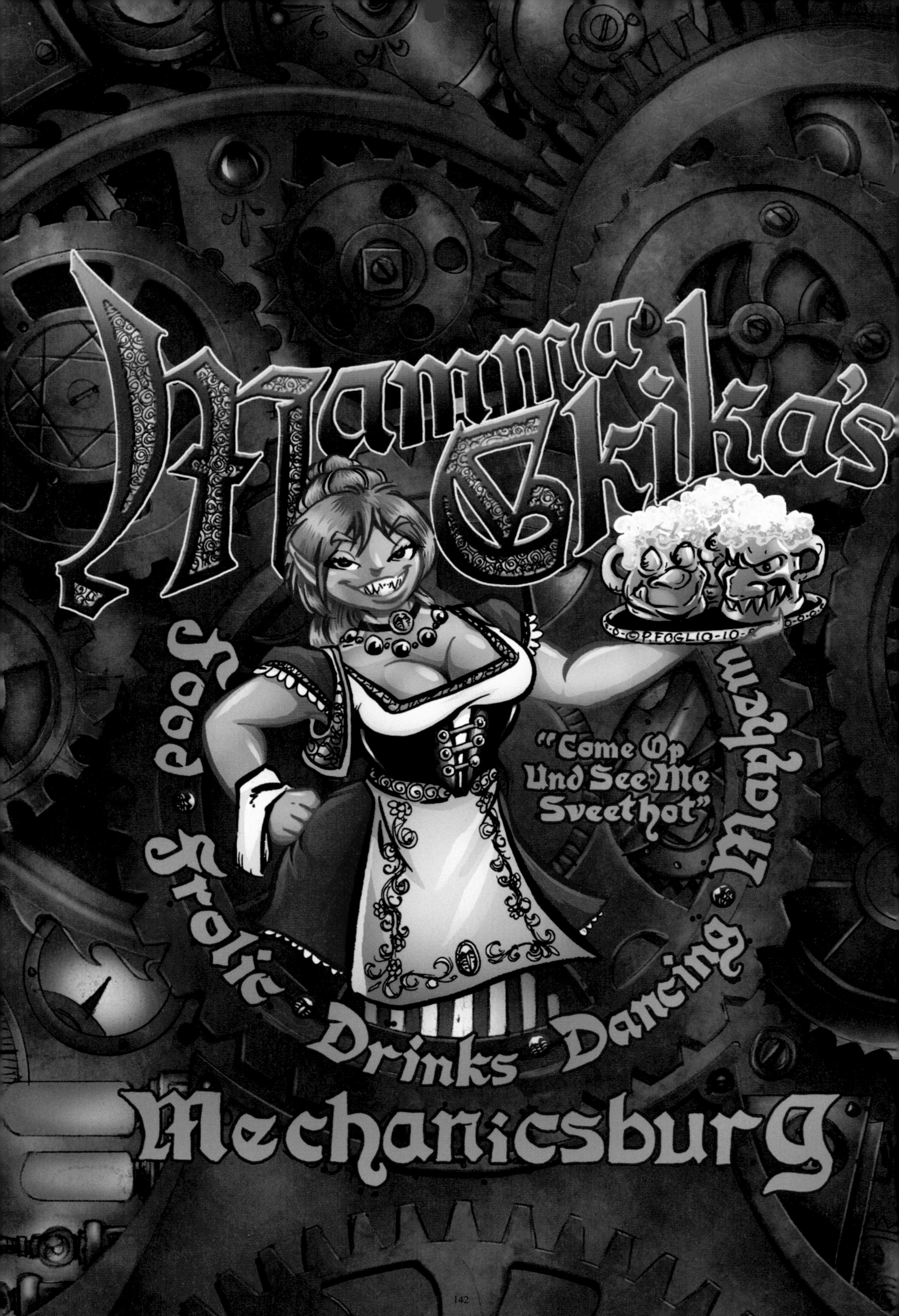
Mamma Gkika's
Food · Frolic · Drinks · Dancing · Mayhem
"Come Op Und See Me Sveethot"
Mechanicsburg
©P.Foglio-10

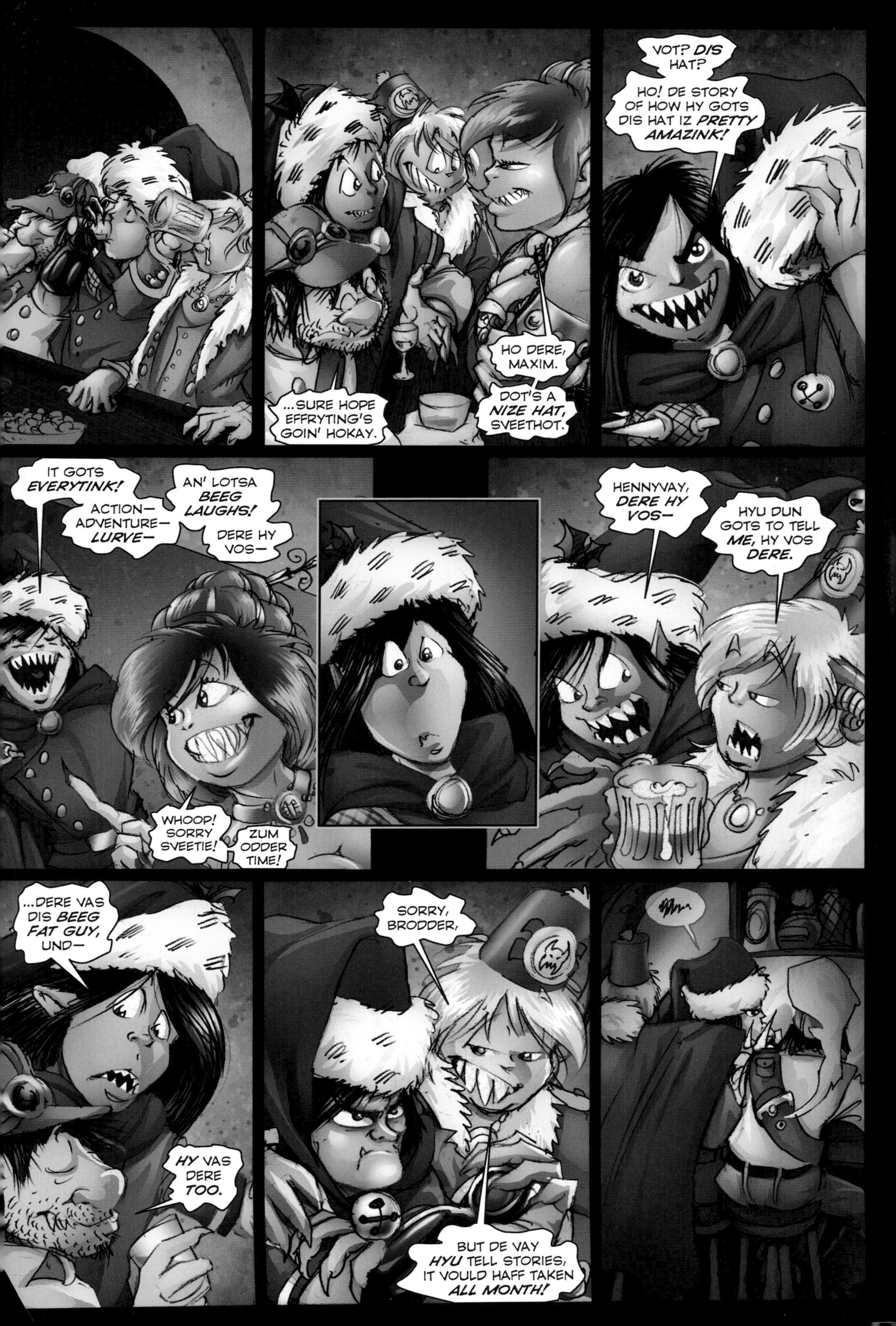

...SURE HOPE EFFRYTING'S GOIN' HOKAY.
HO DERE, MAXIM.
DOT'S A NIZE HAT, SVEETHOT.
VOT? DIS HAT?
HO! DE STORY OF HOW HY GOTS DIS HAT IZ PRETTY AMAZINK!
IT GOTS EVERYTINK!
ACTION— ADVENTURE— LURVE—
AN' LOTSA BEEG LAUGHS!
DERE HY VOS—
WHOOP! SORRY SVEETIE!
ZUM ODDER TIME!
HENNYVAY, DERE HY VOS—
HYU DUN GOTS TO TELL ME, HY VOS DERE.
...DERE VAS DIS BEEG FAT GUY, UND—
HY VAS DERE TOO.
SORRY, BRODDER,
BUT DE VAY HYU TELL STORIES, IT VOULD HAFF TAKEN ALL MONTH!

READ MORE COMICS ONLINE AT:

WWW.GIRLGENIUS.NET

MONDAY · WEDNESDAY · FRIDAY